Soviet Policy toward India: Ideology and Strategy

Russian Research Center Studies, 74

Soviet Policy toward India: Ideology and Strategy

Robert H. Donaldson

Harvard University Press   Cambridge, Massachusetts   1974

To my parents

Preface

The postwar emergence into world politics of the new states of Asia and Africa, with their own distinctive value systems and political cultures, has posed a conceptual as well as a diplomatic challenge to the more established actors on the world stage. Not even the policy-makers of the Soviet Union have managed to escape the conceptual problem, even though their Marxist-Leninist image of the world as an arena of constant struggle between the imperialist purveyors of evil and the oppressed classes and nations had a special appeal to the leaders of the young states. In confronting the diplomatic challenge of the "third world," the Soviets have found it necessary to revise some of the analytical tools and doctrinal assumptions employed by Marx in his analysis of the social order of mid-nineteenth-century Europe.

This study seeks to relate this process of doctrinal revision to the changing Soviet policy toward India. The analysis focuses on India both for the features that this country shares with other emerging nations trying to forge national unity and achieve rapid economic development while pursuing a policy of nonalignment in the East-West struggle, and for its unique position as the largest noncommunist Asian state and a potential counterweight to China.

It is in part because the Soviet Union has also come to look upon India as a vital link in any projected barrier to Chinese expansionism, and in part because of the disunity, and even ineptitude, of the local communist organizations in India itself, that the Soviets have for some time shown little enthusiasm for the prospect of communist rule in India. With respect to South Asia, "stability" has replaced "revolution" in the Soviet lexicon. Doctrinally, the Soviet Union remains committed to the long-term goal of building a communist India. But as the Soviets have become more committed operationally to the present Indian government on the diplomatic, economic, and military levels, the time perspective for the achievement of the ultimate objective of socialism (and even of the intermediate goal of "national democracy") has lengthened. This study investigates the manner in which the Soviets have attempted to reconcile this conflict between short-run expediency and long-run ideals, developing in the process their own version of "de-eschatology." It examines as well the challenge this process has called forth in recent years from the Chinese "true believers."

A word should be said concerning what this study is *not* about. Its focus is on the relationship of Marxist-Leninist doctrine to Soviet policy, that is, upon how the Soviet assessment is arrived at rather than upon how it is implemented on a day-to-day basis. Thus it does not purport to be a diplomatic history of Indo-Soviet relations. Nor does it claim to be a study of Indian policy toward the Soviet Union, though brief consideration is given to this subject. Finally, while attention is necessarily given to the Chinese communists' doctrinal stance and to the relationship of China with both the Soviet Union and India, I am not a "China scholar," and I have had to rely in these matters on translated sources and secondary accounts.

The main sources for the study are largely Soviet sources; this in itself requires a note about methodology. Like most analysts of Soviet policy, I have had for obvious reasons no access to interviews with Soviet officials, to the memoirs of Soviet policymakers, or to such vital information now reposing in a foreign ministry archive or Central Committee Secretariat file cabinet as might be expected by a scholar seeking to write, say, an analysis of United States policy toward India. Nor in my use of published Soviet materials available in the West have I found any analysis independent of the official line set down by political authorities, where such a line has been determined. This latter proviso is necessary because it is possible to find discussion and debate among Soviet authors on matters which have not yet been resolved by higher authorities (or on those matters not considered important enough to resolve in such a manner).

But not all published material is treated with equal awe, either inside or outside the Soviet Union. There is a certain "source hierarchy" which this study employs in determining which part of the material published on a certain issue reflects more accurately the views of the Soviet leadership. At the top of the hierarchy, of course, are the pronouncements of the top party leadership itself. Thus, during the period from the mid-1920's to 1953, for example, the pronouncements of Stalin— even those made during the years he held no government positions and was, as Molotov put it, "just" a party secretary—are treated as the most reliable indicators existing in published works of what "the Soviet assessment" was. Also considered highly authoritative are the resolutions of international and party congresses. Among Soviet journals, the publications of the CPSU, especially *Pravda* and *Kommunist* (*Bol'shevik* before 1952), are most authoritative, and within these journals unsigned articles or editorials are more to be respected than signed ones (unless, of course, the signature happens to be that of, say, Stalin or Khrushchev).

This study often refers to the views of Soviet "Orientalists" or "Indologists," academic specialists most often employed in the research institutes of the Academy of Sciences or in the universities. As Chapter IV argues, these men do not determine either Soviet policy or the Soviet assessment of social forces in the East, except perhaps on issues of minor importance. The general policy line is the work of higher officials in the CPSU, who may in turn instruct the director of a certain research institute to have an "expert" fill in the details and publish an article under his own name. More probably, there will be no direct instructions; rather, an academic will discover for himself—from a speech by a Politburo member or an unsigned editorial in *Pravda*, for example, or from a "self-critical" editorial in the publication of his own institute—that the authoritative assessment has shifted, and he will conduct his own research in the light of such guidelines. Even within the "scholarly community," however, there is often a recognizable hierarchy; certain "experts" of wider reputation who often double as writers for party journals or even party officials (A. M. D'iakov, E. M. Zhukov, or R. A. Ul'ianovsky on India, for example) can be taken as expressing more authoritative views than those of a lesser-known academic, writing in a more obscure publication. But, as we shall see, the academic profession can be a hazardous one in the Soviet Union, and even the views of a recognized expert can be harshly criticized if he has been so unfortunate as to have been an "official" spokesman for a discarded assessment.

In sum, it is an assumption of this study that, in the absence of more direct evidence, published Soviet materials on India, when utilized by the analyst in the context of a "source hierarchy," can serve as an indicator of the shifting assessments and objectives of Soviet decision-makers. By combining this method of evaluating published Soviet materials with observation of Soviet behavior over the past fifty years, a conclusion can be reached about the role of Marxist-Leninist doctrine in the formulation of Soviet foreign policy. The Soviets' own view was well expressed in a 1964 publication: "As a well sustains life in the desert, the constructive approach makes Marxism-Leninism an ever living and ever valid guide to action" ("Constructive Approach," *New Times*, no. 23, 1964, pp. 3–4).

The findings of this study indicate that the well has long ago gone dry. The barrenness of the Marxist-Leninist approach, as wielded by its Soviet practitioners, is strikingly evidenced in Soviet policy toward India. Marxism-Leninism may still serve Soviet policy-makers in providing them with a broad and cohesive image of the external world. But as a guide to action, communist ideology has long been relegated to a role secondary to the more traditional impulses of diplomatic expediency aimed at ensuring Soviet security—even at the expense of the revolutionary advance of international communism.

I am indebted to Vanderbilt University and to its University Research Council for grants which assisted me in revising the original manuscript and making possible its publication.

Portions of chapter six have appeared in my article, "India: The Soviet Stake in Stability," *Asian Survey*, XII, 6 (June 1972), 475–492.

Adam Ulam and the late Merle Fainsod of Harvard, Melvin Croan of the University of Wisconsin, and Derek Waller of Vanderbilt made helpful suggestions. Barry Master, John Tressler, and Konrad Kressley provided research assistance. The responsibility for errors, of course, is mine alone.

Jacqueline Greer, Mildred Tyler, and Betty McKee typed a difficult manuscript with skill and patience. My wife Judy assisted tangibly in proofreading and searching out awkward prose, and intangibly in countless ways.

Robert H. Donaldson
Nashville, Tennessee

Contents

Soviet Policy toward India:
Ideology and Strategy

I Marx and Lenin on India: Communist Theory and Practice through 1924

Analysis of the Soviet approach toward independent India—especially an analysis which seeks to emphasize the influence of doctrine—must begin with a backward glance at earlier Marxist-Leninist theory and practice. For by examining the doctrinal tenets and operational strategies of the founders of the Soviet state and of the pioneer Marxist-Leninist "experts" on Asia, the Western scholar is replicating an exercise engaged in by contemporary Soviet (as well as Chinese and Indian Marxist) scholars as they shape their own assessments. Not only recent "scholarly" works, but official pronouncements and documents concerning Soviet policy toward the third world are replete with citations and references to prewar, and indeed prerevolutionary, communist theory and practice. Marxist-Leninists, with their keen sensitivity to the dynamics of history, to the definition of the "nature of the present epoch" as it has developed out of past epochs, continually inform the assessment of the present with the experience of the past.

1. Marxism-Leninism and the East: Before the Revolution

Karl Marx himself, primarily in his role as journalist for a New York newspaper, had occasion to describe from a distance the socioeconomic conditions of British India from the perspective of "scientific socialism." The objectively "progressive" nature of the British development of India was evident to Marx: modern industry stimulated by the railway system would dissolve the hereditary division of labor on which the progress-impeding caste system rested, thus "laying the material foundations of Western society in Asia." [1] The misery and degradation of the masses was a regrettable, but inevitable, by-product of a process which would—once the bourgeoisie had achieved the limits of what it could accomplish—culminate in revolution. Only the overthrow of the ruling classes, either in Britain or in India itself, would allow the Indians to reap the fruits of modernization.

India interested Marx primarily as a source of English strength; the emancipation of the colonies would weaken the bourgeoisie in England itself. Yet from the bulk of Marx's writings it is clear that he considered a socialist revolution in Europe leading to emancipation of the colonies to be far more

1

likely than colonial (and especially Asian) revolutions preceding those in Europe.

It is rather to Lenin than to Marx that Soviet writers turn when they seek the real origin of communist appreciation of the revolutionary potential of the East. That it should have been the Russian rather than the German who directed attention to Asia is not surprising. His acute consciousness of Russia's relative lag in capitalist development, undoubtedly sharpened by the practical difficulties of attaining proletarian revolution in Russian conditions, was expressed by Lenin in what has been termed the "dialectics of backwardness." [2] This standpoint, which did much to heighten the appeal of Russian Marxism in Asia, can be understood only in the context of Lenin's theory of imperialism.

In contrast to Marx's own expectations, Lenin's theory made much more tenable the possibility that revolution would come first to a less-advanced capitalist country—in particular, to Russia. It was at these weakest links, suffering greater strains and lacking the expediential remedies fashioned by more advanced powers, that the imperialist chain was most likely to break.

Though Russia, unlike India, was politically independent and, indeed, one of the Great Powers, Lenin—even after the 1905 revolution—saw similarities between Russian and Indian conditions. In 1908 he wrote: "There is no end to the violence and plunder which goes on . . . in India. Nowhere in the world—with the exception, of course, of Russia—will you find such abject poverty of the masses, and such chronic hunger . . . In India, too, the proletariat has already developed to conscious political mass struggle and, that being the case, the Russian-style British regime in India is doomed!" [3]

Russia and India were, in Lenin's mind, linked not only by similarities of geographical location, backwardness, and oppression, but also by the common character of one of the strains giving rise to their "mass struggles"—the national question. In Asia the movement for self-determination was being led by a bourgeoisie capable of "championing sincere, militant, consistent democracy, a worthy comrade of France's great enlighteners." [4] The principal social support of the bourgeoisie in these movements came from the vast Asian peasantry.

The proletariat, Lenin wrote in 1916, must give "determined support to the more revolutionary elements in the bourgeois-democratic movements" in their agitation for national liberation.[5] Such bourgeois-led movements were deemed worthy of support not only because they created the internal conditions necessary for capitalist (and then socialist) development, but also because they were directed against the imperialist powers. Their success thus weakened the system of imperialism itself. This Leninist position, worked out before 1917, has continued to occupy a central place in the analyses of Soviet policy-makers in the contemporary era.

Yet Lenin's theory by no means justified support of national movements under all circumstances. He was explicit in emphasizing that the degree to which a given nationalism was progressive was very much dependent on the given country's stage of development. The ultimate goal was not national separation, but *"free, voluntary association and merging"* of *socialist* states.[6] Far from supporting efforts to strengthen nationalism, the proletariat must rather support attempts to erase national distinctions.

One further feature of Lenin's thought during this prerevolutionary period—a feature illustrated by his attitude toward the national question—still persists in the Soviet approach to the third world. In devising programs of action and in forming alliances Lenin exploited all the flexibility of which Marxist analysis was capable. He insisted that "due account" be taken of the specific features distinguishing one country or one stage of development from another. The communist analyst must never attempt to " 'fix' for all time the point of view Marx held in a *different epoch*" or to employ "the *letter* of Marxism against the *spirit* of Marxism." [7] Not all nations would arrive at socialism in the same way. The Marxist must be ready to recognize and exploit all progressive manifestations of revolution—however "impure" they might seem—in order to advance the movement toward the attainment of the ultimate goal. "Whoever expects a 'pure' social revolution will *never* live to see it." [8]

2. From the October Revolution through the Second Congress of the Comintern

Having seized power by capitalizing with maximum flexibility on Russian discontents, the Bolsheviks soon discovered the sobering dilemmas of transforming a revolutionary movement into a ruling party. Despite Trotsky's well-known intention as Commissar of Foreign Affairs to issue a few revolutionary proclamations to the peoples of the world and then "close the shop," the failure of the revolutionary spark to spread in Europe necessitated a more serious consideration of the problems of foreign policy.

During the first years of Soviet rule, when the Bolsheviks were preoccupied first with withdrawal from the world war and then with their own civil war, which was complicated by the Allied intervention, some consideration was given to the prospects for an assault on British India, through Afghanistan or Tibet. Here, in light of the ongoing debate over the degree to which Soviet policy was a continuation of tsarist aims, it may be helpful to recall the nineteenth-century Russian designs on India.

In 1801 the "mad Tsar" Paul had hastily assembled an expedition of 23,000 Cossacks under Vasily Orlov whose task was to march on India by way of Khiva and Bukhara. Napoleon, who was at war with Britain, had made preparations to send a French corps to link up with the Cossack expedition. This foolhardy adventure (Orlov was without maps of the area he was to conquer) was terminated in mid-course by the murder of Paul and the accession of Alexander, who recalled Orlov. Seven years later, in the wake of the Tilsit agreement, Alexander himself was cooperating with Napoleon in another scheme—also abortive—to defeat Britain through the conquest of India.

The middle years of the century were marked by British-Russian rivalry in central Asia, as Palmerston strove to ward off the threat he perceived in Russian moves in the Caucasus and Afghanistan. Again in the 1870's British suspicion of Russian designs on India rose as the distance separating the two states' Asian territories shrank. Alexander II ridiculed the British fears in an interview with the British ambassador in 1876 at the same time that General Skobelev was drawing up plans for the invasion of India. According to Michael Florinsky: "Success, in [Skobelev's] opinion, was assured to an expeditionary corps 50,000 strong. He believed, moreover, that India was seething with discontent and that the mere appearance of even a small Russian force on her frontier 'would probably lead to a general uprising in India and to the ruin of the British empire.' The overthrow of the British power in India, Skobelev maintained, might well provoke 'a social revolution' in the metropolis and 'will be the beginning of the fall of England.' " [9] Though Skobelev scrapped his plan as impracticable, his vision of engineering the fall of Britain by first inspiring an Indian uprising was to be revived by Soviet Skobelevs four decades later. Yet with the tsarist legacy then viewed through Marxist-Leninist perspective, there was both a more "scientific" rationale for assuming the hostility of capitalist Britain and a more universalistic mission to be pursued in liberating the oppressed masses of Asia. The difference of perspective—whatever the short-run similarity of strategies—is sufficient to set off Soviet policies as of a different order from the more limited balance-of-power aims of tsarist expansionism.

Of the early Soviet "India-firsters," one of the most outspoken was K. M. Troianovsky. In 1918 he proclaimed that India was to serve as the vanguard of revolution in the East, as Russia had in the West.[10] For Troianovsky, Persia and Turkey were the gates to this Indian "citadel." For other early specialists on the East—including A. Voznesensky, head of the Eastern Department of the Commissariat of Foreign Affairs—Afghanistan, by virtue of its ethnographic and religious similarities, was the "key" to India.[11] A publication of Stalin's Commissariat of Nationalities stressed in February 1919 the crucial role of the Emirate of Bukhara (over which Moscow's rule was reimposed only in September 1920).[12] In the same journal a later article cited yet another road to the crucial "citadel": along "a Mongolian-Buddhist route . . . through Altai, Mongolia, and Tibet, on to India." [13]

The air of unreality in this debate springs from two sources. First, none of the participants—and, indeed, few of the early commentators on the East—were among the top Bolshevik leadership, and all were "specialists" in the sense that their assignments were to the various bureaus devoted to affairs in the East. Among these organizations there was as yet no clear division of labor, and an atmosphere of competition to produce the spectacular was evident. Second, not only were these speculations probably unheeded, but they were undoubtedly inspired by unreliable information on revolutionary prospects in Asia. Soviet control over the areas of the former tsarist empire bordering the countries in question had not yet been consolidated, so that intelligence was sporadic and often exaggerated. For example, some of the earlier Soviet articles concerning the impact of the October Revolution and the strength of local communists in

India cited as sources British officials and journalists in India—men who shared with the Soviet "Asia-firsters" a desire to magnify the immediacy of the Bolshevik threat.[14]

At least one top party leader joined in the discussion of the "road to India." Trotsky, musing over setbacks to Soviet fortunes in Hungary and the Ukraine, had written to the Central Committee in August 1919: "The road to India may prove at the given moment to be more readily passable and shorter for us than the road to Soviet Hungary. The sort of army which at the moment can be of no great significance in the European scales can upset the unstable balance of Asian relationships . . . [and] give a direct push to an uprising on the part of the oppressed masses." [15] Trotsky admitted, however, that preparation for such a venture could in the immediate future take on only a "preliminary" character.

At that very time, one scheme for utilizing unrest on the "road to India" was proceeding beyond mere speculation. In the fall of 1920, the Indian communist M. N. Roy won approval from Moscow for an attempt to train an army of Indian revolutionaries at Tashkent. Roy was a former Bengali terrorist who had worked with an émigré Indian revolutionary party in California and had helped to found the Communist Party of Mexico. According to his plan, an armed Soviet-Indian force would pass through Afghanistan (with the consent of her monarch, recently at war with Britain) to the northwestern Indian frontier. A revolutionary government would be proclaimed, inspiring the oppressed masses to topple both the British and the Indian bourgeoisie, with the further effect of upsetting imperialist rule in Britain itself.[16]

Though the "army's" military equipment (two trainloads of arms and bullion) did get as far as Tashkent, where a number of Indians were schooled in military and propaganda techniques, Roy's grandiose scheme progressed no further.

One of the main obstacles to success was the unreliable nature of the Indian "revolutionaries" with whom Roy was working. Most of those who were not deserters from the army, traders, or mere adventurers were "Muhajirs," young Moslems who had joined the pan-Islamic Khilafat movement which sought to aid the Turks against the Allies. Having set out for Turkey via Afghanistan, a group of them were rescued from Turcoman tribesmen by a detachment of the Red Army and taken to Tashkent. One of them, Shaukat Usmani, records his impressions: "We had imagined the Bolsheviks to be vulgar, rustic and fearsome people, as the cartoons appearing in British Indian newspapers had depicted them . . . [We were] hailed as the 'representatives of the Indian Revolution.' We were amused at this designation." [17] Persuaded to stay in Tashkent, these Moslem Indians formed the bulk of Roy's force. But they were irresolute cadres, "each of them a self-styled leader," who fell out among themselves.[18] Only a handful, including Usmani, ultimately became Marxists.

In addition to the unstable nature of the "invasion force," which caused the Soviets to back away from the plan, Roy's scheme was also doomed by King Amanullah's unwillingness to have Afghanistan used as a base for the expedition. The British had gotten wind of Roy's plan and had delivered a stern warning to the Afghans in March 1921. British pressure was followed by a cooling of Amanullah's relations with the Soviets and the signing of an Anglo-Afghan treaty.

A final factor was British pressure on the Soviets themselves to live up to a promise, included in the Anglo-Soviet Trade Agreement of April 1921, to refrain from military, diplomatic, or propaganda activity directed against the British Empire. The Soviets were not unmoved by the British protest. Following an exchange of notes, the Tashkent schools—which the British had singled out in their note—were abandoned, and the few remaining Indians were removed to Moscow.[19] A rival group of Indian revolutionaries, based in Berlin, were angered when told by Lenin in the same year that the Soviet government could not actively take part in any plan for promoting revolution in India. When referred by Lenin to Karl Radek, then Secretary of the Comintern, they were given an equally unenthusiastic reception.[20]

The Soviet attitude can be understood only in the context of Russia's primary internal and external preoccupations in 1921. It was the year of the New Economic Policy; concern for repairing the economic damage done by War Communism was impelling the Soviet regime to seek normalization of relations, as well as trade and credits, from the capitalist governments of Europe. Still isolated as the only communist state, and no longer faced with the necessity to wage a war of survival, the regime was taking the opportunity to strengthen itself for the struggles ahead. Inspiring revolution in India through Comintern propaganda or schemes of military aid now seemed a less immediate prospect than in the first heady months after the revolution. Thus, to deemphasize overt designs against India in order not to jeopardize the possibilities of British assistance probably seemed to the Soviets to be an acceptable bargain for the short run. By utilizing the breathing space to strengthen their rule—allowing the capitalists with their aid to "dig their own graves"—the Soviets would be better able to capitalize on future revolutionary potential in India.

While the aforementioned were undoubtedly the major considerations leading to the Soviet détente with Britain, the official justifications were phrased in different terms. M. Pavlovich, head of the All-Union Association of Orientalists, wrote of the 1921 agreement that England, fearing that she might lose her hold over India, was actually retreating before the Soviet successes.[21] To Shaukat Usmani, Stalin offered yet another reason for the Comintern's suspension of plans to aid the Indian revolution. To the Indian's complaint ("we were orphans now"), Stalin is said to have replied: "We want to help you, but it is your own people who have quarrelled and spurned all help." [22] Though Stalin's charge was at least partially justified, this was not to be the last time that the failure of revolution to materialize was blamed exclusively on the defects of local cadres.

Although the Soviets in the early 1920's were scaling down operationally in South Asia, the period saw a rich development of revolutionary theory, which was to serve as a framework for future operational strategies. Especially important were the proceedings of the Second Congress of the Comintern, held in July 1920 and attended by delegates from India, Turkey, Persia, China, and Korea. Though it, like the First Congress, was preoccupied with European affairs, the Second Congress devoted two sessions to a lively debate on the "national and colonial questions"—on ways of applying revolutionary doctrine to the colonial and backward countries of the East. A wide range of issues was discussed—issues which have arisen again and again until the present day. A close study of the debates and of the two sets of theses (Lenin's and M. N. Roy's) which were approved by the congress is warranted in view of the continuing theoretical and operational importance of these questions.

The following are the issues to be surveyed: (1) How important to the world revolution are the colonial and national movements in the East? (2) What is the class basis of these movements? (3) What attitude should the Comintern and colonial communist parties take toward movements not headed by the working class? (4) How is the peasant movement to be developed? (5) What is likely to be the future course of development in the colonies?

Lenin himself set the framework for the debate by submitting a set of draft theses to the Commission on the National and Colonial Questions and inviting discussion and amendment. M. N. Roy accepted Lenin's invitation. In discussions with Lenin, Roy challenged the Russian's factual knowledge of the situation in India. According to Roy (who did not number modesty among his virtues and whose memoirs are often self-inflating), Lenin's confidence in his own theses was shaken by the Indian's arguments, and he urged Roy to draw up supplementary theses.[23] After debate in the commission, both drafts were revised and submitted to the full congress, which adopted them unanimously.

On the question of the relative importance of the movements in the East, Roy at first took an extreme position. He argued that superprofits obtained from colonial investments were "the chief mainstay" of contemporary capitalism; only when these were dried up by the overthrow of imperialism in the East could the European proletariat succeed.[24] Thus the first priority of the Comintern had to be the liberation of the East, on which the destiny of the European revolution was absolutely dependent.

On the other extreme of this issue was the Italian Serrati, who argued that the entire debate on the colonies was meaningless since revolutions in the East were bourgeois-national in character; orthodox Marxists should have nothing to do with them.[25]

Lenin, though he defended the need for debate, agreed that "Comrade Roy goes too far in declaring that the destiny of the West will depend exclusively on the degree of development and the strength of the revolutionary movement in Eastern countries." [26] The Eastern peoples constituted the "reserves" of the world revolution; while this meant that their movement was more than a mere auxiliary to the European revolution, one could not expect victory in the East alone to bring victory in the West.[27]

The strength of the opposition caused Roy to revise his position. The colonies, in his final draft, became "*one* of the main sources" of the strength of imperialism, and victory for the European working class was "not easy" without revolution in the

East.[28] Yet in his speech at the July 26 session of the congress
he continued to stress the "huge significance" of the movements in the East, the "very fast tempo" of industrial development, especially in India, and the inadequacy of the attention
which European parties had paid to the colonies.[29]

On the question of the class nature of the movements in the
colonies and dependent countries, Roy again differed with
Lenin. With reference to his native land, he flatly declared:
"The popular masses of India are not reached by the nationalist
spirit; they are interested exclusively in questions of a socioeconomic character." [30] They did not and should not support
the bourgeois-democratic national movement, whose leadership, seeking political independence under a capitalist system,
was not truly revolutionary.[31]

Lenin, characteristically, failed to share Roy's optimism concerning the possibilities for spontaneous development of mass
revolutionary consciousness in India. He observed that, despite
the existence of five million proletarians and thirty-seven million landless peasants, "the Hindu Communists did not succeed
until the present time in establishing a Communist party in
their country, and because of this single fact the views of
Comrade Roy are to a large extent not well grounded." [32] In
most oppressed nations, the proletarian elements were simply
not large enough to head a distinct, purely class-based, struggle.

What, then, should the attitude of the Comintern be toward
these national-liberation movements in the East? For Lenin,
the pressing priority of the struggle of imperialism against the
"Soviet states" temporarily placed in abeyance the orthodox
Marxist position concerning internal class alignments and made
necessary cooperation between the proletariat of the Comintern
and the bourgeois-nationalists of the East against the common
enemy, imperialism. Only in the course of the movement for national liberation could Indian communists develop their organization to the point where they would be able, "once the national demands were satisfied, to attack the Indian bourgeoisie." [33]

Roy's disagreement with this position was fundamental; in
the commission debates he urged that this point be eliminated
entirely from Lenin's theses. The communist movement in the
colonies must remain separate from the bourgeois-democratic
movement, must struggle only for the class interests of the
masses, and must be the exclusive recipient of Comintern aid.[34]

Gandhi, the emerging leader of the Indian nationalist forces, was, according to Roy, a social reactionary, comparable to the Russian Populists and Social Revolutionaries—hardly an ally worthy of communist support, however temporary. The Indian communists should not ally with Gandhi, but should seize the direction of the mass movement in their own hands.

Lenin's reply to Roy stressed that for a long time the Indian communist party would be small and weak, unable by itself to reach large numbers of the masses. But, on the basis of the demands for national liberation, many more of the workers and peasants could be mobilized. Lenin reminded Roy that the Bolsheviks had supported the "liberal-liberation movement" when it had taken a stand against tsarism. Likewise, "the Hindu Communists are duty-bound to support the bourgeois-liberation movement without, however, merging with it." [35] The projected alliance would not only present the greatest challenge to imperialism, but it would also facilitate the strengthening of the ties of Asian communists to the masses.

Lenin, reminding the delegates that a "pure" social revolution was unthinkable, was urging them to adapt to political and social realities in the East. He did, however, in a concession to Roy and his supporters, acknowledge the distinction between reformist bourgeois-democratic movements (those in which the bourgeoisie joined forces with the imperialists against the working-class movement) and "genuinely revolutionary" bourgeois-liberation movements, the main criterion of which was apparently that the communists were left free to organize the masses.[36] The latter movements were to receive the "active support" of communist parties and "temporary relationships and even alliances" with the Comintern.

A parallel concession was made by Roy in the revised version of his theses. He now admitted that for "the overthrow of foreign capital, as the first step to a revolution in the colonies, it is useful to employ the cooperation of the bourgeois national-revolutionary elements." But he continued to insist that the "foremost and necessary task" was the creation of communist parties in the East.[37] With respect to this task there was general agreement that special tutelary responsibilities rested with the communist parties of countries possessing colonies.

Not only in the theses on the national and colonial questions, but also in a separate set of theses on the agrarian question, the Second Congress set forth its position on the agrarian social structure and on the proper attitude for communists to assume toward the peasantry. The issue, of course, was not one which pertained solely to the East; rather, it was a fundamental theoretical and strategical problem for every communist party.

In the latter set of theses, the agrarian population was categorized into the following groups: (1) the agricultural proletariat—seasonal, migrant, and daily wage-workers who possess no land; (2) the semiproletariat, who own or rent only an inadequate plot of land and who must supplement their earnings by wage labor; (3) the small peasants, who work small farms which are barely adequate for their needs; (4) the middle peasants, whose farms yield a small surplus, and many of whom employ hired labor; (5) the large peasants (or kulaks), who run their farms as capitalist undertakings and who employ wage laborers, but who themselves work and by manner of living are connected with the peasantry; (6) the large landowners, who directly or through leasing land systematically exploit their wage-workers and neighboring small peasants, without themselves working.

The first two groups were to be organized as allies by the industrial proletariat. Small and middle peasants would, in the struggle with the bourgeoisie, tend to waver and must be neutralized by the proletariat, that is, prevented from giving active help to the bourgeoisie. They would be promised that they might retain their holdings and even increase them by adding all the land they had hitherto rented. The large peasants were openly hostile to the proletarian revolution, but their land was to be expropriated only if they showed resistance to the regime of the workers. The land of the large landowners, however, must be expropriated, without compensation, at the moment of victory of the revolution.[38]

This analysis of the agrarian social structure and the basic strategy accompanying it have remained in force with little change up to the present time. Categories derived largely from the Bolshevik experience in Russia have been superimposed by Marxist-Leninists on various agrarian situations little resembling either each other or Russia, with the frequent consequence of distorting or blunting Soviet and local communist perceptions of social forces in the countryside. Particular examples of this tendency as it has applied in India will be examined in later chapters. At the Second Congress, little effort was made by Lenin or others to differentiate between the European and Asian countrysides.

One final issue which received the congress' attention, and which has persisted as a much-discussed question among Soviet theorists, was the question of the future course of development communists should expect and promote in the Eastern countries. Lenin phrased the issue thus: ". . . is the capitalist stage of economic development inevitable for those backward nations which are now winning liberation and in which progressive trends are to be observed since the war?" [39] The answer given by both Lenin and Roy was a conditional "no." If the victorious proletariat of the advanced countries were to come to their assistance with all the resources it commanded, then it was not inevitable that the backward countries must pass through the capitalist stage in order to advance to communism.

Despite the congress' decision to adopt revised versions of both sets of theses and the genuine attempt to achieve a reconciliation of the divergent views of Lenin and Roy, the division—especially on the issues concerning the relative importance of the East and the relative degree of support to be given communist and noncommunist movements there—survived the debates.[40] These issues were to reappear throughout the next few decades, climaxing finally in the present unrestrained clash between Soviet and Chinese communists.

3. 1920–1924: Leninist Theory and Indian Reality

With initial Soviet plans for *direct* assistance to the Indian revolution frustrated in 1921 as a result of British pressure and the cooling of Soviet relations with Afghanistan, Soviet and Comintern emphasis shifted in the early 1920's to the fostering of a communist party in India and the forging of ties with the Indian national movement.

India was indeed seething with social and political unrest in the postwar years. Rising prices and heavy taxation combined with disastrous crop failures and a particularly tragic influenza epidemic in 1918–1919 to produce agitation and violence throughout the country. Calamities of climate and economy were compounded by political blunders. The passage in March 1919 of the Rowlatt Acts—antisedition laws which allowed for imprisonment of troublemakers without trial—provided the spark which set off Mahatma Gandhi's first campaign of passive resistance to and noncooperation with the government. Agitation against the British mounted even higher with the Amritsar Massacre in April, in which hundreds of Indians were killed when a British general ordered his troops to fire on an illegal assembly. The Afghan War and the rise of the Khilafat movement provided the Moslem population with additional grievances against Britain.

The Montagu-Chelmsford reforms of December, which introduced the system of "dyarchy" and a limited participation of elected Indian representatives in the central and provincial governments, were spurned by Gandhi and the Indian National Congress. The following September they began a *satyagraha* (noncooperation campaign) and *hartal* (boycott of British manufactures) accompanied by agitation for revival of village industry (symbolized by the spinning wheel). The aim of the Congress-led campaign was a vaguely defined *swaraj* (home rule).

Gandhi's saintliness and simple mode of life, along with his ability to seize upon symbols which could impart to complex constitutional issues a meaning comprehensible to the Indian villager, enabled him to bring the broad masses into the liberation struggle. Gandhi was thus the link between the westernized intellectual of the Congress and the villager. But his resistance to modernity displeased the Westernizers, while the Marxists were dissatisfied in addition by his refusal to appeal to class interests and class struggle. But despite Gandhi's steadfast insistence on nonviolent means of resistance, there were numerous bloody incidents, especially in connection with the peasant movements in the Punjab and Malabar, in which Sikh and Moslem peasants murdered Hindu landlords. This produced a division between the Congress and the Moslem League and further Hindu-Moslem strife. Finally, when a mob of peasants at Chauri Chaura in February 1922 murdered twenty-two policemen, Gandhi, concluding that the nation was not yet prepared for lofty struggle, suspended the noncooperation and civil disobedience campaigns. His own arrest and imprisonment the next month signaled the breakdown of this stage of the mass Indian national movement. In the following year, C. R. Das and Motilal Nehru regained control of the Congress for the moderate faction. They led the Congress in participation in the elections and renewed cooperation with the British, proclaiming as the new goal the attainment of dominion status for India.

From his headquarters in Berlin, M. N. Roy was, during these years, the primary link between the Comintern and the scattered groups of communists existing in an increasingly turbulent India. He continued to regard Gandhi and the Indian bourgeoisie as too inclined to compromise with imperialism to be even a temporary ally. Rather than the united front from above which Lenin had preferred, Roy continued to urge Indian communists to form an opposition bloc within the Indian National Congress and capture its leadership, at the same time working to convert left-wing Congressmen to communism by discrediting the "reactionary" leadership of Gandhi. In Roy's view, Indian social and economic development had passed the stage in which the bourgeoisie could play the leading role. As an aspiring leader of Asian communism, it was only natural that his immediate priority was the strengthening of his own harassed cadres vis-à-vis the Congress leadership.

The revolutionary turmoil in India had not gone unnoticed by the Soviets. In 1922 Lenin had predicted that India and China were "inexorably and with mounting momentum . . . approaching their 1905." [41] An even more enthusiastic spectator, A. Mashitsky, writing in the official organ of the People's Commissariat of Foreign Affairs, had claimed that "India is aflame with revolution," and that she would play "the most important role in the task of winning the international victory over imperialism." [42]

Soviet spokesmen, however, continued to feel both that the Indian proletariat was too weak to challenge the middle classes and that there was enough revolutionary potential remaining in a section of the bourgeoisie to justify a temporary alliance against the "main enemy," the British. [43] This was by no means the last time that Soviet interests prescribed a different strategy than did the interests of local communists.

One clear example of the Soviet position at this time is in the attitude taken toward the nationalist regime in Turkey, which—while engaging in systematic liquidation of local communists—was considered "objectively" anti-imperialist and was Soviet Russia's only ally among the Eastern countries. In a speech to the Fourth Congress, Karl Radek appealed to the Turkish communists thus: " 'Let not the present moment ob-

scure your outlook on the near future!' The defense of the independence of Turkey, which is of paramount international revolutionary importance, has not yet been achieved. You should
defend yourself against the persecutors . . . but you should also
realize that . . . you have a long road before you which you will
have to follow together with the other revolutionary elements of
Turkey for some time to come." [44] Thus it was the interests of
the international revolution—which increasingly came to mean
the interests of the Soviet Union—rather than those of local
communist groups which were of paramount importance in
shaping Comintern policy.

"The Theses on the Eastern Question" of the Fourth Comintern Congress embodied this Soviet priority rather than Roy's.
The communists, while supporting "every national revolutionary movement against imperialism," must keep in mind that
the bourgeois elements begin to turn away from the movement
as the social interests of the masses come to the forefront. But
only when the proletariat had won the struggle for influence
over the peasant masses would it be in a position to challenge
the bourgeoisie for leadership. Until that time, "[t]he refusal of
the communists in the colonies to take part in the struggle
against imperialist tyranny, on the ground of the ostensible 'defense' of their independent class interests, is opportunism of
the worst kind . . . only the extension and intensification of the
struggle against the imperialist yoke of the great Powers will
ensure for them the role of revolutionary leadership." [45] Thus, in
the majority view, the social forces in the colonies had not yet
developed to the point at which the realization of the socialist
program had become the immediate task.

Despite the Comintern's continuing optimism concerning
revolutionary prospects in India, the fortunes of the Indian
communists had by 1924 plunged to new depths. The defeat of
Roy's attempt to capture the Indian National Congress shortly
after the Comintern congress was followed by the victory of the
moderate Swaraj party faction in September 1923. Police harassment of communist groups increased during 1923; Roy's
newspapers were confiscated, and his chief courier between
Europe and India was arrested. British repression reached a
climax in 1924 with the Cawnpore conspiracy case, in which
Roy, Usmani, and six others were charged with conspiring "to
establish throughout British India a branch of a revolutionary
organization known as the Communist International with the

object of depriving the King of the Sovereignty of British India." Only four defendants were present for trial, which was concluded in May 1924. All were sentenced to four years in prison. The judges who heard their appeal acknowledged that the "conspiracy" had been so absurd as to have constituted no real threat, but upheld the convictions. Thus the most active of the communists on the scene in India were temporarily removed, and further progress in forming a united communist party in India was delayed several years.[46]

Against the background of a clear trend of disintegration in the Indian movement, the Fifth Comintern Congress met in July 1924. How poorly most of the delegates understood the true situation was revealed by the manner in which the same optimistic claims and well-worn slogans of the past four years were reiterated. Trotsky proclaimed that in India the "revolutionary movement is penetrating deeper and reaching wider and wider masses," failing altogether to mention the Cawnpore setback.[47] Congress manifestos pledged support to "every honest expression" of the national-liberation movement directed against foreign capital and stressed the need to develop further "direct links" between the Executive Committee of the Communist International (ECCI) and these movements.[48]

Again M. N. Roy played an opposition role, though this time his objections were so strenuous that Manuilsky, chairing the Colonial Commission, charged that Roy's exaggeration of the communist movement in India "to the detriment of the national movement" constituted a deviation reminiscent of the "nihilism of Rosa Luxemburg." [49]

Roy in turn accused Manuilsky of a poor acquaintance with the facts: "He said that during the last year there has been a strong revival of the national movement in British India. But, comrades, actually we witness the opposite . . . the worst depression in the Indian national movement . . . If we determine here . . . our future tactic on the basis of a fictitious picture, we very naturally will fail to reach correct results." [50]

The recently departed Lenin, argued Roy, did not intend that his theses of 1920 be applied "in a purely mechanical way," without regard to actual conditions and changed circumstances. Yet this was the error the Comintern was making in calling for "direct contact" with national-liberation movements. These movements were no longer unified, but increasingly divided by growing class conflicts, and a "direct contact is necessary with the revolutionary organizations of the working class and the peasantry and not with the bourgeois nationalists, who themselves have no desires to have anything in common with the Communist International." [51] Lenin's legacy—a sensitivity to anti-imperialist and revolutionary potentialities in the East, and the willingness to devise new strategies to exploit these possibilities—was being wasted, Roy seemed to be saying, by the Comintern's mechanical application of an outdated approach.

It was a not untypical irony of the Stalinist era which was about to dawn that the course for which Roy had argued in vain was to be adopted by the Comintern only four years later, just as Roy himself was being purged from his prominent position. But between the fifth and sixth world congresses there was to intervene Stalin's disastrous adventure in China, the consequences of which were to have a direct and damaging effect on Indian communism as well as on the entire movement in Asia.

II The Soviet Approach to India in the Stalin Era

It is, of course, far from an idle academic exercise to examine J. V. Stalin's views concerning the Eastern countries. Not only was Stalin operationally concerned with national and colonial problems early in his career, as Commissar of Nationalities, and thus influential in shaping Soviet policy in the East even prior to his rise to undisputed leadership of the party; in addition, for a whole generation of Soviet scholars, diplomats, and journalists, quotations from Comrade Stalin's writings became obligatory accessories to any commentary on Asia (as well as many other subjects). Thus, while personal public pronouncements from Stalin concerning the colonial areas were rare after the 1920's, his stated views from this early period continued to shape Soviet analysis and policy for almost three decades.

1. Stalin and the East prior to the Sixth Comintern Congress

One of the earliest and most famous of Stalin's writings in this area is "Don't Forget the East," written just a year after the October Revolution. Despite the impression conveyed by the title of the article, Stalin did not argue in it that the Bolsheviks should give first priority to revolution in the East. It was only natural, he said, that Soviet attention was focused on Europe, for that was where imperialism must first be defeated. This understandable preoccupation should not, however, cause the Bolsheviks to forget the East, the " 'inexhaustible' reserve and 'most reliable' rear of world imperialism." Communists must assist the peoples of the East in developing a conscious struggle against imperialism—a process which would be "spurred" by revolution in Europe. For without the emancipation of the East, complete victory over imperialism could not be attained.[1]

a. Stalin and the National Question

It was the national movement, and more particularly the question of self-determination, which occupied the central place in Stalin's early writings on the East. As Commissar of Nationalities, he was deeply involved in the problems of gaining control for the Soviet regime over the non-Russian lands of the former empire. While his own writings on the national question are not in conflict with the Leninist theories discussed

earlier, they do evidence a greater sensitivity to the immediate
tactical problems involved.

Like Lenin (and Marx before him), Stalin manifested a dual
attitude toward nationalism: as a movement controlled by the
bourgeoisie and employed by it to delude or oppress the toiling
masses, it was nefarious, but as a "progressive" anti-imperialist
and antifeudalist movement utilized to strengthen the position
of the workers and hasten their development, it was worthy of
tactical support.

Stalin felt that the existence in the platform of the Russian
party of a widely advertised "solution" to the problem of national minorities—many of whom were related ethnically, re-
ligiously, or linguistically to Eastern peoples outside the empire—greatly enhanced the appeal of the noncapitalist path
being taken by Soviet Russia.

India was one of those countries which Stalin had in mind as
being susceptible, for a number of reasons, to the influence of
Soviet nationality policy. First, India was an oppressed colony
and the scene of a national-liberation movement which, if successful, would severely shake the imperialist system. Second,
India had a large Moslem population and was thus linked by
religion to many of the national minorities of Soviet Asia. (This
Moslem population in India had been one of the targets of an
early appeal by Lenin and Stalin to the "toiling Muslims" to
overthrow the foreign "despoilers" and "enslavers.") [2] Third,
Stalin conceived of India, like the Soviet Union, as a multinational state, beset with all the problems of linguistic and cultural diversity to which Soviet nationality policy addressed itself. In 1925 Stalin, in a passage later to be much quoted by
Soviet writers on India, wrote: "Now India is talked about as
one entity. But there can be hardly any doubt that in the case of
a revolutionary upheaval in India, many hitherto unknown nationalities, each with its own language and its own distinctive
culture, will emerge on the scene." [3]

Was a revolutionary upheaval near in India? Like Lenin, and
contrary to Marx, Stalin held that countries where the imperialist system was weakest—and not just those in which capitalism
itself was most advanced—were ripe for revolution. Thus Stalin
did not exclude the possibility that the next "weakest link" in
the "imperialist chain"—after Russia—would be India. In 1924
he observed that, given a certain minimum level of industrial
development, and with it an industrial proletariat led by a

vanguard, allied with the peasantry, and possessed of a revolutionary spirit, "[i]t is not precluded that the chain will break, let us say, in India." [4]

Shortly afterward, Stalin was indeed deeply involved in promoting an anti-imperialist revolution in an economically backward Asian country—but the locus of his efforts was China, not India. Why did Stalin choose to work in the one country rather than the other? What differences did he see between the revolutionary prospects of the two? And what effects did his experiences with China have on his future policies in the East?

b. The Turn toward Asia

After a long period of intense preoccupation with revolutionary prospects in Europe, the Soviets turned their attention and energies to Asia in the mid-1920's. As was to be the case again after the war, a situation of stalemate in Europe combined with an apparent power vacuum in Asia led to the shift of Soviet focus. Following the achievement of de jure recognition from MacDonald's government early in 1924, Soviet diplomatic and trade relations with Britain steadily worsened until they were ruptured in 1927, leaving the Soviets with few tangible gains from their hard-fought offensive to regain diplomatic status in Europe. In addition, the Rapallo arrangements which Chicherin had negotiated with Germany in 1922 were deprived of much of their significance by the Locarno Pact in 1925 and the cooling of Soviet-German relations. Thus the Soviets were isolated on the diplomatic front and unable to see any signs of impending social revolution in the West.

In China, however, they were faced at this time with a challenge and an opportunity. Both arose from the internal political weakness of China, which, while raising the specter of an expansion of European and Japanese imperialist power and a potential threat to Soviet Asia, also presented to both the Soviets and the Chinese communists an opening for increased influence. Thus there took place in China in the 1920's a convergence of the traditional Russian interest in excluding hostile powers from a weak China and of the Marxist-Leninist impulse to strike a blow at imperialism by depriving it of one of its most important "reserves." In terms of Russian national security, the interest was in creating a friendly China unified and strong enough to ward off intervention, especially from Britain or Japan. From doctrinal perspective, the maximum objectives were both the achievement of the national liberation of China from the imperialist system and the liberation of the Chinese masses from oppression by native feudal and bourgeois forces.

The difficulty for Soviet strategists, however, lay in the potential contradiction involved in seeking the dual objectives of national liberation and internal revolution. For it was precisely the "oppressing classes" of China who were at the head of the movement to oust imperialist power. The strategy with which the Soviets proposed to overcome this dilemma called, as George Kennan has suggested, for "killing two birds with one stone"—supporting the Kuomintang movement against the imperialists and the "puppet" Peking government, while instructing and aiding the Chinese communists to penetrate and win over the Kuomintang.[5]

In January of 1923 the Executive Committee of the Comintern gave its ideological blessing to this strategy, declaring: "The Kuomintang is the only serious national-revolutionary group in China. Inasmuch as the independent workers movement in the country is still weak, and inasmuch as the national revolution against the imperialists and their domestic feudal agents is still the central task for China . . . under the existing conditions it is expedient for the members of the CCP to remain within the Kuomintang."[6] This resolution added that the Chinese party must not, however, merge with the Kuomintang and that in the course of these campaigns, it must not "fold up its own banner."

c. Stalin's Speech to the KUTV

Stalin's most detailed statement on China (and India) prior to 1926 came in his speech to the Communist University of the Toilers of the East (KUTV) in May 1925. The university had been established in 1921 for the purpose of providing Marxist-Leninist training to prospective revolutionary cadres from the Eastern countries. According to M. N. Roy, Stalin placed special emphasis on the role played by this institution.[7] Thus, it was in an address to this group of "students" that Stalin set forth the tasks to be performed in the East.[8]

Stalin began by outlining the effects on colonial and semicolonial countries in the East of a developing revolutionary crisis fed by imperialist oppression. The rapid growth of capital in some of the countries—he cited India as an example—had engendered a "more or less numerous" proletariat as well as the oppression of the workers by native and foreign capitalists. The "national bourgeoisie" in these countries had split into "a revolutionary section (the petty bourgeoisie) and a compromising section (the big bourgeoisie), the former of which continues the revolutionary struggle, while the latter enters into a bloc with imperialism." In opposition to this imperialist bloc the workers and revolutionary petty bourgeoisie form an anti-imperialist bloc.

Only in its emphasis on the degree of capitalist development in the colonies and on the differentiation within the bourgeoisie did Stalin's analysis differ from that of Lenin. However, from these distinctions followed a divergence in the operational strategy deduced by Stalin from his analysis of social forces. Specifically, Stalin's strategy embodied the conviction that liberation could be achieved only through a revolution which *followed* isolation of the compromising bourgeoisie and achievement of proletarian hegemony. The proletariat in turn must be led by a communist party bound to the Western proletariat (that is, the Comintern).

However, the strategy was to be applied not uniformly but according to the degree of development in each Eastern country. It was immediately applicable only in "capitalistically developed" countries like India, where the compromising section of the national bourgeoisie, fearing revolution and the loss of its own wealth, had already "in the main" come to an agreement with the imperialists. In such cases, the communists must "concentrate their fire" on the compromisers, emancipate the masses from their influence, and "systematically" prepare the conditions for the hegemony of the proletariat in the liberation struggle. The party must "set up a national revolutionary bloc of workers, peasants, and the revolutionary intelligentsia against the bloc of the compromising national bourgeoisie and imperialism."

But in an industrially undeveloped country like Morocco, where there was neither a proletariat nor a bourgeoisie (much less a differentiated bourgeoisie), a united anti-imperialist front was the order of the day, and a separate communist party would be formed only immediately before or just after the victory over imperialism.

There was, however, a third type of configuration of social forces perceived by Stalin in the East, for which he prescribed yet a third strategy. In countries like China or Egypt, he main-

tained, there was little development of industry or of the proletariat. While there was a "compromising" section of the
bourgeoisie, it had not yet managed to form a bloc with the imperialists. Here the proper form of struggle was neither the
united national front nor the anti-imperialist bloc over which
the proletariat had control. Rather there should be a bloc of two
forces, the communist party and the revolutionary petty bourgeoisie, which might be united in "a single party of workers
and peasants, like the Kuomintang." This bloc, though led by
noncommunist forces, must be a sort that would preserve communist freedom of action and facilitate its leadership. It was to
engage in the task of exposing the compromising wing of the
bourgeoisie and waging a "determined struggle" against imperialism. But the alliance embodied by this bloc was definitely to
be temporary. Thus Stalin in 1927 vividly described the ultimate Soviet intentions toward the Kuomintang: "They have to
be utilized to the end, squeezed out like a lemon and then
thrown away." [9]

But Stalin underestimated the difficulty of properly assessing
the alignment of social forces in a particular situation—
especially whether a given "bourgeois" group was in league
with imperialism, merely vacillating, or still revolutionary.
Moreover, with regard to those elements of the bourgeoisie
which were adjudged "objectively revolutionary," there was no
guideline laid down by Stalin's analysis which could aid in determining how subjectively revolutionary—that is, how favorably disposed to local communists and to the Soviet Union—
they were. This factor proved to be Stalin's undoing in his application of the strategy to China.

That Stalin attempted to distinguish between the stages of development of various Asian revolutions in the mid-1920's helps
to explain why he chose to concentrate his energies on the
Chinese rather than the Indian anti-imperialist movement. For
having adjudged the Kuomintang an objectively anti-imperialist
group not yet confronted with an opposing bloc of compromising bourgeoisie and imperialists, Stalin was deciding to give Soviet and Chinese communist support to a going organization, to
which entry had already been gained. Not simply a bourgeois
party, the Kuomintang represented a bloc of four classes—
workers, peasants, petty bourgeoisie, and the revolutionary stratum of the national bourgeoisie. Communist participation in
such a bloc, he argued, was both ideologically defensible and

tactically sound. Furthermore, the chances of success seemed great, given the power vacuum existing in China and crying to be filled—if not by pro-Soviet forces, then by hostile ones.

In India, on the contrary, imperialist power showed no signs of imminent collapse. The British had already demonstrated their skill in harassing the Indian communists to the point of rendering them disorganized and ineffective. And the colonial power was favored in India by a good system of communications and transportation (which China lacked), making the pursuit of a revolutionary army far easier. India's social structure, still characterized by the caste system, had not collapsed under Western challenge, as had China's. Moreover, the British features of Western education, the rule of law, a national army, and a civil service had imparted to Indian society an increased ability to resist sudden and violent change.

Nor was there a mass organization of sufficiently revolutionary character to which the Soviets and the Indian party could attach themselves. The Indian National Congress had never embraced violent means, and its leadership in the mid-1920's had even moderated some of Gandhi's goals. Thus the immediate situation in India was not one which could, in Stalin's view, quickly pay off in revolution. The vacillating section of the bourgeoisie would have to be removed from its entrenched position of influence over the masses before the communists could ever hope to move the masses in a victorious revolution against the British.

d. The Chinese Revolution

The launching in June 1926 of Chiang Kai-shek's northern expedition aimed at extending Nationalist control toward Peking was followed by strains within the "anti-imperialist bloc." Some Chinese communists, now fearing more intensely the loss of their independence of action and the rise of "new warlords" in the Canton government, appealed unsuccessfully to the Comintern to be allowed to withdraw from the Kuomintang. The Seventh Plenum of the ECCI considered the issue in November–December 1926, with Stalin for the first time playing a large role in that body. The plenum reaffirmed the principle of alliance, realizing that to abandon the Kuomintang entirely would be to sacrifice the peasantry to bourgeois influence. But the ECCI now directed the communists to move toward achievement of proletarian hegemony *within* the Kuomintang.

An emissary was sent to China by the Comintern to win acceptance for this decision. That the emissary was M. N. Roy, who had not himself been an advocate of the alliance, was not without significance for the development of the Indian party in this period.

Chiang's "April coup" in Shanghai, which led to the slaughter of many communists and an open split in the Kuomintang, failed to convince Stalin to end the policy of alliance. Rather, the communists were now instructed to seek hegemony over the Kuomintang left wing, centered in Wuhan, and to cease cooperation with Chiang's right wing. The bloc of four classes simply became a bloc of three. Under heavy fire from Trotsky (who called for abandoning the Kuomintang and forming soviets), Stalin was loath to admit—by severing ties with the Kuomintang—that his policy of alliance had been mistaken. As Benjamin Schwartz has aptly noted, "one is tempted to suspect that the theory concerning the 'class compositions' of the Kuomintang was deduced from the strategic desirability of cooperating with the Kuomintang rather than *vice versa.*" [10] The assessment becomes even more apt if one includes, along with his reading of "strategic desirability" in China, Stalin's view of the tactical necessities of his struggle with Trotsky.

In September 1927, the break with the Kuomintang was finally effected, freeing the communists to press for truly radical agrarian reforms. But in Stalin's judgment, the basic emphasis was to be put not on the peasantry, but on strengthening communist ties with the proletariat and on the preparation for a rising of the industrial working class. This demand led to the last of a series of defeats for the communists in 1927, the crushing of a foredoomed communist-led insurrection in Canton in December.

This ill-fated uprising was apparently timed to coincide with the Fifteenth Congress of the Soviet party, to which Stalin desperately wanted to display a victory in China. The Canton uprising was later hailed as a "heroic rearguard action" which closed the first revolutionary wave and prepared the way for the new upsurge to come. Stalin assured the congress that "the fact that the Chinese revolution has not led directly to victory over imperialism is not important." Revolutions do not succeed in the first round; the Russian revolution experienced "ebbs and flows," and "it will be so in China also." [11]

Stalin's attempt to salvage a victory from the depths of failure did not obscure, however, the need for a fundamental reassessment of the alignment of social forces in the Eastern countries and of the proper strategy for achieving victory over imperialism. Of course, the difficulties in China had not stemmed solely from the basic doctrinal assessment of the bloc of four classes, but from a tactical inflexibility compounded by the power struggle with Trotsky, and from a failure to perceive the subjective factors—the anti-Soviet leanings of an "objectively revolutionary" national bourgeoisie. These shortcomings of application were not to be absent from future Soviet policies, even after the doctrinal basis for those policies had been altered.

Having so focused his energies on the Chinese revolution, to the exclusion of other national-liberation movements in the East, Stalin reacted to the defeat in China not by turning to another Asian country, such as India. Rather, he precluded the possibility of future defeats simply by refusing to reinvest Soviet energies and resources in an Asian revolution. Having been frustrated by his inability to achieve the desired ends working through forces which eluded total direct control, Stalin chose not to attempt a similar exercise with unreliable Asian nationalists and communists again.

Before the doctrinal reassessments of 1928 are considered, it is necessary to update the story of Soviet policy toward India, which, though definitely secondary to China as a focus of Soviet and Comintern attention in the mid-1920's, had been the object of continued interest throughout the period.

e. Communist Prospects in India

Although M. N. Roy's view of the unreliability of the Indian bourgeois nationalists had been rejected by the Fourth Comintern Congress in 1924, his suspicions were shared by some rather prominent Soviet analysts. V. Kriazhin, Pavlovich's chief assistant in the All-Union Association of Orientalists, offered a rather unfavorable assessment of Gandhi's leadership of the national movement in 1924. Outwardly a religious and utopian figure, Gandhi was, according to Kriazhin, a "typical representative of the petty bourgeoisie," utilizing traditionalist prejudices and fears of capitalist progress and offering a political program which was at best "foggy" and at worst "deeply conservative." Kriazhin did not, however, deny the anti-imperialist role of Gandhi, nor did he suggest that the Indian National Congress, despite Gandhi's large role in it, was unworthy of communist support.[12]

Indeed, the Fifth Plenum of the ECCI in March 1925 directed the Indian communists to continue for the present to work within the Indian Congress and the left wing of the Swaraj party. But it warned against overestimating the revolutionary nature of these nationalist organizations. For the future it was both necessary and possible for the communists to rally and organize the urban petty bourgeoisie and "revolutionary intelligentsia" into an anti-imperialist bloc in support of the national-liberation movement through the vehicle of a mass People's Party agitating for independence, democratic revolution, and an end to feudalism. This multiclass party, apparently modeled after the Kuomintang, was felt to be a more reliable vehicle for national revolution than the bourgeoisie-led Congress.

Though this assessment by the ECCI displayed less confidence in the Indian bourgeoisie than had the Fifth Comintern Congress, it differed quite strikingly from the assessment offered by Stalin in his speech to the KUTV only two months later. It will be recalled that in his address Stalin had characterized the Indian economy as relatively capitalistic—an assessment which had led Stalin to conclude that the Indian communists, while forming a bloc such as the People's Party recommended by the plenum, should "concentrate their fire" against the compromising national bourgeoisie.

Stalin's pessimism concerning the revolutionary potential of the Indian bourgeoisie—an assessment which he failed to translate into an actual operational strategy, given his preoccupation with China—set him to the left not only of the Comintern, but also of M. N. Roy. For whatever Roy's past disagreements with the policy of establishing Comintern contacts with the national-liberation movements, he was determined to retain his place as the chief spokesman for the International in dealings with Indian communists. Since 1924 he had been challenged in this role by the Communist Party of Great Britain (CPGB). This pressure had resulted in Roy's making a greater effort to bring his pronouncements into at least superficial accord with the current Comintern line. Thus, in 1925 he conceded, "[o]bjectively, the Indian bourgeoisie are a revolutionary factor," at the same time seriously hedging this concession by complaining that "they are totally unconscious of this revolutionary role of theirs, and what is worse still, they are remarkably inclined towards counter-revolution, or rather, reaction." [13] It is clear, however, that the differences among Roy, Stalin, and the ECCI in 1925 concerning the role of the Indian bourgeoisie were primarily differences of degree; none of them viewed the bourgeoisie with enthusiasm.

One major problem involved in devising alternatives to bourgeois leadership of the Indian movement was the persisting absence of an organized communist party in India. The Indian comrades did not easily recover from the Cawnpore convictions of 1924. A group led by Satya Bhakta had formed a "Communist Party" in 1925, but Philip Spratt, a British communist active in India shortly thereafter, recalls that, with only one exception, they "did not know what a communist party is and did not try to organize it or carry on its work." When Spratt arrived in India in early 1927, he found only fifteen or twenty "nominal members" and little or no activity.[14] Yet at the same time the ECCI was proclaiming that "in India there are sufficiently strong proletarian masses to begin, in the very near future, to play the leading role in the national-liberation struggle just as in China." [15]

The vehicle through which it was proposed to promote communist contact with the Indian masses was the Workers' and Peasants' Party (WPP). By 1926 both Roy and the CPGB had begun to advocate this device, simultaneously de-emphasizing the theoretically broader-based, but still nonexistent, People's Party. The speed with which the communists moved to control these parties is evidenced by the fact that by the end of the year Roy was complaining in a letter to the Indian comrades that communist control of the WPPs had become too open.[16]

One important factor contributing to the continued absence of a party was British harassment, which made activity through the vehicle of a communist party too dangerous. According to Spratt, the communists did not conceal their political colors as they infiltrated the Congress and trade unions, but rather sought to use these organizations as a legal outlet for their activities. The Russians, he contends, poured in hundreds of thousands of rupees to finance this work.[17]

Opportunities for activity were not lacking. The lull of the mid-1920's in the nationalist movement had come to an end in late 1926 with the disorders arising from the boycott of the

Simon Commission. And in 1928 the industrial strike movement reached a peak, both in numbers and in militance, with some of the largest strikes being led by the communists.

Dissatisfaction among Indian nationalists with the moderate course which had been followed by the Congress crystallized in August 1928, after the All-Parties Conference had adopted a report drafted by Motilal Nehru which called for Dominion status as the nationalist goal. Seeing this move as a betrayal of the 1927 Congress resolution in favor of complete independence, Nehru's son Jawaharlal led one radical group in forming the Independence of India League, whose name reflected its opposition to the moderates' announced goal. There was no open split in the Congress, however, and in December Gandhi returned to leadership of the movement with the proposal to resume the noncooperation movement if Dominion status were not introduced by the end of the following year.

The beginning of this new wave of political agitation in India coincided with the reappraisal being undertaken by the Comintern and the Soviet party in the wake of the defeat of leftist forces in China. Discussions were heavily punctuated with talk of the "lessions of China" for the course to be pursued in the rest of Asia. Significantly, it was the reaction to the "betrayal" by the Kuomintang bourgeoisie, more than the changed situation in India itself, which shaped the new strategy being developed for Soviet and Comintern activity in India.

While communist statements had been noticeably cool toward the "compromising" elements of the "big" bourgeoisie since 1925, the "lessons of China" were interpreted in late 1927 as bringing into serious question the revolutionary potential of the entire Indian bourgeoisie. Following his return from China in 1927, Roy wrote that the lessons from that country's experience were that neither the national bourgeoisie nor the petty bourgeoisie could lead the national revolution to victory. Only the working class, operating through an independent party, could fulfill that task.[18] Though Roy had been for some time masking his distrust of the bourgeoisie out of deference to Comintern policy, this latest position was an explicit return to the line which he had advocated in his debate with Lenin in 1920.

More indicative of a reappraisal is the fact that important Soviet figures were also now condemning the "counterrevolutionary" nature of the Indian bourgeoisie. Nikolai Bukharin, in a speech to the Fifteenth Congress of the Soviet party in December, made one of the strongest denunciations yet of the Indian bourgeoisie, concluding that "[a]s far as we are concerned, it is already an actively hostile force." [19] That this assessment was made on the very eve of a resurgence in India of agitation for independence, in which the radical circles of the "bourgeoisie" and "petty bourgeoisie" played the leading role, and that it was not altered for the next several years, during which the independence movement steadily gained in intensity, is a solid indication of the Soviet tendency to assess the social forces in a country on the basis of factors external to that country.

f. Reappraisal of the Strategy

The reappraisal which occurred in 1927–1928 was indeed not limited to India, but resulted in a new general line applied to the entire world. The temporary stabilization of capitalism was declared to have come to an end and to have been replaced by a period of revolutionary upheaval in the capitalist countries and their colonies. Moreover, the capitalists were said to be preparing a new offensive against the USSR. To help ward off this attack, the proletariat of the world was itself to go on the offensive against imperialism and its allies—the social democrats ("social fascists") and colonial national bourgeoisie ("national reformists")—by wresting control of the masses from these groups.

A convincing case can be made that internal Soviet conditions, and not a genuine perception of realignment of social forces in the capitalist and colonial countries, provided the chief motivation for the shift in line. Having defeated the "left opposition" of Trotsky, Zinoviev, and Kamenev, Stalin was in the process of adopting its policies in preparation for his struggle with the "right" forces of Bukharin and Rykov. On the economic front, this involved the scrapping of the New Economic Policy, the rejection of Bukharin's plan for concessions to the peasantry, and the launching of industrialization and collectivization. This dramatic shift was defended as a means of strengthening Soviet abilities to meet the expected capitalist onslaught, while actually it was to render the country more vulnerable than before.

The foreign policy concomitant of the new domestic line was isolationist: the USSR must avoid entanglement abroad during this period of internal transformation. But this requirement alone did not necessitate the militant go-it-alone policy now prescribed for foreign parties. A rightist strategy designed to give least provocation for capitalist attack would have seemed more directly conducive to Stalin's goals. Again the answer to the puzzle lay in the struggle for power in the Soviet leadership, rather than in a purely "rational" calculus of foreign policy goals and resources. For it was Stalin's decision to discredit Bukharin, who had become identified with the policy of cooperation with social-democratic parties, that in the final analysis dictated the switch to Comintern militance. In a touch characteristic of Stalin, the unfortunate Bukharin was chosen—against his own wishes [20]—personally to introduce the new policy at the Sixth Comintern Congress.

That internal Soviet necessities were sufficient justification for a sharp turn in the line of the international movement was implicit in Stalin's notion of "socialism in one country." Far from being a betrayal of world revolution, socialist construction in the Soviet Union was said to be in the common interest of all communists. Stalin was able to carry the theory to its inevitable (if not logical) conclusion: that the world movement in fact now existed primarily as an aid to the achievement of Soviet foreign policy requirements. In 1929, he said: "An internationalist is one who unreservedly, unhesitatingly, and unconditionally is prepared to defend the U.S.S.R. because the U.S.S.R. is the base of the world revolutionary movement, and it is impossible to defend or advance the world revolutionary movement without defending the U.S.S.R." [21] And defense of the Soviet Union in this period entailed, according to Stalin, not a search for noncommunist allies, but a period of militant isolation during which the country could consolidate its strength.[22]

Although the new policy of "class against class" is usually dated from the Sixth Comintern Congress, the Soviets did not wait for the convocation of that meeting to begin to implement some aspects of the new leftist line. At the Ninth Plenum of the ECCI in February 1928, a resolution on China proclaimed that the bourgeoisie had finally reached an agreement with both feudal and imperialist counterrevolutionary forces, thereby foreclosing its future leadership of the bourgeois-democratic revolution.

Likewise the Indian bourgeoisie was proclaimed by the ECCI to have finally proven its bankruptcy. In a report published on the eve of the congress, the committee argued that the Indian bourgeoisie was seeking not the revolutionary destruction of imperialist control but only a change in the character of that control. Even the politics of the younger Nehru, who in 1927 had been elected to the executive committee of the International League against Imperialism (a new Comintern front), and who had followed up a visit to the Soviet Union with a series of pro-Soviet articles,[23] did not escape the critical fire of the ECCI. Of the Congress' left wing, led by Nehru, the committee wrote that it "has evolved into an instrument, in the hands of the bourgeoisie, for the penetration and vicarious leadership of the broad working masses . . ." [24] This characterization of the noncommunist left as a tool of counterrevolutionary forces was to grow more and more virulent in the next few years.

2. The Sixth Comintern Congress

The Sixth Congress of the Communist International, held in Moscow from July 17 to September 1, 1928, was the last to feature genuine public debate. The fact that so much of the divergence of views centered on strategy toward India is a reflection both of the great amount of attention given to India as "the classical colonial country" and of the presence at the congress of several groups who sought recognition as spokesmen for Indian communism.

The struggle for control of the Indian party between Roy and the British communists had reached its climax in 1927–1928. During Roy's mission to China in 1927, the operational control of Indian communism had passed to the CPGB, and especially to Philip Spratt and Ben Bradley, British comrades who were on the scene leading the communist infiltration of the trade unions, the Congress, and the WPP.[25]

Upon his return to Europe and the Foreign Bureau of the Communist Party of India (CPI), Roy had made an attempt to recapture control of the Indian movement. But it soon had become apparent that the Comintern itself did not agree with Roy's claim to represent it in relations with the Indians. In Moscow for the Ninth Plenum of the ECCI, Roy had begun to feel that he was in personal danger and had finally been rushed back to Berlin by friends.[26] It is probable that Roy had been singled out by Stalin to serve as scapegoat for the failures of Comintern strategy in China. Attacks on him, at first indirect and then open, had followed, with his formal expulsion from the Comintern coming in 1929.

These first stages of Roy's decline prior to the Comintern

congress had not, however, cleared up the question who spoke for the Indian communists. The CPGB continued to claim this right, but so did a number of Indians. G. A. K. Luhani, who had been an associate of Roy's in Berlin, spoke in his behalf at the congress. Saimyendranath Tagore was there claiming to speak for the WPP (and denying that there was a communist party to represent). Shaukat Usmani, along with three of his friends, also attended, though, according to Spratt, without a mandate.[27] Though none of these "delegates" had credentials from the Indian communists, Usmani was "unwillingly and unexpectedly" pressed into service on the presidium of the congress.[28]

One of the major points of contention among these factions was the issue of the "decolonization" of India—a question which had been seized upon by the Russians in their effort to discredit Roy. The term had arisen, according to Roy and Luhani, in 1927, when Bukharin had asked Roy to draw up a resolution for the ECCI to the effect that the gradual industrialization of India by the British constituted "decolonization." Roy had complied, but the resolution had never been adopted.

In essence the "decolonization" theory postulated that increased industrialization in India had created a native industrial bourgeoisie which utilized the mass movement only to frighten the imperialists into political and economic concessions. The conclusion—that the industrial bourgeoisie was not a genuine revolutionary force—was neither a new nor a surprising one for Roy to draw.

But in the hands of the Russians, who were bent on destroying Roy, the theory became somewhat different. They described it as maintaining that the British were voluntarily contributing to Indian industrial development and political independence—that is, that revolution was not a prerequisite for India's liberation and the freeing of her productive forces. This distorted and obviously heretical thesis was the version which came under attack at the congress. According to Bukharin, while industrial development had indeed occurred in India, it was only of the type and magnitude desired by the imperialists.

The primary practical conclusion the Soviets drew from their vigorous denial of "decolonization" was, in the words of the ECCI Agitprop Theses, that "[i]ndustrialization of the present colonies is possible only along the path of their non-capitalist development." [29] The imperialists would never allow the Indian bourgeoisie to develop the country's resources through capitalist means. A second consequence of the Soviet theory was that, given the weakness of the proletariat, the agrarian revolution would be "the central axis of the coming mass revolutionary upheaval" in India.[30]

The alternative to "decolonization," according to the Soviets, was liberation and development of the colonies, "the world rural district," by means of their linkage to the proletariat of "the world city." Only the advanced countries—and in particular the Soviet Union—could draw the colonies out of the precapitalist backwardness, through a relationship of "beneficent" tutelage similar to that between the proletariat and the peasantry of the USSR. (What the real nature of this tutelage was is starkly clear when one contemplates what the Soviet peasant was soon to undergo.)

In India, according to the Soviet theory, one stratum of the native bourgeoisie—the commercial or "compradore" section—was directly serving the interests of imperialism and, along with the feudal strata, was consistently "antinational." The other part, the industrial bourgeoisie, whose development was held back by imperialism, supported the national movement, but in a vacillating "national reformist" fashion. For, although it played a positive role in awakening the masses to political struggle against imperialism, it was so frightened of the revolutionary implications of the mass risings that it inevitably was driven to seek a compromise with the imperialists, deserting "to the camp of counter-revolution at the first manifestation of a revolutionary mass movement." Thus, according to Bukharin, in India—unlike China—"it is inconceivable that the bourgeoisie will play a revolutionary role for any length of time." [31]

While temporary and limited cooperation on the part of communists with such groups was possible, the main task was to expose the tendencies to compromise among the national-reformists and to undermine their influence over the masses. Thus the new communist strategy laid down by the Sixth Congress utilized the "united front from below"—any temporary cooperation with noncommunist groups was to have the aim of winning away their mass support by discrediting their leaders.

In order to carry out this strategy, it was necessary for the colonial communists to "demarcate themselves in the most clear-cut fashion" from petty-bourgeois groups. What this implied for the Indian comrades was an abandonment of the organizational form which they had spent the past year developing: the Workers' and Peasants' Party. This judgment was made explicit in Kuusinen's report and in the congress theses: the WPP represented the dual danger of substituting for a communist party and of changing into a petty-bourgeois party.

This conclusion was not acceptable to most of the British and Indian delegates at the congress. Much energy had been invested in organizing and promoting the WPP, and the tactic had been reaping dividends. Tagore, expressing his interest as WPP "delegate" to the congress, called the order to liquidate the parties "pure and simple professorial dogmatism against which Lenin warned us so many times." [32]

Predictably, it was the Soviet viewpoint which was incorporated into the congress theses on the colonial movement. The basic tasks of the Indian communists were the unfinished tasks of the bourgeois-democratic revolution. The actual conquest of power by the workers and peasants and the transition to the socialist stage of revolution would likely come only gradually, unless one mighty revolutionary wave should arise and find the party organized and experienced enough to take advantage of it. [33]

Thus the new period ushered in by the Sixth Comintern Congress—a period in which the danger of war was said to be extremely great—was one in which special attention was to be focused by the Soviet Union on the developing revolutionary situation in India. Greater concern with India and with the threat of the British army did not, however, lead to an abandonment of caution. Usmani discovered this when, at the close of the congress, his requests for weapons, equipment, and training in guerrilla warfare were refused by Stalin and Bukharin. Indeed, Stalin instructed him to dismiss all notions of guerrilla fighting in India as impracticable, while an unnamed Soviet general, more encouraging, assured him that he would have his weapons once Britain declared war on Russia. The British did not oblige, however, and the disappointed Usmani left the communist movement shortly thereafter. [34]

3. Soviet Policy under the "Left Strategy," 1928–1934

At least one delegate to the Sixth Congress had expressed the feeling that, with all its fine doctrinal distinctions and formulas, the new colonial thesis was anything but straightforward: "I

must say that I read a certain statement four times without understanding it, and yet theses are written for people who know
much less than we delegates." [35] If the Comintern strategy toward India did not become clearer over the next few years, it
was not because of neglect on the part of Soviet journalists and
scholars. The period between the sixth and seventh congresses
saw more attention devoted to India in Soviet and Comintern
journals than in any other preindependence period. Unfortunately, however, the volume of commentary was not matched
by quality. Soviet analysis in this period suffered not only from
lack of direct observation and contact but also from the growing
general malady of Stalinist scholarship. Frequent quotations
from Stalin himself and adherence to sterile ideological formulas stifled independent judgment of the social and political
currents in India.

a. Disarray among Indian Communists

The shift to the new Comintern line was not accomplished
smoothly in India. Having had no official representative at the
congress in Moscow, the Indian communists remained unaware
of the change in strategy until December, when one of their
number arrived from Europe with news of the shift. Philip
Spratt has recorded his interpretation of this lapse in communication: "By 1928 the Comintern had ceased to matter, except as a field for the intrigues of the Russian party factions, and
the swing to the left in that year bore no relation to world politics but was merely an outcome of these factional quarrels.
Probably the Comintern bureaucracy in Moscow realized this
and saw that it did not matter whether the Indian party followed the new line or the old. Certainly they took no special
trouble to inform us." [36]

Lest there remain any doubt about the new course of the International, a letter to the Indian comrades from the ECCI declared that the "main obstacle" in the anti-imperialist and antifeudal struggle in India was "the influence of opportunist
bourgeois nationalism" and directed the communists to wage
"determined and relentless exposure of the bourgeois treachery." [37]

Thus informed of the proper strategy, Spratt and his comrades
proceeded to implement it. "What the collective wisdom of the
Comintern said was right, and it was not for us to question
it." [38] The Indian communist leaders were in the process of car-

rying out the Comintern decision to abandon the WPP when, in March 1929, they were again arrested. But the doom of the WPP had already been sealed.

Thirty-one communists and trade union leaders were arrested and underwent an extremely lengthy trial in Meerut. In January 1933 sentences of from three years to life imprisonment were handed down. (On appeal the sentences were reduced, and most of the prisoners were free by the end of 1933.) The effect of the trial in India was not what the British had planned: great publicity was given to the communists and their long speeches of defense, and many noncommunist nationalists, among them Nehru, were rallied to assist the communist victims of British persecution. As Spratt concluded: "Far from damning Communism the Case encouraged it." [39]

The Comintern assessment of the trial likewise failed to see it as a defeat; indeed, it was stubbornly interpreted in Moscow as a vindication of the Comintern charge that the Indian communists had gone astray. But India's isolation from the world proletariat made the overcoming of such errors especially difficult. Reiterating the conclusion drawn at the Sixth Congress, Manuilsky told the Tenth Plenum of the ECCI in September that the CPGB must be relied upon to overcome the isolation of the Indian proletariat: "If the British Communist Party will not help now the Indian Communists who are scattered and unorganized, who is going to help them? The Communist International has *no other levers* to influence the Indian revolutionary movement than the British Communist Party." [40]

This plenum also reaffirmed Comintern belief in the great significance of the Indian struggle, with Manuilsky asserting that the International should devote fully half of its attention to India. Lozovsky, the head of the Profintern, concurred: "This is not a simple revolt in a little colony. The struggle in India is of tremendous importance because it is the ground upon which the fortunes of British imperialism are going to be settled. He who fails to see this is generally a hopeless case. . . . Just imagine for a moment a united front . . . of India, China, and U.S.S.R. This is an invincible bloc." [41]

The Tenth Plenum was also significant for the development of Indian communism in that it was the occasion for the open attack on M. N. Roy. Roy's former close associate, Luhani, was chosen as his principal accuser. In a declaration in which he acknowledged his error in defending Roy's position in the Comintern congress "decolonization" debate, Luhani charged that Roy's recent writings had constituted "an open betrayal" of the Indian proletariat. Roy was branded an agent of the reformist bourgeoisie, in effect, simply "another Nehru." In the classical fashion of communist historiography, Roy's entire career was retrospectively exposed as treacherous, and his ideas were labeled those of a "Menshevik." [42]

b. Elaboration of the New Strategy

During the years immediately following the Sixth Congress, Soviet and Comintern analyses of the colonial revolutions, and of India in particular, were characterized not by theoretical or strategic departures from the ultraleftist line laid down in 1928, but by an elaboration of this line and an application of it to Indian developments.

An editorial in the Comintern journal in 1929 sought to provide perspective for the application of the new line by evaluating the progress that the colonial movement had made and suggesting that shortcomings on the part of member parties had impeded progress in the East.

The main strategic task in the organizational sphere was said to be the coordination of attacks in the East while simultaneously ensuring supporting attacks from the proletariat of the capitalist countries. A basic requirement for success was the support by the Soviet Union of the colonial revolutions. "But this means that the very character of this form of the emancipation movement . . . is defined and verified by its relationship with the Soviet Union." Consequently, in China the turning point in the revolution had been accompanied by a change in the attitude of the Kuomintang leaders toward the USSR, and in India the bourgeoisie had crossed over to counterrevolution "from the moment that it made its position in regard to the British war on the Soviet Union a matter for trading with the Baldwin Government." [43]

Here, then, was an analysis which supplied the element Stalin had originally overlooked in his policy toward China: the assertion that the "subjective" characteristic of the national bourgeoisie, as manifested by its attitude toward the Soviet Union, was at least as important a determinant of its worthiness of communist support as were the "objective" class characteristics.

During the greater part of the Stalinist period the faster

tempo of the movement in China was seen as exerting a strong stimulating influence on revolutionary prospects in India. But in the years following the Sixth Congress the Chinese revolution was "between two waves," and the prediction was assayed that the coming success of the Indian revolution would impart new strength to the Chinese movement by weakening the imperialist forces that were suppressing it.[44] An even more direct relationship between the prospects for success in India and in Britian itself was asserted in 1931: "History will show in which country the revolution will more quickly smash imperialism. In India (which is more likely) or in England . . . The victory in either would rapidly spread to the other . . . *The overthrow of imperialist domination and the independence of India will aim a mortal blow at the capitalist system in England.*" [45]

The basis for this Royist prediction lay, of course, in the economics of the imperialist system. For, by having hindered industrial development and propped up backward social forces, the British had in effect prevented the very expansion of the Indian market which their declining share of the world market required. The onset of the world economic crisis, according to the Soviet analysis, only aggravated the dislocations of the Indian economy, which were rooted in the structural problems of the antagonism of capitalist and feudal relations. Nowhere was this contradiction more evident than in the "degenerating villages" and the agrarian sector of India's economy.[46]

What form would be taken by the revolution which would shatter this imperialist system? P. Prager, in two articles in *Proletarskaia revoliutsiia* (Proletarian revolution) in 1930, attempted to provide the theoretical underpinnings for the Comintern's view that the colonial revolutions could traverse the noncapitalist path of development.[47]

Prager's argument started with the Sixth Congress' thesis that although the bourgeois-democratic revolution was still on the agenda in countries where feudal or semifeudal relations continued to exist and to hinder further development, it was, in the era of imperialism, only in struggle with the bourgeoisie that this revolution could be won. Moreover, only proletarian leadership of the bourgeois-democratic revolution could assure the attainment of real state independence and independent economic development. Turkey was cited as an example of a country attaining formal independence under bourgeois leadership and failing to achieve self-determined development. In

Mexico, where both the national bourgeoisie and the proletariat had been weak, the independence movement had been led by the petty bourgeoisie, with the result that the economic grip of imperialism had not been broken. Yet Mongolia, which had no proletariat and was far more backward than most non-Western countries, had been able to embark on independent development by taking the noncapitalist path, with proletarian leadership provided from outside—by the USSR. With the help of "advanced" countries, and given the leadership of the proletariat in alliance with the peasantry, the less-developed Eastern nations could pass over the stage of capitalism "as the dominant system" and toward socialism even before all the tasks of the bourgeois-democratic stage had been completed.

c. Specific Applications of the "Left" Strategy in India

The Soviet analysts did not, of course, rest content with the theoretical demonstration of the possibility of proletarian leadership of the colonial revolutions. The literature on the East in this period, and especially that concerning India, is replete with specific charges of bourgeois treachery and inability to assume revolutionary leadership. These charges were leveled with greater frequency as the intensity of the Indian national-liberation movement, under the leadership of Gandhi and the National Congress, began to reach a new height. On January 1, 1930, in its session at Lahore, the Congress voted in favor of complete independence and a boycott of government-sponsored round-table conferences on the subject of Dominion status. On March 12, with his famous march to the sea to make salt illegally, Gandhi inaugurated the second civil disobedience campaign. His arrest in May was accompanied by nationwide disorders, peasant and worker uprisings, and terrorist attacks, which continued throughout the year.

Communist analysts continued to insist, however, that bourgeois leadership of the Indian struggle was consciously aimed at its "collapse by stagnation." [48] The bourgeoisie, unable to lead the mass movement to victory because of its ties with the oppressive feudal elements and its fear of revolution, was obliged as in the past to pretend to direct it in order to limit and behead it. It was the duty of the Indian communists and the proletariat to unmask the true nature of the bourgeoisie in order to destroy the illusions which bound the masses to it, and to seize leadership of the movement for themselves. Karl Radek in

1930 made explicit what the Sixth Congress had implied: "The struggle against the national reformists, the struggle against Gandhism, is no less important a prerequisite for victory of the Indian Revolution than the struggle against English imperialism." [49]

It was Gandhi in particular whom the Soviets singled out as the most dangerous class enemy, not only because his views were so alien to the notion of class struggle, but because it was he who was able to provide the vital link between the Congress and the vast Indian peasant masses. An article by a prominent Soviet Orientalist, I. M. Reisner, in 1930 sought to expose the "Class Essence of Gandhism." [50]

Reisner's insistence that Gandhism had from the beginning been a movement in the interests of the bourgeoisie was in contrast to the notion of those, like Roy, who called it a petty-bourgeois movement. The distinction is crucial, for if Roy's analysis were accepted, then Gandhi and his followers, like other petty-bourgeois politicians incapable of being an independent force, could be regarded as susceptible to being won over by the proletariat. If, on the other hand, Gandhism were regarded as a movement of the bourgeoisie, then it would necessarily pose a greater danger to proletarian hegemony.

Reisner reserved his sharpest attacks for Gandhi's doctrine of nonviolent resistance. Gandhi's nonviolence—"the gendarme of the inner spirit" and "political vegetarianism"—was designed to be applied according to a double standard, not to the imperialists and the bourgeoisie but only to the lower classes. By enjoining the workers not to resist violence with violence, it in effect ensured the suppression of the revolution.

Even the imprisonment of Gandhi by the British was interpreted by the communists as part of a bourgeois-imperialist plot. The CPGB explained in May 1930 that since Gandhi's tactics had proven unable to hold the masses in check, it had become necessary to jail him to delude the masses into believing that this bourgeois leader was really an enemy of imperialism.[51]

The most insistent theme of communist writings on India in this period concerned the need to counteract bourgeois influence among the working classes by organizing a communist party.[52] The tasks which such a party would carry out were detailed in December 1930 when *Pravda, International Press Correspondence,* and the London *Daily Worker* published the "Draft Platform of Action of the Communist Party of India." [53]

This document closely adhered to the line of the Sixth Congress in deriving the aims and tactics of the Indian communists.

Only the leadership of an armed agrarian revolution by the working class, the document proclaimed, could ensure the emancipation of India. The main objects of the present stage of the revolution, which would create the conditions for the building of socialism, were declared to be the violent overthrow of British rule and nationalization of all British holdings, distribution of the land of foreigners, landlords, and the church to the toiling peasantry, and establishment of an Indian Federal Workers' and Peasants' Soviet Republic. The "chief and basic task" remained, however, the establishment of a "centralized, united, mass underground communist party" affiliated with the Comintern.

That this latter task was said to have remained unfulfilled is an indication that the "draft platform" was appearing in advance of the "Communist Party of India" itself. Indeed, at the time the document appeared, the most experienced and capable leaders available to the Indian party were still in the Meerut jail. No central organization yet existed, though factional groups had formed in Bombay, Calcutta, and northern India. To complicate the situation further, M. N. Roy arrived in India in December 1930 and quickly formed a rival party with the intent of working within the National Congress! Roy's arrest in July 1931 on charges originally made in 1924 led to five years' imprisonment, but his followers continued to plague the communists with their "splitting" activities in the trade unions.

Despite the authoritative and wide circulation of the Draft Platform of Action, its effects in India were less than spectacular. Splits among the various communist groups continued. Meanwhile the national movement was taking a new turn, which the communists, in their disorganized state, were unable to exploit. In January 1931, at the first Round-Table Conference in London, representatives of the Indian princes and the moderate Liberals agreed with the British on a plan of federation and limited representative government. In March, having been released from prison, Gandhi reached an agreement with the Viceroy, Lord Irwin, to end the civil disobedience campaign and lead the Congress in participating in the next Round-Table Conference in return for the release of those political prisoners who had not been involved in violent uprisings.

Gandhi went to London at the end of 1931 for the conference, but it failed to reach agreement on the problem of political rights for religious minorities and untouchables. Back in India Gandhi, resuming the struggle, was again arrested, and the National Congress was banned. Released again, he announced a new civil disobedience campaign for August 1933, but was arrested yet another time on the day it began. All the while mass political activity on behalf of independence continued to rage, unexploited by the unorganized communists.

At the end of 1931 Spratt, Ben Bradley, and Muzzafar Ahmad appealed to the Comintern for both tactical and organizational guidance. The appeal bore fruit, in the form of an "Open Letter to the Indian Communists" from the central committees of the Chinese, British, and German parties. This document was published in *International Press Correspondence* in June 1932.[54]

The failure of the mass unrest to develop along lines prescribed by communist strategy was blamed by the fraternal parties on the incorrect tactics of the Indian communists, who were lagging behind the masses in their struggle against imperialism, thus allowing the National Congress to continue its influence. The correct tactical line still consisted in exposing the Congress, and especially its left wing, but the communists had erred in isolating themselves from the masses who were under reformist influence. A distinction must be drawn between the bourgeois Congress leadership and those elements of the masses who blindly followed it.

What the three parties were directing the Indian comrades to do was more easily said than accomplished. The leadership of Gandhi and the Congress had inspired the masses to struggle; the communists were to take over the struggle by denouncing the very leadership which had aroused it. That the Indian communists had difficulty in implementing the advice of the three parties was demonstrated by the fact that a second Open Letter, this one from the Chinese party alone, was sent to them in July 1933, a little over a year after the first.

Yet again, "the most important task" before the Indians was said to be the formation of an All-Indian Communist Party, modeled after the Soviet party. "The bourgeois leaders of the National Congress are crawling on their knees before the British oppressors," the Chinese reiterated, and the masses "are seeking revolutionary leadership." [55]

The Indian communists should work to create a united front of workers, peasants, and urban petty-bourgeoisie—through a united front from below, "a bloc of the masses and not combinations of leaders." Yet even while struggling against reformist leadership, especially in the trade unions, it would be wrong to force a split in these organizations. Even the "joining together" of the Red and mass national-reformist trade unions would be acceptable if the communists would continue to expose the treachery of the reformist leaders and to advance their own slogans.

That this latter instruction represented a discernible moderation in the ultraleftist and isolationist policy of the Sixth Congress, at least as it had been applied to the trade unions, was graphically illustrated by the Indian response to the Chinese letter. An intraparty Indian journal recalled in 1950 that at the time the open letter was received, the Indian communists, who had formed a Red Trade Union Congress, were preparing a handbill for the annual meeting of the "reformist" All-Indian Trade Union Congress (AITUC). This handbill was aimed at exposing this latter body as reactionary and calling for its destruction. "We had made 25,000 copies . . . to be distributed the next day in open session. These handbills were brought to [P. C.] Joshi's place. Along with this there was an unopened packet containing *International Press Correspondence* in which we found a copy of the Open Letter . . . telling politely that we were left-sectarians. We looked at each other. What was to be done? We burnt the whole lot of handbills." [56]

The reason for this tactical shift away from all-out denunciation of the larger, "reformist" unions and toward limited cooperation was simply that the old policy had only reinforced communist isolation from the masses. The trade union movement had first split in 1929 when the National Trade Union Federation (NTUF) had been formed by "reformists" who were concerned by increasing communist domination of the AITUC. The communists, however, had been unable even to retain the hold on the AITUC, losing control in 1931 to the militant nationalist, S. C. Bose. Forming their own Red TUC, they had seen its membership fall rapidly, with the communist-dominated Bombay Textile Union, for example, falling in size from 50,000 to 800.[57]

Another of the open letter's pleas was heeded by the Indian communists. In December 1933 at a conference in Calcutta an All-Indian Communist Party (CPI) was finally formed, with a new central committee including some of the recently released

Meerut prisoners. Its Provisional Statutes, which were modeled after those of the CPSU and other parties, were published in the Comintern journal in May 1934.[58] In rapid succession, the new party was accepted as a section of the Communist International and declared illegal by British authorities in India.

While the CPI was seeking to break out of its isolation from the mass nationalist struggle—without, however, abandoning the "left" strategy—developments were taking place which opened up the possibility of a shift in the direction of the anti-imperialist struggle. In London a parliamentary committee in 1933 and 1934 was engaged in reviewing the results of the Simon Commission studies and the Round-Table Conferences with the aim of drafting a new constitution for India. The plan which emerged, and which was passed by Parliament in August 1935 as the Government of India Act, satisfied only the very moderate Indian nationalists, and agitation against the proposed constitution was widespread. Gandhi was particularly active in protesting the proposed voting scheme, especially for its separation of the "scheduled castes" (untouchables) from the caste Hindu electorate. But in October 1934, Gandhi shocked the country by withdrawing from the National Congress, leaving a vacuum in the nationalist leadership which rival forces immediately sought to occupy.

Gandhi's withdrawal was recognized by the Soviets as presenting new opportunities to the CPI. A communist trade-union specialist had advised the Indian communists in 1934 that "one should go where there are masses, even if these masses are under the influence of a group which follows a wrong line." [59] Gandhi's resignation seemed to open a new path to the Indian masses and to the wresting away of leadership from the reformists. K. Mikhailov wrote early in 1935 that Gandhi's departure was the result of a radicalization of the Indian masses and the failure of reformist leadership. The National Congress was not a monolith but an "arena of struggle"—a grouping of parties which stood for a nonviolent approach to reformist goals. One wing of the Congress, expressing the interests of the big bourgeoisie, sought a quick compromise with the English at the price of only small concessions. The other wing—newly formed into the Congress Socialist Party (CSP)—represented the ruined middle bourgeoisie and higher strata of the petty bourgeoisie. While opposing proletarian hegemony in the anti-imperialist movement, the CSP used revolutionary phraseology. But it too was in essence reformist, since it sought large concessions from the imperialists.[60]

But despite the continued attacks on rival Indian leftists, the necessity for the Indian communists to take advantage of the vacuum in leadership by terminating their isolation and "going where there are masses" soon found expression in a significant change of tactics. The Congress Socialist Party, anxious to attain socialist unity, approached the CPI in 1934 with a proposal for limited cooperation on the trade union front. An agreement was reached for joint action by the CSP, the AITUC, the NTUF, and the Red TUC on certain issues. All parties agreed not to advocate either violence or nonviolence at joint functions and not to appeal for support for either party at the expense of the other. Each reserved the right "of genuine and honest criticism" of the other.[61]

Thus, for the first time in the decade, the Indian communists had agreed to form a limited "united front from above" with rival leftist groups. That this trade union consolidation had the blessing of the Comintern was indicated when the International's journal hailed it as "a most important step." [62]

4. The Seventh Comintern Congress and the United Front Strategy in India

To explain the shift which took place in communist strategy in India in 1934–1935 it is necessary again to change perspective—and this time not to the level of the Comintern and the "world revolutionary forces," but to the level of the diplomatic developments which were confronting the Soviet Union. For it was the changing political relationships in Western Europe and the Far East rather than general economic factors in the capitalist world which motivated the change in strategy.

The rise of the fascist regimes in Germany and Italy and of expansive militarism in Japan could have been evaluated in other terms; the Comintern could have recognized the economic and political instability in Europe and Asia as offering opportunities for immediate proletarian revolution. But domestic turmoil and revolutions in Europe and the Far East were not judged to be in the best interests of a Soviet state threatened by the rising aggressiveness of Germany on the west and Japan on the east. Rather, the Soviets opted for joining the League of Nations and furiously attempting to put together through "col-

lective security" arrangements an antifascist coalition which
could deter or defeat the Germans and Japanese. This required
that, in the security interests of the Soviet Union, ideology be
stretched to provide a distinction between fascist and nonfascist
capitalists, between aggressive and nonaggressive bourgeois
ruling circles.

The making of such a distinction and the formation of defensive alliances between a socialist state and capitalist states were
not likely to give much pause, however, to those who accepted
Stalin's dictum that "it is impossible to defend or advance the
world revolutionary movement without defending the USSR."
And by 1935 there were few communists left in positions of influence either in Russia or abroad who had not already sworn
unquestioning fealty to the Soviet leader.

There is little doubt, moreover, but that the power and prestige of communist parties in Europe and Asia increased in the
period from 1935 to 1939, even if most of these gains were
made in the name of antifascist unity rather than in the name of
proletarian revolution. It was basically because the Comintern
had by then become so pliant an instrument of Soviet foreign
policy that the distinction between these goals could be blurred
with so little dissent.

When in 1928 the noncommunist left of Europe had become
the main Comintern target for its "social-fascist" policies, so
had the nationalists of the colonies become targets for their "national-reformism." In 1934–1935 as antifascist popular fronts of
leftist forces rose in Europe, anti-imperialist national fronts
were created in the East. The parallels are more easily discerned than explained. In Europe and in China communist parties joined united fronts in pursuit of a new objective: united
resistance to the threat of aggression. But in the colonies there
would presumably have been no need for a change in objective.
The aim of the struggle was still national independence under
proletarian hegemony; the main enemies were still the imperialist states. But the crucial difference was that the Soviet Union
was now cooperating diplomatically with these very states.

It was true that the existence of this contradiction and the according of priority to the crises in Europe resulted in relative
neglect by the Soviet Union of the colonial struggle. But this in
fact represented no real change from the earlier period, when
Soviet and Comintern enthusiasm for colonial revolution had

been restricted to the verbal level and had not been manifested in actual Soviet behavior.

Given the changing necessities of Soviet diplomacy, but in the absence of admissions that militant Comintern pronouncements of 1928–1934 had been mistaken, how was the shift to the united front strategy in the colonies to be justified? At the Seventh Congress of the Communist International in Moscow in July–August 1935, justifications were offered which, in the absence of real debate, went unchallenged. A Chinese delegate, Wang Ming (Ch'en Shao-yü), presented the main report on the colonies and dependent countries. In the period just ended, he declared, imperialism had waged a savage offensive throughout the East, the consequences of which had been an increase in popular discontent, an accentuation of the antagonisms between the native bourgeoisie and the imperialists, and a weakening of the influence of national reformism and a rise in that of the proletariat. The combination of these effects had given rise to the "most favorable conditions" for the creation of an anti-imperialist united front of the "broadest masses." (These same conditions, it may be noted, could have also been interpreted as favoring the imminent success of the struggle, under proletarian hegemony, against imperialism *and* the bourgeoisie.)

Had there been an opposition to voice objections to this thesis, it might have reminded the congress of the results of such a wide national front in China in 1927. Wang Ming was ready with the answer to this unvoiced objection: in China it had not been "the anti-imperialist united front tactics themselves that were at fault, but the opportunists, who distorted these revolutionary tactics to suit the bourgeoisie and imperialism, who were at fault." [63]

In the absence of Indian representation at the Seventh Congress, Wang Ming also dealt with the specific application of the united front to India. His first task was a critique of the many errors which the Indian communists (even with all the advice they had been given!) had committed in improperly applying the "correct" tactics prescribed by the Comintern. These errors were of the "left-sectarian" variety: "they did not participate in all the mass demonstrations organized by the National Congress or organizations affiliated with it," thus finding themselves isolated from the masses. Even when they set out to correct this, "our young Indian comrades" had blundered by seeking to put such demands as the establishment of a workers' and peasants' soviet regime and confiscation of landlord holdings before the National Congress as items to be included in a common platform. "Such demands . . . can serve as an example of how not to carry on the tactics of the anti-imperialist united front." [64] Only recently, by amalgamating revolutionary and reformist unions and by reaching an agreement with the CSP, had the Indians arrived at the correct policy.

Those demands which were a correct basis for the common platform of struggle were suggested by Wang Ming. Compared to even the "partial demands" put forward in the earlier period, these slogans were mild indeed: against the new constitution; for liberation of political prisoners and abolition of extraordinary laws; against wage reduction and discharge of workers, high taxes, and high rents; for the establishment of democratic liberties. On the basis of this minimum program the Indian communists were to "support, extend and participate in all anti-imperialist mass activities, not excluding those which are under national reformist leadership." [65] The aim of such joint activity, though, was still to win away from reformist leadership the masses under its influence.

The implementation in India of the new Comintern strategy was guided by R. P. Dutt, Ben Bradley, and Harry Pollitt of the CPGB. Commentaries and instructions regarding India on the part of Soviet analysts became rare during this period.

A 1936 article by Dutt and Bradley asserted that while the National Congress was the "principal existing mass organization" of the Indian liberation struggle, it was not yet itself the "united people's front," for its constitution was still undemocratic, its program insufficiently clear, and its leadership still opposed to mass activity. But it was not impossible that the Congress could become "the form of realization" of the people's front. First, however, there would have to be a combination of the mass organizations of the workers and peasants with the Congress, perhaps even on the basis of collective affiliation, as was illustrated by the pre-1927 Kuomintang—"the most powerful and victorious weapon up to then devised for the colonial struggle against imperialism." [66]

The prime requisite for success of the people's front was an end to "mutual sniping" between the left-wing forces and the unification of these forces (CSP, trade unionists, left Congressmen, and CPI) on the basis of a minimum program. A "central rallying slogan" which could be a "most powerful mobilizing force" was the call for a constituent assembly—the very slogan which, on the lips of the "Royists," had been bitterly denounced by the CPI only two years before. But inconsistency could apparently be overlooked, for the achievement of unity was an urgent task. Dutt and Bradley concluded that "[t]he imminence of new world war makes more than ever necessary the unity and readiness of the national front in India." [67]

In a later article the British comrades attempted to deal with the objection—apparently from those Indian communists confused by the rapid shift in line—that the "Constituent Assembly" slogan meant that the slogan "for Soviets and for socialism is reduced to mere words." To combat this impression, Dutt, Bradley, and Pollitt chose to quote Nehru's slogan, "there can be no Socialism without National Liberation," adding that while the "first task" was liberation and the establishment of democracy, communists would continue in their devotion to the socialist goal.[68]

There is strong irony in this argument, for just three years previously the Comintern had cited those same words of Nehru in an attack on his "national-reformism." In 1933 the conclusion had been that "the overthrow of the rule of British imperialism is impossible without the destruction of all its allies at the same time." [69] It is little wonder that the Indian communists found cause for confusion. While only a short time before, Nehru's "socialism" had consisted only of "pseudo-Left phraseology," after the National Congress session of 1936 the Comintern was hailing "his brave plea for *Socialism* in his historic address to the Congress." [70]

The implementation by the CPI of the Seventh Congress line was facilitated by the eagerness of the leaders of the CSP for Marxist unity. In January 1936, the Congress Socialists offered to the CPI a united front between the two parties as well as the right for individual communists to join the CSP as a step toward ultimate merger. The communists, under the leadership of P. C. Joshi as General Secretary, seized the opportunity. Their own activities as a party having been banned by the British, membership in the CSP gave the communists an opportunity both to work legally and to penetrate the National Congress, the All-India Students Federation, and the All-India Kisan Sabha (peasants' union)—bodies with which the CSP was affiliated.

The communists moved with surprising rapidity to a position

of great influence within the CSP and its trade union and student front activities. The AITUC was again dominated by the communists. Entire provincial organs of the CSP, especially in the south, were taken over by the communists. A resolution of the CSP in 1937 deploring factionalism failed to stop the disruptive activity. Despite the decision of the CSP National Executive to stop the admission of communists into the party, those already admitted were by 1938 almost successful in taking over the National Executive itself.

Ironically, the disagreements between Congress Socialists and communists on strategy found the latter group on the right, arguing for a four-class anti-imperialist alliance which included the bourgeoisie. The CPI was placed in the position of answering CSP charges of "revisionism" with countercharges that the Socialists were being "left-sectarian."

Despite its quarrels with the CSP on matters of organization and policy, the CPI had gained greatly from the united front, increasing its influence and membership and achieving entry into the mainstream of the national movement, the National Congress. Had they not been prevented by Stalinist isolationism and by their own lack of discipline from penetrating the independence movement several years earlier, India's political destiny might well have been altered.

The Congress victory in the 1937 elections for the provincial assemblies—majorities in 6 provinces and pluralities in 3 more—demonstrated its great strength. With its decision to form governments in seven provinces under the new constitution, the National Congress gained the opportunity to implement political and economic reforms in India. Recognizing the mass appeal of the Indian National Congress, Soviet writers in 1938–1939 began to hail it as the organ of the anti-imperialist national front [71]—a step which Dutt and Bradley had been reluctant to take only two years before.

Yet at this time the Congress was engaged in a vital test of its unity, as the recurring struggle between moderates and leftists again broke out into the open. Gandhi (again active in the Congress) and his supporters had threatened to leave the Congress executive if S. C. Bose, the extreme nationalist elected as Congress president in 1938 over Gandhi's protest, continued to head the party. The united front policy of the CPI was faced with a vital test: to support the left-wing forces, even to the point of causing the moderates to leave the Congress, or to opt for unity as the first priority. In the showdown vote at Tripuri in March 1939, the communists, to the dismay of other leftists, supported Gandhi. Bose was defeated and forced to resign in favor of a more moderate president.

The CPI, explaining its decision to support Gandhi, argued that the interests of the anti-imperialist front "demanded not the *exclusive* leadership of one wing but a *united* leadership under the guidance of Gandhi." The CPI was not blind to the implications of this argument: it demanded a reversal of the long-standing communist attack on Gandhi. The CPI journal acknowledged this in April 1939: "This necessitates a very close study of and emphasis on every positive side of Gandhism particularly during its militant anti-imperialist phase between 1919 and 1920 . . . This is the Gandhism that we have to resurrect, burnish and replenish." [72]

In effect, the passage from "united front from below" (the attempt to infiltrate the Congress in order to expose and depose its leadership) to "united front from above" (the willingness to work with that "reformist" leadership) had been completed. But it was more than a recognition of the virtues of Gandhi or of the National Congress which had motivated the CPI in its shift of strategy. That the ominous developments in Europe and the seeming imminence of the fascist onslaught were major factors in the communists' decision is illustrated by a message from Harry Pollitt to the Indians in 1939. The fascist threat, he wrote, menaced not only Europe but also those colonial peoples struggling for independence. "In this situation, the greatest need, obviously, is unity of all the forces making for national liberation." [73]

5. From "Imperialist War" to "Peoples' War"

The sudden conclusion of the Nazi-Soviet pact in August 1939 ensured that, at least temporarily, the Soviet Union would be protected from the danger of fascist aggression. The Germans would be unleashed on Britain and France in a long war in which imperialism would destroy itself while the Soviet Union watched from the sidelines.

For European communists this reversal of Soviet policy and the consequent necessity to refuse to support the war effort came as a great embarrassment and indeed a threat to their recently augmented strength. For the Indian party, however, the dilemma was absent: Indian patriotism demanded opposition to the British, and if an imperialist war threatened Britain, so much the better for the cause of Indian independence.

The viceroy's proclamation of September 3, declaring India to be at war with Germany, and the subsequent Defense of India Act giving wide powers to the British in India met with strong disapproval from the Congress, not because it was out of sympathy with antifascism, but because the consent of the Indian people for such measures had not been sought. Demanding that the British grant independence to India, the Congress pledged: "A free democratic India will gladly associate herself with other free nations for mutual defense against aggression." The British reply, promising merely that new negotiations with Indian leaders would be conducted after the war, left the Congress disappointed and undecided on a course of action. The Congress ministries in the provinces resigned, but Gandhi was reluctant to press on with mass resistance to the British, a course insistently urged by the left, including Bose and the CSP. Even when Gandhi was driven to initiate resistance in the fall of 1940, it at first took the form of civil disobedience by selected individuals, rather than mass action.

The line which was to be taken by the CPI was laid down by Comintern leader Dimitrov in November 1939. Characterizing the war as an "imperialist, unjust war," he concluded: "The tactics of the united People's Front are fully applicable, even now, in China and also in colonial and dependent countries." [74] An article by Soviet Orientalist V. V. Balabushevich the same month reaffirmed the previous view that the National Congress was the "organizational expression" of the united front and declared that the conditions for unfolding the anti-imperialist struggle were now more favorable than ever before.[75]

Thus the Soviet and Comintern writers were simply stressing the need to continue the former tactics in the national struggle: there was no hint that the CPI should abandon the national front with the Congress leadership. The CPI, however, in a resolution of its Politbureau published in November 1939 took a position to the left both of the Congress leadership and of the Comintern. Pointing to the prospect of transforming imperialist war into a war of national liberation, the CPI accused the Congress leadership of seeking to restrict mass struggle *"so as to use it as a weapon of compromise."* [76]

In March 1940 the CPI made its stand even more explicit, as

it again attacked Gandhi's leadership of the Congress as no longer "progressive" and demanded "sharpest opposition to Gandhian leadership . . . isolation of that leadership and determined effort to smash its influence." [77] Clearly the CPI did not intend, in the face of the opportunity of achieving hegemony over the anti-British resistance movement, to continue the tactic of cooperation with the Congress leadership. Likewise, a break was made with the Congress Socialist Party, and in March 1940 all communists were expelled from its ranks, taking with them the entire organization of three CSP branches in South India. The same month the communists led 150,000 workers in a strike which paralyzed textile production in Bombay.

Only in the last half of 1940 did Soviet and Comintern commentaries on India follow CPI statements and behavior in a shift toward the left. An authoritative article in *Bol'shevik* in July 1940 characterized Gandhi as upset by the rapid growth of proletarian hegemony in the national movement and again seeking to disorganize the movement.[78] In December two Soviet analysts declared that the economic self-interest of the bourgeoisie was responsible for Gandhi's vacillating policy. Large war orders for Indian industry, said Balabushevich and D'iakov, had inspired the Indian national bourgeoisie to seek a new compromise with the British.[79]

Why the Soviets suddenly approved the new effort by the CPI to attain proletarian hegemony over the Indian national struggle is not immediately evident. One possibility is that the Soviets saw in communist-led mass resistance and strikes in India a means of disrupting the British war effort and weakening her strategic base in India—an aim which continued support of Gandhi's leadership did not seem likely to further. But why the Russians would pursue this objective can only be the subject of speculation. It is helpful to recall, however, the discussions between Molotov and Ribbentrop in Berlin in November 1940 concerning the possibility of Soviet adherence to a new four-power axis. At this meeting Molotov had showed little interest in Ribbentrop's suggestion that the Soviets expand their influence in the direction of the Indian Ocean, and he had countered with the demand for a Soviet sphere of influence in the Turkish Straits and the Persian Gulf.[80] Even if it is admitted that Stalin could not seriously have expected the Axis to agree to such a demand, it can still be argued that the existence of the ambition was genuine. And a weakening of the British power in

India, by means of a communist-led uprising there, would certainly have facilitated Soviet expansion into the oil fields near the Persian Gulf.

The second possible explanation for Soviet policy, less far-ranging in its implications, is simply that, in the belief that the British Empire would soon be destroyed by Hitler's success, the Soviets were concerned for the future political development of India. The immediate achievement of proletarian hegemony in the Indian independence movement could ensure that when the British were forced out of India it would be a Soviet rather than a capitalist India which would replace them.

Whatever the Soviet motives, they were surely pushed into the background by Hitler's surprise attack in June 1941. With Soviet energies now intensely concentrated on the struggle for Nazi defeat, the interests of true communist "internationalists" likewise had to focus on the defense of the Soviet Union. Questions of national liberation or proletarian hegemony in the East became unquestionably secondary to the need to strengthen the war effort against Hitler. Spared the confusion which had gripped communist parties after the Nazi-Soviet pact, the CPI now found itself faced with a bewildering dilemma. Devotion to the Soviet Union called for support of the war effort; devotion to the cause of independence dictated continued noncooperation and pressure on the British.

The immediate reaction of the CPI to the Nazi attack on Russia was to make the natural argument that, while Indians must sympathize with the struggle of the Soviets against Hitler, the nature of imperialism had *not* been changed. In this view the CPI was in agreement with the leaders of the Congress. It was British imperialism which oppressed India, and India must continue to struggle against it. A CPI pamphlet published in July 1941 declared that the "only way in which the Indian people can help in the just war which the Soviet is waging is by fighting all the more vigorously for their own emancipation from the imperialist yoke . . . We can render really effective aid to the Soviet Union only as a free people." [81]

In September 1941, no less a source than *Bol'shevik* took issue with this view of how the CPI would best aid the Soviet Union. I. M. Lemin flatly declared that India had not yet fully mobilized behind the war effort and that, "the further the mobilization of these forces for struggle against Hitlerite fascism proceeds, the better." There was no mention of *prior* attainment of independence by India.[82] Lest there be any doubt concerning the policy which Moscow desired the CPI to pursue, R. P. Dutt also spoke to the issue in September. In the CPGB organ *Labour Monthly* he wrote that the interest of the Indian people in the victory against fascism was "absolute and unconditional, and does not depend on any measures their rulers may promise or concede." [83]

There was a delay between the publication of this unmistakable directive and the change in the CPI line, but the delay was probably as much a factor of the lag in communications as of CPI resistance to the new line. On December 15 (by which time Japan had entered the war against Britain) the CPI Politbureau announced a new slogan for the new stage: "Make the Indian people play a people's role in the people's war."

A pamphlet published in 1942 by P. C. Joshi provided the detailed justification for the new slogan of the CPI. The struggle against the fascist invader was itself the fight for the people's freedom; it gave India the opportunity to fight alongside the Soviet, Chinese, and even British peoples for her national liberation. But the broadest possible mobilization in a united front of the Congress and the Moslem League, implemented by means of joint ministries even under the present constitution, was necessary on the basis of a common platform. Joshi's suggested platform called for recognition of the *right* to complete independence, a National Government, the release of political prisoners, rapid industrialization to supply the needs of defense of the people, granting workers' and peasants' demands and ameliorating their conditions, and equitable distribution of the war effort. There should be no curtailment of the right to strike, but the workers must determine to use this right "with special care."

On the political stalemate between the Congress and the Moslem League, Joshi's statements were balanced. The Congress was "the premier political organization of our people," but Gandhi's neutrality toward the war effort represented only a "path of negation." The Moslem League exercised influence over "a large section" of Indian Moslems; it was not to be dismissed as reactionary, nor was it alone responsible for the lack of communal unity. Though Jinnah's "dreamland of Pakistan . . . leads nowhere except to stalemate," the Congress should concede certain "sectional" demands of the Moslem League.[84]

A fuller analysis of this latter point—and of the Soviet and CPI position on Hindu-Moslem antagonisms and the Pakistan issue—will be undertaken in the succeeding chapter. Here it is necessary to note only that the CPI had modified its traditional policy of all-out hostility toward the Moslem League in the interest of gaining Moslem support for its goal of national unity behind the war effort.

In July 1942, in return for CPI support of the war effort, the British authorities in India lifted the ban on the communist party and released its leaders from jail. Soon afterwards the party found itself almost alone in the legal political arena. For in August the National Congress began its Quit India campaign of mass nonviolent struggle for independence and against the war effort. The Congress was immediately banned by the British, and its most important leaders were arrested. The blame for the wave of violent disorders and sabotage which followed was squarely placed by the British on Gandhi and his followers.

Though the CPI immediately began a campaign for the release of Gandhi and other Congress leaders, the party did not hesitate to take advantage of their absence. Great gains were achieved not only in the size of its own membership, but in communist influence over the AITUC, the All-India Kisan Sabha, and the All-India Student Federation.

Figures cited by a Soviet source in 1952 give a rough indication of the numerical strength and composition of the CPI at the time of its first party congress in May 1943. The party at that time claimed 16,000 members, compared with only 2,000 in 1934 and 5,000 in 1942. Of the total 1943 membership, 4,000 were listed as workers, 5,500 as peasants, and 6,500 as members of the intelligentsia. Among the leadership, the proportion of worker and peasant representation was even smaller. Of the 139 delegates to the party congress, 86 were members of the intelligentsia, 22 were workers, and 25 were peasants. Only 13 of the delegates were listed as Moslem, and 8 were Sikhs.[85]

In the trade union field, the communist party used its augmented influence to enforce labor peace in the name of increasing the production of war materials. At the same time, the CPI demonstrated its continued adherence to the belief that the war effort would be increased if India were granted her freedom. In 1942 Joshi, in a telegram to the CPGB, sought to encourage the British to make political concessions; he argued that maximum mobilization of Indian resources could be achieved only by an Indian national government.

The Soviets, though continuing to maintain that India should not be preoccupied with constitutional questions during wartime, did give token verbal support to the low-key pressure which Joshi sought to apply to the British.[86] An article in 1942, citing Joshi's telegram with approval, also quoted a noncommunist trade union leader's estimate that under a national government India's military production could be increased tenfold.[87] Soviet commentators acknowledged, however, that it was Congress-League discord which was the essential obstacle to agreement between the British and the Indians. After 1942 the Soviet press dropped all references to the question of Indian independence for the duration of the war.

Whatever gains were achieved by the CPI "people's war" policy, in terms both of contribution to the defeat of the Axis and of an increase in CPI membership, must be weighed against the consequent severe strain in relations between the communists and the Congress leadership. In Congress eyes, not only had the CPI deserted the national struggle to aid the British in fighting the war, but it had sought to appease Jinnah by supporting some of his "sectional" demands.

In 1944 Joshi, seeking to defend the CPI against such charges, published a pamphlet on *Congress and Communists*, the tone of which was a combination of flattery and pleading.[88] The same year Joshi engaged in a long correspondence with Gandhi, initiated by the latter on June 11 with a series of questions on communist policy. These queries concerned: the meaning of "people's war," the source of CPI finances, charges of CPI complicity with the police, whether the CPI policy was dictated from outside. Joshi's replies, picturing the CPI as an autonomous and nationalist organization financed by the people and cruelly slandered by its enemies, failed to satisfy Gandhi.[89] At Joshi's request the Congress file of anticommunist charges and Joshi's replies were replaced before Bhulabhai Desai for an opinion. Exonerating the CPI on most of the charges, Desai nonetheless concluded that ever since the Quit India campaign had begun, the communist party had carried on "propaganda contrary to the views and policy of the Congress."

On the basis of this finding a special committee in September 1945 ordered the communist members of the All-India

Congress Committee to show cause why they should not be expelled from that body. The CPI chose to respond by ordering *all* communists to resign from the Congress, and in December the breach was made total by the expulsion of communists from the All-India Congress Committee.[90]

Thus, on the eve of the final stage in India's struggle for independence, the communist party, having chosen to serve the interests of the Soviet Union before those of the nationalist movement, again found itself isolated from the central mass organization in that movement.

III The Soviets and the CPI in Search of a Policy, 1945–1954

In the aftermath of World War II, India—like the rest of Asia—was the scene of great political and social unrest. A victorious Britain, severely weakened by the war and undergoing swift transformations at home, was confronted in India with economic dislocation, communal strife, and increasing nationalist agitation.

The salient political issue, however, was no longer one of British willingness to grant India autonomy, but rather a question of the ability of the contending parties of India to agree on the political future of the subcontinent. The National Congress, claiming to represent the entire Indian community, and the Moslem League, claiming to be the exclusive spokesman for Indian Moslems and after 1940 demanding a separate Moslem state, had repeatedly failed to settle their differences through negotiation. Elections held in 1945 and 1946 also failed to provide a solution, with the League receiving majorities in the separate Moslem constituencies and the Congress winning in most other areas.

A cabinet mission sent by Attlee in February 1946 proposed that a central government be formed with powers over foreign affairs, defense, and communications. Remaining powers would be granted to provincial governments having the option to merge into groups. Continuing disagreement over details of the plan prompted Jinnah to call for a Moslem show of solidarity on August 16. "Direct Action Day" turned into six weeks of communal violence, which ended when the Moslem League agreed to join the Congress in an interim government.

Congress-League bickering continued unabated until February 1947, when Attlee declared Britain's intention to leave India no later than June 1948. At the same time Lord Mountbatten was named Viceroy of India. The deadlock was broken in June when Congress and the League announced acceptance of Mountbatten's plan to partition the subcontinent, on a communal basis, into two Dominions—India and Pakistan—to which the princely states would be free to accede. On August 15 the new constitutional arrangement was effected. But partition was accompanied by mass murders and the exchange of millions of refugees between the two dominions. It took the assassination of Gandhi by a Hindu fanatic on January 20, 1948, to provide the shock that brought the orgy of violence to a close.

Such, in broad outline, was the turbulent setting in which the Indian communists formulated their postwar policies. Since 1942 the CPI had taken advantage of its newly acquired legality and the wartime ban on Congress activity to increase its membership and its influence over trade unions, student and peasant organizations, and other mass organs. Organizationally, the Indian communists had never before been so prepared for playing an important role in a political arena so vulnerable to revolutionary agitation. Yet, the communists' wartime policy of cooperation with the British rulers of India—dictated by the foreign policy necessities of the Soviet Union—had resulted in diminishing the CPI's potential influence in postwar politics by alienating it from the leadership of the largest nationalist organization.

For, by aiding the British—and the Soviet-defined interests of international communism—in the defense of India, the CPI had thereby earned the epithet of traitor to the cause of Indian nationalism. Paradoxically, had India fallen under Axis occupation, the CPI—like the communist parties of so many European and Asian countries—would probably have been able to gain nationalist prestige as well as valuable experience in partisan warfare by heading or participating in an antifascist "people's liberation army."

1. The Communist Assessment of the Hindu-Moslem Antagonism

An analysis of the manner in which Soviet and Indian communist writers dealt with the most sensitive and crucial issue of this period—the Moslem demand for Pakistan—requires a backward glance at the evolution of CPI nationality policy.

The central theme of communist writings on the Hindu-Moslem antagonism during the 1920's and 1930's was the insistence that such strife was almost entirely the product of a British "divide and rule" policy. Religious and national quarrels stemmed not from the economic base of Indian society, but from anachronistic elements of the superstructure which had been deliberately preserved by the colonial rulers as supports for their oppressive regime. Indeed, as early as 1925 a Soviet writer, B. Seigel', declared that the Indian bourgeoisie had reached that stage of economic development in which it had become conscious of its united class interests despite religious,

caste, and racial divisions.[1] When renewed outbreaks of religious antagonism in the next few years forced the revision of
this conclusion, an Indian communist writing in a Soviet journal
placed the blame on religious leaders—especially Moslem fana-
tics—who served as agents of the British in playing on the backwardness of the masses in order to prevent the unification of the
anti-imperialist movement.[2] Yet at the same time the Indian
communists were warned by a veteran communist trade union
organizer to resist the orthodox Marxist temptation to struggle
against Hindu-Moslem antagonism by condemning religion itself and thus isolating themselves from the masses. Rather, the
party, by uniting in its ranks "followers of different religions,"
should strive to serve as an example to the masses of the possibility of "joint struggle." [3]

However, the example of proletarian fraternalism proved no
more successful than did the force of bourgeois class interests
in ending Hindu-Moslem strife. In the late 1930's, as this communal conflict loomed as an even larger obstacle to the communist policy of promoting a united front under National Congress
leadership, Soviet Orientalists betrayed their frustration over
the staying power of religious and caste traditions. A. M. D'iakov conceded in 1939 that the difficulties in organizing an anti-
imperialist front in India were greater than in most other colonial countries. Again he attributed the survival of the problem
to the alliance of British imperialism and reactionary Indian elements. The Moslem masses he found to be particularly subject
to incendiary propaganda, due to their lower rate of literacy and
urbanization and thus weaker "political consciousness." D'iakov was far from neutral concerning the dispute between
Congress and League, condemning the latter organization as a
British puppet not representative of the interests of the Moslem
masses, and hailing the former as the "peculiar form of the
united anti-imperialist front." [4]

Jinnah's success during the war years in broadening the mass
base of the Moslem League and his commitment of the organization to the cause of a separate Moslem state led the CPI to
reassess its position. P. C. Joshi attempted during the war to
move the CPI to a position of neutrality vis-à-vis the Congress-
League disputes in the interests of maximum mobilization of
the masses behind the war effort. The new position of the CPI
did not, however, represent a complete reversal on the issue of
national unity. Following the example of Bolshevik nationality

policy, an August 1942 CPI resolution recognized the right of secession for "every section of the Indian people which has a contiguous territory as its homeland, common historical tradition, common language, culture, psychological make-up and common economic life." But it stressed that the *recognition* of such right of self-determination was sufficient basis for Congress-League unity. For acknowledging the right "need not necessarily" entail actual separation, while it would serve to dispel mutual distrust and achieve increased unity both now and in the "free India of tomorrow." [5]

Gangadhar Adhikari, a CPI specialist on this issue, elaborated on the party's new policy in a 1943 pamphlet hailed by Ben Bradley of the CPGB as a "capable Marxist analysis." [6] According to Adhikari the problem of the national movement had evolved from an issue dividing the Hindu and Moslem bourgeoisie into a question central to the interests of the peasantry. Thus the demand for self-determination in this new stage had become a "progressive lever" for mobilizing the masses of the various nationalities. The essence of the problem remained the need for the revolutionary unity of the people in their antiimperialist and antifascist struggle, but now "diversity becomes the lever for strengthening unity, for enriching and developing that very unity."

The national oppression which the CPI should oppose included both imperialist oppression and the oppression by certain native "dominant nationalities" which used their advanced stage of bourgeois development to hinder the progress of more backward nationalities. Yet this struggle could not be advanced by support of the "bourgeois reformist" slogan of Pakistan, which was aimed at rallying the masses *away* from the "common freedom movement." The Moslem masses had heeded this appeal not from a "religious urge" but in the hope of attaining their democratic rights.[7]

Though Adhikari denied that this policy was "bodily transposed" from Soviet experience, both his proposals and his reasoning borrowed heavily from Stalin's writings on the nationality problem. Moreover, the transparent tactical nature of the switch in CPI policy only alienated both Congress and League leaderships: the communists, by denying both that India was a single nation and the contention that adherents of the Moslem religion constituted a separate nation, had in effect rebutted the policies of both parties.

The CPI alternative was outlined in its 1945 election manifesto. The party called for immediate independence and "transfer of power" to an All-India Constituent Assembly, delegates to which would be elected by seventeen "sovereign" National Constituent Assemblies. (The apparent contradiction over the locus of sovereignty was left unresolved.) The list of "17 free homelands" was said to represent "our peoples as they were till the British came and conquered and disrupted them." The princely states would be conjoined in these homelands and all questions would be settled "on the basis of complete equality." [8] The all-important problem of determining the boundaries between these "homelands" was left unmentioned, though the CPI memorandum to the cabinet mission later in the year declared that boundaries should be redrawn by a commission "on the basis of ancient national homelands." This same document stressed (as the election manifesto had not) that each national unit should have the option to decide whether it would join the All-India Constituent Assembly "or remain out and form a separate sovereign state by themselves, or join another Indian Union." [9]

The Soviet response to this Indian communist particularist appeal was at first ambiguous. Articles by D'iakov in 1945 failed to mention the new CPI proposals. Instead, D'iakov asserted (as Seigel' had 20 years earlier) that "the Hindu-Muslim problem is nearing solution" and that "the obstacle to the settlement of the Indian question is not so much differences among the Indian parties as a certain definite policy conducted by influential circles in the metropolitan country." [10] By early 1946 D'iakov seemed to have accepted the staying power of the communal antagonisms, and he had adopted a vague position on Pakistan which, while still not mentioning the CPI proposals, at least was not inconsistent with them. While acknowledging the "elementary democratic right of self-determination for regions inhabited by Moslems," D'iakov noted that many "progressive" Indians felt that "Moslem reactionaries" were behind the League, and that the division of the subcontinent would only weaken India without even solving the national question. [11]

Finally, by mid-1947, D'iakov elaborated a more detailed analysis of the nationality problem. Though continuing to ignore the specific CPI policy, he disagreed by implication with some of its particular features—most notably, by listing only twelve "nationalities" in India. [12]

Despite Soviet and CPI assurances that implementation of this demand for self-determination would not necessarily result in the division of India, at least one prominent Indian newspaper—the *National Herald*, owned by Nehru's family—characterized communist policy as a design to weaken India by fragmenting her: "It would not at all suit the USSR to have one or two big powerful neighbors to the South. . . . In fact Soviet and Communist policy . . . has opted in favor of splitting the country into many autonomous units. They deny that there is any such thing as an Indian nation. The Communist plan appears to be for a Balkanization of India." [13] While communist public pronouncements on the subject were too vague to merit the word "plan," there is evidence that at least some Soviet observers did indeed anticipate the disintegration of postindependence India. But the Soviet expectation seemed to be more a fear that a fragmented subcontinent would allow the British to retain their predominant influence than a desire for new opportunities for spreading communist power. D'iakov wrote in June 1947 that the Mountbatten Plan—the culmination of the British policy of "divide and rule"—was aimed at splitting India into conglomerates of feeble and mutually hostile states and predicted that the result would be that India, "like the Balkans in the past," would be an arena of constant clashes.[14] And Khrushchev told an Indian official in 1955 that "I was expecting to see civil war." "We had Gandhi," was the official's reply.[15]

2. Caution in a Time of Chaos: Soviet and CPI Assessments, 1945–1947

Not only did Soviet writers on the nationality problem in 1945–1947 fail to give cognizance to CPI proposals, but even the broader surveys of Indian politics appearing in Soviet journals omitted all mention of the Indian party. From two articles by D'iakov appearing early in 1945 a Soviet reader would have gathered the impression that the Congress and the League were the only parties in India.

In January—after the CPI had already broken with the Congress—D'iakov described the latter group as "undoubtedly a progressive organization," no ordinary political party, but an affiliation of nearly all political groups which aimed at complete independence. Gandhi, though his philosophy bore the "strong imprint of backwardness," was still "the most influential and

popular leader," who had "services to his credit which even his
. . . opponents . . . do not deny." [16] In April, D'iakov wrote
that the anti-imperialist struggle in India was a multiclass
movement including, by clear implication, even "big" capitalists: "it is only the most reactionary elements . . . the princes
and the big landowners—who support the present colonial
regime, whereas the main sections of Indian society are uniting
more and more closely for the struggle for India's independence." [17]

The marked absence of any sharp criticism in D'iakov's articles on British policy in India was duplicated in a pair of articles by E. M. Zhukov appearing in December 1945. Rather
than pledging Soviet, or even local communist, assistance to the
national movements in Asia, Zhukov concentrated solely on the
United Nations trusteeship system as the instrument for accel-
erating the development of colonies toward full independence.[18] Stressing the threat posed by colonial oppression to
the prospects for durable peace, Zhukov pointed out in another
article that it had been the Soviet position at the San Francisco
conference that it was necessary from the standpoint of international security to take measures enabling dependent countries
to make the most rapid development possible toward genuine
national independence. International trusteeship, while not a
"complete solution," represented a considerable step forward
and was a scheme for which the Soviet Union was ready to
"bear its share of responsibility." [19]

Such Soviet caution concerning South Asian national-liberation movements, expressed in language stressing broad united
fronts and international peace and security rather than in the
polemical fire-and-brimstone phrases associated with revolutionary crisis, can be understood only in the context of Soviet
policies regarding Europe and China. The direction of Soviet
policy toward these areas, considered vastly more important in
Russian security considerations than South Asia, strongly
shaped the amount of attention or resources the Soviets felt
inclined to devote to India.

With the atmosphere of wartime collaboration not yet dis-
pelled, the Soviets attempted to take advantage of continued Great
Power détente in order to consolidate their gains in Eastern
Europe as well as the concessions granted them in the Far East
at Yalta. Overt assistance or even active agitation on behalf of
colonial independence movements could have not only strained

relations with "imperialist" governments but also lessened the chances of Western communist parties to take power. Even the Chinese communist movement was subordinated to the interests of Soviet expansion, with the Russians concluding a treaty of friendship with the Kuomintang government. Milovan Djilas has recorded Stalin's unusually frank 1948 observation that he and his colleagues had erred in 1945 in underestimating Mao's chances of success and advising the Chinese comrades to reach a "modus vivendi" with Chiang.[20]

It was only with the deterioration of Soviet relations with the West and the rise of Mao Tse-tung's fortunes in China in 1946–1947 that the Soviet assessment of political developments in India began to shift. And even then, the Soviets were clearly responding to past events, remaining far in the wake of an increasingly revolutionary situation. Nor did the changes in the Soviet analysis appear to bear any relation to the evolution of CPI policy, as that party continued to be largely ignored by the Russians.

In the absence of helpful "open letters" in the journals of international communism (the Comintern had been dissolved in 1943), the CPI experienced difficulties in adjusting to the rapidly changing situation. Especially in 1945, when the Soviet Union was still collaborating with the British, the CPI leaders would have needed to be excellent contortionists to continue to urge a united front with both the Congress and the League while simultaneously avoiding undue protestations against the British.

In truth, the CPI toward the end of 1945 was already less favorable in its assessments of the two dominant parties than was D'iakov. This was in part a consequence of the fact that the Indian communists had been spurned by the leaderships of the Congress and the League and that they were seeking to establish an independent identity in order to compete successfully in their first election campaign. While continuing to talk of a "united front of popular patriotic organizations," the CPI evidently did not have in mind as wide a front as D'iakov had written of. Advocating nationalization of key industries and confiscation of the "illegal riches of war profiteers," the manifesto declared that it would be "a crime against our country's future to leave India's economy in the hands of Indian capitalists . . . for one single day longer."

Yet with respect to neither town nor countryside was the emphasis placed on class struggle. The program spoke of planning through cooperation among the state, management, and labor and of "whole-hearted cooperation and close alliance" between the working class and the middle class (a term probably used to designate the "petty bourgeoisie"). The agricultural platform called for nationalization of the land and limitation of individual holdings to 100 acres, yet it promised to seek the support of "every decent element in the village," and in particular not to "touch the small zamindar or rich peasant" while not allowing them to "go the way of traditional leeches." [21]

The communists managed to win only eight seats in the provincial assemblies, but in light of the restricted nature of the franchise, this was not considered a disastrous showing. Confirmation of the CPI's continuing adherence to a peaceful line came in February 1946, when the party failed to take advantage of violence accompanying a mutiny in the Indian Navy, and later in the year when the CPI sought to dampen communal riots. Yet there were signs of the persistence of more radical viewpoints within the party, most notably in an August 1946 resolution and in a pamphlet written by Adhikari early in 1947. The latter document sharply criticized the "compromising, disruptive and anti-struggle policies" of the Congress and League leaderships and called on communists to lead, organize, and spread the struggle against imperialism while exposing the new Interim Government as "appeasers of vested interests." [22]

But such sharp words were relatively rare in CPI documents, even through the late months of 1947. That the moderate "united front" line associated with Joshi's whole tenure as General Secretary remained dominant was evidenced by the CPI's June 1947 statement on the Mountbatten Plan. This resolution professed to see "important concessions" and "new opportunities for national advance" in the plan and promised full cooperation with the Congress ("the main national democratic organization") in the "proud task of building the Indian Republic on democratic foundations." [23]

As the international situation changed, the Soviet analysis of Indian social and political forces evolved in a different direction, with a slow but unmistakable movement away from the "united front from above" policy favored by D'iakov in 1945. E. M. Zhukov contributed to this reassessment in October 1946 with an article calling Gandhists "the most reactionary strata of the national bourgeoisie" and declaring that English reforms in

India had been largely illusory. Yet Zhukov's caution was pronounced; he took pains to deny bourgeois charges that the "hand of Moscow" was behind the national-liberation movements, suggesting that Soviet assistance was limited to the force of example.[24]

However, even the Soviet "example" was a very passive form of assistance, as the interim Nehru government discovered to its dismay during the Indian famine of 1946. In March of that year the Soviets had made a dramatic offer of food to France (where the communists were in a position to profit from claims of the bounty of socialist agriculture), but an appeal for surplus food from Indian officials (and even from a leader of the CPI) fell on deaf ears in Moscow, as the Soviets declined an excellent opportunity to impress Indian public opinion.[25]

There was nothing in the foreign policy of the Nehru government to give offense to the Soviets; if anything, Nehru was more friendly in his statements concerning Russia than in those relating to the West. Rather, as noted above, the change in Soviet policy toward India was a result of a general hardening in the Soviet strategy which followed upon a change in the political situation in Europe—a change dramatized in 1947 by the proclamation of the Truman Doctrine and the Marshall Plan.

Within the Soviet academic community the change was signaled by a concerted attack on economist E. S. Varga for displaying "bourgeois objectivism" in a work denying the imminence of capitalist crisis. Varga's suggestion of growing industrialization and lessening dependence in the colonies—reminiscent of what the "decolonization theory" of the late 1920's was alleged to have maintained—was attacked by those who denied that the colonies could achieve independence through evolutionary development.[26]

3. The Soviet Reappraisal of India: 1947

And so 1945, a year of infrequent but relatively friendly Soviet assessments of Indian "bourgeois" politicians, and 1946, a year of cooled, but still cautious analysis, were followed by indications on the eve of Indian independence that Soviet Indologists had concluded that the new Indian leaders were "reactionary" and "proimperialist" figures.

A highly significant report ("On the Situation in India") read by the "dean" of Soviet Orientalists, E. M. Zhukov, to the Soviet Central Committee's Academy of Social Sciences in May 1947 (and published in shortened form in August) opened a period of discussion among Soviet experts on what strategy should replace the former "united front from above" approach.[27] Zhukov's report, centering on the causes and effects of the Mountbatten Plan, called attention to an alliance of English imperialism and Indian "big capitalist and feudal elements." This nefarious team, having been frightened by the mass national-liberation movement as well as by the American attempt to oust Britain from its colonial markets under the "false flag" of championing their independence, had agreed on the Mountbatten scheme as a "reform" allowing Britain to preserve her decisive military, political, and economic position.

According to Zhukov, the Indian big bourgeoisie, because of its close ties with feudal elements and its own need to utilize the caste system to exploit the masses, was unable to take the "one straight path" toward expansion of its economic position: "clearing away the augean stables of feudalism." Employing Gandhism for "poisoning the masses with disbelief in their strength" and for justifying its deal with feudalism and imperialism, the big bourgeoisie desired no more than "formal" independence. It preserved its economic and military ties with England out of fear of entering the world arena without British support, and it justified these ties with the theory of "neutrality" which argued that without English help India would be drawn into either the American or the Soviet orbit (a theory which was "obviously absurd" for its equating of U.S. and Soviet policies).

Zhukov went on to assess the contending political parties in India. It was incorrect, he said, to counterpose Congress and League as progressive and reactionary organizations, for each contained both rightist and leftist elements, though the leaderships of both were reactionary. Nehru had recently evolved toward the right and was currently supporting the general aims of the big bourgeoisie in preserving contacts with England. Gandhi, the "apostle of backwardness," had played a negative role in the development of Indian social thought. And Jinnah—"more English than an Englishman"—preserved the religious character of the Moslem League which limited its possibilities in the liberation movement. Finally, Zhukov recognized the existence of the Communist Party of India by endorsing its proposals for self-determination, as set forth in the 1946 memorandum.

Zhukov had, by condemning the leaders of the two major parties, clearly excluded from communist options in India the "united front from above" or close Soviet relations with the new Indian government. Yet it would be wrong to conclude, as one analyst has, that Zhukov had "clearly implied" an alternative strategy.[28] For though Zhukov made many references to the Indian "big bourgeoisie," he was not "careful to include only" this stratum of the bourgeoisie among the proimperialist forces; he had occasionally referred simply to "the bourgeoisie" or "capitalists." The possibility of making a clear differentiation of bourgeois groups, and of advocating a "united front from below" that would include the "middle" or "national" bourgeoisie, was not excluded by Zhukov, but neither was it unambiguously suggested.

Despite the questions it left unanswered, Zhukov's report was an important one. But two studies by American scholars have overstated its significance by erroneously asserting that it formed the basis of a full-scale debate among Soviet scholars.[29] This debate is said to have occurred during a joint session of three branches of the Academy of Sciences of the USSR, meeting on June 14–18, 1947. This conference concerned Soviet studies on India and was organized on the initiative of the Academy's Pacific Institute, which early in 1949 published a collection of papers derived from the June joint session.[30] Included in this collection are three reports on the economic and political situation in contemporary India (one by economist S. M. Mel'man on "The Economic Consequences of World War II," and papers by historians A. M. D'iakov and V. V. Balabushevich on "Postwar English Plans for the State Arrangement of India" and "The Worker Class and Worker Movement in Contemporary India,") as well as a number of reports on linguistics and prewar Indian history.

The introduction to this Pacific Institute publication notes that an additional report had been presented to the 1947 conference by E. M. Zhukov. The editor explained that he was omitting it from the volume since it had already been published elsewhere. Previous Western studies of this period, on the basis of this note, have confidently jumped to the conclusion that the Zhukov article summarized above—"On the Situation in India"—is the missing report. They have used this assumption as the basis for their assertion that a full-scale debate occurred at the conference between Zhukov on the one hand and D'iakov and Balabushevich on the other.[31]

But the extent of the error is even greater. Not only did Zhukov not present his opinion of the changes in India's political situation in public debate in June, but D'iakov and Balabushevich also failed at this meeting to voice the views attributed to them.[32]

That both reports were revised at some time between June 1947 and their publication in early 1949 is certain. A reconstruction of what conclusions each man actually presented to the Academy joint session can be arrived at by a comparison of the revised versions with the summaries published in the Academy of Sciences' 1947 summary of the conference. The bulk of Balabushevich's report on the Indian worker movement, which dealt with the relatively small size, uneven distribution, and poor condition of the working class and the gradual rise of its class consciousness, appears not to have been altered. His observations on the antiworker policies of the right wing of the National Congress are identical in the two versions. According to the 1947 summary, however, his conclusions were rather benign. It quotes him thus: "However India now is not what it was after World War I. The democratic forces in the country have grown and become stronger. The same is true of the working class. It is hardly possible to decide the question of the future of India while ignoring the will of the people." [33] The sentences in the 1949 version which immediately follow the above conclusion contain an outright condemnation of the Indian bourgeoisie and were quite likely added after 1947.[34]

D'iakov's report concerning the Cripps plan, the Cabinet Mission plan, and Attlee's declaration of February 1947 notes (in both versions) the increasing tendency of the Indian bourgeoisie to fear the mass movement and its growing inclination to compromise with imperialism. The conclusion reported in the official summary, however, leaves open the possibility of alliance of the masses with part of the bourgeoisie.[35] The 1949 version omits this conclusion and substitutes the view that the entire bourgeoisie, out of "self interest and treachery" and "for the sake of its profits was prepared to sacrifice the independence of its country." [36]

Such an intensive examination of sources and chronology is

necessary only because previous Western studies have based elaborate arguments on their mistaken interpretations of the evidence. Both studies rely on Zhukov's August article as well as on the later appended conclusions of D'iakov and Balabushevich to describe a debate which almost certainly did not take place.[37]

In summing up the Soviet views on India at the time of Indian independence in August 1947, it can be said only that the earlier favorable outlook toward the Indian "bourgeoisie"— including Nehru and the National Congress—was gradually being discarded by Soviet Indologists. The Congress leadership was said to be moving from an "anti-imperialist" to a "compromising" position. Whether the "main enemy" was still imperialism and its feudal allies or was Indian capitalism and whether Indian communists were now to struggle against the entire bourgeoisie or merely against certain top strata had not yet been decided. For the remainder of 1947 the CPI, without contrary instruction from Moscow, remained friendly to Nehru and his new government.

Given the relatively low priority of India in Soviet concerns, there seemed no hurry to conclude the reappraisal. But assurance that a new, more militant posture was inevitable was provided by A. A. Zhdanov's major speech at the founding conference of the Cominform in Poland in September 1947.[38] This address, by the Soviet official considered second only to Stalin in rank, constituted an unmistakably authoritative description of the new epoch which had replaced the temporary postwar collaboration between the Soviet Union and the West.

Zhdanov spoke of "two basic orientations" or "camps" in the world—the imperialist and antidemocratic camp headed by the U.S., and the anti-imperialist, democratic camp headed by the USSR—and of a sharp change in the relationship of forces in favor of socialism. But this was by no means a stable balance, for the U.S. had "proclaimed a new, openly predatory," expansionist orientation which aimed at destruction of socialism and domination of the world. The Truman Doctrine and Marshall Plan were concrete expressions of this expansionism. As for Soviet foreign policy, it "proceeds from the fact of the coexistence over a lengthy period of two systems—capitalism and socialism." But coexistence did not mean complacency, and communist parties must head the resistance to imperialist expansion, rallying, on the basis of an anti-imperialist and democratic platform, "all democratic and patriotic forces of the people."

Zhdanov's remarks were centered on the situation in Europe, but he did allude to the "sharpening of the crisis of the colonial system" resulting from the war and to "increasing armed resistance" to imperialism by colonial peoples. In addition to this general observation, there were two specific references in the speech to India. Zhdanov spoke of the attempts of "instigators of a new war" to frighten and blackmail "in particular" China and India and to represent themselves to these countries as "saviors from the Communist danger" in hopes of preserving China and India under "imperialist enslavement." But this did not mean that these countries had already fallen to the antidemocratic camp, nor were they, like Indonesia and Viet Nam, in the anti-imperialist camp, though "India, Egypt and Syria sympathize with it."

This new analysis, while pointing to the imperialist threat to India, gave no indication as to which of the Indian political forces could serve as anti-imperialist allies of the communists. (Indeed, neither the CPI nor the Chinese communists were mentioned by Zhdanov.) Whether the new strategy in India was to be anticapitalist as well as anti-imperialist was still an open question.

The question remained unresolved during the next few months, despite the labors of another conference and several more articles by Soviet Indologists. The conference was a meeting of the Pacific Institute in November, which heard reports on "The Great October Socialist Revolution and the Countries of the East." Summaries of the papers presented indicate a rather dull session, with no indication of disagreement.[39] There was more attention than usual paid to the leading role of the CPI in the national movement. But this was to be expected, given the nature of the conference topic.

An article by Zhukov entitled "The Sharpening Crisis of the Colonial System" appeared in *Bol'shevik* in December.[40] As its title implies, it was an attempt to relate Zhdanov's speech to the colonies in more detail. The general theme was the contention that, while the bourgeoisie had led national-liberation movements between the wars, the working class and the communist parties were now in the "vanguard" of these movements. The "big national—compradore and industrial—bourgeoisie" had reached a compromise with imperialism because of the threat to its class interests from the worker and peasant movements.

In "many" countries of the East the communist party had become "the soul and organizer of the bloc of national democratic forces," uniting proletariat, peasantry, and "in many countries even part of the bourgeoisie, chiefly petty and middle." The Communist Party of China, for example, represented "the vital interests of the majority of Chinese people," and in Indonesia and Viet Nam the communists led a "coalition of parties" in a broad front against imperialism, landlords, and the "big national bourgeoisie connected with foreign capital."

But Zhukov's article gave no clear indication as to the alignment of class forces in India. Nor were articles by D'iakov and Balabushevich less ambiguous. All used interchangeably the terms "national bourgeoisie," "big national bourgeoisie," and simply "bourgeoisie," and failed to designate which of these middle-class strata were to be written off as hopeless collaborators with imperialism and which, if any, could be admitted to the "anti-imperialist national front." [41]

4. The CPI Moves "Left": 1948–1950

Unlike the Soviet Indologists, who continued after Zhdanov's speech to be undecided about what course should be taken in India to replace the united front from above, the CPI suffered little uncertainty in choosing a new direction. As noted above, a strong leftist group in the CPI had occasionally surfaced during 1946–1947 to indicate its displeasure with Joshi's moderate policy. Conditioned by a long history of looking for a signal from Moscow, these elements seized upon Zhdanov's address, disregarding its many ambiguities, as just such a directive.

They must have seen additional sanction for an abrupt change of line in another address delivered to the Cominform's founding meeting by Edvard Kardelj, the second-ranking figure in the Yugoslav regime. Kardelj's speech, free of the ambiguities concerning the bourgeoisie found in Zhdanov's address, clearly called for an attack on the entire bourgeoisie and an "intertwining" of the democratic and socialist revolutions. That such sanction was seen by the Indian dissidents is evident both from the fact that Kardelj's speech was reprinted in the CPI journal and from statements later made by Ajoy Ghosh and B. T. Ranadive affirming its "powerful influence" in "showing us the correct Marxist revolutionary path." [42]

The result was a meeting of the CPI Central Committee from December 7 to 16, at which Joshi and his faction were outvoted by the radical group, headed by Ranadive. A resolution was drawn up calling for an end to opportunistic illusions about

Nehru, whose government was tied to big business and was increasingly subservient to the Anglo-American imperialist camp. The Central Committee urged unity among "workers and peasants and progressive intellectuals" in an effort to remove the bourgeois government.[43]

Before the CPI party congress could meet to ratify this policy change, yet another event occurred which must have seemed to the Indian communists to be confirmation of the correctness of their decision. In February the Conference of Youth and Students of Southeast Asia Fighting for Freedom and Independence, sponsored by the communist-controlled World Federation of Democratic Youth and International Union of Students, met in Calcutta. Ruth McVey has convincingly demonstrated that this meeting, originally planned prior to the shift of policy in Moscow and chiefly aimed at noncommunist youth, was not, as some have speculated, the scene for "orders from Moscow" which ignited the militant struggles in Southeast Asia.[44] At most, the conference could be said to have broadcast to wider circles the Zhdanov two-camp message. While different speakers sounded divergent themes and there was no general endorsement of armed struggle nor unambiguous condemnation of "neutralist" governments, the dominant themes were praise for the military successes of the Chinese, Indonesian, and Indochinese struggles and hostility toward the national bourgeoisie. At any rate, the tenor, timing, and location of the conference were certainly not likely to discourage the CPI from pursuing the path it had already endorsed.

The CPI Second Congress opened in Calcutta on February 28 and was attended by 632 delegates (another 287 were elected but unable to attend), said to represent 89,000 members. There were fraternal observers from Australia, Burma, Ceylon, and Yugoslavia. These latter delegates—Zokovic and Dedijer—apparently gave instructions in the anticapitalist strategy and, although the opening shots in the Soviet-Yugoslav dispute had already been fired, Ghosh records that "we swallowed all that the Yugoslavs told us." [45] The congress proceedings centered around a self-critical confession by Joshi of cowardice, betrayal, and "right reformism" throughout his career, Joshi's replacement as General Secretary by Ranadive, and the debate on the draft thesis. This document, published soon after the congress, embodies the assessment of social forces and political strategy and tactics pursued by the CPI over the next two years.

The "Political Thesis" examined the economic basis of

bourgeois collaboration with imperialism, drawing the familiar conclusion that the dependence of the native bourgeoisie on imperialism for its markets and capital, along with its fear of the mass movement, led it to compromise. The Indian government was explicitly identified with this treacherous bourgeoisie, and its policies were said to amount to supporting feudal reaction and sabotaging the antifeudal, anti-imperialist struggle. For the working class to base its strategy on alleged differences among various strata of the bourgeoisie (as Soviet analysts continued to do) was said to be "anti-Marxist." Thus "Nehru is as much a representative of the bourgeoisie as Patel is . . . all shades of difference within the bourgeois camp . . . are entirely subordinated to the new basic realignment of the class as a whole, namely its role of collaboration with imperialism." [46]

The "Political Thesis" clearly implied that the CPI-led "Democratic Front" would use armed struggle to overthrow the bourgeoisie. It spoke of a "new stage" of the revolutionary struggle signified by the development of "armed struggle" and leading to the establishment "at one stroke of people's democracy." [47] This people's democratic state would be based on the alliance of workers, peasants, and the oppressed petty bourgeoisie, and all opponents of democracy—clearly meaning the entire bourgeoisie—would be excluded. This state would implement the program of the democratic front while "simultaneously" proceeding with socialist construction, without an intervening stage of capitalism.

It is evident that this "new" policy was anything but novel. In its insistence on proletarian hegemony, opposition to the entire bourgeoisie, and determination to skip the capitalist stage of development by combining the bourgeois-democratic and socialist revolutions, it was highly reminiscent of the views of M. N. Roy in the early 1920's, of the Colonial Theses of the Sixth Comintern Congress, and of the CPI Draft Platform of 1930. Indeed, the "left" strategy was so deeply engrained in CPI history that it is not at all surprising that, at the signal to abandon the "right" Joshi strategy (pursued with minor deviations since 1935), the party returned to the anticapitalist united front from below. Unlike these previously voiced strategies, however, the 1948 Political Thesis paid only scant attention to the potential of the agrarian revolution—an omission which was somewhat surprising in light of its salute to the "glorious fight of the Chinese people," and in light of the emphasis given by the Second Congress to the struggle in the Telengana district of Hyderabad.[48]

But the new leadership's invocation of the Telengana struggle apparently was meant to highlight the violent tactics favored by Ranadive, rather than the agrarian base of the movement. For the course embarked upon by the CPI in 1948—described by Kautsky as "a policy of violent strikes, riots, looting, arson, sabotage, and murder"—was directed primarily at urban areas.[49]

This urban orientation was soon attacked by the Andhra Provincial Committee of the CPI, which, as the organization that had taken over the direction of the Telengana movement, resented the lack of real assistance from the central party leadership. In a letter in June 1948, the Andhra group invoked the example of the rural-based Chinese revolution as more appropriate to India than the Russian model. The strategical form of the agrarian revolution urged by the Andhra committee was Mao Tse-tung's "new democracy," which united not only the poor peasants and working class, but also the middle peasants and even—in areas with strong feudal institutions—the rich peasants, in the struggle against imperialism and feudalism. The objective of this struggle was the establishment not of proletarian dictatorship but of "new democracy." [50]

While there is no evidence that the Andhra group invoked any other authority than Mao in support of its position, it could have pointed to the fact that some of Mao's strategical pronouncements had recently been appearing in the Soviet and Cominform press. Both *Pravda* of January 6 and *For a Lasting Peace, For a People's Democracy!* (the new organ of the Cominform) of January 15—as well as the CPI journal—had printed excerpts of a speech made by Mao in December, which had described the Chinese party's economic platform strictly in terms of opposition to feudalism and "monopoly state capital." In addition to alliance with the "moderately well-off peasantry," Mao in this speech had defended the policy of protecting the "national industry and trade" of the "middle-class bourgeoisie," which was also a victim of Kuomintang oppression. He had urged a "broad united front embracing the overwhelming majority of the population . . . under the firm leadership of the Communist Party," and had explicitly warned against "pursuing an erroneous ultra-leftist policy in regard to the petty and middle-class bourgeoisie." [51] In a later address, reprinted in the Cominform journal in July, Mao had extended the united front even further, including in it the "workers, peasants, artisans, professional people, intelligentsia, the liberal bourgeoisie *and a part of the gentry* who have split off from the landlord class." Even the landlords were not to be eliminated after the revolution and were to be allowed to retain a portion of their land.[52]

The dissemination of these views in the Moscow and Cominform press did not necessarily constitute an endorsement of their application in other Asian countries. Indeed, as shall be shown below, Moscow remained undecided on the general applicability of the Chinese "model" until mid-1949. But Ranadive's response to the Andhra committee's advocacy of Mao's "new-democratic" path contained no hint of indecision. His reply came in four articles published in the CPI's theoretical journal in the first half of 1949.[53]

Defending his strategy with quotations from Lenin, Stalin, and the theses of the Sixth Congress of the Comintern, Ranadive argued that the bourgeois-democratic revolution was virtually over in India, and thus the next stage must be aimed at the destruction of the bourgeoisie and the establishment of a "Democratic Dictatorship of the Workers and Peasants" which would quickly pass over into a proletarian dictatorship building socialism. Thus capitalism at home, rather than imperialism, had become the main enemy. Describing his view of the agrarian situation, Ranadive argued that even in the countryside capitalism was developing into the main enemy; thus the middle peasant was not a firm ally but a vacillating one, and the rich peasant, not vacillating, but simply an enemy.

In the last and most extreme article, published in July 1949, Ranadive flatly stated that "the entire experience of the Russian revolution" was fully valid for India. He ridiculed the notion of "some" comrades who support "what they call the Chinese way": that a communist party can lead the revolution "without setting the working class itself . . . in motion." But he proceeded from this attack on "some supporters" of Mao's ideas to an attack on Mao himself. Some of Mao's ideas were "such that no Communist Party can accept them." Specific ideas were branded as "erroneous," "reactionary," and even "horrifying."

Ranadive's attacks on Mao could well have sealed his doom, but the utter failure of his policies in India and the damage done by them to the CPI would probably have been sufficient indictment against him. The new leadership, supremely confident that a revolutionary situation existed in India, had rushed into the fray without adequate preparation. Its assessment of the mood of the working class and of the degree of disenchantment with the Congress government had been in error. Thus its "left-sectarian" strategy, as in the past, had led only to further isolation from the masses.

Ranadive's failures were at least in part due to effective counteraction by Nehru and the state governments in imposing partial bans on the party (most notably in West Bengal), in conducting raids against party offices, and in arresting large numbers of the party's leadership. In addition, the government, with the cooperation of noncommunist trade union leaders, had been able to blunt the edge of Ranadive's strike campaign, resulting in a serious weakening of the strength and prestige of the CPI-led AITUC. In frustration, Ranadive had instructed his cadres to engage in acts of terrorism and sabotage, a move which created much disaffection both within and without the party's ranks. Joshi, by then expelled from the party, wrote in 1950: " . . . regular contact with the masses is broken. Small squads of regular comrades . . . guided by a fanatical underground worker, with sometimes a lad or two from the working class thrown in, are sent out when a strike call is given . . . the working class is not responding to our practical leadership." [54]

Even the Telengana movement had suffered a serious setback during Ranadive's tenure. Nehru had sent the Indian army into Hyderabad in September 1948 to force the integration of the princely state into the Indian Union. The Telengana communists, declaring the independence of Hyderabad, had called for resistance to Nehru's "fascist" troops. The Indian army was forced to remain in the Telengana districts until 1951 in order to "pacify" the areas. One of the leaders of the guerrilla movement later admitted that "the guerrilla squads . . . indulged in a lot of indiscriminate and unnecessary killing" which has "brought much disrepute to the Party and to the movement as a whole." [55]

Though it must have been small consolation indeed to the Andhra group, which had seen its movement collapse, its debate with Ranadive was to be settled from above in its favor, and the Andhra leadership was to be the next recipient of the mantle of leadership of the CPI.

5. Soviet Endorsement of the "Chinese Model" for India

The Soviets, absorbed with events in Europe and still undecided at the beginning of 1948 about what policy should be endorsed for India in place of the "united front from above" strategy, proved reluctant to approve or condemn the CPI's choice of a militant leftist orientation. Only a single brief article in the Cominform press referred to the Second Congress of the CPI, and none of the CPI publications from the entire Ranadive period was ever reprinted in whole or in part in the Soviet or Cominform press.

The article concerning the Second Congress appeared in April. It reported that the CPI congress had "stressed the need for a democratic front to combat the American and British imperialists and the Indian bourgeoise who have betrayed the national interests and who have entered into a compromise." [56] But even this brief summary clearly implied that the struggle in India was—contrary to Ranadive's view—still very much an anti-imperialist struggle. The CPI congress themes of intertwining revolutions and militant struggle were pointedly ignored. Subsequent Soviet articles in 1948, while stressing the increasingly "reactionary" nature of Nehru's internal and foreign policies, offered nò clear directive on what approach the CPI should take in combatting these policies.

Soviet apprehensions about Anglo-American designs on India centered, one may judge from a pair of articles in *New Times*, on the situation in Kashmir.[57] Since 1947 India and Pakistan had been engaged in an undeclared war, precipitated when the Maharajah of the largely Moslem state had acceded to India and had called for Indian troops following an invasion by Pathan tribesmen from Pakistan. Not only was this area of great strategic (as well as emotional) importance to India and Pakistan, but—bordering on China and Afghanistan and only a short distance from Soviet Turkestan—it was seen by the Soviets as posing a potential problem for their own security. T. Ershov described as "The Truth about Kashmir" British plans to foment armed conflict in order to return its troops to Kashmir as well as to strengthen reactionary chauvinistic elements in both India and Pakistan. O. Orestov conjured up an even more frightening vision: Anglo-American plans to convert Kashmir into a link in a chain of military bases around the Soviet Union. In this plan the imperialists were seeking to enlist the aid of Indian reactionaries who "toady" to Britain and the United States and who ignore the desires of the people of the region for self-determination.

An article by M. Alekseev, appearing in the authoritative

Bol'shevik, was also hostile to the Nehru government's policies.[58] But unlike other analysts, Alekseev clearly described the Congress government as a representative of the *big* bourgeoisie. Ignoring the Ranadive thesis that Indian capitalism had become the main enemy, Alekseev explicitly declared that India remained in a colonial position and that the objectives of the national-liberation struggle continued to be anti-imperialist and antifeudal. But he did not explicitly draw the implied consequences from his limitation of criticism to the "big bourgeoisie"—that is, he limited the democratic front to workers, peasants, and petty bourgeoisie, failing to mention the middle bourgeoisie at all.

R. Palme Dutt, the veteran British communist mentor of the CPI, in a pair of articles published in the Cominform journal, followed Alekseev in distinguishing between the Indian big bourgeoisie and other strata, but he also failed to mention the middle bourgeoisie. Indeed, Dutt's article advocated CPI leadership of a "broad democratic anti-imperialist front" which would unite "the widest sections of the people," but he added a note of confusion by stating that "[t]his general line has found expression in the decisions of the recent Second Congress." Perhaps Dutt was consciously giving a more moderate interpretation to the new "left-sectarian" line of the CPI in order to suggest to Ranadive that his policies should be softened. This hypothesis is strengthened by Dutt's reference in the same article to the "powerful influence" exerted by the Chinese revolution (with its broad four-class front) "throughout the dependent countries of Asia and the colonial world." [59]

a. D'iakov's View of the Nationality Issue

The theoretical basis for a communist alliance with the Indian "middle bourgeoisie" was provided in an important book by A. M. D'iakov, published in October 1948.[60] In this study, *The national question and English imperialism in India*, D'iakov suggested that "nationality" provided the key for evaluating the degree to which anti-Nehru bourgeois groups were "progressive" and thereby worthy of CPI support.

D'iakov argued that British conquest had interrupted the development of the ancient peoples of India into "nations," which—according to Marxist theory—could come into being only after the evolution of capitalist relations and the unification of internal markets. But British rule, by imposing a degree of economic and political unity on the subcontinent as a whole, and by calling forth in opposition to itself a single national-liberation movement, had contributed to the impression—propagandized by the National Congress leadership—that the Indians were one people. Likewise, the theory propagated by the Moslem League (and ultimately supported by the British for divisive purposes)—that India was two "nations" by reason of its two major religious communities—was "unscientific." Moslem Indians, despite shared religion, were not one nation, because they lacked such mandatory features of nationhood as common territory, common language, and common economic life. Thus the differences between Bengali Hindus and Moslems were no greater than those between German Protestants and Catholics. In certain situations, these differences were made more acute by the fact that class conflicts (e.g., between Hindu landlords and Moslem tenants) were diverted into reactionary religious channels.

There were divisions not only among the masses but even among the bourgeoisie. Since capitalist relations had developed at an uneven rate in India, some Indian nationalities —particularly those in the coastal areas and largest industrial centers—had become more developed than others. Thus it was the bourgeoisie of the Gujarati and Marwari nationalities which had led the National Congress in the struggle against the British in hopes of replacing the colonialists in their preeminent position in the all-Indian market. But this unevenness of development also entailed the oppression of the bourgeoisie of less-developed nationalities by the Gujarati-Marwari group.

D'iakov concluded that the post-1947 government of India was dominated by the big (i.e., Gujarati-Marwari) bourgeoisie, acting as "junior" partners of the English imperialists. This government was not only suppressing the workers, peasants, and urban petty bourgeoisie, but was also infringing upon the interests of the bourgeoisie of the weaker nationality groups. Under such conditions, to support the movements of these various nationalities for self-determination was progressive. For these movements constituted both a struggle against the oppression of the big bourgeoisie and a means for attracting the working classes into political life and for raising their cultural level by developing their national language. The 1945–1946 CPI position on the issue of national demands was explicitly endorsed by the Soviet Indologist. D'iakov seemed to envisage an alli-

ance between workers and bourgeoisie of "oppressed" nationalities, yet he explicitly insisted that such an alliance—as in the
states of Andhra and Kerala—be under the leadership of the
working class.

While D'iakov's insights into the "progressive" (i.e., disruptive) potentialities of movements for national "self-determination" in India testified to the growing sophistication of Soviet
Indologists, they represented no basic change from the Leninist-Stalinist views on national movements.[61] That the Soviets
were far from giving movements of "oppressed nationalities"
any more than a tactical endorsement was emphasized in an article appearing in *Bol'shevik* in August 1948. In it, Iu. Frantsev
reiterated the familiar arguments on the debilitating effects of
"bourgeois nationalism" on working class solidarity and concluded that it constituted "the most dangerous enemy" of the
workers' and liberation movements.[62]

There was little Soviet comment concerning India during the
first half of 1949, but those articles which did appear were not
inconsistent in their analysis with D'iakov's characterization of
the social forces in newly independent India. A brief article by
A. I. Levkovsky explicitly echoed D'iakov's conclusion that the
"deal" between the British and the Indian capitalists "was
made not by the whole native bourgeoisie, but only by its
upper strata: the big capitalists, in particular the representatives
of Indian monopolies . . . (Tata, Birla, Dalmia, . . . etc.)."
More novel was the suggestion made by Levkovsky that the
"armed struggles" then occurring in Indonesia, Burma, and Viet
Nam "could spread to other colonial countries, including
India." [63] A similar note was sounded two months later by S. M.
Mel'man, who predicted that a "huge influence" on the national-liberation movement in India would be exerted by the
risings in Southeast Asia and particularly by the "huge success"
of the People's Liberation Army in China.[64]

b. Soviet Appraisal of the "Chinese Path"

The publication in *Pravda* in June of a long article by one of
the foremost leaders of the Chinese revolution, Liu Shao-ch'i,
ushered in a new stage in the reassessment by the Soviets of the
strategy in India.[65] Liu's article had actually been written one-
half year earlier and was primarily a condemnation of the newly
heretical Yugoslav leaders. What may have caused the delay in
the publication of this work in the Soviet press was Liu's dis-

cussion, toward the end of his article, of the "objective progressive historical significance" of bourgeois nationalism "in such
colonial and semi-colonial countries as China, India, Korea, Indonesia, the Philippines, Viet-Nam, Burma, Egypt, etc." In language more hortatory than Soviet spokesmen had theretofore
been inclined to use, Liu directed the communists in a number
of Asian countries to employ a strategy strikingly reminiscent of
that which Lenin had prescribed in 1920. Specifically addressing himself to the comrades in India and other Asian colonies,
Liu warned that it would be a "grave mistake" to fail to conclude an alliance with bourgeois nationalism, adding that the alliance "must be established in all sincerity even if it should be
of an unreliable, temporary, and unstable nature." At the same
time, he pointed to the necessity of a "firm and irreconcilable
policy" against the "big bourgeoisie, which has already surrendered to imperialism." [66]

Whereas Liu's attitude about the potential allies of the Asian
proletariat was close to (or even more permissive than) Lenin's
stand in 1920, the Chinese leader in at least one respect echoed
a position taken by M. N. Roy at the Second Congress. For Liu
asserted that the victory of the national-liberation movements in
the colonies would result in the triumph of the proletarian revolution in the imperialist countries themselves. The essential
points of Liu's exhortations to Asian communists were given
added weight by Soviet Indologists in a number of articles
which emerged from a joint session of the Economics and Pacific Institutes of the Academy of Sciences. The meeting was
held in June 1949, at the same time that *Pravda* was publishing
Liu's article. The main report was delivered by E. M. Zhukov
on "Problems of the national-colonial struggle since the Second
World War."

According to Zhukov, armed struggle in Indonesia, Indochina, Malaya, and Burma and "the peasant uprisings in
India" attested to a higher stage of the national-liberation movements—a stage in which the working class and the communist
vanguard were playing the leading role. Unlike previous
periods, when the immediate goal of such movements had been
a bourgeois-democratic regime, the goal of this stage was people's democracy. In its general pattern, people's democracy in
the East was to be similar to its manifestation in Europe—"a
special form of regime which corresponds to the path of transition from capitalism to socialism and has become possible

owing to the victory of socialism in the USSR and the strengthening of democratic forces throughout the world." However, the Asian variety would differ somewhat—especially in the "more protracted" timing of its transition to socialism—due to the greater range of "bourgeois-democratic" tasks yet to be accomplished by the revolution. Zhukov emphasized, moreover, that "not only the workers, peasants, petty bourgeoisie and intelligentsia unite in the struggle for people's democracy in the colonies and semi-colonies, but even a certain section of the middle bourgeoisie, interested in being delivered from ruinous foreign competition." [67]

Thus Zhukov appeared to side with Ranadive in designating the goal of the Indian proletariat's struggle as "people's democracy" and in including among its enemies the government of Nehru, the "bloody strangler of the progressive forces." Yet the agreement was only superficial, for by "people's democracy" Zhukov meant a "protracted" intermediary stage to socialism rather than one which could quickly pass over to socialist development. And by including the "middle" bourgeoisie in the national front Zhukov was laying stress on the anti-imperialist and antifeudal nature of the struggle, whereas Ranadive had declared it to be primarily anticapitalist. But Zhukov had *not* implied that the Indian struggle would have to be a peaceful one, for he spoke of the peasant "uprisings" there in conjunction with the armed struggles in the rest of Asia. Zhukov concluded that "the fresh wind from China cannot but carry" to India.

A report to the conference by V. V. Balabushevich concurred in the judgment that it was "not precluded" that certain groups of the bourgeoisie—those in competition with foreign capital or in backward national districts—could become temporary, though not reliable, "fellow-travellers of the democratic forces." [68] But the most notable portion of Balabushevich's analysis dealt with the peasant movement in Telengana—an uprising which had been de-emphasized by Ranadive and whose main sponsor, the Andhra Provincial Committee, was a vocal advocate of a "Chinese path" for India. Telengana, according to Balabushevich, was the "first attempt" to create people's democracy in India. Moreover, it was the harbinger of the agrarian revolution, which constituted the "most important content of the present stage of the national-liberation struggle in India."

This theme was picked up in an article by D'iakov which was

published by the Pacific Institute in November. Like Balabushevich, D'iakov wrote that the new stage of the Indian national-liberation movement "can be termed as an agrarian revolution with complete justification." He, too, singled out
Telengana as a place where the peasant antifeudal and national
movements had merged under communist leadership to create a
"people's power" for the first time in Indian history. Finally,
D'iakov repeated his argument of a year earlier that bourgeois-
nationalism could be utilized as a temporary ally of the working
class, though he now seemed to reflect the caution of Zhukov in
assessing how "reliable" the alliance could be: "The progressive role of these national bourgeois strata is extremely relative
and short-lived and on no account must it be overestimated." [69]

In addition to these statements by Soviet Indologists, the Soviet press in the latter half of 1949 gave wide publicity to statements by the Chinese comrades who were at that time successfully completing their struggle for national liberation. In July,
Pravda reprinted Mao's views on the "People's Democratic
Dictatorship," in which he spoke of a four-class alliance headed
by the working class which would, even after establishing people's democracy, follow a policy of "restricting capitalism, not
destroying it." [70] The Cominform journal in September reprinted a speech by the commander-in-chief of the Chinese
People's Liberation Army, who emphasized the need "to win
over the national bourgeoisie or to neutralize it" in a "colony
or semi-colony like China." [71] The same newspaper edi-
torialized, on the occasion of the Red Army's victory, that it
would "unquestionably . . . inspire the peoples of the colonies
and dependent countries to intensify the national-liberation
struggle." [72]

Further confirmation of the parallels being drawn by the Soviets between the Chinese and Indian revolutions came soon
after Chiang's flight from the mainland, when D'iakov speculated in *Pravda* that the American imperialists were planning to
transfer to Nehru's India the role of "main base" of imperialism
in the East which Chiang had forfeited. The main reason behind these plans, according to D'iakov, was the similarity of the
Indian regime "to the anti-popular, reactionary regime which
existed in Kuomintang China." [73]

The most explicit instruction to the effect that the "Chinese
path" should be followed in other Asian countries came in a
speech by Liu Shao-ch'i to the Trade Union Conference of

Asian and Australasian Countries of the World Federation of
Trade Unions (WFTU), meeting in Peking in November and
December 1949. Liu's address, reprinted in both *Pravda* and
the Cominform journal, enumerated four features of the Chinese path to people's democracy: (1) the working class must
unite with all classes, parties, and groups who wish to oppose
the imperialists and their lackeys; (2) the united front must be
led by the working class and the communist party rather than
by the unreliable national bourgeoisie; (3) the party must be
disciplined and armed with Marxist-Leninist theory; (4) it was
necessary to create, "where ever and whenever possible, strong
people's armies of liberation" and "supporting bases" for their
operation. Moreover, armed struggle was the "main form of
struggle" in many colonies and semicolonies, though it was to
be combined with other legal and illegal forms of struggle.
Together, these features had wide applicability; the Chinese
path "must be followed by the peoples of many colonial and
semi-colonial countries in their struggle to win national independence and a people's democracy. . . . This path is Mao
Tse-tung's path." [74] India was specifically named by Liu as a
country in which an armed struggle for liberation had already
begun.

An important editorial appearing in the Cominform newspaper on January 27, 1950, was, however, more cautious on
whether armed struggle was taking place in India. It quoted
from Liu's speech and endorsed his comments on the "Chinese
path." But only Viet Nam, South Korea, Malaya, the Philippines, Indonesia, and Burma were cited by the editorial as
being engaged in armed struggle. India was, however, the subject of a very important paragraph which, while ambiguous on
the question of violence, left no doubt that the other features of
the Chinese path were quite applicable. ". . . the task of the
Indian Communists, drawing on the experience of the national
liberation movement in China and other countries, is, naturally,
to strengthen the alliance of the working class with all the peasantry, to fight for the introduction of the urgently needed
agrarian reform and . . . against the Anglo-American imperialists . . . and . . . the reactionary big bourgeoisie and feudal
princes collaborating with them—to unite all classes, parties,
groups and organizations willing to defend the national independence and freedom of India." [75]

That this was not the path on which Ranadive had chosen to

lead the CPI was unmistakable. The quite profound repercus-
sions produced by this editorial on CPI leadership and policy
will be considered below. But first it is necessary to place the
Soviet pronouncements concerning India in 1949 in perspective, focusing especially on the Soviet attitude toward China
and on the problem of "neo-Maoism."

c. A "Neo-Maoist" Strategy?

Professor Kautsky's book argues in great detail the thesis that
the strategy which the Soviets were urging for India and other
underdeveloped countries after mid-1949 was a unique departure from earlier strategies and owed its essential features to the
revolutionary theory and practice of Mao Tse-tung.[76] Kautsky
distinguishes three major communist strategies: (1) the "left"
strategy, which defines native capitalism as the main enemy
and a one-stage socialist revolution as the immediate goal, and
which utilizes a united front from below, with workers, poor
peasants, and the petty bourgeoisie ranged against noncommunist parties; (2) the "right" strategy, which defines as the main
enemy fascism, feudalism, imperialism, or a combination of
these and which aims at a two-stage (bourgeois-democratic or
national-liberation followed by socialist) revolution, utilizing a
united front with anti-imperialist, antifeudal *parties* from
above; (3) the "neo-Maoist" strategy, which, like the "right"
strategy, seeks a two-stage revolution directed first against imperialism and feudalism, but which relies chiefly on a united
front from below that includes the national bourgeoisie. This
latter aspect, the communist party's direct appeal from below to
a section of the bourgeoisie (as a class rather than to bourgeois
parties), is said to be the distinctive feature of neo-Maoism.
Unlike Maoism itself, reliance on the peasantry as the main
mass base of the revolution is said not to be crucial, and the use
of violence is said to be a matter of tactics, which can be employed with any of the three strategies.

Both the label Kautsky has attached to this strategy and the
uniqueness of the strategy itself are very debatable. By denying
that reliance on the peasant base is essential to "neo-Maoism,"
Kautsky has emasculated the very feature which Benjamin
Schwartz, among other observers, has identified as the essential
feature of "Maoism." [77] And by relegating the use of violence to
the level of "mere" tactics, nonessential to "neo-Maoism,"

Kautsky has ignored Mao's own dictum that the development and consolidation of the CCP *"have been inseparable from guerrilla warfare."* [78] What remains of "neo-Maoism" after these two features have been defined as nonessential did not, indeed, originate with Mao Tse-tung, though he may have been the first to employ this technique successfully.

On the contrary, by returning to Stalin's 1925 speech to the KUTV, one can find the essentials of "neo-Maoism." The notion of an alliance with the national bourgeoisie was itself an innovation of Lenin's, but it was Stalin who prescribed the peculiar form Kautsky attributes to Mao. In the section of his 1925 speech dealing with India, Stalin distinguished between "compromising" and "revolutionary" sections of the bourgeoisie. In advising the Indian communists to form an alliance only with the latter section, he clearly did not identify it with the Congress party as a whole but only with its "left" membership, and thus he was advocating a united front from below which "concentrated its fire" on the "compromising" bourgeoisie. But this "anti-big bourgeoisie" tactic was included in the context of a two-stage revolution to be led by the working class and aimed first at overthrowing imperialism and feudalism and only later at destroying native capitalism. To quote Stalin: ". . . the Communist Party can and must enter into an open bloc with the revolutionary wing of the bourgeoisie in order, after having isolated the compromising national bourgeoisie, to lead the vast masses of the urban and rural petty bourgeoisie in the fight against imperialism." [79]

To cite these passages from Stalin which contain all the essentials of what Kautsky labels "neo-Maoism" is not to argue that Stalin in 1925 was advocating the use of the approach in China itself. For it will be remembered that, at that time, Stalin felt China to be a country where the "compromising" section of the bourgeoisie had not yet entered a bloc with imperialism, and thus he advised a united front of "two forces" within the Kuomintang. Stalin did, however, prescribe this strategy for India, where it proved—thanks both to Stalin's failure to devote sufficient resources to its pursuit and to the tenacious mass appeal of Gandhi and the "compromising bourgeoisie"—to be spectacularly unsuccessful. But following Stalin's failure in China in the 1920's and the "betrayal" of the revolution by Chiang Kai-shek, this approach—in conjunction with reliance on a peasant base and guerrilla warfare—was skillfully employed by Mao with far better results.

Soviet writers in the postwar period, even when they employed the term "Chinese path," were not unaware that Mao's basic approach was not original with him. Chinese leaders, however, were bolder. Liu Shao-ch'i, who spoke in 1949 of "Mao's path," told Anna Louise Strong in 1946: "Mao Tse-tung's great accomplishment was to change Marxism from a European to an Asiatic form." China's path, he said, would influence all other semifeudal lands in Southeast Asia.[80] Such claims must have only deepened Stalin's natural suspicion of communist movements which arose independent of his control and as potential challengers to his authority. At any rate, Soviet Orientalists were soon engaged in the task of showing that Mao's alleged "great accomplishment" was instead based on the strategical innovations of Lenin and Stalin.

A long article by G. V. Astaf'iev in the 1949 volume edited by Zhukov sought to demonstrate the dependence of the entire Chinese movement on Leninist-Stalinist teachings.[81] Numerous quotations from Stalin's works, including his 1925 speech, were reproduced to support the assertion that Stalin "brilliantly foresaw" the entire course of development in China. Moreover it was, according to Astaf'iev, the Soviet victory over the German and Japanese aggressors (directed, of course, by comrade Stalin) which had been decisive in changing the correlation of forces in China and allowing Mao to achieve victory. Only after a series of such points did Astaf'iev concede that the Chinese movement, "which in the conditions of a semi-colonial country, creatively applied the teachings of Lenin and Stalin . . . the directives of Comrade Stalin on the problems of the Chinese Revolution, and which has profited from the tremendous experience of the CPSU (B) and on the basis of this achieved its present successes, is itself a vast treasury of revolutionary experience." [82]

Further contributions to this debate will be considered below, but the writings already examined are sufficient to demonstrate that when the Soviets spoke of the "Chinese path," they did not thereby designate it as an independent contribution to Marxism-Leninism, but as itself a product of Soviet theoretical insights.

The essential feature of a shift in communist policy toward a section of the native bourgeoisie is not, as the partisans of "neo-Maoism" contend, the change in the form of the united front.[83] For this is itself merely the reflection of what is the key factor: a change in the subjective judgment of which bourgeois leaders and parties are "compromising" and which are victims of imperialist oppression. Thus, for example, in the face of what seemed to be Nehru's increasing receptiveness to Anglo-American attempts to build an anticommunist force in Asia—necessitating the enlistment of the broadest possible support for the CPI campaign against imperialism and its big-bourgeois lackeys—D'iakov and Zhukov "discovered" that the bourgeoisie of certain "oppressed nationalities" shared the CPI's immediate goals. The form that the communist alliance with these disaffected groups would take—whether it would be an appeal to party leaders or to the members of these strata directly—was clearly secondary to the very determination to make an appeal to such bourgeois groups. And this decision was itself the product of the resolution of what the Soviets call the "main question." As Zhukov so candidly put it in his June 1949 report to the Academy: "The progressive character of this or that social movement, the revolutionary or reactionary nature of this or that party at the present time is determined by its attitude toward the Soviet Union . . . therefore, the controversy as to what stage the colonial bourgeoisie begins to play a reactionary role can be solved only under the circumstances when an answer is given to *the main question.*" [84]

6. Changes in CPI Leadership and Policy, 1950–1951

At the time of the publication of the Cominform editorial in January 1950, there seemed to be a broad consensus among Soviet academic experts on India concerning the approach to be taken by the CPI. This consensus embraced the main outlines of what was known among some as the "Chinese path"—so named because of its successful application by the CCP rather than because the Chinese had originated it. It called for a broad united front, including the four-class bloc of workers, peasants, petty bourgeoisie, and the "revolutionary" section of the national bourgeoisie, but under working class and communist hegemony, in a revolution—primarily agrarian—against the imperialist–feudal–big bourgeoisie bloc entrenched in India. Both the National Congress leadership and the Nehru government were judged to be proimperialist and antinational, and thus were targets of the revolution.

This assessment remained unaltered in articles appearing in the first half of 1950. India's new constitution was said to be antipeople and proimperialist, Nehru's domestic policy "terroristic" and violently anticommunist, and his foreign policy increasingly bound to United States imperialism.[85] But the "big bourgeoisie" was not the "main enemy" in the first stage of the revolution. The drive for "people's democracy" was primarily anti-imperialist and antifeudal, not anticapitalist.

Whether the people's democratic revolution was to take primarily a violent form seemed to be undecided. Some statements, including the January editorial, excluded India from the list of Asian countries where armed violence was occurring— and, by implication, should be occurring. But other statements, such as D'iakov's and Balabushevich's in 1949, implied that violence in India—the "Telengana way"—was the proper course. An endorsement of this latter view came in May 1950 in another Cominform editorial: "in Malaya, South Korea, and in a number of districts in India, in Indonesia the armed forces of the people are waging [a] heroic struggle for freedom and national independence. . . . In the present conditions, as shown by the experience of China, armed resistance to the imperialist plunderers is the most effective form." [86]

a. The Removal of Ranadive

It was this latter interpretation which Ranadive chose to stress in the reply published by his politbureau in February 1950 to the January Cominform editorial. It had become impossible for Ranadive to continue to ignore the failure of Soviet and Chinese writers to endorse his urban-oriented anticapitalist strategy, much less his attack on Mao Tse-tung. More explicitly than earlier statements, the January editorial had clearly been a directive closing off the continued pursuit of the 1948 policy. Ranadive's response, however, could serve as a shining example to communist parties on the improper performance of the task of self-criticism. Though hailing the editorial as a "brilliant contribution" and acknowledging the commission of "sectarian deviations," Ranadive's reply contained equal parts of self-justification.[87]

Moscow's failure to acknowledge Ranadive's haughty reply

was correctly interpreted by the CPI as a signal to make the leadership change many of its members had long been desiring. When the Central Committee met in May and June to choose a new leadership, it was Rajeshwar Rao, leader of the Andhra committee—defender of the "Chinese path" against Ranadive's "leftism"—who replaced Ranadive as General Secretary.

It would be an error to assume that Soviet intervention in the personnel and policy problems of the CPI in 1950 was viewed with resentment by the Indians. The CPI had never in its history been sufficiently sensitive to changing currents in Moscow to be able to anticipate policy shifts. Numerous instances in which the Indian comrades had needed sharp prodding from Moscow before they finally stepped into line have been recorded above. Thus the Indian faithful had been sufficiently conditioned to believe that there was a "correct" line for the entire movement but insufficiently astute to discover it for themselves. In 1950 the response among some party members was a strange sort of joy at having been taken to task and set aright. S. A. Dange wrote in an intraparty memo in April: "Everyone began to feel that somewhere things were wrong, but none could say it correctly and some would not say it—until the Cominform spoke, and the whole Party felt relieved. Is it not good that we have a Cominform to tell us things . . . There is hope for us there; we shall correct ourselves." [88] It will be seen below that with the disappearance in the late 1950's and early 1960's of the single authoritative voice of international communism, the ability of the CPI to keep itself together also eroded.

But, in mid-1950 at least, what the CPI needed from the Cominform was an even more unambiguous directive on what policy should replace Ranadive's discarded one. The inclination of the new Rao leadership was to insist on a uniform application of the "Chinese path" or "Telengana way," often ignoring local conditions. It retained the reliance on violent tactics, but replaced Ranadive's neglect of the countryside with its own neglect of the urban areas. A substantial faction of the CPI remained opposed to the view that it was necessary for the party to stay on the offensive, rather than to moderate its course in hopes of reconsolidating its forces. Ajoy Ghosh spoke for this faction in October: "It was the international comrades who pointed out our mistakes. Since we are not agreed on the interpretation, only they can help us." [89]

b. The New CPI Line in International Perspective

Again it was a shift in the perceived requisites of Soviet foreign policy which was to influence the new directives to the CPI and other parties. In Europe the militant employment of tactics associated with Zhdanov's speech, and especially the Berlin blockade and the sovietization of Eastern Europe, had met with an unexpectedly sharp United States response. The formation of NATO and the inclusion of a strengthened West Germany in the western bloc seemingly closed off further avenues for Soviet advance in Europe. These moves were met on the Soviet side with a lessening of militance and an increased reliance on nondiplomatic pressure on Western governments through the worldwide peace campaign.

But as in the 1920's, stalemate in Europe had been accompanied by heightened Soviet attention to Asia, where the Chinese communists had achieved an unexpected and spectacular victory. Indications of such increased interest in the East were the Soviet Orientalists' meeting in July 1949 and the Peking WFTU conference in November—both emphasizing the "Chinese path." A pair of editorials appearing in *Voprosy istorii* (Problems of history) in 1949 and 1950 urged Soviet scholars to concentrate more attention on contemporary problems in Asia.[90]

Increased concentration on Asia was again accompanied, however, by a similar Western concern for the area. As in Europe, the militance of communist tactics, especially in Korea and Southeast Asia, was met by an American attempt to firm up a noncommunist bloc in opposition to further expansion. Though not until 1951 was lessened militance to become apparent in Asia, there were a few indications before then that Soviets were having second thoughts about the newly trumpeted likelihood of duplicating the Chinese revolution. Indeed, as early as 1950 there were signs that—as part of a less militant and more long-range alternative strategy—the Soviets were less convinced of the urgency of the task of deposing such leaders as Nehru. For the Indian Prime Minister in 1950 was putting forth peace proposals for Korea, advocating the seating of Communist China in the United Nations, and resisting "imperialist" overtures for a regional military pact put forward at the Colombo and Baguio conferences.

c. The New Path for the Indian Revolution

Both a turn away from militance and a softened appraisal of Nehru were included in the advice given to the CPI in messages conveyed at the end of 1950 by its erstwhile mentor, the CPGB. The British communists enumerated the "left-sectarian" mistakes of the Ranadive era and warned that a call for armed struggle, when the party organization was still weak, would be "suicidal." It would be a "distortion" of the Cominform editorial to apply mechanically the Chinese and Telengana methods, even though ultimately, after the party had been rebuilt, armed struggle would have to be employed in India. For the present, the "paramount task" was "initial mobilization of mass support and activity on the most elementary issues" as well as the strengthening of the peace movement in India. A broad democratic "united front from above" with left parties and organizations, on the basis of a common action program, should be established.[91]

The decisive communication took the form of an interview in Britain between R. Palme Dutt and two Indian communists at the turn of the year. In it, Dutt more explicitly linked the peace movement to the struggle for "real" independence, noting that "the broad front that will emerge out of the peace movement may lay the basis for the formation of the National front for national liberation." He also stressed that, while there could be no doubt that Nehru's government represented the interests of the "big bourgeoisie," those interests were not always identical with the interests of United States imperialism; Nehru's stand on issues like Korea and the atomic bomb should be skillfully utilized by the CPI.[92]

Although the CPI was already moving away from the militance associated with the "Chinese path" and was moving even farther from Ranadive's anticapitalist strategy, it still lacked a comprehensive program. This need was filled, according to some students of Indian communism, when Rao, Dange, Ghosh, and Basava Punniah traveled to Moscow early in 1951, returning with a secret document called the "Tactical Line," which became the basis for a draft program and statement of policy published by the CPI in April.[93]

The CPI's Draft Program, on the basis of which the party proposed to contest the 1951–1952 general elections in India, sought to build a multiclass appeal. Not only the masses and middle classes of India were suffering, it said, but even the industrialists, manufacturers, and traders were being hurt by the policy of a government "totally in the grip of monopoly financiers, landlords and princes and their foreign British advisers."

The CPI was not at the present stage demanding the establishment of socialism; the level of the economy was too low and mass organization too weak. Still "our Party regards as quite mature the task of replacing the present . . . Government by a new Government of People's Democracy, created on the basis of a coalition of all democratic antifeudal and anti-imperialist forces," though it would be "deceptive" to contend that elections alone could end the imperialist-reactionary hold on India.[94]

Of even greater interest is the *Statement of Policy*—also published in April—which was aimed at a party audience and was concerned with the tactics to be employed in implementing the new program.[95] While utilizing the lessons of both Russia and China, comrades must remember that each country has its own peculiarities. India resembled China in that it was faced with an antifeudal, anti-imperialist revolution in which the peasantry would play a large role. But unlike India, China had lacked the unified communications which allow an enemy to make swift attacks, and, unlike the CPI, the CCP had already possessed an army when it had begun to lead the peasantry. Likewise, India lacked China's geographical peculiarities—an industrial base located with the Soviet Union in the rear. Thus, "peasant struggle along the Chinese path alone cannot lead to victory in India." Rather, the *Statement* advocated "a path of Leninism applied to Indian conditions"—namely, an alliance of working class and peasantry acting in unison.

The question of armed struggle was not the main issue. Whether violence was to be used depended on the degree to which the government was isolated and the people were disillusioned. While the present crisis was deep, it would be "gross exaggeration" to say that the country was already "on the eve of armed insurrection or revolution." The growth of the mass movement had simply failed to keep pace with the growth of discontent, and the fault lay in the weakness of the CPI.

Having worked out, with Moscow's sanction and probably with its aid, a comprehensive statement of its new strategy and tactics, the CPI's Central Committee met in May to complete the shift by removing Rao as General Secretary. He was not immediately succeeded by another leader; the entire politbureau functioned as the secretariat with Ajoy Ghosh as "Secretary of the Secretariat" until October 1951, when Ghosh was elected General Secretary at a party conference. This October conference also formally adopted the "Draft Program" and *Statement of Policy,* declaring them to be the basis of the Indian revolutionary movement, "settling all the disputes and differences that existed in the Party over the past few years." [96]

In a statement reprinted in the Cominform journal the same month, Ghosh blamed the former party leadership for an attempt to "skip over the democratic stage of the revolution" and a refusal to see the "semi-colonial nature of our country which demanded the unification of all anti-imperialist classes and forces." The result had been a prolonged crisis in the CPI, "virtually immobilizing it for a long period." [97]

With respect to the elections scheduled for that year, Ghosh promised that the CPI would support a democratic government formed to carry out a minimum program of reform. It is evident that the communists, while holding little hope of themselves winning the elections, were concentrating on achieving the downfall of the Nehru government. The CPI formed united fronts with a number of parties on a regional and local basis. Contesting 60 seats in the national parliament, the party and its People's Democratic Front won 23 seats and somewhat over 4 percent of the vote. The Congress Party (364 seats and 45 percent of the vote) won the elections; the CPI became the major opposition party in the parliament. (The Socialist Party, receiving over 10 percent of the vote, won only 12 seats.) The Cominform journal termed these results a "serious defeat" for the Congress, attributing its retention of a majority only to the "anti-democratic" electoral system.[98]

It was in fact the Communist Party of India itself, as a result of its policies of the previous years, which had suffered the "serious defeat." This is evidenced not only by its small vote in the parliamentary elections, which reflected the Indian people's weariness with violent struggle, but also by the drastic decline in the party's membership. The gains in membership made since the later years of the war were entirely wiped out as a result of the CPI's attempt at revolution. According to the party's own figures, membership dived from a high of 89,263 in 1948 to a low of 20,000 in 1950. And these consequences of "adventurism" were not to be easily reversed; in 1952, the membership figure was still very low (at 30,000), and the previous heights were surpassed only after the decade's midpoint.[99]

7. The Soviet View of India: 1951–1954

The Soviets signified their approval of the changed course in India by elevating the new CPI path to people's democracy into a model for other less-developed countries—an action more understandable in light of the reports that the new "Indian path" had been personally dictated in Moscow to top Indian communists. But, necessarily, the proclamation of an Indian path involved a reappraisal of the previously heralded "Chinese path," the Chinese claims for which had already struck a sensitive nerve in Moscow.

One of the strongest assertions by a Chinese leader of the distinctiveness of the Chinese model had been published in the Cominform journal in June 1951. Lu Ting-yi wrote at that time that Mao's theory of the Chinese revolution was a new development of Marxism-Leninism. The Soviet October Revolution, he said, was the "classic type" for imperialist countries, while the Chinese revolution was the classic type in colonial and semicolonial countries. But its significance was not limited to just a particular type of country: "it is of universal significance for the world Communist movement. It is, indeed, a new contribution to the treasury of Marxism-Leninism." [100]

The direction which the Soviet reply would take was first revealed in an article by A. Sobolev in *Bol'shevik* in October. While citing the Chinese revolution as an "example" of a colonial revolution which was both "bourgeois-democratic" and "anti-imperialist," Sobolev implied doubt that it was "universal" in significance or even "classical." The indirect expression of these reservations came in his description of the new CPI draft program: "In its essence the program of the Indian Communist Party is a model of the minimum program for the struggle of the colonial peoples in present-day conditions." [101]

That this formulation was not accidental was confirmed during a debate at a conference in the new Oriental Studies Institute of the Academy of Sciences the following month. E. M. Zhukov, conceding that the experience of China was extremely important, warned that it would be "risky to regard the Chinese revolution as some kind of 'stereotype' for people's democratic revolutions in other countries of Asia." [102] The reason for this was the inability to presuppose that other countries would have a revolutionary army. V. V. Balabushevich agreed, saying that in India "we have seen the full error of mechanically applying the experience of the Chinese revolution to Indian circumstances without consideration of India's specific features—and, moreover, the interpretation of the Chinese experience applied was incorrect." [103]

Thus, the new Soviet position consisted of a downgrading of the applicability of the Chinese experience, on the grounds that new conditions in Asia were less favorable to armed struggle. These conditions, primarily shaped by increased American willingness to intervene against communist-led attacks (Korea) and by the failure of several Southeast Asian countries to match the Chinese success, led to the advancement of a new model, one more long-term in perspective and less dependent on violent tactics. Other characteristics of this approach, according to V. V. Balabushevich, included the formation of united fronts from above with a number of left parties, the overcoming of trade union disunity, and the utilization of elections not as a means of obtaining victory for the people but as a device for mobilizing the masses in struggle against existing reactionary governments.[104]

The writing of contemporary history is at best a tentative and uncertain task. But the writing of current history in the Soviet Union, as exemplified by Russian studies of Indian political history, has revealed itself as extremely more hazardous, not because of the unearthing of new documents or memoirs, but because of the frequent shifts in the Soviet political line. Thus favorable or unfavorable assessments of a particular political figure or movement are originally made under the influence of a permissive or hard line dictated by foreign policy needs of the moment. When political considerations dictate a shift of line, past "scholarly" assessments are neither ignored nor excused as time-bound, but are excoriated as incorrect and even un-Marxist. Thus it is not unusual in perusing Soviet volumes on India to find them beginning with an essay in self-criticism of past errors, or even with a foreword by a colleague of the author reassuring the readers that past mistakes have been fraternally exposed and contritely corrected. An author who publishes an assessment toward the beginning of a period of great flux in the political line is often doubly cursed. Not only does his volume have to contain self-criticism or comradely criticism of past mistakes, but reviews of his work, often published much later by colleagues who have the advantage of hindsight, are likely to point to further mistakes committed in the most recent opus, which the unfortunate author lacked the vision to foresee.

An example of this tendency is the treatment given a volume by one of the foremost Soviet Indologists, A. M. D'iakov. The work, *India during and after World War II*, published in 1952, opens with a foreword by the equally distinguished I. M. Reisner.[105] A study of recent events in India, especially an analysis of the new CPI Draft Program and of Ajoy Ghosh's writings in the Cominform journal, together with "comradely criticism" by fellow Indologists, had assisted D'iakov, Reisner assured his readers, in understanding his past mistakes. Among these mistakes, appearing in D'iakov's 1948 work on the nationality question and in his articles in *New Times*, was an overestimation of the depth of contradictions between the Indian big bourgeoisie and English imperialists, leading to the incorrect appraisal of the prewar National Congress as a bloc of anti-imperialist parties and of Gandhi's early activities as "progressive." Thus these assessments (which D'iakov had made under the influence of the "united national front" policy of the Seventh Comintern Congress), far from reflecting fault on Soviet political leaders who had shaped the united front policy, were attributable solely to D'iakov's poor scholarship.

Thus chastised, D'iakov proceeded to apply his own hindsight in a vigorous criticism of past policies of the CPI. Indian communists had, prior to December 1947, suffered under the illusion that the Congress and League leaderships were fit allies; they had erroneously supported the League's demand for Pakistan; they had failed to utilize favorable opportunities for exposing the machinations of nationalist politicians to the democratic masses. Even after eliminating its "right-opportunism," the CPI had proceeded, in its "Political Thesis" and in Ranadive's articles in the CPI organ, to commit a number of "left-sectarian" mistakes. "Great help" in correcting these mistakes had been rendered by the January 1950 Cominform editorial, and a correct policy had finally been achieved in the Draft Program—a "creative application" of Marxism-Leninism to India.

But the unfortunate D'iakov had again erred. A review of his book by K. A. Mikhailov, published in *Voprosy istorii* in June 1953, pointed up various insufficiencies of fact and interpretation, taking particular offense at D'iakov's treatment of the CPI. Once a backward and bungling party, the CPI, having produced (though with much assistance) a document hailed as a model for other parties, was now worthy, it appears, of a less supercilious treatment. Mikhailov complained that D'iakov had failed to note that the CPI's mistakes had been overcome by the party's own self-criticism; he had presumed to instruct the Indian com-

munists on what tasks lay before them; he had incorrectly implied that CPI growth was entirely dependent on its success in
exposing the National Congress. Such was an "unsatisfactory
tone for a Soviet scholar." Even Reisner was criticized for having failed to perform properly his obligations as the book's editor. Mikhailov's conclusion was even more sweeping: "The Institute of Oriental Studies and the Academy of Sciences
Publishing House made an error in releasing a book with such
insufficiencies." [106]

With Soviet and CPI policy at this time based on a distinction
between "big bourgeoisie" and "national bourgeoisie," and
with only the former said to be represented by the proimperialist Indian government, Soviet scholars sought to explain
the origin of this differentiation. The evolution of the capitalist
class, rather than following the classical path of small commodity producers growing into owners of small industries, and then
into big manufacturers, had proceeded in a peculiar fashion.
The big industrial capitalists had arisen from the ranks of the
merchant-usurer "compradore" agents of the colonialists, rather
than from the ranks of small producers.[107] As a result the big Indian industries were closely linked to and dependent upon the
English, who continued to occupy the "commanding heights"
of the economy. Below this highly developed stratum continued
to exist small-commodity production, mixed with surviving vestiges of feudal relations. These smaller producers suffered from
the competition of English imports and were consequently hostile to imperialist domination.

According to this view, the big bourgeoisie very early had
concluded a bloc with the imperialists. The fact, however, that
contradictions between them had continued to exist, and that
the "forms and conditions" of their alliance had occasionally
changed, had been mistaken both by the CPI and by Soviet
Indologists as evidence of the participation of the big bourgeoisie in the prewar anti-imperialist movement. Comrade Stalin,
however, had established as early as 1925 that the big bourgeoisie had already become the implacable enemy of the national-
liberation movement.[108]

The peculiar instrument of the Indian big bourgeoisie in this
task of restraining the mass movement, according to the Soviet
analysis, had been Gandhism. Not even D'iakov's 1948 concession that Gandhi had at first played a progressive role in the Indian national-liberation movement had—as noted above—

proved acceptable to Soviet decision-makers. The general Soviet line on Gandhi in the late 1940's and early 1950's was little different from Professor Reisner's 1930 assessment.[109]

The Soviets were not unaware of the antagonism this appraisal had generated among Indians. D'iakov in 1952 confessed that the attack on Gandhism was complex, for, though it was not difficult to "dismantle his theses," any attack on the Gandhist "cult" was interpreted as an insult to India. Yet, D'iakov concluded, without exposure of Gandhi it would be impossible to free the masses from the influence of the compromising big bourgeoisie.[110]

The "fictitious" independence of India, according to the Soviet analysis, had left unchanged the British control of the economy. Even the proclamation of the republic in 1950 made no difference; India remained in the British Empire. England retained control of the banks and continued to direct Indian industry through the new form of "managing agencies." Control of the army, police, and bureaucracy had merely been transferred to the Indian agents of imperialism. The "onerous level" of military expenditures, the exorbitant profits, and the new national plan of starvation and poverty had even worsened the plight of the toiling masses. Despite the increasing penetration of the economy by American imperialism, which sought to displace British domination, India remained a "semicolony" of English monopoly capital.[111]

The Indian liberation struggle was not only anti-imperialist, but antifeudal as well. The existence of strong feudal vestiges in the economy provided a social prop to imperialism and served as a barrier to the development of productive forces, and also hindered the formation of a class-conscious proletariat.

In "proving" the significance of feudal survivals in Indian agriculture, Soviet Indologists would often turn to a 1925 description by Stalin of the Chinese village, in which he had pointed to the joining in the village of money capital with feudal survivals in order to preserve the exploitative methods of the latter. Many Indian "kulaks" were actually playing a semifeudal role; they were, for the most part, merchants or money-lenders buying up the raw materials from the toiling peasantry and in turn selling them to the imperialists. They were not capitalist farmers employing hired labor. Those strata in the village which, in their relation to the means of production, should have been considered agricultural proletariat were still bound by feudal ties and

lacked the degree of personal freedom necessary for their transformation into a proletariat. Even those who did migrate to the
cities to work in factories retained their ties to the village and
the attendant cultural backwardness.[112]

Caste was said to be one of the holdovers from the feudal age
utilized by the English in their attempts to divide the movement for national liberation of India. G. G. Kotovsky wrote in
1953 that the problem of caste was in essence a *class* problem, a
problem of the Indian agrarian proletariat and semiproletariat.[113]

No amount of "reforms," "plans," or constitutional changes
instituted by the existing Congress government could solve the
economic and social crises in India. From its first day of existence, according to the Soviet analysis, the government had
sought to strengthen the position of the big bourgeoisie and its
allies, the feudal landlords and princes. Its economic plans,
requiring for their fulfillment the attraction of foreign capital,
guaranteed that Indian industry would be kept on the Anglo-
American "leash." [114]

Moreover, this anti-industrial policy was interconnected with
national antagonisms. The Congress leadership refused to carry
out its promises to reorganize India's administrative units on
the basis of national languages, while attempting to impose
Hindi as the all-Indian language. The effect of this policy was
not only to hinder the South Indian bourgeoisie, but also to re-
tard the cultural development of the masses.[115]

Soviet studies of India in this period continued to stress that
India's foreign policy, as well as her internal policy, was reactionary. The "progressive" signs which had caused R. P. Dutt to
express optimism in his 1950 advice to the CPI—Nehru's stand
on the Korean question and the Indian refusal to follow American policy on China, for example—were interpreted by Soviet
Indologists as reluctant concessions by a shaky government to
the peace-loving Indian masses, rather than as indications of
genuine "neutrality." In essence, Indian foreign policy remained tied, though occasionally only covertly, to Wall Street
and to London. And the aim of these centers of imperialism was
to turn India and Pakistan into strategic bases against communism. India, in D'iakov's words "the one country of Asia which
in population and in potential economic resources could oppose
China," was in addition a potential bridgehead for an imperialist attack on the USSR.

Although the present stage of the Indian revolutionary movement was anti-imperialist and antifeudal rather than anticapitalist, the big bourgeoisie—represented by the Congress
leadership and government—was manifestly unable to participate in the movement. Even if it was not the "main enemy," the
big bourgeoisie—with its ties both to imperialists and to feudal
strata—was undoubtedly an opponent. Moreover, given the fact
that it had succeeded very early in the century in organizing itself and in establishing influence over the masses, it had retained a significant hold over the toiling workers and peasants.
But a large section of the people—including shopkeepers,
businessmen, and even some industrialists—had turned against
the Congress since it had taken power.

The entire peasantry, despite the differentiation in its ranks
and the unreliability of some of its strata, was the most important ally of the Indian working class. Likewise, those strata of
the national bourgeoisie which were not tied to foreign imperialism or to feudal elements—and especially the bourgeoisie
of the more backward national units—could serve as unstable
allies, though *not* as a leading force in the national-liberation
movement.

8. The CPI and Soviet-Indian Relations: 1952–1954

Fully in accordance with suggestions from Soviet Indologists,
the CPI, in the period after the adoption of its new program and
its participation in the general elections, had concentrated on
problems of organization and of construction of the united
front. General Secretary Ghosh wrote in November 1952 that
whereas past weaknesses of the party had been rooted in incorrect slogans and tactics, current difficulties arose from organizational weaknesses which existed "despite correct immediate
slogans and correct tactics." The roots of this problem he saw in
the party's "worship of spontaneity," its failure to expose the
"pernicious theory of Gandhism," its anarchist conceptions of
inner-party democracy, and poor agitational and propaganda
work.[116]

In April 1954 the party was able to bring out, after considerable debate, a "Resolution on Party Organization," which complained that the CPI's effective organized strength—50,000
members and 20,000 candidates—lagged far behind its political
influence. The result was an inability to transform its influence

into an "effective striking force." The resolution called for more effective functioning both of the party center and of its local organs, stressing that "[m]any decisions are taken which remain on paper." [117]

On the issue of the composition of the united front, the party—like the Soviet analysts—emphasized its breadth. A 1952 party publication assured the Indian bourgeoisie that, when "communism of the Chinese type comes to India . . . patriotic capitalists . . . would have every reason to welcome such a changeover. The ax of the new regime would fall upon half a dozen of the bigger cartel kings of India . . . These would probably be sent to reformatories. The rest of our bourgeoisie would be allowed to coexist, cooperate and coprosper together with the people." [118]

On the agrarian front, also, the party was careful not to alienate its potential allies. Its leadership attacked "so-called Marxists" who sought to expropriate the rich peasants and who called for immediate collectivization.[119] A 1954 Central Committee resolution even acknowledged that since most landless agricultural laborers were "untouchables," it would be necessary to organize them in *separate* peasant unions in order to avoid the alienation of "caste" peasants.[120] The CPI would not hesitate to utilize the tactic of "caste politics" in its pursuit of a mass united front following.

a. The Nationality Issue

Yet another issue of great tactical importance which concerned the CPI in these years was the problem of nationality and language policy. It will be recalled that in the mid-1940's the CPI had given qualified endorsement to regional separatist movements through its formula of national self-determination, including the right of secession. Later the CPI had taken up the cause of regional languages against the "great-power" demands that Hindi be made the national language. This particularist appeal had been given doctrinal backing in D'iakov's 1948 and 1952 studies, in which he had stressed that self-determination movements in Andhra, Kerala, and other "oppressed nations" were worthy of communist support. Significantly, many of these were areas in which the Congress party was weak and opportunities for communist influence and even victory at the polls were relatively much greater than on the all-India level.

One of the most extreme statements on the question of Indian unity appeared in the CPI newspaper in January 1952 in an article by a Tamil communist: "The unity of India is not an article of faith for us. . . . If people belonging to a certain nationality give their verdict in favor of a separate state, the CPI, true to its Marxian principles on the national question, cannot oppose them." [121]

The importance of this issue can be gauged from the fact that the major portion of an interview granted by Stalin to Indian Ambassador Menon in February 1953—only the third interview given by Stalin to an ambassador in five years—concerned Indian national languages. Stalin, having recently become an infallible arbiter of linguistic questions, inquired of Menon whether Urdu or "Hindu" (sic) was the chief language in India, whether all Indian languages were from the same stock, how they had come to develop and—significantly—which language was spoken by the Gujaratis. Having then received a short lecture on Soviet nationality policy—and a further inquiry on whether the Indian army was of sufficient size to defend the country—the puzzled ambassador was dismissed.[122]

While it is tempting to speculate that Stalin himself had a hand in determining whether the CPI should pursue a course of "Balkanization," the evidence allows only the conclusion that it was shortly after this interview that CPI policy on the issue began to shift away from the particularist extreme. In August the communist trade union leader S. A. Dange warned: "The nationalism of the worker must not be allowed to destroy his internationalism as a class." [123] The warning given at the Third Party Congress was even more explicit. Ghosh declared that there were serious implications—including the disruption of the working class movement—in the party's former emphasis on separatism. For in many industrial centers, the working class was multinational in composition; to pursue the old course would be "disastrous." [124] The Third Congress resolution called for the party to combat bourgeois nationalism, disruption, and national hatred. Moreover, to the draft resolution's demand that there be no compulsory all-Indian language was added the stipulation that to strengthen unity and facilitate communication, people in all states should be "encouraged" to learn Hindi. One might speculate—again without firm evidence—that this, the only amendment to the draft resolution, had been added as a result of a trip to Moscow for "medical treatment," from which Ghosh had returned only a short while before the congress.[125]

What reason (besides the ostensible one of "internationalism") could the Soviets have had in 1953 for urging the CPI to put an end to its very promising attempts at subverting Indian unity through regional and linguistic separatism? The answer best supported by the evidence is that, in the interests of the Soviet struggle against "American imperialism," an attempt was being considered—even before Stalin's death—to bring India as a whole into the anti-imperialist camp. CPI chances of coming to power on a national level were slim indeed, but the likelihood of their succeeding in separatist movements in certain regions was great enough to endanger any contemplated Soviet attempts to woo Nehru himself.

b. New Assessment of Indian Foreign Policy

The signs of a change in Soviet foreign policy toward India came only gradually and were at first unaccompanied by any shift in the "scholarly" assessments of India outlined in the previous section. One of the earliest indications that the Soviet Union might be interested in gaining India's favor came in the spring of 1951, when the Russians made a dramatic offer of 50,000 tons of wheat for famine relief, while the American Congress was engaged in a loud and lengthy debate over its own offer. This was in sharp contrast to the situation in 1946, when the Soviets had ignored a similar opportunity to impress Indian opinion.

Beginning in the same year, at a trade conference in Singapore in October, the Soviet Union appealed to Asian governments for expanded trade ties. The Soviet delegate in Singapore suggested that certain raw materials, consumer goods, and agricultural and industrial equipment could be traded in exchange for such Indian products as jute, rice, rubber, spices, and tea. The following January the Soviets, together with the representatives of China, Hungary, and Czechoslovakia, participated in the Bombay International Industrial Exposition.[126] An article in *New Times* in May, noting that "[i]ndustrialization of the underdeveloped countries is one of the most urgent problems of the times," suggested that Soviet foreign trade organizations "could supply countries anxious to develop their industries with machinery and equipment . . . in exchange [for] the national currency of the countries concerned." [127] That Soviet motives were not entirely altruistic was suggested by no less a source than Stalin's *Economic Problems of Socialism*, which declared that the "socialist world market" would soon find it necessary to locate outside markets for its surplus products.[128]

These tentative shifts in Soviet trade policy toward India, together with the CPI shift from militant to legal tactics, confirm in some measure the thesis of Marshall Shulman that Moscow's foreign policy was not wholly stagnant during Stalin's last years.[129] But the magnitude of the change with respect to India should not be overemphasized, nor should it be forgotten that the motivation was defensive—an attempt to forestall what the Soviets perceived to be new imperialist military and economic pressures on India.

Nor were Stalin's successors, in their first year in power, any more hasty in the reassessment of Nehru and his increasingly independent foreign policy. But that a gradual change was continuing was evident in Malenkov's August 8 speech to the Supreme Soviet—a speech in which he both announced Soviet possession of the hydrogen weapon and declared his belief that "there are no disputed or outstanding issues today which cannot be settled peacefully by mutual agreement between the parties concerned." Malenkov went on to say: "Of great importance for the promotion of peace in the East is the attitude of so big a country as India. India has made substantial contribution to the efforts of the peace-loving countries to stop the Korean War. Our relations with India are growing firmer, and cultural and economic intercourse with her is becoming wider. We hope that relations between India and the Soviet Union will become stronger and develop in a spirit of friendly cooperation." [130]

Such Soviet appreciation of the Nehru government, still very tentative and limited to the anti-American potential in Nehru's foreign policy, posed a severe dilemma for the CPI—a dilemma which received full expression at the Third Party Congress. The problem was simple: if the Soviets were to recognize the "progressive" nature of Nehru's foreign policy, as a policy for peace and against imperialism, and if they were at the same time to stress the inseparability of the struggles for peace and for national liberation, would not this then require Indian communists to moderate their struggle against Nehru on the domestic front? The question was posed at the Third Congress in terms of priorities: was the struggle against American imperialism more important to the CPI than the struggle against British imperialism, that is, against that particular imperialism which, in alliance with the big bourgeoisie, was enslaving India's economy? As Ghosh stated the alternatives: "If US imperialism becomes the main enemy not only to peace but also to our freedom, then we could take up no other attitude but one of progressively lining up behind the Nehru Government on the plea of fighting the American threat . . . the way we understand this point will decide our basic attitude towards the Nehru Government itself . . . cooperate with the Government but criticize specific acts; or, oppose the Government but support specific acts." [131] A document circulated at the party congress by the Andhra communists argued that British imperialism was the "main enemy": "We, situated as we are in a country under a particular State, have some concrete tasks to perform. The chief enemy of our national freedom today is British imperialism." [132] Another group at the congress, apparently including Joshi and supported by Harry Pollitt, a CPGB "fraternal observer," stressed that it was American imperialism which constituted the "main enemy."

The choice made by the Third Congress, though it followed neither extreme, tended to favor the option of continued opposition to the Nehru government. The main political resolution noted that while certain acts and declarations of the government had been "helpful to peace," this did not warrant uncritical and unconditional support for Nehru's foreign policy, which was still basically proimperialist. As Ghosh put it in a report to the Cominform journal, the liberation struggle was directed "above all" against British imperialism and its ally—the Nehru government. On the success of this struggle depended the people's well-being. Yet, as if to reassure the Soviets, he added that the party congress recognized the relation between the struggle for peace and for freedom, and "emphasized the necessity of conducting both struggles simultaneously and with equal vigor, for both of them are equally important." [133]

The situation was strikingly similar to the one faced by the CPI in 1941, when the determination by the Soviet Union that fascism had become the main enemy of international communism had forced the Indian party to play down its opposition to British colonialism. The difference, of course, was that in 1941, by cooperating with the British, the CPI alienated Nehru and the National Congress, whereas in 1954, in moving toward cooperation with Nehru, it would risk forfeiting the leadership of "progressive" forces opposing the government. In both cases the choice was a difficult one to make; and in both cases the

CPI lagged behind the Soviets and had to be prodded to a decision.

In 1954 the Soviet movement toward a rapprochement with Nehru perceptibly gathered speed. A trade agreement concluded between the USSR and India in December 1953 was hailed in a 1954 Soviet publication as the "basis for strengthened economic relations and friendly ties." The same work even conceded that "India has become a sovereign state . . . The conquest by the Indian people of state independence creates the conditions for development of a national economy."[134]

Two series of events drew particular attention from the Soviets. The relations between India and the United States took a significant turn for the worse with the conclusion of an American military aid agreement with Pakistan in February 1954. At the same time, the Indian government's attitude toward People's China, which had remained relatively restrained in the face of China's 1950 provocations in Tibet, improved decidedly with the conclusion of an agreement between the two countries on trade relations in Tibet, in April 1954. This agreement included in its preamble the famous "five principles of coexistence" or *Panch Shila*. Though the treaty merely ratified China's tightening control over Tibet, the optimism with which it was hailed in India was probably influenced by the simultaneous opening of the Geneva Conference on Indochina, the results of which—naming India as the chairman of an international commission to police the settlement—undoubtedly encouraged Nehru's hopes of becoming an arbiter in the Cold War. An exchange of visits by Nehru and Chou En-lai in the same year seemed to set the seal on warming Sino-Indian relations. Articles in *New Times* in March and April manifested Soviet pleasure over increasing Indian-American difficulties. These were followed in the summer and fall by Soviet words of praise for the improvement in Sino-Indian relations.[135]

Soviet pressure on the CPI to share in this new assessment of Nehru's foreign policy was at first subtle and then more overt. An article in the major theoretical journal of the CPSU (now *Kommunist*) in August seemed to express its disapproval of the CPI congress' balanced resolution by stressing the increasing danger to the Indian people of American imperialism. The author cited such American maneuvers as the attempt to turn Kashmir into an anti-Soviet and anti-Chinese base, the USIS efforts to recruit an Indian "fifth column," and the American distribution of "pornographic" books and films which sought to distract the Indian people from their struggle for peace.[136]

An article by Dutt in the Cominform journal in October, stressing again that "[t]here can be no separation of the fight for national independence from the fight for peace," so disturbed the CPI Central Committee that it convened a special meeting to discuss the article.[137] A resolution emerging from the meeting stressed that differences of "an important nature" had been revealed which required more "time and thought" to resolve. This language was later disclosed to have been a compromise substitute for an angry draft resolution introduced by the CPI Political Bureau flatly "rejecting" Dutt's article.[138]

Shortly after this incident Ajoy Ghosh returned to India from yet another journey to Moscow. In a press conference held in the same week of his arrival, he made it clear that the message from the Soviets had finally been understood: "The internal policy of the Nehru Government does not suit the interests of the masses, *while the foreign policy does.*" [139]

An important shift in the communist approach toward India had now been clearly signaled in both Moscow and New Delhi. Nineteen fifty-five was to be the first significant year in a new period of Soviet policy toward India and the "third world."

IV Doctrinal and Operational Changes, 1955–1959

The shift in Soviet policy toward India which became dramatically evident in 1955 was, like previous changes, not primarily motivated by actual developments within India itself. However, two significant shifts in India's domestic and foreign policy orientations which occurred in 1955 did not escape the Soviets' notice.

The first of these was the decision taken by the Congress party, at its golden jubilee session at Avadi in January, to proclaim as its goal economic planning "with a view to the establishment of a Socialist pattern of society, where the principal means of production are under social ownership or control, production is progressively speeded up and there is equitable distribution of the national wealth." [1] Nehru took pains to point out that a "socialistic pattern" was not meant as a synonym for "socialism" in the Marxist sense. There would be no indiscriminate nationalization but a private sector under "broad strategic controls" existing alongside the state sector. Still, the decision was hailed by Congressmen as ranking in importance with the 1929 pledge to seek complete independence. The Congress party's action, immediately denounced by the CPI weekly journal as "grandiloquent talk . . . scrupulously confined to generalities," [2] was to receive a more careful assessment from the Soviets.

The second development was Nehru's increasing prominence in the international arena as the spokesman for the forces of nonalignment, anticolonialism, and *Panch Shila*—the five principles of "peaceful coexistence." One of Nehru's major performances in this role was at the conference of Afro-Asian countries in Bandung in April 1955. E. M. Zhukov, an observer at the meeting, wrote that the great Lenin had been the author not only of the principle of peaceful coexistence, but also of the conviction that close cooperation between communists and nationalists against the common imperialist enemy was both possible and necessary.[3]

1. Soviet-Indian Relations: Diplomatic, Economic, and Cultural

That Zhukov's talk of anti-imperialist cooperation was more than mere rhetoric was demonstrated when Nehru was presented with a triumphal and well-publicized visit to the Soviet Union in June. Soviet hopes for a favorable reaction from the Indian Prime Minister were not unfounded. Nehru's trip to Russia in 1927 had resulted in this observation: "Ordinarily Russia and India should live as the best of neighbors with the fewest points of friction . . . Is there any reason why we in India should inherit the age-old rivalry of England against Russia? That is based on the greed and covetousness of British imperialism, and our interests surely lie in ending this imperialism and not in supporting and strengthening it." [4]

The joint declaration released by Bulganin and Nehru at the conclusion of the latter's 1955 visit was in the same spirit of good-neighborliness and anti-imperialism. It pledged that Soviet-Indian relations would be guided by the five principles of peaceful coexistence, under the aegis of which "there is ample scope for the development of cultural, economic and technical cooperation between their two states." Moreover, that each country was following a system "molded by its own genius, traditions and environment, should be no barrier to such cooperation." Finally, the communiqué noted the similarity of the two governments' views on the issues of disarmament, the Geneva agreements on Indochina, and the rights of the Chinese people with respect to Taiwan and China's seat at the United Nations.[5] Nehru's fastidiousness about India's nonalignment, however, caused him to reject the Soviets' desire to include in the statement the pledge that neither country would participate in an alliance or coalition directed against the other—a promise which to the Indians appeared to be a "negative military alliance." [6] The Cominform journal hailed the communiqué as "a document of immense international significance, outstanding in the history of international relations." [7]

a. The Khrushchev-Bulganin Trip to India

The Nehru visit to the Soviet Union marked only the beginning of an era of personal diplomacy in Soviet-Indian relations. Far more significant than that visit or the resulting communiqué in revealing the lengths to which the Soviets were prepared to go in strengthening those relations was the return visit paid by Khrushchev and Bulganin in November–December of 1955. For on this, the first of the famous "B and K" trips, the ebullient Russians—donning "Gandhi caps" to the shouts of *"Hindi-Russi Bhai Bhai"* (Indians and Russians are brothers)—were to sound all the major themes of the new Soviet assessment of India.

The keynote of the Soviet leaders' remarks to the Indians was a constant reassurance that strengthened relations between the two countries need not to be hindered by the differences in their social systems and that the Soviet Union was not seeking to impose its system in India. In Bombay, Khrushchev took particular notice of Nehru's stated intention of leading India on the socialist path: "That is good. Of course, our conceptions of socialism differ. But we welcome this statement and the intention." [8] And on another occasion, in Bangalore, he went farther, promising Soviet assistance to India's development: "You must choose your own path of development, that which pleases you most. Not only shall we not try to deter you; we shall assist you . . . We say, perhaps there is something in our practical experience that may suit you. If so, use it; if not, don't. We do not force anything upon anyone; we are not seeking to impose any political obligations." [9]

The Soviet leaders also sounded notes of praise of India's rich culture—cruelly depicted by the imperialists as backward—and of her experiences in gaining independence. In expending this tribute, Bulganin did not overlook the man whom the Soviets had theretofore singled out for special attention of another sort. Gandhi was praised as a "glorious patriot" who did much for the struggle for Indian independence. "We, Lenin's pupils, do not share Gandhi's philosophical views, but we consider him an outstanding leader." [10]

Yet another theme put forward by the Russians was also aimed at flattering the ego of the Indians, and it had the additional purpose of suggesting that India's merits had been denied by the imperialists: ". . . why is India not considered a great country? Evidently because the colonialists want to belittle your country and your people. To recognize India as a great power would mean altering their position. But we believe that India is a great power and that she ought to rank among the leading great powers of the world." [11]

Accompanying the tribute to India's ambition to be a world power was Khrushchev's assurance of support to India on the issue most crucial to her national pride. Speaking in Kashmir, he declared that the political status of that area was a matter to be determined by its people, but he added his conviction that already the "people themselves have decided" that Kashmir "is one of the states of the Republic of India." [12] For the continued existence of the dispute he blamed not the two combatants but the imperialists.

The Soviet leaders' propaganda campaign, with its stress on flattery of Indian ambitions, attacks on imperialism, and accentuation of the positive area of agreement between the Soviets and Indians, did not, however, include a direct effort to enhance the prestige of the CPI. Khrushchev and Bulganin refrained from appearing in public with any of the party's leaders, and their speeches made no mention of the local communists. The primary purpose of the trip was the promotion of the Soviet Union as the true sponsor for India's desires for peace and freedom; only indirectly and in the long run could the CPI hope to gain respectability from improved Soviet-Indian relations. This conclusion is confirmed by the results of a public opinion poll conducted in Calcutta shortly after the Russians' visit. Of those Indians surveyed, 62 percent reported a favorable change in their attitude toward the Soviet Union, but only 16 percent replied that their opinion of communism had undergone a favorable change.[13]

On their return to the Soviet Union, Khrushchev and Bulganin soon demonstrated that their speeches had not been meant solely as propaganda for Indian ears, but were indeed intended to lay the foundation for a whole new political line. In their reports to the Supreme Soviet, the Soviet leaders repeated and elaborated upon the themes they had sounded in India. Both praised India's culture, blamed her backwardness on colonial "robbery," and saluted her efforts to develop her economy. Bulganin praised India's peace-loving foreign policy, pledged "full understanding" of her neutrality, and declared his conviction that the community of views between India and the USSR on international questions would not be a transitory phenomenon, but stemmed from the fundamental interests of the people of both countries.

Khrushchev, repeating his pledge of Soviet support to India on the Kashmir dispute with Pakistan—a country "increasingly involved into gambling machinations by the sponsors of aggressive blocs"—asserted, however, that this did not preclude a strengthening of Soviet-Pakistani relations: "should Pakistan take up a stand as independent as that in India, for instance, this would create conditions for the establishment of friendly relations."[14] Though the option for change was thus left open, the initial Soviet tactic in South Asia (and in the Middle East as well) was to build its influence by intervening in regional quarrels (India vs. Pakistan, Egypt vs. Israel) on behalf of the party judged to be engaged in struggle against "imperialism and its lackeys."

Both during and after the leaders' visit, the Soviet and Cominform press was full of reports of the warmth of the welcome, editorials proclaiming the immense historical importance of the occasion, and the texts of Bulganin's and Khrushchev's speeches, which in the words of one editorial, "gave a profoundly scientific Marxist-Leninist analysis" of vital problems of Soviet-Indian relations.[15]

b. Cultural and Economic Contacts

The Khrushchev-Bulganin trip to India was only the first of a long series of fraternal visits. In March of 1956 Anastas Mikoyan was accompanied to India by Uzbek party official Sharaf Rashidov who, as a Soviet Asian, was a frequent member of such delegations. Marshal Zhukov made a visit in January 1957, and two years later a government delegation headed by A. A. Andreev and N. A. Mukhitdinov toured India. In February 1960 Khrushchev himself made a return trip. The number of nongovernmental delegations, including groups of engineers, artists, and scholars, in this period was far larger than the number of governmental delegations, and the traffic was by no means one-way. An American observer has counted 196 Indian delegations to the Soviet Union between the years 1954 and 1957.[16]

Nor was Soviet propaganda transmitted to India solely through personal visits. An ever-increasing volume of books, pamphlets, and magazines made their way from the Soviet Union to India; whereas 17,000 books were sent in 1955, the figure had climbed to 4,000,000 copies by 1958.[17] By 1962 the Indo-Soviet Cultural Society had opened 150 city and village branches, operated 80 libraries and reading rooms, conducted 23 Russian language courses, and published magazines in Hindi, Bengali, and English.[18] But in a country where so many persons are illiterate, the spoken word was also heavily employed. In 1955 Radio Moscow broadcast in three languages to India and Pakistan a total of only two and one-quarter hours per day. In 1962, there were transmissions of that length in both English and Hindi, in addition to two and one-half hours each in Urdu and Bengali and one-half hour in Tamil.[19]

Of equal, if not greater, importance in achieving for the Soviet Union a profound impact on Indian consciousness were the offers of economic assistance which usually were announced during official visits and were well publicized in Soviet propaganda organs as well as in the Indian press.

The Soviet-aided project which achieved the most and the earliest public attention was the Bhilai steel mill, announced on February 2, 1955, in the midst of prolonged Indian negotiations with the British and West Germans for two similar mills.[20] Having reaped propaganda gains from its dramatic offer and having thus prodded the two embarrassed Western countries to speed up their agreements, the Soviets proceeded to engage in a production competion. "Victory" was achieved in time for Khrushchev to announce it to the Twenty-first Party Congress in February 1959 as striking proof of both the superiority of Soviet technique and the correctness of the Leninist peace policy. In addition to rushing the Bhilai plant into production prior to the Rourkela and Durgapur plants, the Soviets sought propaganda impact by trumpeting the favorable terms of the Russian loan (2.5 percent payable in rupees over twelve years, as opposed to Western rates of 4.5 percent and 6.3 percent), the maximum enlistment of Indian industry and training of Indian personnel (many in the Soviet Union), and the absence of Soviet demands for participation in management or profits of the Bhilai plant.[21]

Such circumstances—the dramatic announcement of projects on favorable terms designed to stimulate maximum Indian pride and Western discomfiture—were repeated on other occasions. The most notable examples were the discovery of oil deposits in areas fruitlessly explored by Western firms, the 1960 Soviet sale of crude oil at prices which undercut those of the Western oil cartel, and the 1964 offer to build yet another steel mill at Bokaro—after the Indians had long sought unsuccessfully for the United States to aid the project. This latter project was hailed in the Soviet press not only as a "second Bhilai" but also as a "second Aswan." [22] Soviet aid offers, aimed almost entirely at strengthening heavy industry in the Indian state sector, totalled $806 million between February 1955 and February 1961.

Equally important has been the steadily increasing volume of foreign trade between India and the Soviet Union; India soon became the Soviet Union's largest noncommunist trading partner. Problems have occurred in this area, including fluctuations of purchases and Indian resentment over Russian resale of bar-

tered merchandise at reduced prices, but, as Marshall Goldman
has reported, the net Soviet impact has been extremely positive.[23]

Economic motivations, such as the desire to obtain needed
raw materials and to displace Western goods with excess industrial goods from the communist countries, have not been absent
on the Soviet side. But they themselves have admitted their motives to be primarily political. An article in *International Affairs* in 1959 stated: ". . . the Soviet Union utilizes economic
contacts principally as an important lever for strengthening
peaceful relations and establishing the desired confidence between states with different social systems." [24] It is the Soviet
expectation that countries attaining "economic independence"
from imperialism by industrialization in the state sector of the
economy and by the increase of economic ties with the socialist
camp will develop a stronger proletariat and the material
prerequisites for the transition to socialism.

In addition the Soviets have sought to maximize the propaganda impact of their aid by constantly contrasting it with
"phony, so-called capitalist 'aid.' " Again, many of the themes in
this campaign were sounded by Khrushchev in his December
1955 report to the Supreme Soviet. The "new" relations between the imperialists and their former colonies, he said, consisted in giving "a dollar as 'aid' in order to get subsequently
ten dollars for it by exploiting the peoples who accepted such
'aid.' Having achieved this end they enslave the peoples politically as well." The Soviet Union, on the other hand, renders aid
"as friends, without imposing our terms . . . So far some goods
in our country are produced in smaller quantities than needed
. . . notwithstanding this, we consider it our duty to share with
our friends." [25]

Most significantly, according to the Soviet argument, the imperialists—unlike the Soviet Union—forced the developing
countries to deviate from their chosen course of development.
Not only did the United States and other countries demand the
preservation of the agrarian–raw material character of the economy and refuse aid for industrialization, but they also pressured
India and other countries for concessions to private capital investment, foreign and domestic.[26]

In the late 1950's and early 1960's, the Soviets acknowledged
that some genuine aid to the state sector was indeed being extended by the imperialists. But their ingenious argument was

that it should be viewed "as a peculiar kind of Soviet aid to these countries," for if it had not been for the existence and assistance of the Soviet Union, no aid would have been extended by the West. V. Rymalov concluded: "[G]enuine aid of one group of countries to another is alien to the very nature of capitalism." [27]

The Soviet arguments were not implausible to many of the nationalist forces in the underdeveloped countries. There had indeed been a marked reluctance in some of the Western countries to extend aid to heavy industry in the state sector. Such an attitude, accompanied by talk of "inefficiency" and "lack of infrastructure," must have indeed seemed to some to stem from a desire to preserve the former colonies as "the world village." Soviet aid to the state sector, which had in fact stirred a noticeable increase in Western aid, provided both an alternative source for development funds and the material and moral support for the implementation of an independent and nonaligned—though not infrequently anti-Western—stance in international affairs.

And this was precisely the immediate objective of the orchestrated Soviet campaign, with its diplomatic, economic, and propaganda instruments, pursued in the East in the late 1950's: to foil the suspected political, economic, and strategic designs of the West, and particularly of the United States, on these Asian and African countries struggling to win and consolidate their independence. The minimum and largely negative objective was, in itself, not new. Lenin in his early policy toward Turkey, Iran, and Afghanistan and Stalin in his efforts directed at China (as well as in the policy which had begun to emerge toward India shortly before his death) had also sought to break through the capitalist encirclement along the Soviet periphery.

But Lenin, though he had perceived the possibilities of a breakthrough by means of a communist-nationalist alliance in the East, had been preoccupied with the overcoming of political and economic weaknesses at home and with the more immediate prospects for revolution in the West. And Stalin, facing before the war these same domestic problems in addition to an unfavorable balance of forces abroad, had been preoccupied after the war with domestic reconstruction and the need to consolidate his gains in Europe. Even after the lines in Europe had been firmly drawn and the Soviet Union had broken America's atomic monopoly, however, Stalin had failed to move toward an anti-imperialist united front in Asia with all the resources So-

viet power then allowed. For Lenin's perception of the possibilities of alliance with "bourgeois nationalism" in Asia had been
blunted and distorted by Stalin after the humiliating defeat in
China.

Thus it required the fresh perceptions of a new leadership to
take full advantage both of the new international situation and
of the maximum flexibility allowed by Marxism-Leninism in
exploiting dynamic situations. This has allowed the Soviet
Union not only to move imaginatively in defending against
Western encirclement on its periphery, but also to move
beyond this minimum objective and seize the initiative on a
global scale. The prerequisites for this campaign had been
achieved by late 1955, with the relaxation of tensions in Europe
(the Austrian treaty, the move toward establishment of diplomatic relations with West Germany, and the growing "spirit of
Geneva") accompanied by the closing of a stage in the struggle
for power among the new leadership (Malenkov's replacement
by Bulganin and the gradual emergence of Khrushchev as
primus inter pares). And so the autumn of 1955 saw not only
the "B and K" journey to India, Burma, and Afghanistan, but
also the first Soviet sale of arms to Egypt—the opening shots in
the new struggle for the East.

2. Doctrinal Innovations and the Soviet Reassessment of India

Lenin had once written that "without revolutionary theory
there can be no revolutionary policy," and for Lenin's pupils
this necessitated the working out of a new doctrine to match the
new policy. Such a doctrinal retooling was not meant as a mere
pretext to mask the calculations made in the Soviet national interests. Doctrinal pronouncements may in fact do precisely that,
but they also serve to express the more strictly Marxist-Leninist
goals of which the Soviet leaders are the guardians—and in the
implementation of which their very rule is justified.

The Twentieth Party Congress of the CPSU was to perform
this function, along with its necessary concomitant—the freeing
of Marxist-Leninist theory from the dead hand of Stalin. Even
in the period of late Stalinism when Soviet-sanctioned policy
toward India and other Eastern countries had become less militant in its tactics, the Soviets had remained unable or unwilling
to move toward effective anti-imperialist cooperation with the

new "bourgeois" governments. For Stalin's authoritative 1925 assessment of Gandhi, Nehru, and the other top National Congress leaders as members of a treacherous bourgeoisie which had sold out the masses' interests to imperialism—an assessment which was incorrect in 1925 and even more distorted after the war—had continued to stultify Soviet policy by dictating the conclusion that only proletarian hegemony could bring about true political independence in India.

To explain it in another way, there are two interrelated components of Soviet ideology: an assessment of the social forces and an impulse toward action. If, as in the Stalinist strategy toward postwar decolonization, the assessment of the situation is unrealistic, the push toward action may be blunted or distorted, and the Soviets may be forced to adopt a passive or ineffective policy. An erroneous assessment of social forces can also lead to reckless action, such as that which was decided upon in India by Ranadive on the basis of the same Stalinist perception, and which proved to be equally ineffective.

Underlying the Marxist-Leninist assesment of any situation, there exists a basic image of the world which is inherent in Soviet ideology. The ideology, in this sense, serves as a set of spectacles through which the Soviet leaders and their foreign minions view the external world. In terms of this image they react to their enemies' actions and formulate policies to further their own interests.

One comprehensive attempt to explicate this image—or "operational code"—can be found in Nathan Leites' *A Study of Bolshevism.* Leites maintains that the central questions for the Bolshevik are phrased in terms of "*kto-kavo*—who will destroy whom?" [28] Politics is seen in terms of a perpetual war. The enemy is striving for the annihilation of the party (or state), and the Bolshevik must ward off any illusions that the enemy can possibly enjoy benevolent sentiments toward the party. Continuous hostile pressure, rather than appeal to reason, is the only way to modify the enemy's position. The world is seen in bipolar terms. There can be no permanent sharing of power, no lasting compromises. "There are only two stable situations: being dead and being all-powerful." [29]

The image of bipolarity and constant struggle and change thus provided by the ideology was particularly well suited to the politics of the postwar world. When the Soviets assess what they believe to be unstable situations, they see the ever-present enemy applying pressure and striving for advantage over themselves. This image, therefore, carries with it an impulse toward action, toward combatting the enemy's actions with continuous pressure of one's own.

Stalin's image of a "two-camp" world had denied the possibility of neutrality, temporary or otherwise. If an independence movement in the East was not headed by communists, or by a coalition led by communists (and they seldom were), then it was merely a tool of imperialism, a sham movement not to be trusted. This assessment had carried the "he who is not with us is against us" formulation to the extreme, and it had thus precluded effective Soviet action in those areas where communist parties were weak or absent.

Khrushchev's interpretation in 1956, on the other hand, was to revive the Leninist perception by holding that as long as the brunt of the independence movement in the East was aimed against Western imperialism, Soviet assistance to this movement would further Soviet interests. A temporary alliance against the common enemy was possible. But the doctrine was to be kept flexible in preparation for the inevitable moment when Western influence had finally been removed and the national bourgeoisie began to assert the reactionary side of its dual nature, discrediting itself in the eyes of the masses. Then the working classes and communist cadres, which had been building up their strength as the country industrialized, would, with Soviet assistance, be ready and able to seize power. The Khrushchev strategy thus hoped to allow for continuous Soviet action and influence—effective present action, yet maximum flexibility in the future.

Under the temporary alliance with national-bourgeois forces, the Soviet Union would be able to achieve its aim of expelling Western influence and substituting its own. In the meantime, it would be able to work toward ensuring that the future leadership of these new states would be held by forces more ideologically acceptable and more easily controllable. It would thus be the West, and not the Soviet Union, which would find itself isolated in the end.

Khrushchev himself summed up this outlook of flexibility in a speech in 1960: "Communists are revolutionaries, and it would be a bad thing if they did not take note of the new opportunities which arise and did not find ways and means which will lead them surely to the goal they have set themselves." [30]

a. Khrushchev's Report to the Twentieth Congress

The doctrinal innovations set forth at the Twentieth Congress have, with only slight modifications, retained validity for the Soviet leadership up to the present time.

For a Marxist-Leninist, the first step in the determination both of the strategy and tactics of the international proletarian movement and of the foreign policy of communist countries is the proper definition of the "nature of the present epoch." According to Khrushchev's report to the party congress, the main feature of the era was the "emergence of socialism from within the bounds of a single country and its transformation into a world system" accompanied by growing contradictions within the capitalist world.[31] But the socialist world system did not stand alone in its struggle against imperialism; the "forces of peace" had been augmented by the emergence of peace-loving and nonaligned states in Europe and Asia. "As a result, a vast Zone of Peace including peace-loving states, both socialist and non-socialist, of Europe and Asia, has emerged in the world. This zone embraces vast areas inhabited by nearly 1,500 million people, that is, the majority of the population of our planet." [32] So long as imperialism continued to exist, the economic basis giving rise to war could also be preserved. But war was no longer "fatalistically inevitable" as it had been in Lenin's era, for the peace forces possessed "formidable means to prevent the imperialists from unleashing war, and, if they actually try to start it, to give a smashing rebuff to the aggressors and frustrate their adventurist plans." [33]

Viewed from this new perspective, it was possible for the socialist system to achieve victory in the competition by peaceful means. Confidence in the inevitability of Soviet victory and in the noninevitability of war led Khrushchev to assert that the Leninist principle of peaceful coexistence between states of differing social systems now meant not merely their existence side-by-side: "it is necessary to proceed further, to improve relations, strengthen confidence between countries, and cooperation." [34] The "best form" for such relations lay in the subscription by all countries to the five principles advanced by India and China.

Khrushchev had already gone to great lengths, and would continue to do so, to reassure his listeners of all political persuasions that peaceful coexistence between captialism and socialism implied only a recognition of practical necessities rather than a desire to abandon the struggle. It was in Bombay in November 1955 that he had said, "We have never abandoned, and never will abandon, our political line, which was mapped by Lenin . . . And so we say to the gentry who are expecting the Soviet Union to change its political program: 'Wait until the crab whistles.' " [35]

The program of transformation to socialism in all countries would not be set aside, but the possibility that such transitions would come in a greater variety of forms had increased in the new epoch. Moreover, Khrushchev told the Twentieth Congress, violence and civil war need not accompany the implementation of this transformation in all cases. But the mere desire of communists for a peaceful transition was not in itself sufficient: "Leninism teaches us that the ruling classes will not surrender their power voluntarily . . . The use or the nonuse of violence . . . depends on . . . whether the exploiting class itself resorts to violence, rather than on the proletariat." [36] It was even conceivable that the working classes in capitalist and former colonial countries could, by winning a "stable parliamentary majority backed by a mass revolutionary movement" of the proletariat and the working people, create the necessary conditions for fundamental social change.

He thus admitted of the possibility of many paths to socialism. More favorable conditions for its attainment had arisen because of the victory of socialism in the Soviet Union and its impending victory in the people's democracies. But Khrushchev reminded his audience of one fundamental condition which had not changed: "Whatever the form of transition to socialism, the decisive and indispensable factor is the political leadership of the working class headed by its vanguard. Without this, there can be no transition to socialism." [37]

Finally, with particular regard to the countries of the East, Khrushchev declared that the complete abolition of the colonial system was one of the most pressing problems on the agenda of the new era. Countries such as India, which had already won political freedom, were becoming a "new mighty factor" in international relations, seeking to preserve peace and lessen international tensions as they sought to achieve full—that is, economic as well as political—independence. The existence of a powerful socialist system limited the possibilities of imperialist exploitation of these countries which, "although they do not belong to the world socialist system, can draw on its achievements to build up an independent national economy and to raise the living standards of their peoples." [38]

b. The "Scholars" Move into Line

This, then, in broad outline was the new assessment of social forces and of the technique and prospects for development of the national liberation movement in the East. Together with Khrushchev's attack on Stalin at the party congress, it served as an authoritative directive to Soviet Orientalists to break out of the Stalinist framework of analysis and to intensify their study of the East on the basis of the new political line. Two speakers at the Twentieth Congress underscored the high priority which the party leadership placed on the scholarly reassessment.

O. V. Kuusinen noted the "great political importance" of the fact that Khrushchev and Bulganin during their visit to India had "justly acknowledged the prominent role played in the history of the Indian people by Mahatma Gandhi." In so doing they had taken the initiative in correcting the "sectarian errors" in the works of Soviet Orientalists which had denied that Gandhi had played a positive role. More generally, there were grounds for a critical re-evaluation by historians and propagandists of the theses of the Sixth Comintern Congress and especially of the theses concerning the national bourgeoisie. According to Kuusinen (the very man who had introduced the colonial theses at that congress): "This evaluation had a tinge of sectarianism even when these theses were worked out. Under the changed conditions of the present day and now that the prestige of the Soviet Union has greatly increased, this evaluation does not at all reflect the real situation." [39] To Kuusinen's criticisms Mikoyan in his speech added a more sardonic reference to the obsolescent work of the Academy of Science's Institute of Oriental Studies: "While the entire East has awakened in our time, this Institute has been napping up to this day. Isn't it about time the Institute roused itself to the level of the needs of our time?" [40]

Such harsh criticism by two of the party's top leaders (one a member of the Presidium and the other then between appointments to that body) and the institute's own self-criticism which followed should not be taken, at face value, as an indication that the institute itself bore responsibility for the distorted assessments of the Stalin era. For it is not the purpose of Soviet Orientalists to make the authoritative decisions regarding important assessments of the social forces or national liberation movements in the East. The general line was set by the leadership of the party itself—in speeches by party leaders, in resolutions of party and international congresses, or in unsigned articles in authoritative journals. In this particular case, the authoritative statements had been made by Stalin himself.

On such issues it was the function of the Soviet Orientalist to fill in the "scholarly" details and to justify and propagandize the official line according to the prevailing Marxist-Leninist interpretation, though certain of the leading Orientalists might also be called on by the leadership for advice. On lesser issues, or on issues which the leadership had not resolved, individual contributions or debates among scholars might serve a more authoritative function, until higher authorities chose to speak. One such case (see Chapter III) involved tactics to be applied in India and had occurred during the period between the Zhdanov speech and the promulgation of the 1951 CPI Program.

But, as the previous chapter also pointed out, when the political line underwent a change, the scholars responsible for detailing it might be burdened with the blame for "errors" even though they had not been entrusted with full responsibility for decisions. The party itself never erred. Of course, individual leaders might err, but early in 1956 the public criticism of Stalin's dogmas was still rather reserved. With some exceptions, it was not until after the further de-Stalinization at the Twenty-second Party Congress that Orientalists were free to lay the blame for the previous era's mistakes upon Stalin himself.

Nor should it be assumed that prior to the public criticisms at the Twentieth Congress the Orientalists were wholly unaware that "errors" had been committed. Not only the statements of Bulganin and Khrushchev in India, but also an editorial which had appeared in *Pravda* in January 1955, and which had praised both Nehru and his foreign policy, should have been sufficient indication that a change in the assessment of India was in process.[41] But until the scope and dimensions of the shift were more evident, the Orientalists remained reticent in their appraisals of the Indian scene.[42] Thus public criticisms served a positive function in pointing out particular issues on which the higher authorities desired a new interpretation and in suggesting how far such a reassessment should be carried.

Two such critical articles preceded the Twentieth Congress. An authoritative unsigned article in the party journal, *Kom-*

munist, appearing in the late spring of 1955, informed the Orientalists that as friendly ties developed between the Soviet Union and the newly independent countries, "Soviet man wants to know about the life and struggles of the Asian peoples." But scholarly performance in fulfilling that function had been unsatisfactory. A mistaken estimate had been made of the past and present policies of Asian countries, and, in particular, of the role of the national bourgeoisie. This article was the first to suggest that in "investigating the role of Gandhi in the struggle with imperialism our Orientalists do not always proceed from the concrete historical conditions in India itself." [43]

An unsigned article appearing in the journal of the Oriental Studies Institute in September repeated the charge that there had been "incorrect elucidations" of the role of the national bourgeoisie, "whose immediate interests are infringed by the domination of foreign capital." In general, it said, there had simply been too much "mechanical application of Marxist-Leninist classics to a different historical epoch without a consideration of concrete facts," [44] a conclusion which the examples given in the present study have most assuredly confirmed.

The most comprehensive of the critical essays directed at Soviet Orientalists appeared shortly after the Twentieth Congress.[45] Citing Kuusinen's speech as authority, the editorial branded as "sectarian self-righteousness" the one-sided portrayals of the programs of the Asian national bourgeoisie— programs which, though inconsistent, had been supported by the majority of the people. While it was true that only the proletariat is consistent in its fight for liberation, it was wrong both to maintain that only proletarian leadership would assure victory in the struggle for independence and to characterize the achievements of the bourgeoisie as capitulations to imperialism.

Moreover, Orientalists had disregarded such "first modest but important successes of the young states" as agrarian reforms and the industrialization efforts underway in some countries. In general, economists had not given "due evaluation" to the objective trend toward independent capitalist development and toward increasing contradictions between the national bourgeoisie and imperialism; furthermore, they had exaggerated the role of feudal remnants. Moreover, Orientalists were plagued with "dogmatism and blind acceptance" on the ideological front, a condition which stemmed from paying "little attention in their work to the treasury of Lenin's ideas." Thus, the editorial seemed to say, Orientalists must move away from the dogmatism of Stalin's ideas and return to Lenin's more flexible perceptions of the revolutionary potential of the Asian bourgeoisie.

c. Re-evaluation of Gandhi and the Liberation Movement

The performance of this task in reference to the national-liberation movement in India was entrusted to three of the most prominent Soviet experts on India. E. M. Zhukov wrote in *New Times* in February 1956 of "Gandhi's Role in History." [46] Soviet Orientalists, "myself included," said Zhukov, had made "deplorable mistakes" in failing to recognize that under Gandhi's leadership the National Congress had been "a *genuinely popular anti-imperialist movement.*" Interestingly enough, Zhukov's analysis of the causes of these mistakes, published prior to the Twentieth Congress, blamed them not on doctrinal deficiencies but on the fact that "until quite recently, we did not possess sufficient knowledge of the facts of Indian history"—a shortcoming which had now been remedied by the study of Nehru's accounts of the Indian liberation movement!

A much more frank and realistic appraisal of the causes of the Orientalists' mistaken evaluations of the Indian movement was advanced by A. M. D'iakov and I. M. Reisner later in 1956. Their views, republished in 1957 in an Indian weekly, constituted in this period the authoritative Soviet position on Gandhi and the history of the Indian national liberation movement, and thus they warrant extensive summary. [47]

The events of the past five or six years, according to D'iakov and Reisner, had revealed the incorrectness of the Soviet assertion that India's "sham" independence had left her an English "semicolony." Particularly India's peaceful foreign policy and the government's policy of developing heavy industry had demonstrated that "under certain conditions the national bourgeoisie is capable of heading the national liberation struggle against imperialism and of attaining national independence for their countries." [48]

Whence had this long-standing mistake arisen? D'iakov and Reisner unerringly pointed to Stalin's 1925 speech to the KUTV, which had alleged that a large part of the Indian national bourgeoisie had compromised with imperialism, and to the colonial theses of the Sixth Comintern Congress, which had

further developed this viewpoint. Neither appraisal had reflected the actual situation in India, they said, which was characterized by steady intensification of the contradictions between the national bourgeoisie (including its upper stratum)
and imperialism.

Having misperceived the relationship between the Indian
bourgeoisie and the English, Soviet Orientalists had proceeded
to overestimate the leading role of the working class and the
CPI in the liberation movement. D'iakov and Reisner described
this tendency in an uncommonly insightful phrase: "we substi-
tuted what was desired for what was real."

Moreover, it had never been correct to appraise Gandhi as an
ally or agent of imperialism, as Stalin had at the Sixteenth Party
Congress. Rather, "Gandhi was a patriot who was unconditionally devoted to the cause of the liberation of his country.
Those actions of Gandhi with which we cannot agree were determined by his opinions as a representative of his class, i.e.,
the class of the national bourgeoisie. And it is impossible to
treat them as traitorous actions, accomplished in the interests of
imperialism." [49]

This re-evaluation of twentieth-century Indian political history and of Gandhi's role in particular was more than an academic exercise. Not only did the conclusion that the Indian
bourgeoisie had not betrayed the liberation movement enable
Soviet scholars and the CPI to justify a more favorable attitude
toward the policies of Nehru's "bourgeois" government, but it
also constituted a sort of apology for what had been a long-
standing insult to Indian nationalists. That the pre–1955 Soviet
interpretation of Gandhi and the Indian independence movement had wounded Indian pride and damaged Soviet-Indian
relations was made clear in a 1957 speech by the Indian ambassador to a Moscow assemblage celebrating the seventh anniversary of the Indian Republic:

In the past some misunderstandings stood in the way of the
strengthening [Soviet-Indian] friendship. I shall cite one example. We in India were pained by the wrong interpretation
given by some Soviet periodicals to the role played by Mahatma
Gandhi, the father of our nation. . . . But when Mr. Bulganin
and Mr. Khrushchev visited India they came to an understanding of the place Gandhi holds in our hearts and what he
did for the freedom of India. . . . As a result you are now giving

a more correct interpretation . . . I cite this as an example of
how good will can help establish understanding between
states.[50]

But the new Soviet respect for Indian sensitivities did not
mean that criticism of the ideology of the Indian regime was
halted entirely. As Khrushchev put it, peaceful coexistence by
no means included ideological coexistence. In many cases,
however, criticism of Indian policies was indirect and attributed to publications of the CPI or the opinions of "progressive circles." The caution with which direct verbal skirmishes
were marked was well illustrated by an article written in 1958
by academician Pavel Yudin, formerly editor of the Cominform
journal and at that time ambassador to China. The article—entitled "Can We Accept Pandit Nehru's Approach?"—took issue
with an article by Nehru which had criticized communism's violent means and the suppression of freedom in the Soviet
Union.[51] The substance of Yudin's remarks was harshly orthodox in its criticism of Nehru's "abstract and subjective approach," its assertion that in India the bourgeoisie and landlords were using the state machinery as an instrument of
violence against the people, its charge that Nehru's "socialism"
had little in common with "real socialism," and its implied
threat that India's ruling circles had better implement a radical
agrarian reform from above if they wished to avoid an even
more radical reform from below. But this extremely blunt language was sandwiched between lavish assurances that "progressive people" appreciated the "noble and historic" role of
Nehru, who was "an outstanding statesman." As a man experienced in both politics and literature, Nehru should know, said
Yudin, that one's published views are always subject to criticism. The two sides might have their ideological differences,
but they were nonetheless "united by the struggle for peace."

d. Indian Foreign Policy

That the convergence of Indian foreign policy with Russian
interests was the major factor bringing about the Soviet assessment of India was illustrated by the increased volume of attention given to this subject by journalists and scholars. Even such
prominent Soviet experts on international law as professors V.
Durdenevsky and Eugene Korovin were enlisted in the effort to
give a "scientific" analysis of the "five principles" on which

India based her foreign policy and upon which Soviet-Indian cooperation was said to rest.[52]

According to the Soviets, India's adherence to the five principles in her foreign policy was not the result of subjective factors but rested on the persistence of objective contradictions between the Indian bourgeoisie and imperialism. In essence this was an antagonism between imperialism and nationalism, and it found expression in the increasing political and economic pressure placed on the Indian government in an attempt to force it into aggressive military blocs. The result of such imperialist pressure was the Indian policy of neutrality, "an active means of defense" against the West which "strengthens the forces of peace and weakens the forces of war." [53]

The new Soviet analysis of neutrality, derived from the "zone of peace" concept, represented a considerable advance beyond the rigid Stalinist view and permitted a much more flexible approach to the newly independent countries. But the Soviets made it quite clear that only "positive neutrality"—i.e., non-alignment in blocs combined with active struggle against colonialism and warmongering—was to be considered progressive. Passive withdrawal from the vital international questions was not true "neutrality." And since the Soviet Union and other socialist countries were by definition the most consistent fighters against colonialism and in behalf of peace, the ideal neutral would be consistently anti-imperialist and pro-Soviet, without actually being a member of the socialist camp.

One issue which Soviet Indologists found difficult to resolve was the determination of the point at which Indian foreign policy had become "progressive." D'iakov in 1955 ventured the opinion that even the policy of the interim government of 1946–1947 had been "independent." T. Giiasov, in a study published in 1957, asserted that only "during the Korean War and afterwards" had an independent policy been conducted. T. M. Ershov dated the change at the beginning of 1952; previous policy had been largely positive, but sometimes "evasive." [54] And V. P. Nikhamin, in a 1959 monograph, discerned three distinct stages of development in the first decade of India's policy: (1) 1947–1950, during which India had supported independence struggles and the cause of peace, but had vacillated on a number of issues; (2) 1950–1954, during which the struggle for peace had been strengthened due to the proclamation of the Republic (an event which at the time had been described by

Soviet writers as a sham), the victory of the Chinese revolution, and the imperialist aggression in Korea; and (3) 1954–1957, during which progressive tendencies had been "still more strengthened" when the United States–Pakistan alliance and the creation of SEATO had brought the Cold War to the very borders of India.[55]

Nothing in the relations between India and the Soviet Union in this period (1955–1959) caused the Soviet writers to change their estimation of Indian foreign policy. In Nikhamin's words, not even the imperialists' attempts to utilize the "Hungarian putsch" to change Indo-Soviet relations succeeded; though Indian leaders gave an estimate of the Hungarian events which differed from that of the socialist camp, still they failed to support the Western position.[56] Indeed, Krishna Menon's was one of only two noncommunist votes in the United Nations against the resolution calling for free elections in Hungary; he had earlier abstained on the United States–sponsored resolution calling for a withdrawal of Soviet forces. Preoccupied at the time with the Suez question, India seemed to prefer to take her stands on clear-cut cases of "imperialist aggression" against non-Western countries and to stand on the sidelines when Soviet aggression in Eastern Europe was at issue.

The Soviet Union did not let India's "independent policy" go unrewarded. In February 1957, a Soviet veto blocked a resolution opposed by India calling for a United Nations force to demilitarize Kashmir. And in 1961, following India's military take-over of Goa, the Soviets again used the veto in the Security Council to stop a Western resolution calling for a cessation of hostilities and Indian withdrawal.[57]

On at least two occasions during this period, the Soviet posture as protector of India's rights had more far-reaching implications. Both situations arose during 1958 in connection with Khrushchev's obsession with top-level personal diplomacy. A Soviet proposal for a summit conference in February 1958 was addressed to the United States, Britain, France, Italy, Poland, Czechoslovakia, Rumania, Yugoslavia, Sweden, and India. The meeting never took place, but only a few months later, during the crisis in Lebanon, Khrushchev again called for a summit meeting, this one to include the Soviet Union, the United States, Britain, France, and India—"one of the leading states, a country whose voice is heeded not only in Asia, but throughout the world."[58]

On neither occasion had another great—and very jealous—
Asian power been included on Khrushchev's invitation list. But
on this second occasion, the Soviet leader quickly heard a complaint from the uninvited guest; he flew to Peking in great se-
crecy at the end of July, announcing on his return that there
would indeed be no summit meeting.

The issue of the Chinese reaction to Soviet-Indian relations
will be considered in fuller detail in the next chapter. Here it
should simply be noted that it was not the "imperialists" alone
who were to feel displeasure over the warming of relations between the Soviets and Indians.

e. Internal Indian Politics

The improvement in Soviet-Indian relations in 1955 also produced a modification in the Soviet appraisal of current issues
of Indian domestic politics. Recognition was given both to the
"progressive" measures taken by the Congress government on
social, political, and economic issues and to the popularity of
such programs among the masses.

Concerning the language and nationality issue, which remained a highly controversial problem in India throughout the
period, the Soviet assessments continued to reflect the anti-
separatist course first set in 1953. There was praise from the
Soviets for the work of the government-appointed States
Reorganization Commission, whose recommendations on the
reorganization of state boundaries on a linguistic basis were
implemented in December 1956.[59]

Whereas earlier Soviet writings on this issue had referred to
Stalin's nationality theories as authority for support of the right
of secession, post-1953 assessments quoted Lenin as opposing
" 'the idiotic system of small states and national particularism
. . . We are not in favor of preserving small nations at all costs;
other conditions being equal, we favor centralization.' " D'iakov
and T. F. Deviatkina concluded, on the basis of this Leninist
principle, that "the separation from India of independent national districts, weak in their economic aspects, will lead to loss
of their political independence." Worse still, such seceded
areas would "inevitably fall under the economic and political
influence of the strong imperialist powers." [60]

The one general election held during this period—in
1957—saw the Congress party increase its share of parliamentary
seats to a total of 371 out of 494. Rather than bemoaning the

continued dominance of the "bourgeois" party, the Soviet press chose to attribute the Congress' success to its turn toward progressive policies at home and abroad. There was no hint in the press either of expectation of a communist victory or of disappointment at the CPI's relatively poor showing on the national level.[61]

f. Indian Economic Development

To consider the Soviet assessment of the Indian economy only after an examination of Soviet views on Indian foreign and internal politics would appear to orthodox Marxist-Leninists, of course, as a rather perverse reversal of their own thought processes. Yet it is suggested here that this is precisely the order in which the Soviets themselves have made their assessments. Soviet Orientalists do not determine the extent to which this or that political group is "progressive" by examining its economic position—its place in the "relations of production"—or the economic policy which it supports. Nor are objectively similar land reform policies pursued by a bourgeois politician in a proimperialist government and by one in an anti-imperialist administration likely to be judged by a Soviet scholar according to a single criterion, such as the degree to which they result in increased production or redistributed income. Rather—as Zhukov frankly admitted in 1949—the "progressiveness" of a political group is derived from its position on the "main question" of the era—its attitude to the Soviet Union. And it is on the basis of this judgment that the economic position and policy of the group in question are assessed.

Only with this principle in mind is it possible to understand how one prominent Soviet economist, in studies of the Indian economy published in 1953 and in 1956, could conclude in the former case that the attainment of formal independence by India had not at all altered the semicolonial character of her economy, and on the basis of the same facts and arguments could in 1956 find that "the very fact that the British imperialists lost state power in India" meant that "the position of British finance capital in the Indian economy was seriously weakened." [62] The primacy of political criteria can also explain why *New Times*, which in 1955 criticized India's First Five-Year Plan on the basis that it had "not yet resulted in any appreciable change in the structure of Indian industry or the economy as a whole," could conclude only eight months later that "definite progress in developing an independent economy was achieved by India in the period of her first five-year plan." [63] In both cases the discovery that a national bourgeois government formerly held to be an agent of imperialism was indeed a progressive and peace-loving friend of the Soviet Union led to a rapid reversal in the assessment of its policies and position. By no means did this result in a complete cessation of criticism; rather, the tone of such criticism shifted. Policies once denounced as hopelessly proimperialist were now viewed paternalistically and even solicitously as the basis on which more progressive policies could be built.

The reassessment by Soviet Orientalists of the policies of the national bourgeoisie in India and other liberated countries opened, interestingly enough, with a spirited debate on the very definition of "national bourgeoisie." A key issue in this discussion, which occurred in 1956 in the Institute of Oriental Studies' Section for the History and Economy of India and Countries of Southeast Asia, was the relative weight to be given to economic and political criteria in arriving at a definition.

In the main report, economist A. I. Levkovsky chose to concentrate on the economic content of the concept "national bourgeoisie" in prewar India. The national bourgeoisie, he said, exists in colonial or dependent countries in which precapitalist forms of exploitation survive. It "represents local industrial capital in the broad sense of this word" and is characterized by both close ties and contradictions with foreign capital and the landlords. Levkovsky identified three substrata—big, middle, and petty—which he defined according to the type of economic holdings and source of income. [64]

On no single part of Levkovsky's exposition were his colleagues able to reach agreement. But it was Levkovsky's use of economic criteria as the sole basis for the definition which drew the most fire. G. I. Levinson preferred a definition which was not divorced from political criteria. The national bourgeoisie, he suggested, was that group whose interests temporarily coincided with the interests of the economic and social progress of the country. V. I. Pavlov, on the other hand, felt that in determining whether a section of the bourgeoisie was "national" or "proimperialist," it was necessary to give equal weight to political and economic factors. If only the economic position of the Indian bourgeoisie was to be considered, he suggested, the term "national bourgeoisie" should be avoided altogether. [65]

If the foregoing discussion seems to be pervaded with abstraction, artificiality, and general confusion, it is by no means an uncommon or accidental phenomenon. Such problems have always plagued Soviet Orientalists in their efforts to apply to a highly complex Indian social and economic structure analytical constructs borrowed intact from Marx's and Lenin's studies of quite different situations. Debates such as the one in 1956 only highlighted the difficulties faced by these scholars in attempting "scientific" analyses by means of artificial labels on whose meaning they were unable to reach agreement. Only in the 1960's did Soviet Orientalists become publicly conscious of the difficulty and seek to minimize it.

Further disagreement in the reappraisal of the Indian economy in the late 1950's arose over the role of the state sector in influencing the future course of India's development. Again the difficulty was in part semantic. India's economy was recognized as being no longer "semifeudal." Nor was it yet "socialist" either in its productive relations or in the material development of productive forces. The sole available alternative— "capitalist"—hardly seemed to be a proper label for policies pursued by a ruling class now recognized as "progressive." Nationalists and communists seemed to agree that capitalist development as it had evolved in the West could not produce the desired levels of achievement in the shortest possible time. Nationalist leaders in many of these states sought a "third path"— neither capitalist nor socialist in the Marxist-Leninist sense, but a "national" type of socialism. Soviet Orientalists, unable to accept this label, turned to the concept of "state capitalism" to describe this form of rapid industrialization under the direction of a state sector which coexisted with a privately owned capitalist sector.[66]

One of the earliest attempts to apply this concept to India was made by Modeste Rubinshtein in *New Times* in 1956. Despite the continued strong existence in the Indian economy of foreign capital investment and native monopoly capital, in India "the objective possibilities exist for obviating the continued growth of monopoly capital and, by peaceful means, in conformity with the will of the overwhelming majority of the people, taking the socialist path." The existence of state-capitalist enterprises, which help to weaken the imperialists' position in the economy, facilitated this transition, though further steps to change substantially the ownership of the means of production, to ensure a considerable increase in output, and to achieve higher living standards for and increased political activity by the working classes would also be necessary.

Such a conclusion itself would not have been so striking had not Rubinshtein gone on to declare—pointing to the Avadi session of the National Congress—that such a "socialist path . . . has been advocated for many years by Jawaharlal Nehru." Given friendly ties with the socialist countries and close cooperation among the progressive forces in India itself, India could develop along socialist lines, for as Lenin had "repeatedly emphasized," state capitalism is "a step toward socialism." [67]

Not unexpectedly, this article produced a shock wave in the CPI. For Rubinshtein had seemingly excised from the doctrine the requirement that proletarian hegemony precede the transition to socialism. Citing Khrushchev's Twentieth Congress statement to that effect as authority, Ajoy Ghosh wrote in his reply to Rubinshtein: "The replacement of bourgeois-landlord rule by the rule of the people headed by the working class—without this, socialism is inconceivable . . . To conclude: there undoubtedly exists a non-capitalist path of development for the underdeveloped countries like India. But it would be an illusion to think that the present government, headed by the bourgeoisie, can advance on that path. The CPI does not suffer from such illusions." [68] Rubinshtein's relatively unqualified praise of Indian "state capitalism" and of Nehru's "socialism" had thus suggested to the Indian communists the quite correct implication that—if the theory were allowed to stand—their own "historical mission" would in effect be transferred to the national bourgeoisie.

Only after some delay did higher authorities among Soviet academicians make it clear that the theory would *not* be given an official stamp. B. G. Gafurov, director of the Oriental Studies Institute and former first secretary of the Tadzhik party organization, addressed himself to the Rubinshtein-Ghosh dispute in 1957. "Some scholars," he wrote, had misinterpreted the "instructions" of the Twentieth Congress and had made the "mistake" of regarding the Indian state sector "as a point of departure for socialist transformation of the economy. According to this conception, in essence the possibility of building socialism is permitted under the leadership of the bourgeoisie." [69]

In effect this statement ruled out the possibility that state capitalism within the framework of the existing bourgeois state could simply "grow over" into socialism. It did not, however, preclude a continuing optimistic assessment of bourgeois policies of state capitalism so long as such assessments were qualified with explicit recognition that a change in class relationships must precede the transformation to socialism.

The resolution of this issue only made more obvious the continuing disagreement among Soviet Orientalists concerning the criteria by which the "progressiveness" of a given state capitalism could be judged. A debate on this question, highly reminiscent of the 1956 debate, took place in the Oriental Studies Institute's Economics Section in 1958. Again Levkovsky presented the main report, which concerned state capitalism in India, and again he seemed to prefer the use of economic criteria. State capitalism arose from the contradictions between a country's economic backwardness and its requirement for rapid development. Its class content, he admitted, was determined by the class nature of the state, which in India expressed the vital interests of the national bourgeoisie. But having made this qualification, it was possible to state that insofar as state capitalism is directed to the liquidation of economic backwardness or assists independent economic and political development, it is progressive and corresponds to the interests of the masses.[70]

In reply to this argument, one group of scholars, led by R. A. Ul'ianovsky, accused Levkovsky of overstressing the economic criterion. If the chief criterion of the progressiveness of state capitalism is the degree to which it aids economic development and the conquest of backwardness, Ul'ianovsky pointed out, then the systems found in the Philippines and in Israel would qualify as the most progressive—clearly an unacceptable conclusion. Predictably, a third group, led by A. A. Poliak, condemned Ul'ianovsky in turn for overemphasis on the foreign-policy criterion, concluding that internal and external factors deserved equal stress.[71]

Although this particular debate proceeded with typical abstraction and irresolution, Ul'ianovsky sought on later occasions to develop in more detail his analysis of Indian state capitalism. It was, he argued, anti-imperialist, for it strengthened the independence of the country and aggravated the crisis of imperialism, and thus it differed from the "state-monopoly capitalism" found in the West. The development of the state sector did not remove the contradiction between socialist production and capitalist appropriation. The issue concerning which classes would direct the state enterprises, and in whose interest, was as yet unresolved. State capitalism was in effect a new form of class struggle. There was the danger that the attempt by monopoly capital to subordinate the state sector to its own interests might succeed. But in conditions of "bourgeois democracy" the state sector could serve as a step toward socialism, though "it is not yet socialism and not a finished point of departure for the noncapitalist development of the country." [72]

Ul'ianovsky summed up his views on Indian state capitalism in a 1960 article which stressed the political factor: "The circumstance that a given state capitalism develops productive forces is not yet the decisive criterion of its progressiveness. Whether it develops on a national, anti-imperialist, anti-colonial basis . . . is the most important criterion." [73] Indian state capitalism, in its current stage of development, met this criterion and thus could be adjudged progressive.

Both Ul'ianovsky and his colleagues singled out certain features of the Indian path of development which posed a possible threat to the continued progress of Indian state capitalism. The Second Five-Year Plan, praised for its stated goals of priority development of heavy industry and expansion of the state sector, was criticized for its proposed means of financing this development. Instead of increasing taxes on high incomes or profits, suspending compensation payments to landlords, or nationalizing foreign-owned enterprises, the plan proposed even heavier indirect taxes—an increased burden on the working classes—and a dangerous overreliance on external sources of capital. This allowed foreign capital to retain its important position in the economy and allowed Indian monopoly capital to expand side by side with the state sector.[74] None of these criticisms, however, destroyed the basic optimism of the Orientalists that, given the internal pressure of progressive forces and the strengthening of ties with the socialist countries, India could continue her independent economic progress.

Soviet economists were forced to concede that Nehru's "progressive" policies had brought little in the way of concrete benefits to the Indian proletariat. The Indian workers, according to L. A. Gordon, received no net benefit from small increases in their real wages if their indebtedness rose simultaneously. Furthermore, the existence of a growing army of urban unemployed threatened to depress living standards even more.[75]

Finally, if Soviet strategists had hoped that assistance to In-

dian industrialization would result in an increase in the size of
the Indian proletariat, they must have been disappointed in
reading in a 1960 study that, thanks to capitalist "rationaliza-
tion," the number of factory proletariat had remained almost
unchanged in the years since independence.[76]

As for the mass of the Indian peasantry, Soviet Orientalists
saw little to point to in the way of improvements. The picture
they drew was one of gradual and painful capitalistic development in agriculture. The land reforms of the bourgeois government had had as their goal "gradually to convert the landlords
and rich peasants into small and medium capitalist farmers,"
but this had not led to a distribution of the land to the majority
of peasants. Land ownership, no longer primarily on a feudal
basis, was still concentrated in the hands of an extreme minority.[77]

Nor had such bourgeois policies as the Community Development Program aided the village poor. The implementation of
these programs on the local level was in the hands of the most
prosperous stratum of the agrarian population. The poor peasant
and agricultural worker contributed free labor and received no
positive benefit. The attempt to improve agricultural production
by means of national planning had had only limited success
given the private basis of land ownership. In essence the
agrarian problem was rooted in the existing social relations and
not in the low level of technique, lack of resources, or "overpopulation" of the land. This latter feature was in fact a "bugaboo" of the bourgeois economists. Overpopulation was a relative rather than an absolute factor—India's population density
was no more than that of some advanced European countries—
and even this would disappear as soon as India's industry developed.[78]

Not only did Soviet Orientalists turn "thumbs down" on all
the current government programs of land reform, but they also
gave a negative estimate of Vinoba Bhave's *Bhoodan* (landgift)
movement. Bhave, a disciple of Gandhi, had begun the movement after the climax of the Telengana uprising; he presented it
as a nonviolent and harmonious alternative to agrarian revolution. According to one Soviet analyst, its positive results had
been minimal, and the entire movement was but a "propaganda
song and dance over a limited charitable and philanthropic
measure." [79]

Ul'ianovsky's conclusion was that the bourgeois policy of

gradual agrarian reforms from above, while it had involved some compromise with the landlords, had nevertheless succeeded in ending the dominance of feudalism on the land, had produced some modernization of the social order in the village, and had increased somewhat the level of agricultural production. The results had been the growth of differentiations among the peasantry, a loss of its former class unity against the common enemy, and the increasing contradictions between the rich and middle peasantry on the one hand and the poor peasants, sharecroppers, and agricultural workers on the other.

Though this entire analysis had borrowed the conceptual framework used in the analyses of the Russian village, Ul'ianovsky—unlike most Soviet students of the Indian village—did explicitly recognize that differences existed between the two situations. Indian "feudalism" had been of a different type—there had been no large seignorial estates or corvée system. Indian land reforms were proceeding under the direction of the national bourgeoisie, whereas in Russia they had occurred under the monarchical regime, and the international conditions under which the two situations had developed were dissimilar.[80]

On the whole, the main theme of the Soviet reassessment of the Indian economy was thus the conviction that for the most part the "state-capitalist" policies of the Indian national bourgeoisie, though still capitalist and involving many of the burdens and limitations inhering in that system, were contributing to the clearing away of feudal and colonial features which had hampered India's development, and they thus constituted a progressive step toward the inevitable and perhaps peaceful transformation to socialism.

3. The CPI Reaction to Soviet-Indian Rapprochement

Chapter III has already pointed out the reluctance with which the Communist Party of India had yielded to Moscow's insistence on, first, the priority of the anti-imperialist struggle and, second, the contributions (still considered in 1954 to be "limited") of Nehru's foreign policy to the struggle for peace. It was with even greater hesitation that the CPI finally began to echo Moscow's reassessment of the internal situation in India. For the CPI, by accepting the Soviet appraisal of Nehru's policies, was forced to smooth over many of its differences with the bourgeois regime and thus to sacrifice its clear-cut oppositional role. In effect, the CPI was gradually deprived of its internal enemy, while the Nehru government in its turn was largely freed from whatever danger a radically oppositional CPI had posed to it. Thus the Soviet reassessment, while allowing for revived flexibility and activism in Soviet foreign policy toward nationalist regimes such as Nehru's, simultaneously blunted the activism of the local communist parties—in the interests of Soviet policy—and led to a kind of semiparalysis.

It will be recalled that at the beginning of 1955 the CPI had just begun to operate under Ghosh's formula of opposition to Nehru's internal policies and support for his foreign policy. The first test of the popularity of this new line came in the February 1955 elections in newly created Andhra state. This was an area in which the CPI had long been strong; it included the Telengana districts in which the party had conducted a lengthy agrarian uprising. In the 1951 elections in the districts which now constituted Andhra, the CPI had won a surprisingly large number of seats in the legislative assembly. It had skillfully exploited both the popularity gained from its active struggle to achieve a Telegu-speaking state and the caste-based split in the local Congress party organization. Thus the CPI entered the 1955 elections so fully confident of emerging with a victory that it had not sought an electoral alliance with the other anti-Congress parties.

The result, as the CPI itself admitted, was a "big political defeat" which shook the party's confidence and lowered its prestige. From a strength of 48 seats in a house of 140, it had emerged with only 15 seats in a house of 196.[81] The Congress' election propaganda had featured the wide distribution of the *Pravda* January editorial praising the achievements of the Nehru regime. This maneuver had effectively blunted whatever gain the CPI might have hoped to achieve from its association with the prestige and achievements of the Soviet Union. But as Selig Harrison has pointed out, the real secret of the CPI defeat in Andhra was the Congress' ability to beat it at its own game of caste politics.[82]

The same phenomenon of regionalist, caste-based politics, as opposed to a politics built on competing social and economic programs, was to play a vital role—this time to the CPI's advantage—in the 1957 elections in Kerala, when the CPI managed to form in the state (with the help of five independent legislators) the first popularly elected communist-led government in history.

Kerala, the southernmost state in India, was characterized by both the highest literacy rate and the highest unemployment rate in all India. Its four equally balanced communities—the Ezhava and Nair castes and the Christian and Moslem groups—had long been engaged in a bitter rivalry. In 1957 the skillfully led Kerala Communist Party had utilized this communal rivalry and the widespread unpopularity of a corrupt, faction-ridden local Congress organization to win 40 percent of the votes and form a government.[83]

In other areas of India, however, the communists had not been so skillful. Outside the states of Andhra, Kerala, and West Bengal—and especially in Hindi-speaking areas where Congress strength was based—the CPI was far less potent. The 1956 reorganization of Indian states on a linguistic basis, together with the decision taken by the CPI in 1953 (and strongly supported by the Soviets) to abjure separatism, has perhaps limited the further spread of CPI regionalism, but the party has remained, in Harrison's words, "concentrated . . . in regional strongholds that have been located, by and large, where their leadership has 'belonged' within the social and economic power structure and where this leadership has appropriated particularist disaffection." [84]

In the wake of the 1955 defeat in its Andhra stronghold, the CPI found itself divided and groping for a new strategy. Only after a month-long debate was the Central Committee able to produce a compromise resolution in June 1955. This resolution, acknowledging the "radical change" in the Indian government's foreign policy, declared that the main internal tasks—the confiscation and nationalization of British property and the complete abolition of feudalism—remained unfinished. Since Nehru's government, dominated by the big bourgeoisie, had refused to implement these policies, then the mass movement for the completion of the antifeudal and anti-imperialist tasks would have to develop in general opposition to the government's internal policies. The goal for which the party would work would continue to be the "people's democratic revolution," for only a people's democracy "which includes all the democratic classes, including the national bourgeoisie, but is led by the working class, can fulfill these tasks speedily and effectively." [85]

That this compromise resolution had not in Soviet eyes gone far enough in its reappraisal of Nehru's economic policies was evident from the manner in which the Cominform journal reported it. Detailing those parts of the resolution which praised Nehru's foreign policy, the article added that a "considerable part" of the resolution dealt with internal matters. But the article failed entirely to indicate either the substance or the tone of the CPI's comments on the domestic situation.[86]

The attempt to reconcile this divergence of opinion followed the usual pattern: Ghosh traveled to Moscow in July for a visit of two months. On his return he published a series of four articles in the CPI journal, in which he gradually moved away from the position of the June resolution and in the direction of the emerging Soviet reappraisal. In October he wrote that, while the bourgeoisie could not complete the tasks of the bourgeois-democratic revolution, it was now possible for the government to follow "an increasingly independent policy." [87] In November, reaffirming the policy of struggle against the big bourgeoisie, Ghosh declared that "this is not and cannot be the *dominant* aspect of our movement in the present stage. That aspect is and must be anti-feudal, anti-imperialist." [88] In December he went even further, denying that there was a differentiation between a "national" and a "collaborationist" bourgeoisie and declaring that the interests of the entire bourgeoisie in India came into conflict with those of imperialism. Moreover, Ghosh admitted for the first time that the conditions in the country were not yet conducive to the call for a coalition, interim government to replace that of the Congress.[89] Finally, in January, Ghosh acknowledged that the government's strengthening of the state sector, though it was not "socialism," was a progressive step toward strengthening economic independence. The CPI's task was not to deny this, but to ensure more progress.[90]

The gradualism of Ghosh's reassessment was caused not by his own uncertainty as to what the Soviets desired but by the strong reluctance of leading party cadres to accept it. The amount of resistance they were able to muster can be gauged from the fact that at the CPI's Fourth Party Congress in April 1956 Ghosh was not able to win the delegates' permission to incorporate the new position in the form of amendments to the 1951 Program.[91] He did, however, succeed in gaining its adoption as a Political Resolution of the party congress.

Before examining that resolution, it would be useful to summarize Ghosh's report to the party congress concerning the decisions of the CPSU's Twentieth Congress.[92] Ghosh told the delegates that Khrushchev's concept of the "zone of peace" demanded a linking of the struggles for peace and for national freedom in the East. It would now be "doctrinaire and dogmatic" to deny the progressiveness of India's foreign policy or to maintain that neutrality was impossible.

Ghosh went on to outline for the congress the implications of Khrushchev's thesis on the peaceful transition to socialism. He stressed that the possibility of such a transition was dependent upon the prior weakening of the capitalist system and on the democratization of the state apparatus. Thus a "sustained struggle for extension of democracy" would be the necessary prerequisite of peaceful transition in India.

Finally, Ghosh addressed the issues raised by de-Stalinization. On the basis of the agonizing appraisal he presented to the congress, it can be concluded that the issue had produced a profound shock in the CPI—a party which had been exceptionally dependent for its guidance on the "infallible" pronouncements of the CPSU. The undoubted harm to the Soviet party's prestige which stemmed from Khrushchev's revelation of Stalin's crimes was to make it far more difficult for Stalin's successors to impose their will on the already faction-ridden CPI. As Ghosh himself admitted later in 1956: "We agree that we were wrong in idealizing everything in the USSR. . . . We are deeply conscious of the damage this has done to the cause of Communist-Socialist unity and even to the cause of Socialism. We are determined to abandon this attitude." [93]

The CPI's Political Resolution at the Fourth Congress was straightforward in its praise of the "radical change" in Nehru's foreign policy and in its determination to strengthen the anti-imperialist features of that policy. It declared that the Third Congress had been "sectarian" in its refusal to recognize the progressive measures of Indian foreign policy.[94]

On internal issues there was more ambivalence. The resolution recognized "a certain amount of strengthening of the national economy," but declared that the "crisis of semi-colonial economy continues." However, the approach of the CPI's Third Congress to domestic problems had been "grossly subjective" in overestimating the strength of the peasant movement, of working class unity, and of the party itself, and in declaring that the establishment of a "Government of Democratic Unity" was an immediate prospect. In truth, said the resolution, the building of the democratic front would demand "a policy of simultaneous unity with and struggle against the bourgeoisie." The main targets of the struggle were imperialism, British capital, and feudal survivals. Every step taken by the government "for strengthening national freedom and national economy, against imperialists, feudal and monopoly interests will receive our most energetic and unstinted support." [95]

The CPI had thus made great strides away from the militancy of the late 1940's and had even moved far from the position embodied in its 1951 program. Its position after the Fourth Congress was similar to the one it had occupied in the late 1930's and immediately after the war. Recognizing the durability of the Congress' hold on the masses, the CPI had lowered its immediate sights from the goal of replacing the Congress government with a communist-led coalition to the aim of pressuring the existing government to move leftward. The ultimate goal—the attainment of people's democracy—remained unchanged, but the expectation that its implementation was near at hand had vanished except among a group of extremists.

In the 1957 elections the CPI called for the formation of alternative governments only in the states of Kerala and West Bengal, where the party urged "democratic Congressmen" to join the struggle "not against the Congress as such but against those elements and trends inside the Congress which are helpful to the landlords." [96] In the pre-election pamphlet just quoted, E. M. S. Namboodiripad, who was to become Chief Minister of Kerala, called for redistribution of land, suspension of compensation payments to landlords, and lifting the rent, debt, and tax burdens from the peasantry, thereby expanding the domestic market.

Once in power in Kerala, the CPI matched the moderation of its slogans with its practice. Namboodiripad, in a 1957 pamphlet, stated his agreement with the approach of the Second Plan but complained that Kerala was not receiving its "fair share" of the benefits. On the labor front, he called for a policy of "industrial peace"—avoidance of work stoppages and the "most rapid and peaceful solution of labor disputes." His government banned the eviction of tenants from the land and proposed an agrarian reform bill which sought "partial satisfaction to both the tenant cultivator and the small landlord." Direct ac-

tion by the masses should not do "violence to person or property," and the police should render due protection to propertied
classes. Namboodiripad declared his awareness that on the success or failure of the communist government in Kerala depended the future of the movement in the country as a whole.
The achievements of the Kerala communists would prove to the
country that they were "noble and patriotic," and that communists and nationalists could work together.[97] And once in office
the Kerala communist government, claiming that it was cir-
cumscribed by the Indian Constitution and by the policies of
the central government, declared that while it would be unable
to lay even the basis for socialism, it would strive to carry out all
the "bourgeois-democratic" tasks that the Congress party had
pledged—and failed—to do.

Encouraged by its success in winning power in Kerala, the
CPI sought after the elections to become a "mass party" by
doubling its membership to 250,000, a goal that it claimed to
have achieved in the space of a year.[98] In April 1958 the party
held an "Extraordinary Congress" at Amritsar for the purpose of
adopting a new party consititution. The preamble to this document, reaffirming the aim of people's democracy led by the
working class and declaring that its policies would be worked
out by "applying the theory of Marxism-Leninism to the realities of the Indian situation," pledged the party to strive "to
achieve full democracy and Socialism by peaceful means." In
other words, the CPI ". . . considers that by developing a powerful mass movement, by winning a majority in Parliament and
by backing it with mass sanctions, the working class and its
allies can overcome the resistance of the forces of reaction and
ensure that Parliament becomes an instrument of people's
will." [99]

In his clarifying remarks issued after the congress, Ghosh
stressed that the pledge of nonviolence was conditional; "the
preamble merely means that the party perceived a 'possibility'
that the working people could achieve power through a parliamentary majority." [100] There remained also the possibility that
the ruling classes would resist violently, in which case the party
would respond in kind. Such reassurance, however, failed to
satisfy a powerful leftist faction within the party. One year after
the congress this faction issued a document, "On the Revisionist Trend inside the CPI," which ridiculed the notion of a
peaceful path. Quoting *Peking Review*, this group suggested

that the necessary alternative was the Chinese path, which dictated, that through "revolution in one form or another the working class must smash the bourgeois state apparatus and replace the bourgeois dictatorship by proletarian dictatorship." [101]

But not even the ouster of the Kerala government and the imposition of "President's rule" in that state in 1959 shook the party leadership's adherence to the "peaceful path." Indeed, Ghosh went so far as to reaffirm explicitly the party's commitment to the Amritsar decision.[102] But the intraparty dispute concerning the correctness of this policy was soon to be aggravated—to the point of splitting the CPI—by parallel developments which began to unfold at the end of the decade: the growing enmity of Peking toward both India and the Soviet Union.

V From Tibet to Tashkent: The Challenge of China, 1959–1965

A qualitative change had occurred in Soviet policy toward India in 1955, when for the first time the diplomatic, economic, and cultural instrumentalities of the Soviet state were employed in an effort to build Indian support for the "anti-imperialist" objectives of Soviet foreign policy. Yet another qualitative change began to take shape at the end of the 1950's, when both the Soviet Union and India were increasingly forced to take into account in their policy equations the menacing claims of their common neighbor, the People's Republic of China.

Of most direct concern to this study are two facets of the Chinese challenge: the effects of her border disputes with India on Soviet-Indian relations and the effects of her diplomatic, organizational, and ideological competition with the Soviet Union, particularly with respect to the "third world," on the Soviet assessment of India.

Viewed on one dimension, the Sino-Soviet conflict has included a number of clashes at the level of state-to-state relations, some of which (including the Sinkiang boundary and the status of Mongolia) predate the rise of Marxism-Leninism in either state. The border incidents between the USSR and People's China date back at least to 1958 and have been the most explosive source of tension. When, in a 1964 interview, Mao Tse-tung brazenly challenged the legitimacy of Soviet frontiers, both west and east, the Soviet reply was a veiled but impassioned nuclear threat.[1]

Antedating such baleful exchanges concerning their common border was a more general Chinese complaint against the Soviets' unwillingness to employ what Khrushchev claimed and Mao believed to be superior Soviet strategic power in order to regain from the imperialists and their minions such Chinese territory as Formosa and the Pescadores. As early as 1957, with the first demonstration of Russian space technology, Mao had proclaimed that "the east wind prevails over the west wind." But Khrushchev's carefully calculated strategic bluff was designed to further Soviet interests in the West, especially Berlin, and relied on the inclusion of periods of détente with the NATO states.[2] There was no room in such a strategy for the risks of employing Soviet power on behalf of Chinese national interests, as Khrushchev demonstrated first in the Quemoy and

Matsu incident of 1958 and then more openly in the 1959 and 1962 Chinese clashes with India.

More was involved here than simply a quarrel over the time-table and means for advancing communism in Asia; soon this facet of the dispute was revealed as an active rivalry for pre-dominant influence throughout the "third world." According to a Soviet diplomat who defected to the West from the embassy in Rangoon in 1959, a "gentlemen's agreement" in 1955–1956 which had recognized Southeast Asia as a "Chinese sphere" and India, Afghanistan, and points west as a "Soviet sphere" had been ended in 1958 by Chinese "intervention" in India.[3] Moreover, one Soviet author has claimed that as early as 1956 the Chinese leaders told a group of foreign communists that "European Communist Parties should not meddle in the revo-lutionary struggle in colonial countries," but should leave these affairs to the Chinese, "who were best able to judge such mat-ters." [4] At any rate, by the early 1960's the Soviets and Chinese were engaged in a frenzied scramble to outbid each other for the support of not only Asian but also African and Latin Ameri-can regimes and movements.

In addition to their insufficient defense of Chinese territorial claims, the Soviets were—in Chinese eyes—guilty of failing to devote sufficient resources to Chinese economic and military development. For their part, the Soviets were probably no more willing to build China up to the point where she could pursue her risk-laden ambitions (and perhaps involve her allies in such risks) than they were to encounter such risks in China's behalf. Khrushchev, who had promised in October 1957 to aid the Chi-nese in developing nuclear weapons, went back on his pledge in June 1959.[5] Insult was added to injury in 1963 when by agreeing to the test-ban treaty Khrushchev appeared to be seeking to freeze China permanently out of the "nuclear club."

The Chinese case on the issue of economic aid appears to be weaker. One of the first acts of the post-Stalin Soviet leadership had been to increase considerably the niggardly aid program to China and to abandon the concessions Stalin had exacted from Mao in 1950. While Khrushchev did attempt to use aid levels to pressure the Chinese leaders in the late 1950's, he did not ter-minate the aid program even after the provocations which re-sulted in the departure of Soviet technicians from China in July 1960. In the entire period from 1949 to 1965 loans totaling over $2 billion in goods and services went from Russia to China.[6]

The Chinese, of course, have pointed to the $4 billion in Soviet aid to nonsocialist states as evidence that "proletarian internationalism" has been betrayed. But this argument can cut both ways; the Soviets cannot have been pleased to see that during the years of their heaviest disbursements to China the Chinese had embarked on their own program of aid to nonsocialist states (totaling about $900 million by 1966).

These clashes of interest on the state level were amplified by the personal rivalry between Khrushchev and Mao. Chapter III has already detailed the early Chinese claims on behalf of Mao's theoretical contributions. But such claims were muted in the face of Stalin's evident resentment and the counterattacks from Soviet scholars. With Stalin's death and subsequent removal from the Marxist pantheon, Mao could again step forward as the senior Marxist theoretician. It was thus no small blow to Mao's substantial ego when Khrushchev—a man of similar-size ego but without prior philosophical contributions—arrogated to himself the right unilaterally to revise Marxist-Leninist doctrine. Regardless of the strength of his ideological convictions, there was undoubtedly an element of personal vindictiveness in Mao's challenge to Khrushchev's doctrinal innovations. Nor was either man's concern limited to his rival's theoretical standing. Each sought in addition actually to have the other removed from power. Even after Khrushchev's ouster, the Chinese have been haunted by his personality, labeling both his successors and Mao's own internal enemies, "Khrushchev revisionists."

The next dimension of the dispute concerns the organization of the communist movement. On this level the Chinese challenge began quite early, with their assumption in 1956–1957 of the role of adviser to the Soviets in the handling of the turmoil in Eastern Europe. Thus, while insisting at the 1957 Moscow Conference that the Soviets retained the "leading role" in the camp, the Chinese sought to establish their right to a veto over the Soviet exercise of that role. The Soviets not unexpectedly resisted a title to leadership that included a "unanimity rule" allowing the lesser members of the camp a voice in the disposition of Soviet resources.[7]

While not claiming to be "leader," the Chinese did however seek to win adherents to their particular "path of socialist construction." But the Chinese campaign on this level was not limited to the force of example. As early as 1960 they began their "fractional" activities, seeking first to capture and then to split both the international front organizations and the member parties. Khrushchev countered in 1963 and 1964 with his own attempts to call an international conference for the purpose of reading the Chinese out of the movement. For those, like the Rumanians, who were skillful enough to take advantage of this situation, it resulted in a greatly increased amount of autonomy in the former "bloc." But for those unfortunates, like the Indian communists, who lacked the internal cohesion necessary for such delicate maneuvers, the Sino-Soviet competition so magnified existing fissiparous tendencies as to result in an actual split.

The ideological dimension of the conflict, while it tended to elevate all quarrels to the level of principle and made pragmatic compromise difficult, was perhaps also responsible for preventing a total break. Neither side could afford to alienate those "fence-sitters" who sought to retain formal unity at all costs. Nor, for all the polemics accusing each other of aid and comfort to the imperialist enemy, could either take the risk of actually cutting the other adrift into a possible real-life coalition with that enemy.

With all the endlessly repeated polemics of the past few years, it is not difficult to identify the chief points of contention on this ideological level and the rival strategies which they express. The main thrust of the Chinese argument is that the Khrushchevian assessment of the nature of the epoch and of the balance of forces has sacrificed the international activism of the revolutionary movement on the altar of Soviet enrichment. The Soviet counterattack centers on the need to abandon the sterile and stilted assessments, inherited from the past era, which produce a policy of inflexibility—either the irrelevance of Stalinism or the reckless adventurism of Maoism. Each side has long since despaired of persuading the other to change its foreign policy as a result of this debate and has instead concentrated on winning over, by pressures as well as persuasion, as many as possible of the member units of the international proletarian vanguard.

According to the Soviets, the Chinese were first to make the dispute public in the appearance in April 1960 of "Long Live Leninism"—a reply to Khrushchev's doctrinal revisions—in the journal *Red Flag*. But the Chinese place on the Soviets the blame for opening the dispute to outside observation, through Moscow's refusal in September 1959 to side with China in her border conflict with India.

1. The Sino-Indian Border Dispute

As early as 1957, when a Soviet writer was hailing the Sino-Indian border as a "border of peace and friendship," [8] the Chinese were engaged in building a strategic military road across India's Aksai Chin plateau—the only route by which western Tibet could be linked with Sinkiang. Chinese maps had long showed this desolate area of Ladakh, as well as large sectors of the Northeast Frontier Agency (NEFA), to be part of China, but Chou En-lai had personally assured Nehru in 1954 that these were merely reproductions of old maps the Chinese had not yet revised.

The prelude to the 1959 border clashes was the bloody Chinese suppression of the short-lived Tibetan revolution of March 1959. Described by the Chinese as a rebellion of the "reactionary clique of the Tibetan upper strata," this uprising evoked a wave of sympathy among the Indian press and public. Far worse in Chinese eyes was India's decision to award sanctuary to the Dalai Lama after his fight from Lhasa. In the Chinese press, "Indian expansionists" were charged with having conspired with Tibetan reactionaries to "abduct" the Dalai Lama and with having aided the rebellion, though Nehru himself was said to remain an advocate of Sino-Indian friendship.[9]

Sino-Indian tension continued during the summer and led the Indians to attempt to outflank the Chinese outposts in Ladakh. But it was in the other disputed border area, in the NEFA, that the first Indian blood was spilled on August 25. Nehru's protest—the first Indian admission of border trouble—was answered by a letter from Chou on September 8 which accused India of unilaterally seeking to change the established border and which challenged India's treaty rights in the buffer states of Sikkim and Bhutan. A more conciliatory message from Chou on October 6 was followed two weeks later by the ambush of an Indian patrol in Ladakh, in which nine Indians were killed.

There was evidence that the most concrete Chinese objective was a settlement which would cede the Aksai Chin area to China, while accepting the McMahon Line as the boundary in the east. But the timing of the border incidents suggests that China's purposes were more far-reaching. For September 1959 was the date of Khrushchev's trip to the United States and his meeting with President Eisenhower at Camp David—the high point of his drive to prove that détente and peaceful competition could serve the communist cause better than military force. But if the Chinese sought to sabotage the détente by forcing Khrushchev into a militant stand in support of Chinese claims in India, Khrushchev's reaction was far from obliging.

According to a later Chinese version, the Soviet chargé d'affaires in Peking was informed that the Indian government had "provoked" a conflict and was warned against being "taken in by Nehru who was striving to put pressure on China by utilizing the Soviet Union." [10] On September 9 the Soviet diplomat replied by showing to the Chinese an advance text of the TASS statement to be released the following day. This statement opened by denouncing the "Western campaign" to poison Sino-Indian relations and to "complicate the situation" on the eve of Khrushchev's visit to the United States. The statement continued:

It would be wrong not to express regret that the incident . . . took place. The Soviet Union enjoys friendly relations with both the Chinese People's Republic and the Republic of India. The Chinese and Soviet peoples are tied together by indestructible bonds of fraternal friendship . . . Friendly cooperation between the USSR and India according to the ideas of peaceful coexistence is developing successfully.

Attempts to take advantage of the incident . . . for the purpose of fanning the "cold war" and of disrupting friendship between peoples should be condemned decisively.[11]

The statement closed with an expression of the conviction of "Soviet leaders" that China and India would, in the traditional spirit of friendship, settle the misunderstanding to their mutual interests.

The Chinese have reported that they "intimated in principle that it would be better for the Soviet Government to refrain from making a public statement on this question," later providing the Soviet chargé with a copy of Chou's letter setting forth the Chinese views and proposals.[12] The Soviets not only ignored the Chinese advice, but Khrushchev reiterated Soviet "regret" in a speech to the Supreme Soviet following the Ladakh incident, adding that it "would gladden us if there were no repetition of the incidents . . . and if the frontier disputes were settled through friendly negotiations to the mutual satisfaction of both sides." [13] TASS covered this later border clash by reprinting Indian and Chinese accounts side-by-side and without comment.

Moreover, between the two border incidents Khrushchev had been in Peking for the celebration of the tenth anniversary of the People's Republic of China. At a banquet in his honor, he had publicly warned against attempting to "test by force the stability of the capitalist system." According to the Chinese article of 1963, "the entire world" recognized this as an "insinuation that China was being 'bellicose' regarding Taiwan and the Sino-Indian boundary." They further reported that they had given Khrushchev an explanation of the "true situation and background" of the conflict during his visit and informed him that "it would not do to yield to the Indian reactionaries all the time." But Khrushchev, they said, "did not want to know the true situation and the identity of the party committing the provocation, but insisted that anyway it was wrong to shoot people dead." [14] On November 7, Khrushchev told a correspondent for the CPI journal *New Age* that the border incident was "sad" and "stupid." Reminding his listener of the manner in which the Soviets had settled their own dispute with Iran, he asked: "What are a few kilometers to the Soviet Union?" The implication was clear: China had no business quarreling over a few scraps of worthless territory.

The Chinese thought otherwise and called in the Soviet ambassador on six occasions in December and January to explain their position and protest that Soviet "neutrality" had in effect "censured" China. The Soviet censure in fact moved beyond the realm of implication when a "verbal notification" to the CCP from the CPSU Central Committee in February declared that "one cannot possibly seriously think that a state such as India . . . immeasurably weaker than China" would really launch an attack. China's posture during the incident had expressed a "narrow nationalist attitude." [15] Only two months later China, considering her differences with the Soviet Union now "in the open," went on the attack on the ideological level with the publication of "Long Live Leninism." Three years later the Chinese cited the Soviet behavior during the 1959 crisis as ". . . the first instance in history in which a socialist country, instead of condemning the armed provocations of the reactionaries of a capitalist country, condemned another fraternal socialist country when it was confronted with such armed provocation." [16]

During the interval between the 1959 and 1962 attacks, both China and India, as well as the Soviet Union, were engaged in frenzied diplomatic activity. For his part, Nehru moved quickly to reassure the Soviets that he viewed the border dispute as Chinese rather than communist aggression. The TASS statement, he acknowledged in a press conference, had been both "fair" and "unusual." On the other hand, the Indian ambassador to the Soviet Union, who had been warned by Khrushchev in March 1959 that India was responsible for Sino-Indian differences on Tibet, was assured by the Soviet leader in December that both India and China were "dear" to the Soviet Union.[17]

The Soviets further reassured the Indians of their continued friendship by stepping up their diplomatic contacts. A delegation headed by Voroshilov, Kozlov, and Furtseva attended the celebration in India of the tenth anniversary of the Republic in January 1960. And the following month Khrushchev himself returned for a brief visit in the course of a journey to Burma, Indonesia, and Afghanistan. The trip was largely in the form of an inspection tour of the Soviet-aided Bhilai steel plant and Suratgarh state farm. In between his generously disbursed advice to Indian engineers, Khrushchev praised India's foreign policy and her efforts to build heavy industry (the "mainstay of independence"), attacked Western aid and theories of development, and concluded that Indian-Soviet relations "have never before rested on a more solid basis of friendship and understanding than at the present time." [18] The shrill denunciations of the West that had characterized the 1955 visit were absent; Khrushchev exuded the "spirit of Camp David." Nor was there a single public mention of the border problem or of China. But it could not have been lost on the Chinese that Khrushchev was in India on the tenth anniversary of the signing of the Sino-Soviet alliance.

Khrushchev used the occasion of his visit for the signing of an agreement spelling out the terms of the $375 million loan the Soviets had presented to the Indians the previous year, in the midst of the quarrel with China. In addition, negotiations were under way for the sale to India of about $30 million of Soviet airplanes, to be used for transporting troops and war matériel along the Himalayan border, as well as a sizable amount of earth-moving and street-building machinery to be employed by India in the construction of roads along her northern frontiers.[19]

The Chinese were occupied in these months in talks with the

governments of Nepal, Burma, and Pakistan aimed at settling their border disputes with these countries—and perhaps also at isolating India from her neighbors. The contrast between these negotiations and the state of Sino-Indian relations was heightened when talks between Nehru and Chou—preceded by an angry demonstration by an Indian mob of 5,000 people shouting, "Chou En-lai, *hai, hai*" (death to Chou)—in April 1960 came to nought.

In the wake of this failure, the Indian government began to implement its "forward policy," the effect of which was both to underline India's inflexibility on the issue of the disputed border and to contribute to the heightening of Sino-Indian tensions. Beginning early in 1962 the Chinese delivered to India, through diplomatic channels and the press, an increasingly bellicose series of protests against alleged Indian violations of the border.[20] Nehru joined the Chinese in this game, most notably by his announcement in August that the Indians had accepted an offer made by the Soviets in May to supply MIG-21 fighter planes (which had not been supplied to China) and by his October 12 declaration that he had issued instructions to the Indian army "to free Indian territory" in the NEFA of "Chinese intruders." This order, which was not followed by actual implementation, provided the occasion for an impassioned *People's Daily* editorial on October 14, entitled "Mr. Nehru, It Is High Time for You to Pull Back from the Brink of the Precipice!"[21] The Indian "reactionary ruling circles," the editorial said, did not "scruple to use the lives of Indian soldiers as stakes to satisfy their insatiable greed." Nehru had made up his mind to attack Chinese border guards "on an even bigger scale," but the "heroic Chinese troops . . . can never be cleared by anyone from their own territory."

Fighting began in the NEFA area on October 20. Only four days later a Chinese statement, expressing shock at the "Indian aggression," proposed a ceasefire and mutual withdrawal of troops twenty kilometers from the line of de facto control. The Indians, maintaining that this would leave Indian territory under Chinese control, spurned the offer and declared a state of emergency. The fighting turned into a general Chinese offensive in mid-November, with the Indians losing over twoscore posts in Ladakh and being pushed back in the NEFA to within thirty miles of the Assam plains. On November 19, Nehru appealed to the United States and Britain for military aid.

The position of the Soviet Union during the initial stages of this crisis was even more ambiguous than it had been in 1959. The Chinese later claimed to have notified the Soviet ambassador as early as October 8 of their "information" of an impending Indian attack and their "resolute" determination to defend themselves. Accompanying this message was the statement that the use of Soviet-made transport planes by India was "making a bad impression" on Chinese frontier guards. The same Chinese source goes on to note that Khrushchev informed the Chinese ambassador on October 13 and 14: "Their information on Indian preparations to attack China was similar to China's. If they were in China's position, they would have taken the same measures. A neutral attitude on the Sino-Indian boundary question was impossible. If anyone attacked China and they said they were neutral, it would be an act of betrayal." [22]

Thus made aware that trouble was imminent, Khrushchev's response was to seek to avoid renewed fighting by urging Nehru to negotiate the issue. A letter to that effect had been sent to the Indian on the very day of the Chinese assault. The Soviets, once they were faced with a fait accompli, sought to make the best of a bad situation. Thus on October 25, *Pravda* and *Izvestiia*, in their first mention of the new fighting, reprinted the Chinese statement charging India with aggression and proposing a cease-fire. A *Pravda* editorial the same day sided with China in opposing the "notorious" McMahon Line boundary in the NEFA, though placing the blame squarely on the "imperialists" rather than on India. Noting the "inviolable" Soviet friendship with China and the friendly Soviet relations with India—though voicing concern that "reactionary circles" and even some "progressive-minded people" had succumbed to chauvinism—the editorial endorsed the Chinese proposals as "constructive." An editorial in *Izvestiia* the next day stated that the USSR and other socialist countries could not "remain indifferent" to the situation and voiced the Soviet desire that "the difficulties generated by the colonial legacy be removed as quickly as possible." [23]

While still refusing to renounce hard-won gains by openly joining in the Chinese denunciation of India, the Soviets had strayed far from their studied neutrality of 1959 by reprinting only the Chinese version of the incident and endorsing Peking's proposals for a settlement. This apparent shift can be understood only in light of the radically different context in 1962. Far from the "spirit of Camp David" was the atmosphere in October 1962: the world had just been plunged into its first nuclear confrontation—the Cuban missile crisis. Khrushchev was later to express his anger at the Chinese for engaging in conflict with the Indians at this most sensitive moment for the socialist camp. But until he had weathered the Cuban confrontation, he could not risk provoking further disunity in the camp by siding against China, either directly or indirectly. The Soviets went so far as to announce on October 29 that the USSR supported Chinese territorial aims and would provide no arms to India. Temporary assurance that the Sino-Indian conflict would not escalate could be found in the fact that the United States was equally preoccupied with the Caribbean.

Only after the Soviets had (in Rusk's immortal phrase) "blinked" in the Cuban crisis, and that danger had passed, did the Soviet press resume comment on the Sino-Indian conflict. While the Soviet Ambassador to the United Nations, Zorin, had appealed to the Indians in the General Assembly as late as October 30 to accept the Chinese proposals for a ceasefire, a *Pravda* editorial on November 5, entitled "Negotiation Is the Way to Settle the Conflict," failed to mention either the Chinese proposals or the McMahon Line. Rather, it warned of the drain on Indian resources and the threat to her nonalignment which could result from continuation of the conflict, and it reminded the combatants that the imperialists "would like to warm their hands at the fire of the military operations" taking place on the border. "The Soviet people cannot remain indifferent when the blood of our brothers and friends—the Chinese and Indian peoples—is being shed. . . . The Soviet people are of the firm opinion that in existing situation the most important thing is to cease fire and open negotiations on peaceful settlement of the conflict." [24] Unlike the *Pravda* piece of October 25, this editorial—with its return to neutrality—went unreported in the Chinese press.

On November 6, Deputy Prime Minister Kosygin, speaking at the celebration of the anniversary of the Bolshevik Revolution, repeated the Soviet view that only the imperialists benefited from the Sino-Indian conflict and added that the Soviets were convinced "there are no fundamental divisions between them, no disagreements that could not be resolved around the negotiating table." [25] If this opinion came as a surprise to the Chinese—who had been emphasizing their "divisions" with Nehru throughout the year—even more unsettling must have been Nehru's announcement on November 10 that the Soviets had reversed themselves and had given assurances that they would not back out of their agreement to sell MIG-21's to India.

Within the next few days, the Chinese both intensified their invasion of India and launched an attack on Khrushchev's handling of the Cuban crisis.[26] But on November 21, having routed the Indian army and clearly demonstrated their ability to drive as far into the subcontinent as they wished, the Chinese announced a ceasefire and unilateral withdrawal to positions twenty kilometers behind the autumn 1959 lines of control.

The motivations behind this action can be understood only in the context of China's original objectives in the 1962 conflict, which did not include—as some in the West had feared—the actual conquest of India. The timing of the Chinese ceasefire is significant, for it came on the very eve of the arrival in India of the Harriman mission from the United States. The Chinese could thus claim to have exposed to the Afro-Asians the "sham" nature of Nehru's nonalignment, without actually running the risk of substantial Western involvement in the fighting. It had certainly been no secret to the Chinese that even if the United States had been invited by the Indians to conclude an actual alliance, American hands would have been tied by their involvement with India's other antagonist, Pakistan. Indeed, a joint US-UK effort to arrange the Pakistani government's assurances that it would not take advantage of Indian military difficulties and would work to settle the Kashmir dispute was subsequently torpedoed by Nehru's declaration to parliament that he had no intention of upsetting the "present arrangements" in Kashmir.

Not only Nehru's prestige but his ambitions to develop India's economy along a noncommunist path which would serve as a model to the "third world" seemed to have been wrecked. India's military posture had been exposed as extremely vulnerable. She could not avoid the diversion of a larger share of her resources to defense; expenditures in this area rose by three times in the period from 1959–1960 to 1963–1964. Even with the added expenditures, there could never again be confidence among the Indians or her neighbors that she would be able to defend her borders. Thus the Chinese could not but have been pleased to see Ceylon declare its neutrality in the dispute, Nasser to hesitate for a long period before endorsing India, and Ghana to condemn the British for their military assistance to Nehru. Even Pakistan hastened to reach, before the end of the year, an "agreement in principle" with the Chinese on the delimitation of their common border.

The vacillation of the Afro-Asian states was perhaps one of the many object lessons the Chinese had prepared for Khrushchev. The Soviet leader could certainly have derived little comfort from the whole experience. Though he had finally moved to salvage the fruits of his long cultivation of India by shifting to a neutral and ultimately pro-Indian stance, Khrushchev's initial vacillation on the Sino-Indian war had damaged his cause in the eyes of many Indians, while his subsequent change of position probably lost him the allegiance of many more in the communist movement. The first conclusion is borne out by a pair of public opinion polls conducted in India in the summer and fall of 1962 (immediately before and after the Sino-Indian war). In the period between the surveys, the number of respondents concluding that India should "cooperate very closely" with the Soviet Union fell from 43 percent to 16 percent, while those wishing cooperation with the United States and the United Kingdom rose, 49 percent to 58 percent and 26 percent to 36 percent, respectively. In November 1962, only 1 percent felt India should "side" with the USSR, while 36 percent felt she should align herself with the United States and the United Kingdom.[27]

The reaction among Indian politicians was more balanced, with a larger proportion of them declaring unwillingness for India to abandon her side of the long-nourished Soviet-Indian friendship. But there was an undeniable increase in the polarization of positions of the Indian political elite, with most of the change occurring not among those who had theretofore favored one side or the other, but among those devoted to nonalignment. The pressure on Nehru was so great that the controversial pro-Soviet Defense Minister Krishna Menon was first given a new position of Minister of Defense Production and only a few days later removed from the cabinet altogether.

Nehru himself, though profoundly shocked by the 1962 war, was by no means prepared to cast his "neutrality" to the winds. Even his request to the West for arms was preceded by his informing the Soviets of his intention. As Nehru later described their reactions to Harriman, "the Soviets had replied that they understood both the request and the need for it." Nor was the United States mission anxious for the Indians to abandon nonalignment; in Hilsman's words, it "seemed best for India, if at all possible, to continue to maintain its good relations with the Soviet Union." [28] The subsequent Chinese charge of United States–Soviet cooperation against China in the conflict with India was thus not completely without foundation.

The new Chinese assessment of Nehru's India represented a retreat to the inflexible theory of the Stalinist era and stood in stark contrast to the emerging Soviet assessment. The Chinese views, which have remained in force to the present time, were contained in a *People's Daily* editorial published on October 27, 1962, and entitled "More on Nehru's Philosophy in the Light of the Sino-Indian Boundary Question." [29] The conclusions in this article were much harsher than those drawn two years previously in the first Chinese discussion of "Nehru's philosophy." No longer was there an attempt to distinguish between Nehru and the Indian "big bourgeoisie," but rather the policies of the Prime Minister were now said to express the class interests of that stratum. "Nehru's philosophy" was centered around the goal of establishing "a great empire unprecedented in India's history," toward the furtherance of which goal he had become a "lackey of the imperialists." Internally, Nehru's policies were "antipeople." The "socialist pattern of society" was, in simplest terms, a "hoax."

Nehru's foreign policy, the Chinese held, had once been "helpful" to world peace, but even then it had been marked by a failure to oppose the major acts of imperialist aggression. But recently Nehru's policies had become openly proimperialist, as a result of which the United States had dropped its opposition to India's "sham" nonalignment. In such circumstances, Tito and "his ilk" (the Soviets were not yet being named directly in Chinese polemics) were exposing themselves as renegades by urging the Soviet Union to "stand by the bourgeois reactionaries and play a 'pacifying' role in relation to the invaded socialist country." Moreover, "some self-styled Marxist-Leninists, such as S. A. Dange" in the CPI had "trailed closely behind" Nehru in his adoption of an anti-Chinese strategy. Only those communists and progressives in India who urged "unflinching struggles" would be proved by history to "really represent the interests of the great Indian nation and people." [30] The Chinese message was clear: this was no time for currying Nehru's favor or engaging in false patriotism. Rather, the situation was ripe for all-out struggle against the "reactionary" Indian government from both within and without.

Chinese advocacy of such an extreme strategy could have

only confirmed the Soviets in their decision to dissociate themselves further from the Chinese actions. The next step in this
process, following the November 5 retreat to neutrality, came in
Khrushchev's December 12 speech to the Supreme Soviet. An
indication of what was to come in this speech might have been
gathered from the presence of Tito and Rankovic in the audience.

Though he stopped short of an open attack on China's actions,
Khrushchev's thinly veiled criticisms were not hard to deci-
pher. He began his survey of the "deplorable" Sino-Indian
clash with a reaffirmation of the TASS statement of 1959—a document which had already called forth displeasure from the
Chinese. Moreover, Khrushchev declared his belief that the territory over which the conflict had occurred was "virtually unin-
habited" and thus "apparently of no great value for the life of
man." As for the Soviet Union, it adhered to Leninist views on
the question of border disputes, that is, that there were no disputes of this nature which could not be settled without resort to
arms. The Sino-Indian war could have served the interests only
of imperialists and chauvinists.

While Khrushchev declared "sensible" the Chinese ceasefire
and withdrawal, he answered affirmatively the question,
"would it not have been better if the sides had not resorted to
hostilities at all?" Then, in what might be interpreted as a reply
to Chinese charges that the Soviets had been guilty of *both* "adventurism" and "capitulationism" in the Cuban crisis, he went
on to declare that there were people who were asking: was the
Chinese withdrawal "not a retreat?" Khrushchev's own answer
to this question was that those who said that China had ceased
hostilities because of the American and British support India
had begun to receive were evidently correct. Finally, Khrushchev made it clear that, though it would be "slander" to say that
China's aim had been the invasion of India, still "we likewise
absolutely do not accept the idea"—clearly put forward in
China's press—"that India wanted to start a war with China." [31]

Khrushchev did not, however, rest content with a rejection of
Chinese motives and explanations, but added—as if in answer
to China's charges that India had cast her lot with the imperialists—a gratuitous insult to China's unwillingness to clear the
vestiges of colonialism from her own soil.

One must be very careful not to cast irresponsible accusations,
such as . . . that some wage an offensive against imperialism

. . . while others allegedly show liberalism. . . . India, for example, achieved the liberation of Goa, Diu and Damao. These were vestiges of colonialism on Indian soil. . . . The aroma coming from [Macao and Hong Kong] is not a bit better than the smell from colonialism in Goa. But would anybody condemn [China]? . . . it is by no means because the Chinese take a less sharp attitude toward colonialism than the Indians that they show greater tolerance of Salazar than India does.[32]

Late in December a confidential memorandum was sent from the CCP to eleven other ruling parties; twenty-one pages of it were devoted to answering Khrushchev and defending the Chinese action against India. This document flatly accused the USSR of being "on the side of the imperialists" by joining the United States and the United Kingdom in supplying arms to India. According to a summary of the document, it declared that India "takes orders from Washington and London. Soviet aid to India is equivalent to direct military aid to India against China." [33]

The Soviet reply to this letter, also confidential, was equally frank. It charged that the Chinese had failed to inform the Soviets of their decision to invade "though the latter had many times willingly offered to mediate in this delicate question." The Soviets had supported the Chinese in their contention that the McMahon Line is "artificial," but "as was always emphasized in talks with China," there was no reason for provoking military operations "bound to throw India into the arms of the capitalists."

Soviet and Indian policies "have much in common," but the establishment of this state of cooperation and mutual trust "required many years of difficult negotiations and patience." China was aware of the Soviet Union's relationship with India, yet this "unfaithful ally" had "invaded" India and moreover "requested from the USSR aid in the invasion which it had itself provoked."

What else could the Soviets have done than to "beg" the Chinese to stop military operations and accept Soviet mediation, "for which India was ready"? But China failed to "leave aggression to the capitalists," and the Soviet hope of preventing India from being forced to turn to the West for military aid had been shattered. Moreover, "we lost one of our most faithful friends among the Indian leaders"—a clear reference to the purge of Krishna Menon. China herself was now negotiating

a pact of friendship with Pakistan, an "appendage of the capitalists." The Soviet complaint against China was succinctly
summed up in one sentence: "Thus years of hard striving for
Indian friendship and Indian neutrality went for nothing." [34]

Later, when the two parties were publicly detailing their
charges against each other and no longer relying on the Yugoslav and Albanian surrogates, some of the complaints at which
the Soviets had previously only hinted were made more explicit. Thus, for example, *Pravda* took the Chinese to task in
August 1963 for taking advantage of the critical moment of the
Caribbean crisis to achieve their "selfish purposes." *New Times*
in October charged that the border dispute "objectively hinders
the revolutionary process" in India and "helps the counter-
revolutionaries." Another article in the same month accused
China of utilizing the conflict to show the correctness of its
thesis on the necessity of pushing the revolutionary process
from without; the "depravity" of this line was said to have been
confirmed by the development of events.[35] Editorials in *Pravda*
in September 1963 and in *Kommunist* in April 1964 accused
China of departing from the general line "collectively worked
out" in 1957 and 1960 by disrupting the national-liberation
movement with her attack on India, by finding fault with the
doctrine of the "zone of peace" with the assertion that the
Nehru government sought to set up a huge empire, and by attempting to substitute a geographical and racialist approach for
the proletarian approach.[36]

In summary, the Chinese conflict with India was more than
simply a factor complicating the path taken by the Soviets in
their relations with India since 1955. It was in itself a major
issue in the Sino-Soviet dispute and helped to force the Soviets
to reappraise and articulate many of the premises of their general policy toward the "third world."

2. The Chinese Challenge to the Soviet Strategy toward the "Third World"

The assessment of the newly independent states which had
been worked out on the basis of Khrushchev's doctrine of the
"zone of peace"—as Chapter IV emphasized—was linked to the
degree of anti-imperialism manifested in the foreign policies of
these regimes. A foreign policy which was responsive to Soviet
influence, rather than the path of economic development cho-

sen or the degree of freedom of action allowed to local communist parties, had constituted the overriding criterion for judging
"progressiveness." Such an assessment had allowed great flexibility for Soviet foreign policy, but it had not offered much hope
for the imminent transition of any of these states to communism.
Khrushchev had reaffirmed the Leninist doctrine that working-
class leadership was a prerequisite for socialist transformation,
but the original optimism that Soviet aid to industrial development would strengthen the size and influence of the proletariat
in countries such as India and bring closer the peaceful establishment of people's democracy had proved illusory.

Communists in parties such as the CPI, seeing no evidence
that their support of "national bourgeois" governments had
brought them any closer to power, had grown increasingly frustrated over what seemed to be a self-paralyzing policy. The
other side of the coin was that even the nationalist leaders
whom the Soviets were courting could not feel overly comfort-
able with the Soviets and their minions when the declared communist goal was a "socialism" and "people's democracy" which
assigned the national bourgeoisie to at best a temporary purga-
tory.

By 1960 the new Soviet policy was in great need of renova-
tion. In most Afro-Asian countries, the struggle against overt
Western colonialism was easing. While these states could still
play a major role in supporting such anti-imperialist struggles as
the one in the Congo and in opposing other aspects of Western
foreign policy, the focus had largely shifted in Asia and Africa to
a concern with the future path of internal development. An assessment based chiefly on foreign policy criteria was becoming
more and more irrelevant to the new issues which faced local
communists.

Not surprisingly, it was the Chinese who took up the case
against the lack of ideological purity in the Soviet policy toward
the national bourgeoisie. As has been pointed out above, the
Chinese motivation was not simply an obsession for theoretical
rectitude; they were not at all pleased to see Soviet largesse
which could have been of assistance to their own faltering development program flowing into noncommunist (and especially
the rival Indian) development efforts.

The initial Soviet reaction to the Chinese challenge was to
defend the progressive potential of the national bourgeoisie. An
authoritative article by E. M. Zhukov in *Pravda* in August 1960

undertook to answer the "profoundly erroneous" views of un-named "petty bourgeois 'leftists' and hopeless dogmatists" who denied the historic importance of the formation of national states in Asia and Africa. Lenin had considered it natural, Zhu-kov reminded his antagonists, for the bourgeoisie to play the leading role in the first stage of the national-liberation move-ment. With the struggle against the remnants of feudalism still on the agenda in many of these states, it was possible for the workers, peasants, and intelligentsia to cooperate with the anti-imperialist bourgeoisie "over a long period" on the basis of the solution of "general national democratic tasks." While this did not mean that the question of noncapitalist development would everywhere be "postponed indefinitely," still it was necessary to guard against a "most dangerous form of sectarianism that leads to self-isolation." [37]

Unimpressed with this argument, the Chinese replied that it was the Soviet position which was anti-Leninist and led to iso-lationism: "If we view the movement led by the bourgeoisie in colonial lands as the mainstream of the national-liberation movement and do nothing else but clap our hands and give full support to it . . . then it will in fact mean the adoption of the bourgeois viewpoint and the violation of Lenin's views." [38]

Despite the harshness of the language employed in this de-bate, neither side had at this time concluded that the Sino-Soviet dispute was beyond the point of reconciliation. Accord-ingly, a meeting of leaders from eighty-one communist parties was convened in Moscow in November. On December 6 a statement was issued purporting to represent the common in-terpretation of the Marxist-Leninist position on the major issues of the day. The section of the Moscow statement concerning the national-liberation movement bore unmistakable signs of com-promise and even contradiction. Yet subsequent Soviet state-ments on this subject indicated that, unlike the Zhukov assess-ment of August, the Russians had indeed recognized the necessity of giving ideological justification for their continued support of the neutralist states not merely in terms of anti-im-perialism but in terms of assisting likely prospects for non-capitalist development.

The central feature of the new assessment was the concept of the state of "independent national democracy," which repre-sented an attempt, in a single doctrinal formula, to take account of a multiplicity of interests: the aspirations of local nationalist leaderships, the interests of local communist cadres, and, finally, Soviet foreign policy interests. The concept had the advantage for the Soviet policy-makers of being broad enough to justify either a hard- or a soft-line policy and of being flexible enough to serve either as a description of a current situation or as a goal to be attained.[39]

The statement, asserting that the "complete collapse of colonialism is imminent" thanks to the strengthening of the world socialist system, set forth a description of the "urgent tasks of national rebirth" facing the ex-colonial countries, the implementation of which required a determined anti-imperialist and antifeudal struggle waged by "all the patriotic forces of the nation united in a single national-democratic front." The basis of this front was the alliance of the working class and the peasantry; on the strength and stability of this alliance "in no small degree" depended the extent to which the national bourgeoisie participated. More than in Soviet statements of the preceding period, the national bourgeoisie was characterized as "inclined to compromise" and "unstable," though "objectively" it was interested in the solution of anti-imperialist and antifeudal tasks. But as social contradictions grew, the national bourgeoisie was more and more inclined to seek agreement with reactionary forces. Thus the workers and peasants must play the "leading part" in solving the problem of noncapitalist development, which was "the best way to abolish age-long backwardness." As for local communist parties, they supported anti-imperialist actions of national governments while firmly opposing antidemocratic actions and those which endangered national independence, and they exposed the "demagogic use by bourgeois politicians of socialist slogans."

Finally, the statement affirmed that in many countries conditions were arising favorable to the establishment of an "independent national democracy," defined as

. . . a state which consistently upholds its political and economic independence, fights against imperialism and its military blocs, against military bases on its territory; a state which fights against the new forms of colonialism and the penetration of imperialist capital; a state which rejects dictatorial and despotic methods of government; a state in which the people are ensured broad democratic rights and freedom . . . the opportunity to work for the enactment of an agrarian reform and other domestic and social changes, and for participation in shaping government policy.[40]

In short, a national democratic state, in addition to following a pro-Soviet foreign policy, must allow sufficient "participation" by the working class (that is, by the communist party) for it to exert pressure on the domestic policies of the ruling groups. There was, however, no insistence that such "representatives of the masses" actually hold power, but only that they play a "leading part" in implementing the noncapitalist path. In effect this supplied a new intermediate objective, a seemingly more attainable goal than "people's democracy." [41] It constituted a way station on the road to socialism, which guaranteed both the working classes and the bourgeoisie an active role.

The postconference statements of the Soviets and Chinese showed the existence of continuing disagreement on the new concept. Khrushchev's January 6 report on the conference not unexpectedly emphasized flexibility. He called for maximum utilization of the revolutionary possibilities of "all allies, no matter if inconsistent, shaky and unstable" in the anti-imperialist struggle. While urging that "special note" be taken of the national democracy concept, he likewise pointed to the necessity of taking cognizance of national peculiarities and declared that "a variety of ways of solving the task of social progress is bound to emerge." [42] The Chinese, for their part, simply refused to mention the "national democratic state," evidently considering it unsatisfactory as a proletarian objective.

Soviet statements concerning national democracy in the course of 1961 displayed more caution than Khrushchev's January speech might have led an observer to expect. Not untypical in its tone was an article appearing in *Kommunist* in May and written by Boris Ponomarev, then a member of the Central Committee apparatus concerned with nonbloc communist parties (and subsequently in 1961 elevated to a secretaryship). Ponomarev put special stress on the contradictory nature of the policies of bourgeois politicians, and especially on the limitations inherent in state capitalism. National democratic states, he indicated, would not simply arise from the "growing over" of national bourgeois regimes but would be created "only through the struggle of the masses." Nor was a national democracy, once created, to be considered "socialist." Rather it made possible the break from the world capitalist system and the entry onto the road toward the noncapitalist path. For the achievement of socialism itself, "revolutionary changes in one form or another" were required. Finally, while denying that the concept was the "fruit of ivory-tower meditations," Ponomarev warned against the temptation to make the concept more concrete by "lining up states and assigning them to categories." [43]

This relative Soviet caution in the assessment of the Afro-Asian states was also reflected in the Twenty-second Party Congress and the program of the CPSU which it adopted. According to the program, the national bourgeoisie, its progressive role not yet exhausted, was increasingly inclined to compromise with imperialism and domestic reactionaries. The working class was the most consistent fighter in the national liberation movement, and its alliance with the peasantry was the "nucleus" of the broad national front. The goal of local communist parties was the establishment of national democracies and the beginning of noncapitalist development. This task was not easy, however; these parties were being persecuted by reactionary circles (Khrushchev cited the Pakistani regime as an example in his speech to the party congress) who sought to disrupt the national front.[44]

In essence, this formulation represented the 1956 "zone of peace" concept tempered with a decreased optimism about the national bourgeoisie and supplemented by the new middle-level objective of national democracy, with its greater focus on domestic problems. Simply stated, the difficulty with this assessment, for all its built-in flexibility, was that it remained wedded to a class analysis which had become increasingly artificial in its applicability to an ever more variegated "third world." There was difficulty enough (as we have seen) in applying the class analysis of feudalism-capitalism-socialism to *relatively* developed countries such as India, which did indeed have an identifiable (though proportionately small) bourgeoisie and proletariat. But the early 1960's were the years of African statehood, and the communists (as well as noncommunists) found themselves confronted with cultures they little understood and socioeconomic structures which defied analysis in terms derived from the European experience. In countries such as Guinea there simply was no "national bourgeoisie," "feudal" exploitation in agriculture, or viable "proletariat."

Moreover, revolutionary nationalism in Africa was primarily a movement of the intelligentsia. But Marxist-Leninist analysts portrayed this group not as a class but as a free-floating stratum, and they had thus concluded that it could be of no great consequence. Chained to their traditional categories, Soviet theorists in the early 1960's were thus unable to admit that class interests as such had not been decisive in the policies of such leaders as

Nkrumah, Touré, and Lumumba. Moreover, this fundamental defect in the Soviet assessment of such non-Western social forces was to be reinforced by certain manifestations of instability in "third world" politics which have tended to puzzle both East and West.

To summarize the point, the concept of "national democracy" with its insistence on a "leading role" for the working class and freedom for the local communists, while it might have been credible in the more advanced new states, seemed to condemn those states largely devoid of both proletariat and national bourgeoisie to a sort of limbo. In the assessment of India and her prospects for socialism this problem did not cause as much difficulty as in the African and Middle Eastern countries. Yet it is of interest to survey the manner in which Soviet scholars and officials dealt with the problem, for in the process they sought to sharpen some of the analytical tools which were used by Soviet Indologists as well.

A directive encouraging Soviet scholars to research some of the problems appeared in March 1962 in the journal of the Academy's Institute of World Economics and International Relations.[45] This institute, until 1956 a section of the Economics Institute of the Academy, devoted itself to theoretical economic and political research on the noncommunist countries and was to take the lead in the creative reappraisal of the mid-1960's. In contrast to a research directive appearing earlier in the journal of the more established Oriental Studies Institute (renamed Institute of the Peoples of Asia in 1961), which called the investigation of the "national democracy" concept the most important problem,[46] the March 1962 directive called on researchers to reveal "the inevitability, *under certain circumstances,* of the development of the national democratic state." More emphasis was placed on the complete elimination of "deadening schemata, dogmatic cachets and labels inherited from the days of the Stalinist personality cult," in the study of such problems as the character of industrialization, the acceleration of the speed of economic development, and radical solution of the agrarian question. Most interesting was the call for "profound study of the rather complex devetailing of class relations" in the newly liberated states.

a. Soviet Discovery of "Third World" Diversity

The result of the "profound study" by Soviet scholars was the discovery of a surprisingly large variety of "intermediate strata" between the national bourgeoisie and the proletariat and of an equally large number of possible forms in which the newly independent states could make the transition to noncapitalist development. Having in effect given the researchers free rein to experiment with refining Marxist categories to fit contemporary conditions, Soviet policy-makers were rewarded with an assessment so flexible that it justified almost any course of action with respect to the nationalist regimes which the political leaders saw fit to adopt.

An early example of the new trend in Soviet analysis was a report delivered by R. M. Avakov and G. I. Mirsky to a conference sponsored by the Institute of World Economics and International Relations in the spring of 1962. This paper, "The Class Structure in Underdeveloped Countries," began with the argument that in the countries of the "third world" the process of class formation was not yet completed and that, in contrast to the social structures of highly developed capitalist countries, "extreme heterogeneity, many social strata, and fluidity of class composition" characterized the underdeveloped countries.[47] To prove the point, Avakov and Mirsky proceeded to distinguish the following "basic classes": (a) two strata of the proletariat (neither "pure" in the Western sense); (b) six strata of the peasantry; (c) five strata of bourgeoisie classified according to the branch of the economy in which capital was invested, as well as three additional strata designated according to the scale of holdings and two more groups classified according to their attitude toward foreign capital; (d) the intelligentsia (including the officer class), which could be divided according to whether it supported the interests of the workers or of the national bourgeoisie; (e) the feudalists, including the "fairly widespread . . . 'bourgeoisified' feudalists."

This, however, was just the beginning, said Avakov and Mirsky, for the analyst must also differentiate at least six groups of countries: (1) those relatively highly developed in capitalist relations and in which the national bourgeoisie held power (India); (2) those which were less developed and in which the national bourgeoisie might share power with feudalists who support nonalignment and economic independence (Iraq); (3) those which were "formally" independent and in which the proimperialist bourgeoisie held power (Pakistan); (4) a special group (Ghana, Guinea, Mali, and perhaps Indonesia) in which capitalist relationships were rudimentary, a national bourgeoisie was virtually absent, and a proletarian class was only "evolving," but in which ever-increasing weight was being acquired by forces favoring noncapitalist development; (5) most other countries of sub-Saharan Africa, sharing many objective features with the states in the above group, but still dependent on imperialism; (6) those states exceptionally weak in capitalist development, but ruled by a feudal class which was "for reasons of a historical and international nature" neutralist in its foreign policy (Afghanistan).

Avakov and Mirsky freely admitted that this formidable list of classifications was "arbitrary." And if they themselves could not decide in what category to place such states as the UAR, then it is not surprising that their colleagues found fault not only with the placement of particular countries, but with the criteria by which the groups had been defined as well. But as Ponomarev had pointed out, it was not for the Soviet scholars to assign states to categories. That, he had concluded in the 1961 article, was a matter for the peoples themselves to decide.[48] Rather, the benefit to be derived from such an exercise in classification as Avakov's and Mirsky's was the suggestion of a larger number of ways by which *any* state, no matter how backward, could be said to be moving toward socialism.

b. Alternative Paths to Socialism

Thus, for example, the total absence of a working class and communist parties need be no obstacle to the development of African states toward national democracy. At least three alternative ways were said to exist: nonproletarian leaders might adopt working class viewpoints; a strong, progressive (but noncommunist) single party might be able to lead the state on the path of noncapitalist development; or, in the absence of these alternatives, the proletariat of the "advanced countries" might be able to lead the local peasantry to "national democracy."

Concerning the first alternative, V. L. Tiagunenko wrote as early as March 1962 that in countries such as Ghana, Guinea, and Mali, which had already taken "a step to the creation of conditions for transition to the noncapitalist road of development," the possibility had become real "that the most farsighted representatives of the radical petty bourgeoisie in the course of a genuinely popular revolution can go over to the position of the working class and join the ranks of active fighters for the socialist reconstruction of society." [49] Mirsky in a 1963 article described the leaders of Ghana, Guinea, Mali, and the UAR as representatives of the "progressive intelligentsia and revolutionary democrats" and suggested that if they "leaned on the masses" and utilized the aid of the socialist camp, they could develop the national democratic revolutions in their countries.[50] The conclusion of A. Sobolev, published in *World Marxist Review* at the same time, was similar: "If a revolutionary democrat or a member of the national bourgeoisie is willing to take one step forward, it is the duty of the Marxists to help him take two. . . . National democracy can be established under the leadership of any democratic class." [51]

The second alternative had been manifested as early as the Twenty-second Party Congress, when precedent had been broken to admit to the proceedings representatives of the ruling parties of Ghana, Guinea, and Mali. Less than a year later, G. B. Starushenko wrote in *Kommunist:* "The general democratic program is being successfully carried out in young African states led by mass democratic parties, such as in Mali and Guinea." Individual communists or sympathizers in such countries, according to another scholar, should support such "progressive" ruling parties, at the same time seeking to "work inside . . . in order to isolate Right-wing elements . . . and gradually win leadership." [52]

But if a state lacked both a progressive single party and acceptable individual leaders, and if the proletariat was also non-existent or small, did this mean there was no hope for its revolutionary advancement and that Soviet aid should not be given to it? On the contrary, in such a case it remained for the working class of the "advanced countries" to provide leadership to the peasant mass. This theory, embellished with the example of Soviet aid to Mongolia, has already been encountered in Chapter II. But, while Prager had stipulated in 1930 that only countries contiguous to the Soviet Union could hope to receive this assistance, the existence of the powerful world socialist system was said in 1964 to make this limitation no longer necessary.[53]

Nor did Soviet scholars rest content with devising alternative methods by which the transition to national democracy could be achieved in the absence of local proletarian leadership. Pointing to the example of the Cuban revolution, G. B. Starushenko suggested in *Kommunist* in 1962 that neither proletarian leadership nor the direction of the communist party was an inviolable prerequisite for socialist transformation. If such a transition is based on class struggle in the welfare of the people and is conducted in conditions of expanded ties with the socialist camp, then the "experience of history shows that *national leaders of revolutionary inclination* can implement a general democratic program and lead their countries to socialism." [54]

Somewhat later, Mirsky, admitting that proletarian leadership of the socialist revolution was "best," chided the "dogmatists" for believing that in the absence of such leadership the revolution must wait. Rather, Mirsky said, the only "subjective" prerequisite was "a political leadership that accepts socialism." Given the support of the socialist camp, performing the function of proletarian vanguard, "elements close to the working class" can take up the historical mission of revolutionary leadership. "Nature abhors a vacuum." [55] It will be recalled that a similar notion, advanced by M. Rubinshtein in 1955, had so aroused the ire of local communists (including the CPI) that it had quickly been disavowed by higher Soviet officials. This time, however, the utility of the idea was found to outweigh its unorthodoxy.

c. Emphasis on Transitional Stages

Far more typical than statements such as Mirsky's, however, were writings which de-emphasized the goal of socialism and concentrated instead on the intermediate stages. Most Soviet analysts seemed to imply that once a country had achieved the beginning stages of the "noncapitalist path," there was no need to hurry toward socialist transformation itself. Starushenko, despite his willingness to mention the possibility of rapid transformation to socialism, placed far more emphasis on gradual and peaceful transition. Warning against "groundless infatuation with socialist slogans," he declared that "neglecting the general democratic tasks and spurting forward will narrow the mass base of the socialist revolution and compromise the noble idea of socialism in the eyes of the peoples." [56] In a similar vein, Tiagunenko warned against premature narrowing of the united general-democratic front by such measures as exclusion of the national bourgeoisie before its revolutionary potential had been exhausted. Quoting from Stalin's 1925 speech to the KUTV, he declared: "Life has shown the mistakenness of the Stalinist position that the national front must be created 'against the bloc of the compromising national bouregoisie and imperialism.' " Neither unity "against" the bourgeoisie nor "around" the bourgeoisie, but "unity with the possibility of participation of the bourgeoisie" was the present-day task.[57]

Even nationalization of foreign-owned enterprises and the exclusion of domestic private capitalist development would require a long period of preparation. In the first stages of the noncapitalist path revolutionary forces must avoid the alienation of the peasantry; the "expedient" course was to satisfy peasant land-hunger in preference to nationalizing all the land. Tiagunenko was quite explicit about his reasons for giving such advice: he feared that premature nationalization would place too much of the burden of developing the material base of socialism onto the socialist camp. Countries of Asia, Africa, and Latin America "cannot count on the socialist states to guarantee all the capital requirements, equipment and technical aid," but would need to satisfy part of these requirements by accepting imperialist aid—something a country which had prematurely declared socialist transformation (Cuba?) would not likely receive.[58]

Two years after it had opened the discussion, the editorial board of *Mirovaia ekonomika i mezhdunarodnye otnosheniia* sponsored another exchange of views among historians, economists, and journalists.[59] Summing up the discussion, Tiagunenko prefaced his remarks with the statement: "It is particularly gratifying to note that the conclusions and assessments which until quite recently were shared by a comparatively small circle of people have now begun to be shared by many." Experience had refuted the "schematic attitudes" of only four or five years ago, he said. Among the views now held to be discredited he listed the following: that the national bourgeoisie was in power in most former colonies; that these countries were ripe for an accelerated development of capitalism and that only working class leadership could advance the revolution further; that there were no intermediate stages in the development of the national democratic revolution; and that this struggle could not proceed under nonproletarian leadership.[60]

Tiagunenko emphasized that a direct transition to socialism was impossible in most countries. But this should not be allowed to paralyze the revolutionary parties or to imply the abandonment of the country to capitalist development. It was clear from his remarks that Soviet scholars were aware that the very notion of intermediate stages of the revolution proceeding under direction of a broad united front had provided both new justification for Soviet support of the development efforts of noncommunist states and new middle-level objectives toward which local communist parties (where they existed) could strive.

d. The New Assessment in Action

Nor had these contributions of the recent scholarly reappraisal escaped the attention of Soviet policy-makers. An important editorial in *Pravda* in December 1963 had acknowledged that certain features of noncapitalist development recognized by the 1960 Moscow Statement only as "tendencies" had since developed rapidly, demanding profound theoretical interpretation. In particular, *Pravda* pointed to those "national" varieties of socialist doctrine which had previously been condemned for combining "religious, petty-bourgeois or utopian" ideas with "scientific" notions, and which were now recognized as playing a "positive" role "when they serve as a foundation for carrying out anti-imperialist, revolutionary-democratic and anticapitalist undertakings. Supporting everything that directly or indirectly serves the cause of social progress, Marxist-Leninists are actively propagandizing the ideas of scientific socialism." [61] And in the same month Khrushchev himself, stressing that "there is no universal recipe suitable for all countries," endorsed measures taken by "revolutionary-democratic statesmen . . . [who] declare their determination to build socialism." [62]

Khrushchev set out to implement these notions in the spring of 1964. The Algerian National Liberation Front (FLN), once considered a "national bourgeois" party, was hailed as a "fraternal" party, and "Comrade" Ben Bella was awarded the "Hero of the Soviet Union" medal. On his May 1964 visit to Egypt, Khrushchev bestowed this same award on Nasser and Amer, again hailing them as "comrades" and declaring that the UAR was "embarking on the path of socialist construction." Such comments were not at all pleasing to the much-persecuted Arab communists; the Syrian party leader Khaled Bagdash even declared in July 1964: "the possibility of a restoration of capitalism is not excluded in Egypt." [63] Nor were all of Khrushchev's colleagues, and especially those in charge of dealings with nonbloc parties, prepared to accept the flamboyance with which he embraced nationalist leaders. Among the charges Suslov is reported to have made against Khrushchev in October 1964 was his failure to consult the Presidium on such matters as his journeys to underdeveloped countries, the expensive presents he was wont to bestow during these trips, and his decision to award to the Arab leaders the "Hero" medal which, according to Suslov, "may under no circumstances be awarded to any non-communist leaders." [64]

There is ample evidence, however, that the post-Khrushchev leadership has decided to curb only the flamboyance of the approach to "revolutionary-democratic" forces in the developing countries. Suslov himself, in his February 1964 speech to the Central Committee, had virtually equated the "non-capitalist" and "socialist" paths and had declared that nationalist leaders of many countries were supporting a "transition to the path of socialism" and taking "practical measures" in this direction.[65]

Moreover, the unorthodox theories worked out by such scholars as Mirsky and Tiagunenko from 1962 to 1964 and endorsed by Khrushchev were reaffirmed many times in the months following Khrushchev's ouster. Thus, for example, F. Burlatsky wrote in *Pravda* in August 1965: "Communists and the working class have supported and continue to support all progressive social forces sincerely striving for socialism." [66] While communists would not merge with such groups and would continue to conduct a "principled and at the same time flexible approach" in the interests of introducing true scientific socialism, they considered it "sectarian" to reject cooperation with adherents of non-Marxist "socialisms." As Mirsky put it the following year: "Non-proletarian socialist trends and scientific socialism are not separated by an insurmountable wall." [67]

Even more authoritative was an article in *Kommunist* by Ul'ianovsky (who had become deputy chief of the Central Committee's International Department). Urging a "solid alliance" between communists and social forces "leaning toward socialism," Ul'ianovsky reaffirmed the possibility of a gradual transition from the "general democratic" to the socialist stage of a revolution, beginning without a national proletarian dictatorship or even an organized Marxist-Leninist party. Ul'ianovsky went on, however, to stress that as the struggle developed further, some form of "vanguard party"—as a nucleus of a left-wing bloc in which Marxist-Leninists play the role of "friend and assistant"—would have to be created. And he expressed confidence that "in the final analysis" left-wing and other affiliated national-democrats would be won over to Marxism-Leninism.[68]

Another indication of continued optimism concerning these "progressive" regimes in the months following Khrushchev's ouster can be found in the Central Committee's May Day and Anniversary slogans. The 1965 Anniversary slogans reversed the previous practice of listing the "progressive" Arab and African states below such "capitalist-path" states as India. Another innovation was in the assessments given of these states' policies: the UAR was said to be "building an independent, national, democratic state" and struggling for socialist development; Algeria was "building an independent national state" and struggling for "social progress"; Burma's people were "struggling for an independent, democratic state" and social progress; the peoples of Ghana, Guinea, the Congo (Brazzaville), and Mali were "building independent, national, democratic states" and struggling for social progress.[69] Thus it was authoritatively confirmed that several third-world regimes were deemed to qualify as "national democracies," with one even said to be fighting for "socialist development."

e. Sino-Soviet Polemics on "Third-World" Strategy

It should come as no surprise that the Chinese have vigorously attacked the new Soviet assessment. Rejecting the notions both of "national democracy" and of a peaceful and gradual transition to socialism led by "revolutionary democrats" following a noncapitalist path, the Chinese have in the strongest terms accused the Soviet Union of betraying the national-liberation movement. The Soviets have replied with a counterattack against the Chinese theory that the "third world" has become the "storm center" of world revolution. Such a position, say the Soviets, is utilized by the Chinese to alienate the national-liberation movement from the world socialist system and to attempt to substitute a geographically and racially based alliance. Thus it has become obligatory for every Soviet assessment of revolutionary prospects in the underdeveloped countries to include an affirmation of the necessity of moral and material assistance from the socialist camp as a prerequisite for victory.

The Soviets have displayed special sensitivity to the Chinese charges that they are devoting insufficient resources to the liberation movement and that theories of peaceful coexistence and peaceful transition to socialism are reflections of a "bourgeois" preoccupation with building the material wealth of the Soviet Union. The Soviet reply has been that the fulfillment of their own economic plans by socialist countries assists the developing countries by making possible "mutually advantageous" trade and aid, as well as by both preventing the imperialists from imposing their own trade terms and pressuring them to increase their own aid.[70] The very existence of a strong and wealthy Soviet Union is said both to deter the imperialists from imposing their will on the newly independent states and to provide an inspiring example for those states to emulate. Ponomarev has expressed this point by offering a strange new definition of "internationalism" as the efforts by the USSR to attain the "peaks of communism," thus increasing the possibility of curbing imperialism and helping Soviet allies.[71]

Peaceful coexistence, by facilitating Soviet progress toward communism, thus assists the liberation struggle. On the other hand, the Chinese preference for armed struggle, as manifested in the conflict with India, had actually harmed the national-liberation movement. According to the deputy chief editor of *Pravda* in July 1963:

Neither Marx nor Engels nor Lenin ever thought of armed uprising as a form of struggle that must always be employed under all conditions . . . An atmosphere of war hysteria makes it easier for the forces of reaction . . . In India, reactionary circles are attempting to make use of the . . . [border] conflict . . . to organize a campaign against all progressive forces. . . . On the other hand, a slackening of tension and successes of the policy of peaceful coexistence are accompanied by an intensification of the workers' movement.[72]

In addition to facilitating the anticommunist hysteria provoked by domestic reaction, Chinese adventurism had in some cases encouraged nationalist leaders to "disregard laws of economic development" and to embark on "pseudorevolutionary utopianism." The result of such a rejection of coexistence and "reliance on their own forces" was that these leaders had bankrupted their countries and discredited the idea of socialism.[73]

This emphasis on peaceful coexistence and the possibility of peaceful transition to socialism, as well as the accompanying stress on the Soviet contribution to the liberation movement, was subsequently reaffirmed by the post-Khrushchev leadership. In one of the most forceful statements of this point of view, a *Pravda* editorial of October 1965 argued that the forcible implementation of one country's will upon another not only was alien to Marxism-Leninism, but (worse yet) could lead to thermonuclear war. The peoples of the socialist countries should concentrate their main efforts on the building of socialism and communism in their own countries, for this was their chief contribution to and the decisive precondition for development of the liberation movement.[74]

3. The Soviet Assessment of India

In general the Soviets were able, as a result of the reassessment of social forces in the underdeveloped countries, to discover new "progressive" strata and new way-stations on the road to socialism which could allow them to justify their support of certain nationalist leaders on grounds more doctrinally acceptable than simple diplomatic expediency. But on a more specific level, their findings with respect to India were not so encouraging. For unlike the leaders of some of the African and Arab countries and unlike the regimes of Burma and Indonesia, the Indian political elite could not conceivably qualify as "revolutionary democrats," nor could their domestic economic and social policies be characterized as leading to the "noncapitalist path" of development. Nor, in the presence of a genuine proletariat and a long-suffering communist party, could direct support to the Congress party be justified as a revolutionary alternative.

Thus, that the Soviets nonetheless continued to give aid and support to the "bourgeois" Congress regime in India was testimony to the continued preeminence of the foreign policy criterion in determining Soviet policy toward India. It evidenced as well both the increasing Soviet fear of Chinese hegemony in Asia and Moscow's calculation that a less forthcoming policy might well have opened India to greater Western influence.

a. Soviet Perceptions of India's Internal Politics

In the 1962 article by Avakov and Mirsky which had discerned so many gradations of intermediate strata into which leaders formerly classified as "national bourgeois" could be placed, there had been no attempt to rescue the Indian government from its previous niche. The Indian bourgeoisie, distinguished by a large "monopolist" upper stratum and by "intricate links" to foreign capital, was said to possess "incomparably" more opportunities to influence its government than did the Egyptian or Indonesian bourgeoisie. The most favorable feature that Avakov and Mirsky could perceive in the class orientation of the Indian government was that it "has to consider the interests not only of the bourgeoisie but also of other classes." [75] Mirsky appeared to be even less optimistic a year later when he declared that Togliatti had been correct in noting (at the Italian party congress) that there had recently been a "shift to the right" on the part of the Indian national bourgeoisie. [76]

Articles by Soviet Indologists early in 1964 pointed to "deep-going" contradictions among the various strata of the Indian bourgeoisie, which had been reflected both in the continued vacillations of Congress party policies and in the emergence on the Congress' right flank of the "proimperialist" Swatantra party. [77] The death of Nehru in May 1964 (he was eulogized by Khrushchev as "an outstanding statesman of our time, the close and sincere friend of the Soviet Union") [78] was soon to be lamented by the Soviets as more than the loss of a friend. It was viewed as well as an event whose result was the further strengthening of Indian reaction. Although the domestic policies of the Nehru regime had been condemned shortly after his death for having allowed the fruits of India's progress to be enjoyed chiefly by the rich while real wages had remained stagnant and unemployment had increased, they were appraised more favorably by the Soviets in further retrospect. An article appearing in August 1965 found no comfort in the disorganized state of the post-Nehru Congress party but asked, almost plaintively, how long the Congress could maintain influence "unless tangible steps are taken to realize [its] promises?" Nehru's achievements in the field of socioeconomic reform, the article recalled, had been "substantial," but his successors were finding themselves thwarted by the reactionaries. [79]

The Indian right, according to Soviet estimates, was growing stronger both politically and economically. Whether the Indian state sector would continue to play a progressive role or would develop in the direction of state-monopoly capitalism was an open question whose resolution depended upon the outcome of the struggle within the Indian bourgeoisie. [80]

b. Economic and Social Phenomena

Soviet economists studying the Indian agrarian situation perceived a similar growth in class differentiation. In contrast to the earlier uncertainty concerning the degree of capitalist development in Indian agriculture, a report published by the staff of the Institute of the Peoples of Asia in 1965 was firm in its conclusion that the strengthening of rural capitalism had furthered the class contradictions between the rich and poor peasants. Moreover, it was recognized that this phenomenon made more difficult the organization and maintenance of a united front among the peasantry. While the "objective basis" of any united front was the struggle against imperialism and feudalism, the struggle of the peasant masses was becoming more and more a struggle against bourgeois elements—something the Soviets were not yet prepared to sanction.[81]

One interesting change in the Soviet assessment was the conclusion reached by some economists in the mid-1960's that the overpopulation problem was no longer to be considered a "bugaboo." To the assertion by V. Chevrakov that "birth control cannot solve social problems" and that the "people of the third millennium, living under world communism," would find a solution to the population problem, Boris Urlanis replied that the problem could not be so easily dismissed. Industrialization would eventually lead to a reduction in the birth rate, he argued, but many countries required an immediate solution to the problem and needed a "demographic policy." [82] While much had changed since the previous decade, when the Soviets had universally regarded planned parenthood as "fiendish racism," still Soviet economists were agreed on the principle that no form of birth control could be made to work unless accompanied by "radical" socioeconomic transformations.

A less sharp but extremely significant evolution has been evident in the Soviet assessment of the role of Gandhism in Indian society. It will be recalled that the truly dramatic shift in the Soviet perception of Gandhi's role had come in 1956, when D'iakov and Reisner had disavowed the Stalinist notion that Gandhi had been a traitor to the Indian national-liberation movement, peddling pernicious ideas totally lacking redeeming virtues. Not quite a decade later there appeared in *Voprosy filosofii* (Problems of philosophy) a new, more sophisticated analysis by O. V. Martyshin suggesting a further evolution of Soviet thought on this matter.

What is new and significant in Martyshin's analysis is his attempt to show that the claims of the Indian national bourgeoisie to be following Gandhi's teachings were baseless. Gandhism had served its purposes in allowing the bourgeoisie to attract the masses and subordinate them to its leadership in the struggle against the British; after 1947 it became an embarrassment and even a danger.

For Gandhism contained elements which were not "narrowly bourgeois" but were "all-national" in content, and these entered into conflict with the exploiters. In particular, his "sociological concepts" contained a revolutionary potential which had not yet been exhausted; Indian communists, for example, utilized some of these concepts and methods in their agitation among the masses.

Thus, Martyshin was saying, to label Gandhism as the ideology of the Indian bourgeoisie was in effect to forfeit complete control of this doctrine to the most reactionary circles of that class. But to take note of the petty-bourgeois utopian elements of Gandhi's thought, to demonstrate that they were an expression of social protest, and to show that bourgeois practices had little in common with Gandhi's teaching was to prevent the bourgeoisie from using the name of Gandhi, "sacred to millions of Indians," for its own political interests. In short, then, Martyshin was urging his fellow Indologists as well as the Indian communists to make positive use of this link to the Indian masses, to "justify the demands of the working people from the standpoint of Gandhism." [83]

Though the Soviets could make an argument in favor of utilizing Gandhism in order to take advantage of its popularity among the masses, there was in India another type of movement with widespread mass support which Soviet analysts continued to condemn. This was the agitation among various ethnic, linguistic, and religious groups for autonomy within or even separation from the Indian republic, an agitation which continued to gather steam during the 1950's and 1960's. The veteran Indologist A. M. D'iakov addressed himself to this issue in a 1963 book on the nationality question.[84] In many respects, the work is a reaffirmation of D'iakov's earlier views concerning the origin and nature of the "multinational" Indian state, but some of his observations concerning issues vital to contemporary Indian politics bear noting. For D'iakov himself views the problems confronting India as "typical" of the third world and presents his analysis of the nationality question in India as one which "can greatly contribute to the understanding of the national development of newly liberated states in the future."

D'iakov's theme is one which the Soviets had stressed since the early 1950's: separatist movements are a grave danger to the consolidation of political unity in India and are likely to be exploited by the imperialists as they attempt to "dismember" and "subjugate anew" the newly independent states of Asia and Africa. Nowhere is there the slightest indication that D'iakov perceives an advantage to be gained by the Soviet Union from these separatist movements; rather, his overriding concern is the preservation of India's unity and stability.

But the way to deal with this secessionist threat is not to impose a common language and culture on minority groups, for this only aggravates the internal strife. D'iakov in effect counsels India's government to follow a cautious and conciliatory policy, aiming toward the removal of all traces of "national oppression" and granting to national regions the right and opportunity to develop their economies and cultures. However, he reaffirms his conviction that the problem cannot be finally solved under a bourgeois regime. A "consistent democratic national policy" cannot be implemented while "capitalist relations prevail, because the more powerful groups of the bourgeoisie try to dominate over the weaker ones, which often leads to the rise of separatism and the weakening of the state." Only a radical transformation which puts an end to the political monopoly of the bourgeoisie can ensure a "stable multinational state."

c. Prospects for Socialist Development

That such radical changes could soon be effected by the Indian proletariat was placed in doubt by the conclusions of a thorough and relatively sophisticated study of the Indian working class published in 1963 by L. A. Gordon and L. A. Fridman.[85] They began with the argument that the overwhelming majority of the working class in countries such as India was "semiproletarian." Neither workers in handicraft industry, nor agricultural workers, nor workers in the service industries were true proletarians in their economic position or class outlook. The actual industrial proletariat in India was not only comparatively small, but was itself strongly influenced by petty-bourgeois notions. Moreover, the development of state capitalism was in at least one respect harmful to future prospects for

Indian political development, for it tended to blur the conflict of interests between labor and capital. These peculiarities of the Indian scene made the organization and political education of the working class extremely difficult, though not totally impossible. But such a discouraging picture of the Indian proletariat could only confirm the Soviet conviction that socialist revolution in India was not at hand.

Of course, the weakness of the proletariat in other underdeveloped countries had not been an impassable barrier to the conclusion that socialist transformation was possible in those states, given a "revolutionary" leadership which believed in "socialism." But in such cases the Soviets had in effect been arguing that the *farther* a country was from capitalist development and bourgeois rule, the *more likely* were its chances for the achievement of socialism through noncapitalist development. Soviet denials to the contrary, such a theory was an utter reversal of Marx's theories—but it had found substantial confirmation in the history of communist revolutions.

With respect to India, however, this theory could not, even in the hands of "creative Marxist-Leninists," be made to fit the facts. State power in India was firmly in the hands of groups which by Soviet standards could not be called "revolutionary democrats" or "radical intelligentsia," nor were such "intermediate strata" found to be waiting in the wings. Capitalism was admitted by Soviet Indologists to be the "leading" if not the "dominant" mode of production, and the Indian bourgeoisie, very much in evidence, was among the strongest in the "third world." [86]

It must be recognized that over the past three decades and more of Indian history the weakness of the working class had not served as an obstacle to the proclamation that proletarian power (either "soviet" or in "people's democracy" form) was the direct objective of Indian communists. But as numerous examples given in this study have confirmed, the Soviets had always in the past, at least in their public pronouncements, deluded themselves as to the actual strength of the Indian proletariat. In the middle 1960's this fiction was no longer necessary, for the concept of "national democracy" provided a middle-level objective which was said to be attainable even in the absence of "proletarian hegemony." Indeed, the overestimation of proletarian strength in India was no longer even desirable, since—as will be argued below—the Soviets were becoming increasingly uncomfortable with the very notion of communist revolution or rule in India.

But if neither "revolutionary democracy" nor "proletarian hegemony" were considered to be viable objectives in India, what were the doctrinally sanctioned desiderata? Soviet Indologists were unanimous in the opinion that India could not achieve rapid industrialization if she remained on the capitalist path. Even state capitalism, in the absence of fundamental changes in the social system, could do no more than create favorable conditions for the struggle to achieve democratic reforms and economic independence. But state capitalism would require "extensive" ties with the socialist camp, and even these links could only mitigate but not eliminate the dislocations inevitable for an underdeveloped country located in the world capitalist economy. Thus, even in such relatively more developed "third world" countries as India, the vital task was to *interrupt* capitalist development and to transfer the country onto the "rails of noncapitalist development." [87]

The national bourgeoisie was firmly committed to the capitalist path. So long as it retained a monopoly of political power, India would be simply "incapable of profound development" in an antifeudal and anti-imperialist direction. Thus the task immediately on the agenda for progressive Indians was the formation of a democratic coalition opposed to the bourgeois monopoly of political power.[88] Though little mentioned by Soviet Indologists in recent years, and even then only as "*one* of the expedient sociolegal forms of noncapitalist development" [89] in India, "national democracy" was the sole remaining alternative form of state power. And so, since 1961, this had been the stated objective of the Indian Communist Party.

4. The Split in the CPI: 1959–1965

As the two preceding chapters have pointed out in detail, the history of the CPI since the mid-1940's has been a story of one factional dispute after another. Each successive factional victory, accompanied by assurances that the "basis for unity" had at last been found, soon crumbled as a result of renewed indecision (see Table I).

No small part of the CPI's difficulty, especially in the first postwar decade, had resulted from those changes in the Soviet foreign policy line which had produced one after another reas-

Table 1. CPI Leadership, Policy, and Factionalism: 1935–1972

Period	Leader and Approved Policy	Major Opponent(s)
1935–1947	P. C. Joshi: "Right" strategy. United front from above. Anti-imperialist and national-liberation struggle.	B. T. Ranadive: "Russian model."
1948–1950	B. T. Ranadive: "Left" strategy. "Russian model." Armed, urban-based struggle for people's democracy and socialism; struggle against (undifferentiated) bourgeoisie and government. Main enemy Indian capitalism.	Andhra Committee: "Chinese path."
1950–1951	Rajeshwar Rao and Andhra Committee: "Chinese path." Violent struggle in rural areas. Broad antifeudal and anti-imperialist struggle under CPI leadership against big bourgeoisie and government, for "New Democracy."	A. K. Ghosh: Seek Cominform advice, slow down pace of struggle.
1951–1954	A. K. Ghosh: "Indian path" ("neo-Maoism"). Less militant, multiclass appeal, with emphasis on anti-imperialist and antifeudal struggle, seeking coalition government of people's democracy under CPI leadership, but not skipping "democratic stage."	
1954–1955	A. K. Ghosh: Continued opposition to government domestic policy, but grudging support of some foreign policies. U.S. imperialism main enemy. Goal of people's democratic revolution, in alliance with "national bourgeoisie."	
1955–1960	A. K. Ghosh: Support for "progressive" features of government domestic policy. "Simultaneous unity with and struggle against bourgeoisie." Possibility of peaceful transition.	B. T. Ranadive and B. Gupta: "Chinese path" of violent revolution. Sup-

ing Congress left) under working class hegemony, seeking people's democracy and socialism. No condemnation of Chinese attacks.

National-democratic front (including Congress left) seeking establishment of coalition government of National Democracy; socialism in distant future. Opposition to Chinese attacks.

B. T. Ranadive and E. M. S. Namboodiripad (CPI Marxist): Working class hegemony over national front; quick transformation to socialist revolution and people's democracy. No electoral alliance with Congress. Lean to China on international issues, but critical of both China and Soviet Union.

1964–1972

S. A. Dange (CPI): United national-democratic front engaged in parliamentary and mass struggle against reaction and imperialism. Electoral alliances with Congress against right permitted. Establishment of coalition National Democracy with exclusive leadership of neither national bourgeoisie or working class. Adoption of noncapitalist path, with gradual shift to working class leadership and socialism. Pro-Soviet.

1969–1972 Charu Mazumdar (CPI Marxist-Leninist): Chinese path: armed struggle (against government domestic and foreign policy) under leadership of working class, to achieve people's democratic revolution based on rural areas. No electoral participation. Pro-China.

sessment of the Indian government. But on each occasion the
Soviets had been able to impose their reinterpretations upon
the CPI and to guide the Indian party to the strategical-tactical
line considered most conducive to Soviet interests.

But not all the blame for the stormy history of the CPI can be
placed on the Soviets. For the CPI leadership, largely composed of middle-class intellectuals, has been no stranger to the
internal rivalries which have marked the history of other Indian
political parties. Chapter IV has already pointed to the strong
Indian regional differences reflected within the CPI. Tactics
successful for one regional branch may prove fatal for another,
but in the absence of a strong party center, such divergences are
extremely difficult to reconcile. Finally, the CPI has been far
from immune to the tendency for policy differences to become
weapons in the hands of individuals or factions struggling for
power, and thus to be magnified and made less amenable to
compromise.

Only in this context of long CPI factionalism, produced by
both internal and external stresses, can the effect of the Sino-Indian and Sino-Soviet conflicts be properly assessed. It is not at
all unusual that the former episode produced differences of
opinion among Indian communists. What made this conflict,
unlike previous ones, end in an actual split in the party was the
simultaneous erosion of that unified international communist
authority on which the CPI had so long been dependent for the
settlement of its quarrels. In summary, then, on top of long-
standing strategical-tactical differences magnified by personal
and regional considerations was placed the additional problem
of a conflict between the "motherland" and a revered socialist
state, long a mentor and model for the CPI. In the absence of an
authoritative international center to mediate these differences,
the CPI, lacking its own authoritative center, rushed headlong
into a split.

a. CPI Reaction to the 1959 Sino-Indian Conflict

The CPI first reacted to the events in Tibet in March 1959 by
pretending that there was no Sino-Indian conflict of interest involved. But as the magnitude of the rebellion became clearer
and the Dalai Lama's presence in India was announced, the
party was forced to drop this fiction. Accordingly, a May 1959
statement of the Central Executive Committee (CEC) publicly
echoed the Chinese line in accusing "some Indians" of seeking
to sabotage *Panch Shila* and in regretting Nehru's interference

in China's "internal affairs." Privately, however, the CPI sent a protest to the Chinese, asking them to cease their references to "Indian expansionists." The reply, as Ghosh described it later, was "curt." [90]

When the actual status of the Sino-Indian border became the main issue in August 1959, the CPI realized that siding openly with China could pose a great danger to its political strength. An evasive public statement calling for negotiations on the border was accompanied by another private letter from Ghosh to the Chinese, warning that continuation of the border clashes would result in increased "chauvinistic" right-wing pressure both against the CPI and against Nehru's nonalignment policy. This, together with a second private appeal in September, "fell on deaf ears." [91]

Ghosh's response to the Chinese silence was instinctive: he flew to Moscow for advice. It was during his consultations with Soviet leaders that the TASS statement of September 10 was released, thus minimizing, in Ghosh's opinion, the damage done to the "peace camp." But on his return from Moscow, Ghosh presided over a stormy session of the CEC which eventually produced a resolution devoid of criticism of China. The CPI's statement that socialist China could not be guilty of aggression and that the McMahon line was subject to negotiation was met by epithets of "treason" from broad sections of the Indian public.[92]

Confirmed in his fears that CPI prestige was suffering, Ghosh arrived in Peking in October for the anniversary celebrations with the hope of producing moderation in Chinese policy. Though refused an audience with Mao, Ghosh received—perhaps from Khrushchev, who was also in Peking—what he took to be assurances that Sino-Indian differences would soon be settled. This message he relayed to a press conference in New Delhi on October 21, only a few hours prior to the bloody massacre of Indian troops in Ladakh.

This public embarrassment of their leader, combined with another snub by the Chinese in response to a fourth letter from Ghosh, finally exhausted the CPI's patience. In mid-November the entire National Council of the party met to pass a resolution for the first time upholding the Indian position on the McMahon Line (while urging negotiations on the Ladakh border) and praising Nehru for his determination to continue an independent foreign policy.[93]

It was soon evident that the CPI resolutions were not the

unanimous views of its leadership. Rightists such as Dange preferred a more open avowal of support for Nehru in the dispute, while leftists such as Ranadive and Bhupesh Gupta backed the Chinese position. Gupta was a member of the CPI delegation to the Rumanian Party Congress in June 1960 at which Khrushchev privately attacked the Chinese for, among other things, their conflict with India. When Gupta failed to support the CPSU position, Khrushchev was said to have replied: "Go back and convince your own countrymen about the just nature of the Chinese action." [94]

That Gupta's faction was a CPI minority was confirmed in September, when the CEC passed a secret resolution, "On Certain Questions before the International Communist Movement," which praised the Soviet party's "correct" stand on the Sino-Indian question while condemning the "grave and serious mistake made by China" in fomenting the border dispute. The paramount issue was said to be not the correctness of historical territorial claims but the need to strengthen the unity of the "peace camp." [95]

But the leftists were by no means ready to abide by the rules of "democratic centralism" and accept the condemnation of China. Leftist-dominated party committees in the Punjab and West Bengal passed resolutions denouncing the CEC stand. Undeterred, Ghosh took his case against the Chinese before the international meeting in Moscow in November 1960, declaring that while "we have no illusions about the Indian national bourgeoisie," the Chinese attack, in the face of CPI pleas, had endangered the Nehru government's position as a "very significant force for world peace." [96]

The Russians, however, were not pleased by the excessive ardor Ghosh employed in defending them against the Chinese. They were hoping to paper over the differences within the communist movement by means of the Moscow Statement, and Ghosh's speech had not contributed to this end. Thus, Suslov reportedly called the CPI delegation for a conference after the Moscow meeting had concluded, informing them that, while the Soviets still did not support the Chinese action, they also did not approve the CPI's overly critical attitude toward China.[97]

b. The CPI Debate on "National Democracy"

The CPI heeded Suslov's words, but its subsequent scaling down of the dispute with the CCP did not lead to a cooling off in its own internal factional strife. A heated debate broke out in the February 1961 National Council meeting concerning the new draft program to be presented to the Sixth CPI Congress, which was scheduled to meet in April. In the end, two rival programs were submitted to the congress, the "left-wing" program by Ranadive and the official "right-wing" program supported by Dange's group. Both drafts endorsed collaboration with a section of the national bourgeoisie in the formation of a "national-democratic front," but the left-wing program excluded mention either of bringing the congress "left" into this front or of establishing a government of national democracy. Rather it expressed confidence that India "will emerge as a victorious People's Democracy and advance on the road to socialism." This was in contrast to the right-wing program's call for bringing a large section of Congress party masses and part of its leadership into a united front whose immediate objective would be the "establishment of National Democracy in order to advance on the road to socialism." [98]

As might be expected, the Soviets—represented at the party congress by a delegation led by Suslov—supported the right-wing formulation, with its use of the "national democracy" concept. Though the Indian government's refusal to grant visas prevented the Chinese from sending a delegation, the weight of CCP influence was clearly behind the left-wing draft. This document, like Peking's own statements, avoided the "national democracy" formula and retained the "people's democracy" concept. Both concepts embraced the idea of a multiclass government, but only the latter insisted upon working-class hegemony in the state.

There are indications that Suslov, having seen firsthand the strength of the CPI leftist faction, advised Ghosh to avoid a showdown at the congress by making some concessions to the leftist viewpoint. Accordingly, to forestall a split, Ghosh employed the tactic of including in his speech to the party congress much of the harsh rhetoric employed in the left-wing draft's assessment of the Nehru government's internal policies, while nevertheless implying a preference for "national democracy" as the immediate goal. Ghosh's speech was in fact adopted as part of the official political resolution, and both sides agreed to Namboodiripad's suggestion that the adoption of the new program be postponed again.[99]

An article by Ghosh published in *World Marxist Review* early in 1962 made more explicit his basic agreement with the Soviet assessment of India and his endorsement of the Soviet conclusion that socialism was not on the immediate agenda of the CPI. While pointing to the inadequacies of the Indian economy and asserting that they could not be corrected by the national bourgeoisie on its own, Ghosh rejected the notion that the Indian bourgeoisie was politically bankrupt. India's need was not for a struggle directed solely against the government, but for "simultaneous unity with and struggle against the bourgeoisie." The goal of the struggle was not socialism but "democracy"— the replacement of the exclusive rule of the bourgeoisie with a state led by a "democratic coalition" in which the working class and its peasant allies would "acquire an increasingly important position." [100]

It is doubtful that Ghosh could have unified the CPI around such a program, even with strong Soviet backing. But it is not inconceivable that he could have done it, especially in view of Ghosh's demonstrated skill at—in Marshall Windmiller's apt phrase—"standing on all sides of an issue at once." [101] But such unity was never to be, for in January 1962 Ghosh died. A long struggle for the succession was temporarily resolved in April by the naming of the centrist Namboodiripad as General Secretary and the appointment of the leading rightist, Dange, to the new post of Party Chairman.

The new duumvirate inherited a party which had emerged from the 1962 general elections with its parliamentary holdings unchanged. But there was significance in the fact that the CPI had made gains in the leftist strongholds of West Bengal and Andhra Pradesh, while losing seats in the areas of north India and Bombay where the party's rightist faction was centered. Nationwide the Congress party had again emerged with a strong majority, but it had lost seats to the rightist Jan Sangh and Swatantra parties.

c. The CPI and the Sino-Indian War

Before the new leadership could set about the task of rebuilding the party in these areas where it had lost strength, the CPI suffered a new setback with the resumption of Sino-Indian hostilities. And in October 1962, the CPI's reaction was far less ambiguous than it had been in 1959. A resolution of the party secretariat declared in no uncertain terms that the McMahon Line was the border of India and that all attempts to defend it were justified. Two days later Dange, attacking China's "militarist and recalcitrant attitude," declared: "We are neither Peking patriots nor Washington patriots. We are citizens of India which is neither aggressive nor expansionist, which in its foreign policy is a nonaligned and peaceful country. Anyone who attacks such a country must be rebuffed." [102]

That Dange's views were a reflection of the sentiments of the majority of the CPI leadership was confirmed at the beginning of November when the National Council released a resolution entitled, "United to Defend Our Motherland against China's Open Aggression." This resolution, which preceded by three days the Soviet switch to neutrality on the 1962 Sino-Indian conflict, included the statement that the party was not opposed to the buying of arms "from any country on a commercial basis." It also contained a passage, not publicly released until 1963, which accused China of violating the understanding of the 1960 Moscow Conference in relation to peaceful coexistence and the communist attitude to newly independent countries. China, this passage declared, "has fallen victim to narrow nationalistic considerations at the cost of the interests of world peace and anti-imperialism, in its attitude towards India." [103]

The intensification of the Chinese attack in mid-November called forth from the CPI secretariat a letter to "fraternal parties" which named China as the aggressor and declared that, as a result of her actions, the CPI and the "democratic movement" were in "extreme jeopardy." The Chinese reassessment of the Indian government contained in the editorial "More on Nehru's Philosophy" was condemned in the strongest possible terms: it was "grossly subjective, perverse, full of falsehood . . . and has nothing to do with any Marxist-Leninist analysis." This unprecedented letter, which fully revealed the extent to which the CPI felt in danger of losing its position in India, concluded with an appeal to fraternal parties to halt China's present policy, which could only contribute to "ruining of the relations of India with the Soviet Union and other socialist countries." [104]

Evidently the letter failed to produce among the "fraternal parties" immediate sympathy with the CPI's position, for on December 4 Dange left India for a visit to Moscow. He arrived in time for Khrushchev's speech to the Supreme Soviet, in which the Soviet leader implicitly attacked the Chinese position. In the same edition of *Pravda* in which Khrushchev's speech was printed, note was taken of his visit with Dange. The circumspection characterizing this dispatch suggests that Khrush-

chev was by no means ready publicly to embrace, at least at that
time, the CPI's unrestrained attack on China's actions.[105]

One factor which may have contributed to the Soviet restraint
was the wholesale arrest by the Indian government of over 900
communist and trade union leaders, including fifty National
Council members and the entire provincial leaderships of West
Bengal, Punjab, and Kerala. Nor could it have escaped the notice of the Soviets that only leftist communists had been de-
tained. The rapid reaction by the rightists in reorganizing the
beheaded provincial organizations led to speculation that
Dange had cooperated with the government in the betrayal of
his comrades.[106] Whether or not they shared these suspicions,
the Soviets did not let the factional coloration of those arrested
diminish the scope of their propaganda campaign aimed at attacking the "chauvinists" who "senselessly hounded" the communists and at securing the release of those arrested. This campaign formed part of an increasing series of expressions of
concern over the growing strength of Indian "reactionaries"
and their threat to Nehru's nonalignment policy in the wake of
the Chinese invasion.[107]

Only a few months after Dange's visit with "fraternal parties," the Chinese party leveled a most unfraternal attack on
Dange's "revisionist clique," which was said to be seeking to
turn the CPI into a "lackey" of the Nehru government. The editorial ended with a thinly veiled call for an overthrow of the
CPI leadership, "the Dange revisionist clique . . . a handful of
pygmies." [108] Dange's reply, entitled "Neither Revisionism nor
Dogmatism Is Our Guide," defended the CPI's "joining in a
united front with its national bourgeoisie" as consistent with
proletarian internationalism and made it clear that Dange had
no intention of switching that line or surrendering his leadership.[109]

d. The CPI Split

At the time Dange's reply was published, the CPI had already begun to split apart. Following the November 1962 National Council resolution, three leftists had resigned from the
secretariat, and a fourth member, the prestigious Namboodiripad, had withdrawn his resignation only under pressure
from the rightists. But at the subsequent National Council meeting in February, Namboodiripad submitted a document, "Revisionism and Dogmatism in the CPI," purporting to be critical of

both the right and left, but in fact more sympathetic to the leftist position. His theses having been submitted to a committee, Namboodiripad again offered his resignation and this time was not asked to reconsider.

Only in April 1964 was the split in the CPI formalized, with the resignation of thirty-two members of the National Council. What precipitated the walkout was Dange's refusal to yield the chair during an investigation of the so-called "Dange letter." This document, denounced by Dange as a forgery, had been published in the Indian press in March and purported to be a letter written by Dange to the British in 1924, in which he had allegedly offered to work as a "police spy" in return for his release from prison. The National Council majority accepted Dange's denial of the letter's authenticity, but the thirty-two "splitters" made it a central issue in their attempt to discredit the "right-reformist" Dange leadership. Already they had established rival party newspapers in five provinces and had even put up a rival candidate against the official CPI candidate in a local election in Andhra.[110]

A "unity meeting" held in July failed to heal the split, which was interpreted by the rightist majority as "an integral part of a world-wide move" by the CCP to split communist parties.[111] The leftist factions, with the support of key centrists such as Namboodiripad, declared themselves to be the true communist party in India, the CPI (Marxist), and held their own Seventh Party Congress in Calcutta in October. Although, in light of the continuing popular hostility to China, this group did not openly call itself "pro-Peking," its positions on questions of internal and foreign policy and on the issues dividing the international communist movement clearly marked it as sympathetic to the CCP in its dispute with the CPSU.

Thus, the program adopted at the Calcutta congress emphasized the "compromising" tendencies of the bourgeoisie and declared, "only when the anti-imperialist national front is under the leadership of the working class does the democratic revolution not only get completed . . . but quickly passes over to the stage of socialist revolution." Like the leftist draft program submitted to the Sixth Party Congress, the new program of the left CPI failed to mention intermediate stages to proletarian hegemony but called for the replacement of the "bourgeois-landlord state" by a "state of people's democracy led by the working class." While affirming that the new party would try its utmost to achieve a peaceful transformation, it reminded its adherents that the ruling classes never relinquish power voluntarily and that it was necessary to be prepared for "all contingencies." [112]

The CPI "majority," estimating its own membership at 107,000 and that of the left CPI at 40,000, held its own Seventh Congress in Bombay in December and adopted a program of its own. This document was wholly consistent with the Soviet assessment of Indian social forces and of the strategy to be pursued by "progressive forces." It noted a "growing differentiation" in the ranks of the national bourgeoisie which would permit all but the "monopoly" stratum of this class to join with workers and peasants in a National Democratic Front. This front would be forged through parliamentary and extraparliamentary mass struggles aimed at isolating Indian reactionaries. On assuming power, hopefully by peaceful means, it would establish a national democracy, a transitional state in which "the exclusive leadership of the working class is not yet established," though the exclusive leadership of the national bourgeoisie would no longer exist.

The program of this government, aimed at transforming the social and political order and laying the foundation for building socialism, would consist of a strengthened "independent policy of peace," the curbing of state bureaucracy, the completion of the formation of linguistic states, the gradual elimination of foreign capital holdings, nationalization of banks, a ceiling on profits, the expansion of the state sector, and the implementation of agrarian reforms (including a ceiling on land holdings and the development of producers' cooperatives). Capitalist relations would not be immediately liquidated, though the growth of capitalism would be progressively restricted. Ultimately the working class would occupy the leading position in the democratic coalition, allowing the transition to the ultimate goal of socialist development.[113]

In the interval preceding the establishment of national democracy, the CPI vowed to continue support of "progressive" manifestations of government policy, while conducting mass struggles (some taking the nonviolent Gandhian form of *satyagraha*) to "induce the government to change its policy." Moreover, its election strategy, in contrast to the left CPI strategy of forming anti-Congress alliances including parties of all shades, would consist of fighting the Congress party when there was a chance of communist or leftist victory and supporting the

Congress wherever there was a danger for a victory of reactionary forces.[114] Thus, in the view of the right CPI, as in that of the Soviets, the Congress party was far preferable to parties on its right and should not be weakened to the benefit of "reactionary" groups.

On questions concerning the international communist movement, the right CPI congress took a consistently pro-Soviet stand. This action was applauded by B. N. Ponomarev, who headed the Soviet delegation to the congress. The CPI, he declared, was an "outstanding detachment of the international communist movement." Both Ponomarev's speech to the congress and *Pravda*'s subsequent coverage of its accomplishments indicated full Soviet approval of the new "rightist" program.[115]

On the issue of the CPI split, the Soviets, as they had done since 1963, placed the blame not on the Indian leftists themselves but on "monstrous" interference in CPI affairs by the Chinese party. The Soviets continued to express their hope that, by emphasizing "specific problems of struggle" and playing down ideological issues, the two CPI's could be reunited.[116]

5. The Road to Tashkent

Although Soviet and CPI analysts agreed on "national democracy" as the goal toward which Indian communists should march, there was in Soviet policy the clear implication that for the present the widening of the class composition of the Indian government and the achievement of strictly internal "national-democratic tasks" was definitely secondary to the need to guarantee that India remain nonaligned and as economically and militarily strong as possible. As long ago as 1961 one Soviet publication had explicitly stated that the "main thing is that India is developing successfully as an independent state, firmly following a peace-loving foreign policy." [117]

Ever since the October 1962 Chinese attack on India, Soviet press accounts of India's internal political situation had stressed the theme that her nonalignment was under increased attack from a coalition of Indian reactionaries and United States imperialists. In March 1963 Lev Stepanov noted the temporary failure of efforts by the Kennedy "regime" to subvert the policy of nonalignment, which he termed "a policy that follows logically from the newly emerged nations' position in the world." [118] A

year and a half later, *Pravda* was warning of an even greater
threat on the part of Indian "reactionary parties": their demand
that India arm herself with nuclear weapons. Such an action,
Pravda warned, would be "fraught with dangerous consequences." [119]

The Soviets did more than issue warnings in their campaign
to keep India from aligning with the West or matching China's
atomic armament with her own. Between October 1962 and
May 1964, the Soviets sold India $130 million in military equip-
ment. This sum was more than doubled in September 1964,
when Indian President Radhakrishnan was promised in Moscow $140 million in additional military aid (including forty-four
MIG-21's, fifty surface-to-air missiles, seventy tanks, and six
submarines) to be financed by a long-term, low-interest Soviet
loan. [120]

Nor did the Russians keep a tight hold on the purse strings
when the Indians came to Moscow for assistance with their
Fourth Five-Year Plan. On his visit to the Soviet Union in May
1965, Prime Minister Shastri was promised up to $800 million
in Soviet loans—an amount equal to what the Soviets had
pledged to India in the entire preceding decade. The following
January representatives of the two countries signed a trade
agreement which foresaw a doubling of the 1964 level of Soviet-Indian trade by 1970. [121] During the Shastri visit Kosygin
defended Soviet assistance as an "internationalist duty" to aid
peoples in strengthening economic independence. He added:
"We wish for the people of India that their country become a
prosperous state as quickly as possible, that India continue to
exert an important positive influence in all international affairs." [122]

Of course, the Soviets were not able to achieve with their aid
a completely subservient Indian foreign policy. The two governments had their differences on various international issues,
such as the Khrushchev-Nehru dispute over the proper handling of the United Nations force in the Congo. The Indian
Prime Minister not only criticized the Soviet demand for a withdrawal of UN forces following Lumumba's murder, but he provided Indian replacements for those contingents which were
withdrawn. Another area of disagreement throughout the 1960's
was the long-standing Indian refusal to recognize the Ulbricht
regime in Germany. And on the issue of the Vietnam War, the Indians consistently refused to join the Soviets in an across-the-

board condemnation of U.S. policy. But the areas of Soviet-Indian agreement on international issues remained sufficiently broad to allow Kosygin to state, "we believe in the development of India, we believe in its future," and to add, perhaps with an eye to more than one type of "imperialist": "Soviet-Indian friendship *helps to stabilize the situation in South Asia,* hampers the imperialists' intrigues in this region and thus strengthens the cause of world peace." [123]

If Kosygin's words were indeed meant to apply to those Chinese "imperialists" who sought to destabilize the situation in South Asia, the Chinese soon let it be known that the Soviet message had been received in Peking. "Observer" wrote in *People's Daily* on May 27 his views about "What Shastri's Soviet Trip Reveals." It was well known that "long ago" India had entered into a military and political alliance with the United States, but the reason "why the Soviet leaders set such store by Shastri and praise him to the skies is that he is a rare anti-China cavalier as well as Washington's pet." The Soviet "capital investment" in India was evidence of the Soviet-Indian alignment against socialist China.[124]

The Chinese had cause to worry not only about the solidification of Soviet-Indian relations, but also about a developing Soviet rapprochement with Pakistan. China had assiduously courted Pakistan ever since the outbreak of Sino-Indian hostilities. And Pakistan's receptiveness to closer ties with China had grown markedly with the increasing military assistance from her nominal allies, the United States and the United Kingdom, to India, her sworn enemy. No Western assurances could alleviate Pakistan's suspicions that this Western aid to India was equally as useful against her as against China. Such Pakistani anxiety was tailor-made for Peking's intentions further to isolate India from her neighbors.

Pakistani Foreign Minister Z. A. Bhutto was thus accorded royal treatment when he journeyed to Peking in March 1963 to sign the border agreement negotiated the previous year. Not long after his return, Bhutto, hinting that far more than a border problem had been discussed in Peking, told the Pakistani parliament that an attack on Pakistan by India would involve the "largest state in Asia." A year later, during a visit to Rawalpindi by Chou En-lai, China for the first time supported the Pakistani demand for a plebiscite in Kashmir.

The Soviets, who had long indicated willingness to better

their relations with Pakistan, were forced to conduct their approaches delicately, given the tenderness of Indian sensitivities. But the effort was considered to be worth the risks and was clearly preferable to abandoning Pakistan to the exclusive blandishments of Peking. Moreover, success in the campaign to woo Pakistan would mean a further weakening of the "containment" alliances constructed by the United States on Russia's south flank.[125] Thus, a month before Shastri's visit, Ayub Khan had been received in Moscow to negotiate the full range of trade, aid, and cultural agreements. Included in the final Soviet-Pakistani communiqué were pledges of "resolute support" for peoples fighting for self-determination and demands that "international agreements" be implemented. Both points could be regarded by eager Pakistanis and nervous Indians as an indirect Soviet acknowledgment of Pakistan's position on Kashmir.

To forestall such claims, Kosygin was at pains to assure Shastri that "when the Soviet Union strives to improve its relations with other countries, it does not do so at the expense of Soviet-Indian friendship." But the absence in the final Soviet-Indian communiqué of the customary acknowledgment that both sides regarded Kashmir to be a part of India provided an indication that, at the least, the Soviets had returned to a position of neutrality on this issue.[126]

A clear sign of the shift in the Soviet position can be found in a further examination of the Central Committee slogans. Since the late 1950's and throughout the remaining Khrushchev years, India had held pride of place in the listing of noncommunist countries, while Pakistan had not been mentioned at all. As previously indicated, a major rearrangement of the list of third-world countries greeted in the slogans appeared with the 1965 Anniversary slogans. India's slogan (the thirty-third in the entire list) was now placed behind those of the "progressive" regimes judged to have embarked on an anticapitalist path. Equally significant, however, was the appearance—in both the May Day and Anniversary lists—of slogan forty-seven: "May the friendly relations between the Soviet people and the peoples of Iran, Pakistan, and Turkey develop and grow stronger." This greeting was unmistakably linked with the emerging Soviet diplomatic effort on its southern flank, and in fact it first appeared only a few days after Ayub's historic visit to Moscow.

Just as dramatic was the further rise in Pakistan's position in the slogans of 1966. The May Day slogans not only devoted a separate greeting to Pakistan for the first time, but also placed it immediately below that addressed to India. The slogan urged that "friendly, good-neighborly relations develop between Pakistan and the Soviet Union!" In October, the appeal was made even more positive with a further change now implying that good relations already existed: "May the friendly, good-neighborly relations between Pakistan and the Soviet Union develop and grow stronger!"

In the final set of slogans including these country-by-country lists, issued for May Day 1967, the Pakistani slogan again followed immediately after India's. They were differentiated only by the reference to "traditional friendship and cooperation" in the Indian case, and the presumably less ardent "friendly, good neighborly relations" in the Pakistani case.[127] For those in India who paid attention to such signs, this Soviet shift in only three years from unabashed favoritism to careful evenhandedness must have evoked much concern.

No sooner had the Soviets begun their rapprochement with Pakistan than fresh hostilities broke out between India and Pakistan in the saltwater marsh and desert known as the Rann of Kutch. The brief war may have been Ayub's way of indicating his displeasure over India's proclamation in December 1964 that Kashmir was an "integral" part of India. The Soviet interpretation was more imaginative and was consistent with its long-held thesis that only imperialist maneuvers had kept India and Pakistan apart: "Everyone who has followed American press reports about the methods of the U.S. Central Intelligence Agency will at once see that the conflict in the Rann of Kutch . . . [was] provoked by customary CIA methods in order to sidetrack attention from the war in Vietnam." [128]

Far more serious, however, was the bloody Indo-Pakistani war which broke out on August 5 in Kashmir. Provoked by the infiltration of Pakistani irregulars into Kashmir, to which the Indian army had responded by crossing the cease-fire line into Pakistani-held territory, this undeclared war was ignored by the Soviet press for nearly three weeks.

Finally, on August 24, a *Pravda* "Commentator," declining to discuss either side's version of the origin of the conflict, declared that the "main thing is to find a way to stop the bloodshed immediately and to liquidate the conflict" by means of negotiation. Soviet "traditional friendship" with India was growing stronger and relations with Pakistan were "improving" and therefore the Soviet Union could not "remain indifferent" to the conflict, from which only imperialists and reactionaries would gain. Using a phrase now common in its references to South Asia, *Pravda* declared: "We would like Indian-Pakistani relations to be a stabilizing factor in Asia." [129]

But the situation became more destabilized on September 7 when the Chinese government entered the conflict with a "stern condemnation" of India for its "criminal aggression" and an expression of support for Pakistan. The United Nations, where efforts to end the conflict were in progress, was denounced as a "tool of United States imperialism and its partners." Far more ominous, however, was China's complaint that "India is still entrenched on Chinese territory on the Sino-Sikkim border and has not withdrawn." The statement continued: "Aggression is aggression. India's aggression against any one of its neighbors concerns all of its neighbors. Since the Indian Government has taken the first step in committing aggression against Pakistan, it cannot evade responsibility for the chain of consequences arising therefrom." [130] In rapid succession there followed Chinese statements accusing the Indians of provocation along the Sino-Indian border and demanding that they dismantle all "aggressive military works" on the Sikkim border within three days or face "grave consequences." Immediately before the second of these statements was issued, the Soviets issued what amounted to a stern warning to the Chinese not to stir up further troubles: "There are also forces trying to derive advantages for themselves from the exacerbation of Indian-Pakistani relations. Through their inflammatory statements they are instigating a further heating up of the military conflict . . . If matters take this course, many states, one after another, may find themselves drawn into the conflict." [131]

The Chinese escalated the war of words with a return blast at the Soviets, denouncing them for working "hand in glove" with the imperialists themselves to add "fuel to the flames." [132] China's verbal bluster was not, however, matched by willingness to enter the fighting. In addition to the Soviet warning, the Chinese had received from the United States a warning of retaliation against China if she should attack India.[133] In the end, China's threats had probably only hastened a halt to the fighting by intensifying United States and Soviet pressure on the combatants. As India and Pakistan were agreeing to United

Nations cease-fire proposals, the Chinese withdrew their ul-
timatum with the explanation that Shastri had met their demands. In fact, India had made no real concessions (Shastri had
even denied that the offending "military works" existed) and
the Chinese statement was taken as purely a face-saving matter.[134] Chinese belicosity in this crisis had not succeeded in
winning support or influence, and while her charge of United
States-Soviet cooperation may have been confirmed, the Soviets
ultimately managed to turn their efforts for peace into a major
propaganda and diplomatic success.

For on September 17 Kosygin had sent to Shastri and Ayub an
offer of "good offices" in the conflict, which included a proposal
that the two sides meet "in Tashkent, for instance," with—"*if
desired by both sides*"—Kosygin, for the purpose of establishing a "direct contact in order to achieve agreement on
the re-establishment of peace between India and Pakistan."
This offer, dictated "by one thing and one thing only, a sincere
desire to contribute to the earliest restoration of peace," [135] had
not been the first made by Kosygin, though it was the most
concrete. Kosygin had twice before sent letters offering his
"good offices," and Deputy Prime Minister K. T. Mazurov had
been in New Delhi seeking to restrain the Indian military efforts. On September 22, Shastri indicated his willingness to accept Soviet "good offices." Ayub was less enthusiastic, first
seeking Anglo-American mediation of the conflict and finally
agreeing (on November 16) to the Soviet offer (reportedly only
after being pressured to accept by President Johnson).[136] By
early December, arrangements had been completed for a meeting at Tashkent to be convened on January 4, 1966.

What did the Soviets hope to gain from their efforts to facilitate the settlement of the Kashmiri war? In this case (though not
as a general rule) major Soviet objectives had been stated quite
explicitly in Kosygin's letters and in the Soviet press. At least
three themes had repeatedly been stressed. The first was the
desire to restore stability to South Asia. The second theme was
that the conflict played into the hands of "external forces" and
invited both intervention from outside (the West and/or China)
and increased pressure from "chauvinists" and "reactionaries"
within. Finally, Soviet statements stressed the war's damaging
effects on the development efforts of both India and Pakistan. In
both countries the Soviets already had a sizable investment to
protect.

The Russians ran a risk in staking their prestige on the achievement of some kind of settlement of the issue which had inflamed the Indian subcontinent for two decades. But the potential rewards far outweighed the risk. For if the Tashkent conference, guided by the paternal hand of the Soviet Union, could produce the beginnings of a rapprochement between India and Pakistan, then it would have contributed enormously to the primary—and unspoken—Soviet objective in this area: the containment of Chinese influence and expansion in Asia. If India and Pakistan, instead of expending their treasure and energies in quarreling between themselves, were to unite against China in the defense of the subcontinent, then the security of the southeastern flank of the Soviet Union, as well as that of the subcontinent itself, could be markedly heightened.

Prior to the rise of Soviet concern over the Chinese threat to their security, the Russians had been primarily motivated by a desire to prevent the United States from building a solid phalanx in South Asia to contain the Soviet Union and China. The Kashmir issue had served as an instrument to prevent such unity in the service of containment. But by 1965 the locus of the main threat had shifted, and Kashmir had become a thorn in the Russian side.

The Soviet interests in the Indian subcontinent were thus remarkably parallel to those pursued by the United States. Both superpowers shared the desire to contain Chinese expansion and both had recently found Indo-Pakistani hostility an obstacle to that goal. This is not to argue that this limited convergence of interests was destined to be permanent or that it had overridden other sources of conflicts, including those in the ideological realm. But, for at least a limited time and in a limited area, India had become—in Nehru's words—"a kind of an area of agreement between opposing ideological forces." [137]

The Chinese, of course, were as sharply aware of this fact as anyone. They had first accused Khrushchev of cooperating with "imperialism" and Indian "reactionaries" to betray the interests of the revolutionary movement, and in 1965 they found his successors even more guilty of this offense. The attacks of Khrushchev on the Chinese position in the Sino-Indian dispute, they said, "pale into insignificance in comparison with those of the present leaders of the CPSU. They have discarded even the small fig-leaf Khrushchev used in order to feign neutrality.

Small wonder that the U.S. imperialists are gleefully hailing a 'new era' in U.S.-Soviet cooperation." [138]

It was not a good year for China. Besides the setback to her prestige suffered in India, a far more serious blow was dealt to the Chinese strategy by the coup and countercoup in Indonesia in September–October 1965. By the time the Indonesian events had worked themselves out, it was clear that the losers in the upheaval had been President Sukarno—who had since 1963 been one of Peking's closest allies and a collaborator in the scheme to organize a "third-world" bloc of "New Emerging Forces"—and the Indonesian Communist Party, whose almost total decimation deprived Peking of its largest and closest non-bloc supporter in the Sino-Soviet dispute. Peking had thus suffered a grievous blow to its strategy in Asia, from which the Soviets could not but take satisfaction (though it was not clear that the Soviets themselves had won any more positive benefits).

Nor had the Chinese been any more pleased by the new direction toward neutrality in the Sino-Soviet dispute taken in 1965–1966 by its two allies among the Asian ruling parties— North Vietnam and North Korea. Indeed, at the very time that Kosygin was greeting Ayub and Shastri in Tashkent, Aleksander Shelepin was in Hanoi winning the agreement of the North Vietnamese party to send a delegation to the forthcoming Soviet party congress in return for a substantial increase in Soviet aid in the Vietnam war. Thus it was against a background of declining Chinese influence in Asia—as well as of the rise of the debilitating Cultural Revolution within China—that the Tashkent Conference opened in January 1966.

The declaration produced by the conference after a week of difficult negotiation pledged the Indians and Pakistanis to exert "all efforts to create good-neighborly relations" and, in accordance with the United Nations Charter, "to settle their disputes through peaceful means." Agreement was reached on the principle of "noninterference in the internal affairs of each other," on discouragement of hostile propaganda, on resumption of diplomatic, economic, and cultural relations, and on the holding of future meetings on "matters of direct concern to both countries." But each side failed to achieve its major objective: Ayub received no explicit guarantee of further talks on the political future of Kashmir, and Shastri failed to get the "no war" pact he sought.

On the substantive issue, Shastri and Ayub agreed that armed personnel would be withdrawn not later than February 25 to the position held prior to the outbreak of hostilities, and that prisoners of war would be repatriated. The declaration closed with an expression of "deep appreciation and gratitude" to the Soviet leaders and to Kosygin personally "for their constructive, friendly and noble part in bringing about the present meeting which has resulted in mutually satisfactory results." [139]

In the Soviet view, this declaration, which left the most sensitive issue—the political future of Kashmir—unmentioned, was "the maximum of what could be expected at the present stage." Though substantive progress in resolving the issue of Kashmir could come only with time, the Soviets did not hesitate to take maximum propaganda advantage of the "great international significance" of the meeting itself. As *Pravda* commentators Yuri Zhukov and Viktor Mayevsky put it, for the first time in history a dispute between two Asian powers, arising from the colonial legacy, had been discussed under the "good offices" of a socialist power. The time had passed when such problems could be settled on instructions from the imperialist powers, *New Times* proudly asserted. And in the opinion of *Kommunist*, the Tashkent conference had been both a demonstration and a vindication of the Soviet policy of peace.[140]

Nor were the Soviets alone in their praise of the achievement, which was widely hailed as a victory for Soviet diplomacy. The statesmanlike and benevolent image of Kosygin at Tashkent as he sought to increase Soviet influence by presiding over the restoration of peace in the subcontinent could easily be contrasted by the "third world" with the belligerent ravings of the Chinese. It could also be contrasted, by those who knew of it, with another scene at Tashkent almost half a century before— when M. N. Roy, with Lenin's approval, had set out with a motley army on an aborted attempt to bring communist influence to India by force.

VI From Mediation to Alliance: Soviet Policy, 1966–1972

The tragedy of Indo-Pakistani relations was all too evident in the aftermath of the Tashkent meeting. The great hopes engendered there for an end to the enervating conflict on the subcontinent were not to achieve fruition, though the credit widely given to the Soviet Union for its efforts was not thereby diminished. On the fourth anniversary of the conference, *New Times* wrote that, although the course outlined by the declaration had been correct and had had a beneficial influence on the political climate in South Asia, relations were, unfortunately, "still somewhat strained" between India and Pakistan.

The reasons adduced for this understated "strain" were the same ones that the Soviets had been advancing for decades: the complexity of problems left over from colonial days and the "intrigues woven by the reactionaries and extremist elements as often as not egged on from without." [1] But Soviet arguments laying all blame on extremists and external scapegoats rang stale and hollow. For the Indian and Pakistani leaders were caught in a web of their own making: long years of fanning popular hatred and suspicion were not easily overcome, nor were the large amounts of prestige invested by each side in the emotional issue of Kashmir easily sacrificed by either state.

But the tragedy was by no means a two-character drama. A parallel, self-created web held the Soviet Union and the United States: the spiraling arms race entrapping them on the subcontinent. Although the Americans sought to free themselves from such a self-defeating involvement by an extended suspension of arms shipments to India and Pakistan, unilateral extrication did not prove possible. For India, there was the alternative source of supply in the Soviet Union; in May 1968, the Soviets added one hundred SU-7 fighter-bombers to the threescore MIG-21's and 500 tanks previously sold. But for Pakistan, in the absence of military aid from either the United States or the USSR, the alternative source of supply was Peking. Indeed, a 1966 Sino-Pakistani agreement called for China to supply $120 million in tanks and aircraft. Neither the United States nor the Soviet Union felt it could long afford to sit by while Pakistan again grew more dependent on China.

The Americans resumed the sale of spare parts in the spring of 1967, but continued the suspension of arms sales until 1970.

In October of that year came reports that the Nixon Administration had provided Pakistan with bombers, fighters, and armored personnel carriers. Despite American assurances that the sale was a "one-time, limited exception to the embargo" and that the existing military balance on the subcontinent would not be upset, the Indians voiced their "gravest concern" in a formal protest.[2] Though American sales were suspended during the Pakistani civil war of 1971, shipments of arms already licensed were continued until November, triggering a further sharp decline in U.S.-Indian relations.

In the months following the Tashkent conference, the Soviets had provided jeeps, trucks, and sample helicopters to Pakistan. But the vigorous Pakistani protest over the above-mentioned 1968 SU-7 deal with India—a deal which the Pakistanis claimed would nullify the Tashkent agreement—was soon followed by a visit to Rawalpindi from the Soviet premier. Three months later, while Ayub was serving notice on Washington that it would have to give up its Peshawar intelligence base, the Soviets concluded a significant arms deal with Pakistan and began deliveries of tanks, artillery, and armored personnel carriers. The resulting protests from India were accompanied by riots at the Soviet embassy in New Delhi. The widespread disillusion over India's alleged "special relationship" with the USSR included the introduction of a motion by a parliamentary opposition group calling for the censure of the government for its friendly policy toward the Soviet Union. The reaction of the left CPI was to urge that India pursue closer relations with China.

Kosygin hastily sought to reassure the Indians, using the same argument that the Nixon Administration was to employ two years later: Moscow had no intention of altering the military balance on the subcontinent. *Pravda*—avoiding explicit mention of the arms deal—blamed "reactionary leaders" for the riots and asserted that they had met with a "worthy rebuff from progressive deputies and representatives of the Government," including Mrs. Gandhi, whom it quoted: "We must not allow our friendship with the Soviet Union to be weakened." [3] But the entire incident must have brought home to the Soviets the lesson the Americans had learned in South Asia and the Middle East about the unpopularity which can be reaped by a supplier to both sides in an arms race.

1. Soviet Diplomatic Activity

Although the Soviets had failed to realize the goal of uniting India and Pakistan in the joint defense of the subcontinent against China, and while they had been the recipients of outbursts of popular and official displeasure, their diplomatic and trade relations with both India and Pakistan continued to be generally cordial through the end of the decade.

India remains a major third-world aid recipient and trading partner for the Soviet Union. But the Soviets have in recent years grown increasingly cool to Indian requests for additional credits aimed at rapidly expanding the size of the public sector of the economy. The concern shown by Kosygin in his September 1965 speech announcing the planning and production reforms in the USSR—that efficiency and "profitability" had too long been sacrificed to considerations of sheer gross output—extended as well to the economic effectiveness of Soviet rubles expended abroad. The immediate propaganda impact and doctrinal desirability of aid devoted to increasing the size of the state sector began to be overshadowed by arguments based on economic criteria and on long-term political considerations. Sweeping reforms and excessive nationalization, it was now recognized, could lead to economic chaos, discrediting both the idea of socialism and those radical leaders who sponsored it.[4]

India's economic difficulties in the 1960's in fact forced the scrapping of one Fourth Five-Year Plan and the substitution of another, much more modest, plan de-emphasizing the role of the state sector.[5] Soviet concern over the low efficiency and mismanagement of state-owned heavy industry was evident. In December 1966, the Indians were granted a credit to be applied not toward the new projects they had requested, but toward increasing the capacity of existing enterprises. When Kosygin visited India in January 1968, he was reportedly appalled by the mismanagement and underutilization of plants in the public sector. Two months later a deal was negotiated calling for the delivery to the USSR of 600,000 tons of steel from the Bhilai plant, which was operating well below capacity.

Since 1955, the Soviets had helped or were currently assisting India with 70 major projects, primarily in the heavy industry sector, for a total of $1.4 billion in credits. Moreover, the Soviet

Union had become India's second leading trading partner; according to Indian trade statistics, the percentage of India's foreign trade turnover accounted for by trade with Moscow had risen from 2.4 percent at the beginning of the 1960's to 11 percent in 1969–1970.

Yet the continuing stagnation of Indian industry and the disastrous crop failure of 1972, which depleted India's grain reserves, must have brought home to Indian officials the point that the Soviet capacity for assistance was indeed limited in these areas in which the USSR itself was so noticeably deficient. And indeed, by 1970–1971, India's repayments to the USSR for past assistance were already running ahead of new Soviet disbursements, creating a "negative aid flow" of about $28 million. Almost one-fifth of India's exports to the USSR were going toward the servicing of past debts.[6] By the end of 1972, there was considerably less optimistic talk of "dovetailing" the Soviet and Indian economic plans or bringing India into a relationship with the Council for Mutual Economic Assistance (COMECON), and there were signs of spirited Soviet-Indian haggling over the details of the trade relationship.

The Soviets themselves continue to stress the theme that aid and trade from the socialist countries lessen India's dependence on Western sources and strengthen her industrial development. Moreover, Kosygin claimed on his visit to India in May 1969 that Soviet aid had enabled India to defend her territorial integrity and sovereignty in the face of "adventurist encroachments" by unnamed "foreign forces striving for hegemony in Asia."

The element of personal diplomacy, which had been cherished by both Khrushchev and Nehru, has survived changes of leadership and remains characteristic of Soviet-Indian relations. Kosygin visited New Delhi four times in the four years following the Tashkent conference. Mrs. Gandhi made trips to Moscow in July 1966, November 1967 (when she was the only noncommunist head of government at the fiftieth-anniversary celebrations), and September 1971. The late Indian President Husain made a state visit to the USSR in June 1968, and his successor, President Giri, spent ten days in the Soviet Union in the fall of 1970. On this last occasion, the Soviet press reported that talks took place in an atmosphere of "sincere cordiality and mutual understanding." Views of the two sides on such international issues as Indochina and the Middle East were said to "come close together or coincide." President Podgorny was quoted as saying that Soviet-Indian relations were "marked by that precious quality which distinguishes true friendship and cooperation from temporary agreements pursuing momentary advantage." The Indian people, he concluded, could "rest assured that the Soviet people will remain their loyal and reliable friend." [7]

Soviet writers continued to describe the relations between the two states as a "classical example of peaceful coexistence." Despite differences in their political and social systems, "progressive" forces in India "have always sided with the Soviet Union in the struggle to unite and coordinate the efforts of the Asian and African peoples with those of the world socialist system." [8] At the same time, the Soviets have also continued to emphasize the dangers inherent in using a policy of "nonalignment" as a "convenient pretext" for nonparticipation in anti-imperialist struggles, as an excuse for failing to see such "political realities" as the differences between the "NATO bloc" and such benevolent groupings as the Warsaw Treaty organization, or as a basis for advancing such "harmful doctrines" as the notion of a world conflict between rich and poor nations.[9] Finally, though they have professed the belief that friendship with such countries as India was not a transitory phenomenon and could "withstand the test of time," Soviet commentators have reminded their readers of the "dual nature" of the national bourgeoisie and of the presence of "reactionary circles" among Indian capitalists who are inclined to cooperate with imperialism.

The Indian government, however, has taken pains to dispel such fears by avoiding incidents which might prove offensive to their Soviet benefactors. These steps have ranged from the censorship of alleged anti-Soviet sections of the Western film "Dr. Zhivago" before allowing it to be shown in India, to the strong discouragement given to Svetlana Alliluyeva's wishes to stay in India rather than return to Moscow. A more recent example occurred in the summer of 1970, when the removal of Dinesh Singh from the post of foreign minister occasioned a visit to New Delhi from a Soviet deputy foreign minister, reportedly concerned over reports that Dinesh Singh's successor would seek to reverse some of his pro-Soviet policies. Mrs. Gandhi was quick to reassure the Soviets that there would be no policy changes.[10] As if to offer proof, her government announced the impending official visit of Madame Binh, the foreign minister of the Vietcong government. Two weeks later, the Indians announced that they had established relations at the consular-general level with the German Democratic Republic.

This disinclination to alienate the Soviet Union was also evidenced at the August 1968 session of the United Nations Security Council when India (as well as Pakistan) abstained on the vote calling for condemnation of the invasion of Czechoslovakia by Warsaw Pact forces. The Indian press was less sensitive to Soviet reactions. The *National Herald,* for example, declared that the Soviet Union had "squandered, in a few days, the prestige and goodwill gathered through the years." [11] Even the pro-Soviet CPI failed to speak out in favor of the Soviet action, maintaining silence for nine months before finally proclaiming the invasion "inevitable and justified." But like the invasion of Hungary a dozen years before, this Soviet application of force in Eastern Europe has not appeared to disturb the official Indian conscience so much as have the incursions of "imperialists" into the third world.[12]

The Pakistanis, however, were still relatively recent recipients of Moscow's good will and did not feel so strongly the necessity to avoid offense to the Soviets; eventually, they joined the call for withdrawal of invasion forces from Czech soil. Pakistan in this period was still a military ally of the United States and remained one of Peking's closest friends. Yet the degree of Soviet-Pakistani cooperation was clearly on the increase in the late 1960's.

Soviet aid commitments to Pakistan in the 1960's amounted to $265 million. An additional $207 million Soviet offer for construction of a giant steel plant near Karachi, in the form of a twelve-year credit at 2½ percent interest, was signed in January 1971. In the sphere of trade relations, there was a fourfold increase in the volume of trade between the two countries in the period between 1964 and 1967. In December 1969, the two governments agreed to barter arrangements for 1970 estimated at a level of $50 million. Pakistan was to provide raw materials such as jute, cotton, rice, wool, and hides, as well as textiles; the Soviets were to trade pig iron, chemicals, fertilizers, and machinery. This agreement was notable not only as testimony to increased trade relations, however, but also for its indication of a certain persisting wariness on the part of the Pakistanis, who insisted that the agreement include a clause forbidding reexport of the bartered goods.

In the diplomatic sphere, there were frequent personal contacts between the leaders of the two states. Ayub Khan visited Moscow twice during his presidency (in April 1965 and in September 1967), but there is no evidence that the Soviets experienced feelings of regret when he was ousted in March 1969. Indeed, they were probably pleased at the prospect that the succeeding military regime headed by Yahya Khan would put an end to the mounting chaos in Pakistan. A pair of articles by Pakistani leftists sympathetic to the USSR, appearing in *World Marxist Review* in 1969 and 1970, gave indirect indication of the Soviet-favored view concerning Pakistan's internal turmoil.[13] "Ultra-left" and "Pekingite" forces were condemned for their advocacy of an armed anticapitalist struggle aimed at establishing "people's democracy." Such radical demands were said "to objectively aid" reactionary forces by narrowing the united front. The correct course was rather the utilization of bourgeois-democratic reforms as a means of carrying forward a more gradual struggle for national democracy and noncapitalist development. Internal change was the goal, but less destabilizing means were clearly preferred.

Upon assuming the presidency, Yahya received a message from Podgorny and Kosygin expressing confidence that the "relations of friendship and all-round cooperation" between their two countries would "strengthen and develop." Kosygin traveled to Pakistan in May 1969 (only thirteen months after his first visit to that country) and was assured by Yahya that recent internal developments did not affect his country's relations with the Soviet Union. The joint statement issued at the conclusion of the visit emphasized the need for rapid and peaceful settlement of unresolved disputes between Pakistan and India, and it included a pledge of expanding the spheres of Pakistani-Soviet cooperation, which was "not directed against any third state." [14] In fact, Kosygin stated, Moscow was determined to do "everything in its power" to encourage the development of friendly and cooperative relations among Pakistan, India, Afghanistan, and "other states of this region."

Yahya Khan returned Kosygin's visit in June of 1970. "Complete agreement or close similarity" of views on international issues, including the Middle East and Indochina crises, was reported by the Soviet press to have resulted from the talks. Anticipating the reaction from a number of quarters where increased Soviet-Pakistani cooperation would be disquieting, *New Times* declared that it was "obviously subversive" to claim that such cooperation militates against the interests of other countries.[15]

The immensely destabilizing and enervating conflict which broke out in East Pakistan in March 1971 evoked a stern message of official concern from the Soviets. On April 2, President Podgorny requested that Yahya "take the most urgent measures to stop the bloodshed and repressions against the population in East Pakistan" and work toward peaceful resolution of the conflict.[16] In June, Premier Kosygin urged that steps for safe and secure return of refugees from East Pakistan be taken without delay.[17] And in July, an article in *Izvestiia*, noting the reports about deaths and injuries resulting from clashes on the Indian-Pakistani border, concluded that tension between the two states had come to a head, raising the danger of more widespread military conflict. Expressing sympathy for the adverse effect on India's "already tight economy" of the influx of millions of Pakistani refugees, the writer urged a solution based on a "political settlement with consideration for the legitimate rights and interests of the people of this portion of the country." Taking note of forces, motivated by "greedy interests," which were seeking to heighten tension in the area, *Izvestiia* declared that the maintenance of peace on the subcontinent "is the only correct path and conforms to the national interests" of the peoples of both countries. In what amounted to a wistful epitaph for the "spirit of Tashkent," the article added: "After the signing of the Tashkent Declaration, the entire world community hailed the desire of the Indian and Pakistani governments to avoid direct military confrontation. India and Pakistan were able to reach a settlement of the border incidents by quickly holding meetings between their representatives. This method has justified itself *until recently.*" [18]

2. "Collective Security in Asia"

The concern for South Asian stability, so insistently voiced by the Soviets since the Indo-Pakistani war of 1965 and so evident in their dealings throughout the rest of the decade with both India and Pakistan, had begun to take a more concrete form during Kosygin's travels in South Asia in the late spring of 1969. His attempts to promote a settlement of Indo-Pakistani and Pakistani-Afghan differences were reported to have been placed in the context of a new regional cooperation arrangement. Kosygin hoped to have these three states and Iran meet in Kabul to discuss transit arrangements which would facilitate greater intraregional trade. But the Pakistanis feared that the ultimate Soviet aim was an anti-China political grouping. A spokesman for the Pakistani foreign ministry in July 1969 said that he saw little economic advantage in the proposed arrangements and openly declared that Pakistan would refuse to join any alliance opposed to China.

At the very time that Kosygin was engaged in these talks in Pakistan, a significant article appeared in *Izvestiia* concerning the problems of Asian security. Written by commentator V. V. Matveyev and entitled "A Filled 'Vacuum,' " the article focused on talk of a "vacuum" in Asia following the British withdrawal from east of Suez. Not only the Americans, Australians, and Japanese were casting greedy looks on this area, but also the Chinese; Matveyev cited "undenied reports" that Chinese soldiers were currently active in northern Burma. But, Matveyev predicted, there would be no "vacuum" for these intruders to fill, for India, Pakistan, Afghanistan, Burma, Cambodia, Singapore, and other Asian states were making efforts to consolidate their sovereignty and strengthen their economic autonomy. These independent states could resist interference from foreign powers in their internal affairs by setting up "the foundations of collective security" in this region.[19]

Matveyev's article commanded little foreign notice at the time. But, a little more than a week after its publication, Brezhnev, speaking to the Moscow Meeting of Communist and Workers' Parties, declared toward the very end of his lengthy address: "We are of the opinion that the course of events is also putting on the agenda the task of creating a system of collective security in Asia." [20] Foreign diplomats and journalists who inquired of Soviet officials about this single cryptic statement were directed by them to Matveyev's article.[21]

But the *Izvestiia* piece had been no more specific than Brezhnev on what the Soviets meant by a "collective security" system. Were they in fact proposing to sponsor an Asian military and political pact aimed at the containment of China? This was certainly the interpretation offered by the Chinese, who identified themselves as the target of this "sinister" plan picked up by the Soviets "from the garbage heap of the notorious warmonger Dulles." According to Peking, India and Japan were to serve as the linchpins of this projected security system in which the revisionists and imperialists were collaborating.[22]

The Soviets, denying that these were their intentions, still refused to say more than what their proposal was *not*. In fact, at the end of June the Soviet ambassador to Japan confessed that there were no specific plans as to the form such a collective security system should take or as to which countries should be invited to participate.[23] In its broadcast to South Asia on July 6, Radio Moscow protested that Brezhnev's proposal had been misinterpreted as calling for "filling a vacuum" with a new military alliance. The negative attitude of the USSR toward military blocs of any kind was common knowledge. Two days later, Radio Moscow's commentator V. Volokholansky specifically accused the Americans and Chinese of distorting the Soviet plan. The "genuinely peaceful" forces in Asia had long been seeking ways to create a "zone of peace"; the Soviet proposal simply proceeded from this urgent need to oppose aggressive forces in Asia with a "collective system." Such a system would be different from existing groupings; not only would it guarantee peace, but it would also "produce conditions for creative endeavors to boost the economic development" of Asian peoples, by which, of course, the "Soviet people also mean themselves." Closing of foreign military bases and the establishment of such a "zone of peace" in Asia should not offend anyone, for it "tallies with the interests of all nations." [24]

Foreign Minister Gromyko, in his foreign policy report to the Supreme Soviet two days later, reiterated this concern over the "misinterpretation" of the Brezhnev initiative. There was simply no foundation for the belief that it was directed against some other country or group of states; the proposal was an idea advanced in the common interests of all states, and the Soviets hoped that it would receive "very serious study." [25]

India's government did not appear sufficiently disillusioned with its traditional nonalignment to be prepared publicly to embrace the Brezhnev proposal, but neither was it inclined to offer an immediate and explicit rebuff. Mrs. Gandhi's own reaction put the most benevolent face possible on the Soviet plan; she said that she felt the Russians were more interested in economic cooperation—to which India was not averse—than in a military alliance. CPI chairman Dange likewise put his own interpretation on the proposal, viewing it as a "healthy" anti-American (not anti-Chinese) measure.[26]

Judging from the number of times that they have quoted it, the Soviets must have been more gratified by the reaction of Foreign Minister Dinesh Singh after he discussed the idea with Brezhnev and Kosygin during his visit to Moscow in September: "India welcomes the proposal by the Soviet Union on the creation of a system of collective security in Asia . . . the essence of the Soviet plan is the development of cooperation among the Asian countries for the purpose of strengthening peace." [27] But in a more considered reaction in December, Dinesh Singh said that his government did not believe in the notion of big powers acting as the guardian of security for India or her neighbors. Indonesia's foreign minister, Adam Malik, delivered an even sharper rebuff at the ministerial meeting of the Association of South East Asian Nations (ASEAN) the same month. Declaring that there was simply no need for a collective security system in Asia, he warned his colleagues against overestimating the threat of China and thereby being driven into reliance on the major powers.

The Soviets, who had been promoting the Brezhnev initiative with renewed vigor at the time of the ASEAN meeting, received a similarly cold response from the Japanese. *Izvestiia* concluded that Japan's participation in such a collective security system would require, as a prior step, the formation of a new government which would support "democracy," neutrality, and the liquidation of the Japanese-U.S. security pact. If such a government would disband Japan's existing alliances, renounce nuclear weapons, and demand the withdrawal of foreign troops, it would thereby be taking a "concrete step" toward the strengthening of peace.[28]

On balance, the Soviets could not have been overly encouraged by the reactions to the Brezhnev proposal. On the other hand, given the purposeful ambiguity with which the whole Soviet "plan" was shrouded, it must be concluded that since they had ventured so little, they could not have expected much to be either lost or gained. Brezhnev's cryptic comment in June had probably been intended as no more than a "trial balloon," a "testing of the wind." This is not to suggest that it was a casual afterthought, however, for we have seen that the ground for this initiative had been carefully prepared by the

Kosygin trip to South Asia and by Matveyev's *Izvestiia* article. Indeed, it was reported that the Soviet ambassadors to fifteen Asian countries had been called to Moscow at the time of Brezhnev's speech for briefings and discussions of the likely Asian reaction.[29] And the Soviets took pains in the six months following the speech to keep the idea alive, frequently alluding to its intent but without ever committing themselves to more details.

The probable reason for this studied ambiguity lies in the variety of potential purposes that the proposal for a "system of collective security" could serve. On a very modest level, the proposal was an effective way of reminding the world that the Soviet Union considers itself to be an Asian as well as a European power and that it intends to play a more active role in Asian security matters. This, of course, was one of the themes which had been emphasized by Kosygin's role at Tashkent and reiterated in the annual remembrances of that event.

A second possible purpose was to serve further notice that the Soviets were aware of the potential change in the military balance in Asia as Britain began to withdraw from "east of Suez" and to alert smaller Asian states to the danger of allowing American or Japanese "imperialism" to take up the British role, as well as to suggest that alternative arrangements could gain Soviet support. Even if no Soviet-sponsored "collective security system" were to result, by promoting the erosion of existing security arrangements and forestalling the construction of new Western-backed pacts, the Soviets could have achieved a net gain.

Despite their loud protestations against the theory of "filling the vacuum," the behavior of the Soviets—especially in the Middle East and the Indian Ocean—has indicated that they are indeed sensitive to such opportunities. The Soviet naval presence was first noticeable in the Indian Ocean in the spring of 1968, only shortly after the British declared their determination to withdraw from "east of Suez." Since that time, from six to fifteen Soviet warships have been present in the Indian Ocean, calling at some twenty ports in fourteen different countries from India (where the fleet has access to dockyards) to East Africa. Should the Suez Canal be reopened, the ability to link up this fleet with the more formidable force in the Mediterranean would represent the fulfillment of an ambition even greater than that of which the tsars once dreamed. Without immediate prospect of a large Western presence in the Indian Ocean, the Soviets can already calculate an increased political impact from the present limited force.

The intensive post-Tashkent Soviet diplomatic activity in South Asia which has been described above must surely be viewed in light of the changing military context in this area. If the United States continues to follow the British in reducing its Asian commitments, the leaders of South Asia may well be left to feel that a "collective security system" under Soviet guarantee is a viable alternative. The Brezhnev initiative, then, may be seen as an invitation to the states of this area to discuss with the Soviet Union, collectively or individually, cooperative defense arrangements for the post-Vietnam era.

Just as the Soviet denials of an interest in "filling the imperialist vacuum" in Asia have doubtful credibility in light of their military and political behavior, so also their protests that the collective security proposal had nothing to do with an anti-Chinese grouping ring hollow. For Brezhnev's speech followed by only three months the bloodiest and most far-reaching clash of Soviet and Chinese troops on their common border, and rumors of an impending full-scale Sino-Soviet war were very much in the air. In 1969–1970 Sino-Soviet polemics reached a new peak. On the very day of Brezhnev's speech to the Moscow Conference, *People's Daily* was charging that he and his colleagues had "turned the world's first state of the dictatorship of the proletariat into a dark fascist state of the dictatorship of the bourgeoisie." [30] The Soviets in turn were accusing "Mao's clique" of having established an antisocialist "military-bureaucratic dictatorship" in China. One Soviet writer has gone so far as to characterize "Mao Tse-tung Thought" as "a hodge-podge of Confucian postulates preaching obedience for the masses and deifying the supreme ruler, of feudal arrogance, petty-bourgeois chauvinism, Trotskyite 'Left-wing' radicalism and downright ignorance." [31]

According to the same *New Times* article, the chauvinistic ambitions of the "Peking empire-builders" are without limit. The Maoists rejoice over conflicts between India and Pakistan and are doing everything possible to hinder normalization of relations between the two. They are taking "practical steps" to bring South and Southeast Asia under their domination, though they "do not care a straw for the interests of the Asian peoples and the fate of those whom they are exhorting to rise in a 'people's war.' " [32] In the face of such charges, Soviet claims that the proposed "system of collective security" in Asia is not directed against any country must be taken rather lightly.

As noted above, Peking has publicly labeled the scheme a device for the containment of China. The Chinese have accused the "new tsars" of having turned Mongolia into a military base, of encouraging Japanese militarism, and of engaging, in coordination with U.S. imperialism, "in a futile effort to make the Indian-Pakistani subcontinent a link in the anti-China encirclement." [33] Moreover, they have labeled the Soviet presence in the Indian Ocean "expansionist," and they accuse the "revisionist chieftains" of plotting to fill the vacuum left by British withdrawal in order to build up Soviet "sea supremacy from the Black Sea, via the Suez Canal and the Indian Ocean, to the far East." [34]

Identifying India as an "important link" in the projected Soviet "encirclement" of China, Peking has continued its bitter attacks on the Indian government. In March 1970, calling attention to "intensified war preparations along the China-India and India-Pakistan borders," *Peking Review* assailed the Congress government's "mad course of arms expansion and war preparations in its efforts to serve U.S. imperialism and social-imperialism as a pawn in opposing China, to carry out an expansionist policy towards its neighbors and to put down the Indian people more ruthlessly." [35] India's acceptance of Soviet military aid has been a special target of Peking's fury. In March 1969, as Soviet Defense Minister Grechko was leaving India after a week's visit, he was quoted by the Indian press as saying that the Soviet Union would assist India if China again attacked her. Reminding the Russians that "Indian aggressor troops had fled helter-skelter in panic" during the last military engagement with China, Peking then accused the Soviets of seeking to turn Indian nationals into "cannon fodder" for Soviet "military adventures" against China. Between 1960 and 1967, the Chinese estimated, the Indian "reactionaries" had received $900 million in arms from the Soviet Union.[36]

In their reactions to Soviet-Indian cooperation, the Chinese did not limit themselves to verbal blasts at the two "collaborators." Rather, they stepped up their efforts to keep the Pakistanis out of any putative Soviet "encirclement" scheme. At a banquet in Peking in July 1969, honoring Pakistani Air Marshal Nur Khan, Chou En-lai described the Brezhnev plan as a new step "to rig up" an anti-China military alliance, and he praised the "Pakistan people and the righteous world opinion" for "exposing and rebutting" such schemes.[37] And when Pakistan's chief of state visited Peking in November 1970, his reception and the press coverage accorded him can only be described as lavish. "Several hundred thousand revolutionary Chinese people" were said to have shouted slogans supporting the Pakistanis in their struggle to safeguard national independence and to oppose foreign interference and backing the Kashmiri people in their struggle for self-determination. An editorial in *People's Daily* avowed that "no one can wreck" Sino-Pakistani friendship. And in the communiqué issued at the conclusion of Yahya's visit the Chinese expressed "willingness to render to Pakistan further assistance within China's means and capacity to help make the economy of Pakistan self-reliant." [38]

In summary, then, the Soviet proposal for a collective security system in Asia only accentuated trends which had been established in the mid-1960's. The Soviets continued military aid to and diplomatic courtship of both India and Pakistan, seeking to turn their attention from their quarrels with each other and toward a common effort to meet the Chinese "threat." The Chinese, meanwhile, intensified their war of words with both the Soviets and the Indians, engaging in limited military conflicts with both, while they sought both to solidify their friendship with Pakistan and to encourage her leaders to press their claims against India.

3. The Soviet-Indian Treaty and the December War

It is undoubtedly in the context of "collective security" against the Chinese that the main thrust of the twenty-year Soviet-Indian Treaty of Peace, Friendship, and Cooperation, signed on August 9, 1971, must be viewed. Negotiation of the treaty had reportedly begun two years before, in an atmosphere of sharp Sino-Soviet conflict and splits in Mrs. Gandhi's ruling party.[39] The Indians were apparently motivated to resume their discussions with the Soviets in the summer of 1971 by the increasing pressure to create an independent Bangladesh and return East Pakistani refugees to their homes through military action. President Yahya Khan made it clear that such action on India's part would set off a general war—a conflict in which Pakistan expected to be supported by China.

The other decisive new element in the situation came to light in July, when President Nixon revealed that his assistant, Henry Kissinger, had traveled to Peking to arrange a visit by the U.S. President in 1972. A detail of special interest to the Indians was Pakistan's role in facilitating Kissinger's secret journey. Thus, with the cooperation of India's sworn enemy, the American President was making overtures for a new relationship with China, India's second major antagonist in Asia. In her two wars of the 1960's, India had enjoyed first the support and assistance of the United States against China, and then its strict neutrality in the 1965 war with Pakistan. As India faced the prospect of another round with Pakistan—supported by China—in 1971, could she count again even on American neutrality? [40] Or had the seeming convergence of interest of the two superpowers in the 1960's in supporting India as a bulwark against Chinese ambitions been outdistanced by events in the 1970's?

The Soviets, no less concerned over the prospect of a Sino-American rapprochement, saw the Indian dilemma as an opportunity both to gain influence in New Delhi and to deter another enervating conflict in the subcontinent. A large-scale Indo-Pakistani war could only intensify the drain on India's resources, thus likely wasting not only the Soviet economic investment in India, but substantial Soviet arms investments in both of the belligerent countries as well. In Soviet eyes, the only gainers from such a conflict would be those "forces beyond their borders that are striving to damage India and Pakistan by pursuing their own definite political purposes." [41] The formal linkage of Soviet and Indian interests by means of a treaty might succeed in deterring the Chinese from providing military backing for Pakistan, while placing additional pressure on Yahya to reach a political solution in East Pakistan, thus allowing the removal of the refugee burden from India.

The treaty itself cost the Soviet Union very little. What little influence the USSR had in Pakistan had already been lessened by what Yahya considered meddlesome Soviet statements concerning Pakistan's "internal affairs." That the Soviets intended nonetheless to try to minimize the treaty's alienating effect on Pakistan was evident both from the absence in the joint Soviet-Indian communiqué of any reference to an independent Bangladesh, and from the repeated assurances by the Soviets that the treaty was directed against no third party.

The Pakistani foreign secretary, two weeks after the treaty was signed, stated his belief that the Soviets would exercise their influence on India to restrain her from attacking Pakistan. "That is good enough as far as we are concerned." He traveled to Moscow in early September to receive from Gromyko direct assurances of the Soviets' "very positive desire of maintaining and further strengthening relations" with Pakistan.[42]

As Foreign Secretary Khan was undoubtedly aware, the actual obligations the Soviets incurred from the treaty itself were minimal. Apart from pledges to strengthen economic, scientific, and cultural cooperation and to continue regular contacts on international problems, each party to the treaty promised: (1) not to enter into any alliance or commit any aggression directed against the other (Article 8); (2) not to undertake any commitment incompatible with the treaty (Article 10); and (3) in the event of an attack or threat directed toward either by a third party, to "immediately start mutual consultations with a view to eliminating this threat" (Article 9).[43] In his speech to the Supreme Soviet Presidium on August 12, Gromyko paid special notice to this last provision, remarking that it had "drawn attention in many capitals and corresponding conclusions are already being drawn from it." [44] The careful adherence in comments by Gromyko and the Soviet press to the exact wording of this article ("with a view to") suggests that the ambiguity in its phrasing was deliberately designed to create maximum uncertainty about Soviet actions in a crisis situation, and thus a maximum deterrent effect.

In short, the treaty's main purpose, from the Soviet point of view, was to formalize and extend Russian influence for the immediate purpose of *stabilizing* the situation in South Asia, both by deterring the Pakistanis and their Chinese patrons, and by providing a psychological crutch to the Indians designed to forestall an emotional drift toward war on the part of New Delhi. Technically, the Soviets were under no greater obligation to give material assistance to India in case of attack than they had been prior to the treaty's signing. In fact, even in the absence of the treaty, the Soviet umbrella was likely to have been extended to cover India if she had become involved in a war with Pakistan supported by China.[45]

India, on the other hand, though she had not denied herself the option of unilateral military action against Pakistan, had solemnly declared her intention to consult the Soviets in the event of any threatened attack, thus formalizing and displaying for the benefit of third parties the strong Soviet political influence in subcontinent affairs. Of course, the interpretation placed upon the treaty by Mrs. Gandhi's government was that it served to strengthen India's traditional policy of nonalignment, and indeed the treaty formally notes the Soviet "respect" for that policy. A *Pravda* editorial, commenting further on the Soviets' "great respect" for Indian nonalignment, added, in a novel interpretation of the meaning of that term, "India *invariably* shows understanding and support for the peaceful Soviet foreign policy." [46] One parliamentary critic in India, noting the irony in the fact that the treaty had been signed on the anniversary of Gandhi's "Quit India" movement of 1942, asked whether "three decades after we ask the British imperialists to get out, we are going to ask the Russians to come in." [47]

There were few such critics in India, however. Only the Swatantra party, among the non-Marxist political groupings, opposed the pact. The leader of Swatantra's erstwhile ally on the Indian right, the Jan Sangh, declared that the treaty gave India "a friend who can be trusted and who can stand by us through thick and thin." [48] Not unexpectedly, the CPI was loudest in its praise for the treaty. In the opinion of CPI parliamentary deputy Hiren Mukherjee, the pact "lifted much of the gloom" which had resulted from India's humiliation at the hands of the "crude but craftily evolving Washington-Islamabad-Peking axis." [49]

The first consultations following the signing of the treaty took place in Moscow in late September, when Mrs. Gandhi conferred with Brezhnev, Kosygin, and Podgorny. Though discussions were held on a long-range program of economic cooperation and a decision was made to set up an intergovernmental commission on economic, scientific, and technical cooperation, the main item on the agenda was the evolving crisis in East Pakistan. In a joint statement issued at the conclusion of the talks, both sides announced that they would seek "urgent measures" to reach a political solution "with due regard to the wishes, the inalienable rights and lawful interests of the people of East Pakistan." In the Soviet view, this clearly excluded for the present the imposition of a military solution by India. As Kosygin put it: "As regards what authority there should be in Pakistan, it is for the Pakistan people to decide. It is not a question for India to decide. You agreed to this. Therefore, we appeal that this problem had to be solved by peaceful political means. Every effort should be made to prevent a military conflict from breaking out." [50]

However, the Soviets also "took into account" Mrs. Gandhi's statement of India's determination "to take all necessary measures to stop the inflow of refugees" and to ensure their speedy return.[51] For their part, the Soviets reaffirmed Podgorny's April statement on East Pakistan, though Kosygin added in a speech in Mrs. Gandhi's presence that it was "impossible to justify" the actions of the Pakistani government. While the Soviets would do everything possible to maintain peace on the subcontinent, they "expected" from Islamabad an early political settlement of the crisis.[52]

Although the Soviet Union had taken its strongest position to date, there was disappointment expressed in the Indian press at the posture of the Soviets with regard to what they still referred to as "East Pakistan." The *Times of India* felt that the Russians were trying to close off the Indian option for military action, while *The Statesman* observed that the Soviet commentary indicated that "the vital issue is not independence but the preservation of peace in the subcontinent." [53] Both were probably quite accurate assessments of the Soviet purpose at this time.

During October and November, however, articles in the Soviet press grew steadily more critical of Islamabad's policy, perhaps reflecting the official frustration at the lack of response to Soviet pressure on Pakistan. An article in *New Times* in October spoke of "mass reprisals" and "bloody terror" in East Pakistan on orders of the military administration, and it declared that the Soviet people were "demanding" that Pakistani authorities stop the persecutions and reach a political settlement. Significantly, the author of this piece went beyond "humanitarian" arguments in his support for the Bengali cause. Noting that the platform of Sheikh Mujibur Rahman's party called for Pakistani withdrawal from SEATO and CENTO, he concluded that "the East Pakistanis' struggle for their national rights is part and parcel of the Pakistani people's overall struggle for democracy and progressive socio-economic reforms." [54]

A month later, the same writer declared that the refugee problem was "no longer an 'internal affair' of Pakistan." He accused the Pakistani authorities of "banking on a military solution" by deploying troops on the Indo-Pakistani frontier and thus forcing the Indians—who were "displaying great restraint and a high

sense of responsibility"—to take measures to safeguard their security. Yet that there were still limits on the Soviet position
with respect to Pakistan was evident from the author's call for a
settlement based not only on the "will and interests" of the
East Pakistanis, but also on "respect for Pakistan's territorial integrity." [55]

Indeed, the major thrust of the Soviet press commentary was
an emphasis on the need to avoid war on the subcontinent. To
illustrate his contention that there could be "no military solution for the existing problems," one writer recalled the consequences of the 1965 war: a crisis in the Indian economy from
which it took two years to recover, activization of reactionary
forces in India, and an economic and political crisis in Pakistan.
The September 1965 TASS statement, arguing that only hostile
external forces could profit from Indo-Pakistani war, was, according to this article, "more timely today than ever." [56] But as
the situation continued to deteriorate, subsequent articles in
Pravda and *Izvestiia*—bearing titles such as "Hindustan Needs
Peace"—reported "war hysteria" among "reactionary and chauvinistic forces" in Pakistan and clearly placed the blame for the
rising level of military hostilities on Islamabad.[57]

A frenetically paced diplomacy on the part of all the involved states was accompanying the escalation in military preparations by India and Pakistan. President Podgorny stopped
briefly in New Delhi on October 1 on his way to Hanoi, and he
met with Yahya Khan at the celebrations in Persepolis, Iran,
later the same month. Deputy Foreign Minister Firyubin arrived in India for a six-day visit on October 22 amidst reports
that Mrs. Gandhi's government had levied new taxes, called up
the militia, and activated the army reserves. Firyubin's talks
were pointedly labeled as in accordance with the obligation for
"consultations" stated in Article 9 of the August treaty. To rein-
force the message that these consultations concerned "effective
measures" to remove the threat, Air Marshal Kutakhov arrived
in India for a six-day visit shortly after Firyubin's departure.
Moreover, in the period between August and the end of November, eight shiploads of Soviet arms were reported to have
arrived in India.[58] Clearly, though the Soviets were publicly
counseling against war, they were ensuring that India would be
well armed should she find a military solution necessary.

Mrs. Gandhi departed India in the midst of these visits from
Soviet dignitaries to travel in six Western nations. She arrived

in the United States in an atmosphere of administration displeasure over her rejection both of Yahya's offer of a mutual troop pullback and of U Thant's suggestion that United Nations observers be stationed on the borders of the two countries. Despite the Nixon Administration's decision finally to halt the flow of military equipment to Pakistan, Mrs. Gandhi—who had complained that India had had a "far more understanding approach" on the part of the Soviets than on the part of the Americans—continued to refuse to negotiate with Islamabad prior to a favorable settlement in East Pakistan.

At the same time that the Indian Prime Minister was in Washington, a Pakistani delegation headed by former foreign minister Bhutto (and including high-ranking military officials) was engaged in consultations in Peking. Expressing China's "great concern" at India's "crude interference" in the internal affairs of Pakistan, acting Foreign Minister Chi Peng-fei declared that China would in case of foreign aggression, "as always, resolutely support the Pakistani Government and people." Twice more during the month high-ranking Chinese officials publicly expressed "concern" over Indian "provocations," but in general the Chinese were observing a public restraint which must have disappointed their Pakistani friends.[59] In the meantime, the Pakistanis were receiving what Bhutto later labeled "tremendous pressure" from the Soviets to make political concessions in the East.[60]

By the end of November the busy movement of diplomats had come to an end. On the same day that President Nixon was dispatching personal messages to India, Pakistan, and the Soviet Union urging an end to border skirmishes and requesting the Soviets to exert more influence for peace, Mrs. Gandhi took the significant step of declaring that her government considered the very presence of West Pakistani troops in East Pakistan as "a threat to our security." Full-scale war broke out four days later. The conflict in the East ended on December 16 with the unconditional surrender of Pakistani troops, whose logistical situation had been virtually impossible. The war on the western front, which had been limited throughout, was ended the following day, when Yahya accepted a cease-fire. But while the fighting on the subcontinent was proceeding, as well as in its aftermath, a torrent of impassioned, often vitriolic words poured forth from Moscow, Peking, and Washington, and acrimonious around-the-clock debates occurred at the United Nations—all of

which revealed much about the perceptions and stakes of the
"great powers" in this tragic war.

The Soviets, in their unabashed partiality in defense of India,
surely lived up to the expectations of many Indians following
the August pact. Most notably, Ambassador Malik used his
vetoes in the Security Council to block cease-fire resolutions
while the Indians completed their military operations in East
Pakistan. Malik's arguments in the United Nations were amplified by articles in the Soviet press. According to the Russians,
Pakistan bore sole responsibility for both the immediate and
underlying causes of the conflict. Yahya's campaign in the east
of "terror and lawlessness on a scale unprecedented in history,"
and his repeated refusal to listen to reason, culminating in the
"unprovoked aggression" by Pakistani planes on December 3,
forced India to take measures to defend herself. United States
imperialism, angry at the policy of socioeconomic reform pursued by India's government and anxious to divert attention from
its aggression in Indochina, had taken a stand which was interpreted by authorities in Islamabad as "encouragement of the
peace-imperiling moves." For its part, the USSR could not ignore a conflict taking place in the "immediate vicinity of its borders" and "consequently affecting its own security." [61] While
the Soviets according to their own version, had supported
moves to stop the bloodshed, they had also insisted (for example, in a TASS statement of December 6) that such moves
should be linked to a solution of the political causes of the war,
which were (in Brezhnev's words) "brutal suppression of the elementary rights and the clearly expressed will of the population
of East Pakistan and the tragedy of the ten million refugees." [62]

The United States, pressing for a cease-fire resolution in the
United Nations, took a stand which reflected irritation with both
India and her Soviet patrons. Ambassador Bush labeled India
the "aggressor" in the conflict (a term later disavowed by the
State Department), and the Nixon Administration quickly
moved to cut off $87.6 million in development loans to India
(though economic aid to Pakistan was not terminated). The
President told the new Pakistani ambassador that "we have followed with sympathetic interest" Yahya's efforts to reduce tensions and achieve an amicable political settlement. In a "background" briefing designed to explain this partiality, Henry
Kissinger, denying that the administration was "anti-Indian,"

nevertheless claimed that India had attacked Pakistan without justification while the U.S. was in the process of promoting a political settlement. The subsequent publication in the American press of "secret" notes of administration deliberations, gleefully picked up and trumpeted in the Soviet press, cast embarrassing doubt on Kissinger's explanations.[63] Administration disquiet at the perceived pursuit of unilateral military advantage by the Soviets in the subcontinent, and at the Soviets' failure to restrain India in the conflict, went so far as to move Kissinger to suggest that "a new look might have to be taken at the President's [Moscow] summitry plans." [64]

The Chinese, who had been relatively silent on subcontinent affairs prior to December, unleashed a verbal assault on the Soviets and Indians after the outbreak of war, while eschewing actual military involvement. In the United Nations, Ambassador Huang Hua introduced a resolution not only calling for troop withdrawals but also condemning India for her "creation" of Bangladesh and "aggression" against Pakistan. But the major thrust of Huang Hua's argument was directed against the Soviet Union, which—under the terms of its "military alliance" with India—acted as "supporter, encourager and protector" in her aggression against Pakistan. According to Huang, the Soviet aim in encouraging the dismemberment of Pakistan was to gain control of the subcontinent and the Indian Ocean "and enlarge its sphere of influence in its contention with the other superpower for hegemony." Huang saw a parallel with the Soviet tactic in the Middle East; in both cases, the USSR was taking advantage of the dependence of another state in order to extend its own sphere of influence. But through its efforts to fix its "security borders" at the Indian Ocean, the Soviet Union was in reality copying the tactic used by the Israelis in the Middle East conflict.[65]

According to *People's Daily*, the Soviets had "stage-managed" India's long-planned scheme to annex East Pakistan. The Indians carried out this plot by encouraging secessionists, "cooking up" the so-called "government of Bangladesh," and injecting this "puppet regime" into East Pakistan by "open, direct invasion." India's "naked aggression" was covered up by "absurd pretexts, arrogant in the extreme." The "so-called refugee question" was simply a product of Indian interference. The Chinese were familiar with such practices: "Didn't the Indian reactionaries also create the 'Tibetan refugee question' more than ten years ago? When the rebellion of serf-owners they engineered failed them, they abducted tens of thousands of Tibetan inhabitants of China to India and made use of this incident to carry out frantic anti-China activities." [66]

The Soviets, too, in carrying out "subversion and splittist activities against China," had used the same tactic by coercing "several tens of thousands of Chinese civilians" from Sinkiang; were they also going to take it as a pretext for launching armed aggression against China? In the Chinese view, the entire "Bangladesh" incident followed the same "gangster's logic" that had led the Japanese militarists to "rig up Manchukuo" and then demand the withdrawal of Chinese troops from their own territory.

A statement by the Chinese government, issued on the day the Pakistani forces in the east surrendered, reminded India that such logic could also be used against her. "It is known to all that India has its own nationality problems, whose complexity and acuteness are rarely seen elsewhere in the world. . . . He who plays with fire will be consumed by fire." [67] But the dire consequences predicted by China for India and her "backstage manager" were clearly reserved for the future. Though she promised to continue to give material and political assistance to Pakistan, China's intervention during the fighting was limited to two "strong protests" to Indian over "encroachments" by Indian troops across the Sikkim boundary. For the present, China could only advise "our friendly countries" threatened by superpowers and their clients to exercise vigilance and strengthen their defensive capabilities.

Much attention was paid in the Soviet press to the fact that both Peking and Washington had aligned themselves with Pakistan in the conflict. The Soviet press approvingly reprinted the comment of the *Times of India*, to the effect that cooperation between the U.S. and China had developed so rapidly that one could not dismiss the possibility that the two had already arrived at an agreement aimed at the Soviet Union and its friends. Similarly, James Reston's observation in the *New York Times* concerning the threat of separatist disintegration in India itself was labeled by the Soviets as a "transparent hint." [68]

In the Soviet view, the American stand could have been predicted, given the class nature and "imperialist essence" of the U.S. regime. But the Chinese policy could only be seen as a "flagrant betrayal of class principles." Peking evidently saw nothing wrong in "consorting with the conservative bourgeois-landowner circles" of Islamabad who were seeking to "strangle the democratic liberation movement" in East Pakistan. China's "rabid anti-India and anti-Soviet campaign" merely made manifest her intention of sowing distrust of the Soviet peace policy and paving the way toward realization of her own "Great-Power ambitions and hegemonic plans" in Asia. By acting in the crisis as the "accomplice of imperialism," the Chinese were clearly seeking "to obtain the United States' consent to their penetration into certain areas in Asia, to their subversive activities there." [69]

Moscow's assessment both of China's position during the Indo-Pakistani war of 1971 and of its subsequent activities, and the consequent revival of the Soviet campaign for collective security in Asia, must be viewed in the context of the emerging triangularity of global relationships, most dramatically demonstrated in the summitry of 1972. The events of that year pointed to a choice by the Soviets (after some internal debate) to accept for the immediate future a limited-adversary relationship with the United States, based on strategic parity. This choice, however, by no means relegated the Soviets to foreign policy "quietism" or to a position as a "satisfied power." They were still capable of engaging in "fishing operations," in the course of which they might fully expect their newfound status of nuclear equality to bring political advantages in crisis-bargaining situations. A world of parity is not necessarily a world in which risk-taking is foresworn.

Though the Moscow summit might have established some important ground rules for the conduct of the rivalry, the Soviets clearly expected that their competition with the United States would continue. However, the Soviet-American "limited adversary" relationship was being forged in a world which was no longer strictly bipolar. Soviet analysts have explicitly noted that the absence of a zero-sum situation may allow both parties to make gains (or suffer losses). Yet they are also quite aware that the burgeoning presence of China complicates the question of relative gains and losses even further. The recent expansion of Soviet military capabilities has reflected this awareness: Soviet forces on the Sino-Soviet border *trebled* between 1968 and 1971. And though relations between the parties have improved since the low point of 1969, both Soviet and Chinese decision-makers still consider the other side to be a major security threat.

The Soviet side's judgment of the unlikelihood of any imminent return of Sino-Soviet relations to a "fraternal" basis was
evidenced by Brezhnev's remarks to the Soviet trade unions
congress in March 1972. At that time he accepted the possibility
of conducting relations between the two socialist states under a
formula at which the Soviets had recoiled in horror when the
Albanians had suggested it as a basis for their own relations
with Moscow a decade earlier: ". . . we are now prepared to
construct Soviet-Chinese relations on [the] basis . . . of the
principle of peaceful coexistence." [70]

The Chinese, of course, had not been inactive in the conduct
of their own diplomacy, and it was this fact which had brought
the dispute more squarely into the international arena and
made life even more complicated for the Soviet leaders during
1972. In Moscow's judgment, the Sino-American talks
amounted to imperialist exploitation of China's "anti-Soviet-
ism." Brezhnev himself expressed skepticism in the March
speech that the U.S.-Chinese dialogue was limited to matters of
bilateral relations. Earlier, an article in *International Affairs*
had suggested that China's "anti-Soviet" policy was compensation to the Western states for their aid in developing China's
economy and "turning China into a state capable of realizing its
territorial claims on the Soviet Union, and of bringing under its
influence the neighboring states in East and Southeast Asia."
Mao, who had covertly sought to improve relations with the
U.S. since 1964–1965, was acting as the "Trojan horse of imperialism in the international revolutionary movement, this forming
the essence of the intensified diplomatic flirtation" between
Washington and Peking.[71]

Because their interests are more directly and concretely in
conflict, it is the Soviet and Chinese leaders who must most fear
being "odd man out" as they perceive the triangular relationship—Washington, Peking, and Moscow—as a struggle on
two fronts. Thus, as China perceives the USSR as "adversary
number one" and undertakes to reduce its antagonism with the
U.S. in order to struggle more effectively against the Soviets,
this in turn alarms the Soviets and causes them also to appeal to
the Americans. So long as the Chinese and Americans were
simply not in contact, the Soviets occupied the advantageous
position. After 1971, however, the continued sorry state of their
own relations with Peking, together with their perception that
the Americans and Chinese were teaming up in anti-Soviet ma-

neuvers, had put the Soviets in a more disadvantageous position in this triangular relationship.

4. The Revival of the "Collective Security" Campaign

But in the immediate aftermath of the December war, the Soviets had every reason to be exultant. Though they had failed to bring about the removal of the refugee burden from India by peaceful means, they had at least played an essential role in India's victory over Pakistan, while their American and Chinese rivals had both lined up on the side of the loser. In the eyes of India (and much of the rest of the world), the first encounter by the new Washington-Peking alignment had ended in defeat. One Soviet official at the United Nations crowed: "This is the first time in history that the United States and China have been defeated together." [72]

As American influence in India had declined dramatically, so Soviet influence had never been greater. Soviet military and economic aid was bound in the future to loom even larger in India's calculations. The meaning and effectiveness of the Soviet-Indian Treaty had been strikingly demonstrated to all concerned—but especially to the Indians, who had, with Soviet help, achieved in one stroke the dismemberment and elimination as an effective military threat of their main antagonist of nearly a quarter of a century. In the words of the London *Economist*, the destruction of the approximate balance of power on the subcontinent had left the Soviets as the "patron and protector of the local cock of the roost." [73]

The Soviets, reluctant to destroy all their ties with Pakistan, moved cautiously after the war in establishing relations with Bangladesh; nonetheless, the USSR was the first great power to recognize Dacca. Sheikh Mujibur Rahman's visit to Moscow in March of 1972 was the occasion for the announcement of Soviet assistance in construction of several large industrial projects, in the restoration of rail and sea transport, and in training prospective Bengali economic specialists.[74] The atmosphere of cooperation, bolstered by a communiqué in which Mujib stated his agreement with a number of Soviet positions on international questions, has been accompanied by the establishment of a noticeable Soviet presence in Bangladesh.

Only two weeks after Mujib's visit to Moscow, President Bhutto of Pakistan was received in the Soviet capital for a "frank and useful exchange" on the prospects for developing "good-neighbor relations" between the USSR and Pakistan. The ideological predispositions of the new regime in Pakistan had already been certified by the Soviet press as more acceptable than the preceding military oligarchy had been. Bhutto's visit, and the consequent announcement that Soviet aid and trade would be resumed, indicated that Moscow had chosen to rebuild its relations with Pakistan rather than abandoning it completely to Peking and Washington. The Soviets immediately began to employ their influence for the purpose of pressuring Bhutto away from what Kosygin called "a policy of confrontation" to a "policy of peace and cooperation" with India.[75] The degree of Bhutto's susceptibility to such blandishments was in doubt, however. Already he had signed a new $300 million economic and military aid agreement with Peking, and by the beginning of the summer the Chinese were reported to have delivered 60 new jet fighters and 100 tanks as replacements for Pakistan's losses in the war.[76]

In the changed circumstances of 1972, however, Pakistan and Bangladesh were overshadowed on the subcontinent by a strengthened and confident India. And for the Soviets, the essential point was that whereas prior to 1971 the balance of forces had dictated the well-nigh impossible task of uniting India and Pakistan in a common grouping against Chinese influence, the situation after the December war seemed far more manageable. India, grateful for Soviet assistance and dependent on further aid, was in the new circumstances an even more valuable partner in the effort to outflank China. As Brezhnev put it in December 1972, Soviet-Indian friendship, as based on the treaty, had not only led to the strengthening of "progressive anti-imperialist forces in India," but was also "having an important positive influence on the international situation as a whole." [77]

In the longer perspective, and on the other side of the ledger, there were great risks in the increased Soviet involvement on the subcontinent. As the Soviet press acknowledged, the Chinese were likely to be more involved than ever in sponsoring separatist and "Maoist" movements in both India and Bangladesh. Vast quantities of assistance would be required in both areas; an American official had already commented with relief that the "international basket case" that Bangladesh was likely to become would not be "our basket case." [78] In short, the Soviets were likely to be faced with a greater burden of both military and economic aid in an area in which prospects for stability had by no means been enhanced. But there seemed to be no alternative open to the Soviet Union but to shoulder the greater burden as the price for greater influence, for the maintenance of this influence seemed still to require that the Soviets seek *stability* in South Asia.

Finally, it is significant that, in the months following the Soviet-Indian Treaty, the Soviets revived the long-dormant notion of a "system of collective security in Asia." An article in *New Times* in September quoted approvingly the view of a left-wing Indian newspaper that the treaty could become the first step toward establishment of a collective security system.[79] This theme was elaborated in another article in the same journal, which asserted that the Soviet Union was working steadfastly toward the realization of this idea, which was "bound to assert itself gradually." [80] Shortly afterward, Gromyko, addressing the General Assembly, reiterated the same message: "As is known, the Soviet Union has advanced the idea of creating a collective security system in Asia which would guarantee an atmosphere of security on this continent. Time and effort are needed to realize this objective. But the situation that has taken shape in Asia requires that such efforts be made, and made persistently." [81]

Brezhnev himself returned to the idea in his speech of March 1972. Noting the Soviet-Indian treaty and the subsequent strengthening of Soviet relations on the subcontinent, he then praised the recent "turn for the better in our relations with Japan." Gromyko in January had made his first visit to Tokyo in six years. His trip—obviously timed to exploit Japanese disillusionment with the United States and to divert Tokyo from following the American lead in conducting talks with China—had won from the Japanese the promise of a resumption of talks on a Moscow-Tokyo peace treaty. It was thus in the context of Soviet relations with Tokyo and New Delhi that Brezhnev went on to say:

The idea of guaranteeing security in Asia on a collective basis is arousing increasing interest in many Asian countries. It is becoming increasingly clearer that the real path to security in Asia is not the path of military blocs and groupings but the path of good-neighbor cooperation among all the states interested in this. Collective security in Asia must, in our view, be based on such principles as renunciation of the use of force in relations between states, respect for sovereignty and the inviolability of borders, noninterference in internal affairs and the broad development of economic and other cooperation on the basis of full equality and mutual advantage. We . . . are ready to cooperate with all states with a view to the implementation of this idea.[82]

A new wave of articles in the Soviet press echoed Brezhnev's idea. Prominent among them was a piece appearing in June in *Pravda* by Viktor Mayevsky, entitled "Collective Security in Asia is an Urgent Problem." Why the sense of "urgency" in Moscow about this long-standing notion? One probable reason was the increasing evidence that an Indochina peace arrangement was imminent.[83] Rather than allow this area to slip under Chinese influence following an American withdrawal, Moscow might well have wanted to include it as part of a larger Soviet-sponsored security system in Asia. The other, perhaps stronger, reason for urgency was Soviet concern at the increasing pace of Peking's diplomatic activity; the Chinese were simply refusing to be "contained." To prevent Tokyo—and even New Delhi—from becoming ensnared in Peking's active net, the Soviets were offering to these and other Asian countries the alternative prospect of their own security grouping—which was not, of course, "directed against any other country."

For the immediate future, the Soviets seemed likely to continue their campaign for a collective security system in Asia, pursued through the use of both diplomatic and economic inducements for closer cooperation with the states of South Asia as well as through continued negotiation with Japan. Though they characterized Peking's fears of encirclement and Washington's talk of "counterbalances" as reminiscent of the practices of "bourgeois and monarchist diplomacy in Metternich's time," the practical thrust of the Soviet effort was toward consolidation and ratification of the territorial status quo. In the words of *Izvestiia*'s commentator Viktor Matveyev: "Such a system answers its purpose when it covers an extensive region and stipulates the appropriate commitments: renunciation of the use of force between states; respect for their sovereignty and integrity; and nonintervention in their internal affairs—that is, those conditions essential to maintaining peace among states." [84]

Yet at the same time the Soviets would be likely to continue to exploit opportunities for the cautious expansion of their own influence in Asia at the expense of Peking. Such efforts, in

South Asia at least, would probably remain outside the military realm. The Soviets, while pointing with alarm at alleged American efforts to turn the Indian Ocean into an "American lake," continued to describe their naval operations there as aimed solely at ensuring the safe descent of Soviet spacecraft. Though both arguments strain credibility, they do not lend support to any putative scheme on the part of Moscow greatly to enlarge its own military presence. Rather, in the context of existing alignments, the Soviets would most likely continue their policy of providing India with sufficient military aid to ensure her regional hegemony.

Whatever may come of it, the collective security campaign serves as further evidence of the continuing Soviet interest in India as a bulwark of containment of Chinese influence in South Asia. As A. M. D'iakov had said in 1952, in the quite different context of condemning American plans for containing Chinese communism, India is "the one country of Asia which in population and in potential economic resources could oppose China." [85]

5. India's Domestic Politics: The Soviet Assessment

In accordance with this long-standing estimate of India's potential, the Soviets have continued to display no small interest in her internal political situation. The recent visible disintegration of Congress unity, climaxing at the end of 1969 with the formal split of the ruling party, was seen by P. Kutsobin in *New Times* as ushering in "the most crucial period since independence." [86] Mrs. Gandhi's success in holding on to power despite the opposition of the Congress "syndicate" was, in the Soviet view, not a "fortuitous" event, but reflected the fact that the prime minister's program of socioeconomic reforms "has received the support of the broadest circles of the Indian public." [87]

In fact, the entire confrontation in the Congress party was perceived by Soviet analysts as an inevitable result of class polarization between, on one hand, the Indian "monopolists" and large landowners backed by imperialist support and, on the other, the "broad masses as well as certain groups of the middle and small bourgeoisie." This antagonism, which had been present ever since the national bourgeoisie had taken command of the Indian state, had been "papered over" for many years because the bourgeoisie had been so busy accumulating wealth that the competition from the growing state sector had not proved very frightening to them. But further consolidation of the public sector, as represented in the crisis-precipitating step of nationalization of India's banks, had proved unpalatable to the "monopoly" sectors of the bourgeoisie.[88]

These right-wing forces, which had long blocked implementation of "progressive" socioeconomic measures by the Congress and which had favored greater cooperation with imperialism, had now split off from Mrs. Gandhi's Congress supporters. And according to the Soviets, although the "dominant trend in recent years"—the "steady strengthening" of the right-wing elements—had thus been checked, the danger was by no means over. For the new danger was that the Syndicate Congress would form a parliamentary and electoral alliance with the Swatantra and Jan Sangh parties, whose mass support was based on the exploitation of communal and religious hostilities. Only the unity of left and center forces, the Soviets said, could defeat the reactionary bloc, implement consistent reform, and return the country to political stability.

Such a united front had long been urged by the CPI, and when Mrs. Gandhi lost her parliamentary majority after the Congress split, there was increased hope that she would be forced to implement a more radical policy in return for leftist support. Her decision to dissolve the parliament ahead of time and to call for new elections in 1971, while opening the possibility that her "New Congress" would win an absolute majority and be able to rule without the support of other parties, also posed an opportunity for the CPI and other leftist parties to increase their representation, as well as the danger that both these strategies would be defeated by a victory of the united right.

To the surprise of most observers, it was the first-named possibility which became reality in the March 1971 elections. Mrs. Gandhi's landslide victory was termed by a Soviet observer both a triumph for her and her party and a "defeat for Indian reaction." Passing over without comment the failure of the Moscow-backed CPI to increase its strength in Parliament, B. Kalyagin wrote that the Congress' absolute majority put it in a position "to carry out the important democratic reforms it has promised and which the masses are eagerly awaiting." [89] Three months later, another Soviet journalist indicated that a satisfactory start on reforms had not yet been undertaken. Criticizing Mrs. Gandhi's new budget indirectly (by reporting the views of "Indian democratic opinion" and "informed observers"), this writer again showed alarm at the continuing strength of the Indian right wing and the persisting disunity among "democratic and Left parties." [90]

The question at issue in this struggle, in the Soviet view, was at once simple and yet of vast significance. As Kutsobin posed it: "In what direction is the country to move, in the interests of which classes and sections of society is its socioeconomic and political development to proceed?" [91] In the two decades since India had achieved independence, progress had been made in overcoming the colonial legacy and in building the foundations of an industrialized economy. But at the same time that the state sector had been built up, the government had also been promoting the concentration of capital in the private sector. That this had not contributed to rapid growth was due to what Mirsky called the "historical shortsightedness" of India's bourgeoisie, which was "rooted in the very nature of that money-grubbing class." For no more than 50 percent of the profits from the private sector had been invested in productive fields. Unlike the capitalism of the nineteenth century, the capitalism developing in India could only be a "degenerate, parasitic, speculative-bureaucratic capitalism" connected with the neocolonialists and perpetuating exploitation and vast inequalities.[92] For India to become a truly industrialized state following the capitalist path would require, according to Ul'ianovsky, a minimum of 100–150 years. For the national bourgeoisie was simply "incapable of profound development" of the anti-imperialist or antifeudal revolution or of fulfilling the general-democratic program in the interests of the people.[93]

Thus in India, more than in any other emerging country, "the tragic contradictions of the capitalist model of development" had been manifested, according to an editorial in *New Times* marking the twentieth anniversary of the republic. Such successes as had been registered had occurred "in spite of capitalism, rather than thanks to it." And now the forces of monopoly capital were seeking to restrict further the role of the state sector, to drive India further down the capitalist road and anchor her more solidly in the imperialist world market. But at the same time, forces advocating a transition to the noncapitalist path were growing stronger. Their victory would not be easy, however. The interruption of capitalist development and transition to a noncapitalist path would be impossible to achieve without "a sharp social and political struggle" which would break the political monopoly of the Indian bourgeoisie.[94]

a. "Creative Marxism" and the "Intermediate Stages"
High-level public affirmation of this thesis concerning the utter bankruptcy of the capitalist path and the need for third-world countries to move toward socialism by way of intermediate stages followed in a few months. As Brezhnev put it in his address marking the hundredth anniversary of Lenin's birth, the path toward socialist development in the third world was not likely to be an immediate or direct one. In his opinion, "this road of development, as Lenin said, must include a whole series of 'gradual preliminary stages,' of 'special transitional measures.' "[95] This explicit recognition of the complex and extended nature of social change in the third world, the result of a decade and a half of full-scale Soviet activity in Asia and Africa, is a far cry from the confident optimism concerning the prospects for rapid development toward socialism which had characterized the early Khrushchev years. It represents an even greater advance in sophistication from the Comintern era—a fact which was candidly acknowledged by A. A. Iskenderov in a 1967 publication.[96]

As the external and internal conditions of the national-liberation struggle have changed, he wrote, the estimates and conclusions of the Comintern—some of which were "sectarian" even when they were adopted, as Kuusinen had admitted at the Twentieth Party Congress—are today "even further from reality." But, according to Iskenderov, Marxist-Leninists are not afraid of abandoning "old, erroneous conceptions stemming from a dogmatic approach." Far from being a sign of weakness, it is a confirmation of the vitality of the ideology, which is being "constantly developed and enriched." Unlike the "dogmatic distortions" of the doctrine, "creative Marxism" does not proceed from "ready-made schemes but deals with existing and constantly arising problems, which vitally concern the masses."

And Iskenderov did not hesitate to identify the principal peddlers of such distortions—the Chinese—or to admit unashamedly the source of their errors—the "dogmatic postulates contained in some documents of the Comintern."[97] Such "creative" Soviet-sponsored ideas as the possibility of noncapitalist development had simply been ignored by the Chinese. By promoting the thesis that armed risings are the only road to socialism, they had in fact hampered the development of the revolution. For unless armed uprisings have broad mass support, "they can only degenerate into skirmishes of small armed detachments, having no links with the the people, and result in putchism [sic] and petty-bourgeois adventurism which has nothing to do with revolutionary struggle." What Iskenderov seemed to be saying is that the Chinese, in their advice to third-world revolutionaries, as well as in their own domestic practice, were ignoring a truth the Soviets had long since enshrined in their own version of the doctrine: *"It is easier to start a social revolution in an economically underdeveloped country than to lead it to ultimate victory,* since it is necessary to cope with the gigantic task of amassing the material requisites of socialism there." [98]

The same theme was emphasized by A. Yakovlev in a book published the following year. Whereas the Soviet theorists had come to recognize the "multiformity of historical, social and economic conditions" which distinguished one newly independent country from another, the Chinese have generalized their own experience—the establishment of people's democracy by armed struggle—as the sole valid form of revolutionary struggle. In so doing they have ignored the intermediate stages toward socialism which had been discovered by Soviet "creative Marxists." Such an attitude "has nothing in common with Marxism-Leninism, which rejects adventuristic notions of leaping over objectively necessary and unavoidable stages of revolutionary development and mass movement—notions which lead to a senseless dissipation of the revolutionary energy of peoples and ultimately discredit slogans and targets which are perfectly correct in other circumstances." [99]

b. Meaning of the "Noncapitalist Path"

As Soviet scholarship concerning the third world has become more sophisticated, the earlier tendency toward optimistic generalizations concerning revolutionary prospects has been checked. In the process, according to the editors of *International Affairs,* "[i]t goes without saying that some of our concepts which took shape in the stormy period of the national-liberation movement are now undergoing certain changes." [100] The major effort by Soviet analysts in sharpening their theoretical framework has gone toward a full-scale inquiry into the meaning of the "noncapitalist path of development"—a concept about which there had been considerable ambiguity in the past.

Though they did not themselves use the precise term, the founders of Marxism-Leninism are said to have first formulated the notion that nonindustrialized countries could achieve socialism without ever enduring the capitalist stage. Writers such as Mirsky and Kim have emphasized continuity between Lenin's statement at the Second Congress of the Comintern, which affirmed the "possibility" of backward countries' bypassing capitalism with the support of proletarian regimes in advanced countries, and their own usage of the term.[101] Kim acknowledged the fact that present-day underdeveloped countries lack the advantage enjoyed by Soviet Central Asia and Mongolia in their own "noncapitalist development"—that is, proletarian leadership and a common border with or even incorporation into the Soviet state. Yet he still contended that, given the lessened importance of the geographical factor in contemporary world politics, the political, economic, and ideological possibilities for noncapitalist development have "increased beyond measure."

A considerably different position on the matter is taken by B. S. Nikolayev. Contemporary noncapitalist development, he argued in 1970, "is far from being an exact replica of the model dealt with by the founders of Marxism-Leninism in their lifetime." Lenin's own works, as well as the Comintern documents, presented the concept as follows: ". . . in the event of the socialist revolution winning out in the leading countries of the world, there would be no obstacle to the accelerated socioeconomic development of the former colonies if, as Lenin put it, the Soviet governments came to their assistance with *all the means at their disposal,* and the *Marxist parties headed the revolutionary transformations* in these countries." [102] A study of the relevant documents confirms that Nikolayev's position is closer to the historical facts. As Nikolayev implies, and as we shall see below, current Soviet theory on this subject has moved away from the Leninist position by allowing for *non-Marxist* leadership of noncapitalist development as well as by specifically denying that the Soviets either feel obliged to assist the process with all means at their disposal or consider such assistance to be a prerequisite of successful development.

Less controversial than the origin of the concept is the propo-

sition that not all underdeveloped states will proceed to socialism by way of this path, and that even those that do embark on
noncapitalist development may make the transition in different
ways. According to V. L. Tiagunenko and V. G. Solodovnikov,
in their respective contributions to a 1970 *International Affairs*
forum on this subject, the noncapitalist way is by no means
obligatory for all developing countries. In those third-world
countries where capitalism is relatively developed (some Latin
American countries and Nigeria are listed by Solodovnikov), "in
all probability the question of socialist revolution is going to
arise." But until it does, these countries "will apparently travel
the more excruciating way, via mature capitalism." [103] Tiagunenko's view is that while socialist revolution without any intermediate stages is "quite possible" in such countries, it is also
possible that "in these also there may well be a period of development (especially at the initial stage) which will not be strictly
socialist (in the composition of power)" but will have features
identified with the "noncapitalist way." [104]

In the opinion of Professor Ul'ianovsky (the deputy head of
the Central Committee Secretariat's International Department),
India is one such case. It is a country which has attained "a
middle level of capitalist development," but in which the
slogan of "noncapitalist development" helps to unite the "progressive forces" with the objective of setting up a national-
democratic front, halting the further development of monopoly
capital and putting it in the hands of the state.[105]

Some of these same theorists earlier in the decade had implied that those third-world countries which were *least* developed, by virtue of the absence of a bourgeoisie or of capitalist
development, were the most likely candidates for a rapid transition onto the noncapitalist path. The disappointing experiences
of many of these countries, especially those in Africa, as they
had tried to rush ahead toward a "socialist" program, had had a
sobering effect on Soviet observers. Tiagunenko, for example,
had been one of the most optimistic earlier in the decade, but in
1970 he wrote: "The most economically backward countries
are, to put it mildly, not the best examples for demonstrating
the advantages of the noncapitalist way." More backward countries, with more difficulties to overcome, would take longer to
catch up, and would demonstrate the advantages of the noncapitalist path "only gradually." [106]

One of the most respected of Soviet Orientalists, E. M. Zhukov, wrote quite candidly about this change in mood among his colleagues. The relative ease with which the first stage of the national-liberation movement—the achievement of political independence—had been achieved had created "illusions" about the possibility of a "similarly simple and one-act solution" for the second stage, the achievement of economic independence. But the further progress of the movement had proved "much more drawn out than some political leaders and scientists had expected." In some countries that had been "reckless" attempts by petty-bourgeois leaders to skip stages of development or to ignore the absence of "objective conditions" for revolutionary advance. Zhukov frankly declared: "Proclaiming socialism is not the same thing as building it." Yet even while condemning such impatience, Zhukov did not seem to be advising Soviet policy-makers to withdraw support in these circumstances. Marx and Lenin, he reminded them, had given "every possible support" even to those revolutionary actions of the proletariat which had had no chance of success. Rather, Zhukov was saying, Soviet policy-makers and scholars needed to be more realistic concerning the likely slow pace of further advance toward socialism in the third world.[107]

c. The Question of Leadership

In addressing the question which class was capable of leading a country on the noncapitalist path of development, Soviet writers were in full agreement on only one point: the national bourgeoisie, by virtue of its "dual nature" and its tendency to form temporary alliances with "exploiter forces," was excluded from a leading role. Echoing a phrase employed by Tiagunenko in 1964, D. Zarine wrote with respect to the united anti-imperialist front that it was "no longer a question of unity under the bourgeoisie's leadership, but of unity with its possible participation." [108] Yet Zarine was also rather pessimistic concerning the strength of more "progressive" forces in the third world: the proletariat possessed a "semipeasant psychology," many of the working class were only "semiproletarian" by virtue of their employment in nonproductive fields, semiproletarian strata in the countryside were "passive" and would join the struggle "only by force of circumstance," whereas the "bureaucratic bourgeoisie and military-parasitic groups" retained much influence. In light of this estimate, the conclusion that the "working class alone" could direct the revolutionary transformation places Zarine in the camp of those Soviet observers who saw little immediate prospect for such a transformation.

Professor Kim, while sharing this estimate of the deficiencies of the national bourgeoisie and proletariat, and while agreeing that the peasantry could not lead the revolutionary movement, was more sanguine concerning the possibility for leadership of the movement by petty-bourgeois "revolutionary democrats." He did acknowledge that though such leaders had a "socialist aim," and their programs were marked by a "highly progressive character" that made it "inevitable" that their outlook would be revolutionized even further, still the "duality" of the petty bourgeoisie would occasionally lead them to such retrograde measures as the attempt to "cut off Communists from the revolutionary process." [109]

Rostislav Ul'ianovsky's position was similar. The national bourgeoisie was capable of continuing for some time its struggle against imperialism, but the experience of the past two decades had revealed the inclination of that class to compromise with foreign capital, thus disqualifying it from continuing "at the head of the struggle" though not from participating in that struggle. Either the proletariat in alliance with the petty bourgeoisie and other working masses, or—where the proletariat had not yet become an organized class force—"revolutionary" or "national democrats" (Ul'ianovsky does not clearly distinguish between them) will lead the noncapitalist advance. It would be "sectarian" to rule out very close cooperation between communists and such nonproletarian forces; to insist on working class hegemony at the first stage of this process was to ignore the revolutionary potential of these masses and the petty-bourgeois intellectuals who lead them. It was also to disregard the role of the world socialist system, which seeks to safeguard these regimes and give them aid, though of course socialist countries lack "the potential to deal with the full range of economic tasks" in these countries.[110]

Noncapitalist development, then, could take place in the framework of a number of forms of state power; the "decisive criterion" was simply that the national bourgeoisie have been removed from a monopoly hold on political power. The state might, in the first place, be organized as a "national democracy." Ul'ianovsky made it clear that this concept was now to be applied more loosely than when it had first been formulated in 1960; he himself defined it as a "revolutionary dictatorship of proletarian, semiproletarian and nonproletarian social groups and sections who have a stake in independence and steady socioeconomic development towards socialism." Such a state has only "limited possibilities" by virtue of its class character, heterogeneous social base, inadequate economic resources, and the absence of the leadership of a Marxist-Leninist party. Its specific structure need not "coincide in every detail with that theoretically advanced by, say, the 1960 International Communist Conference." [111] By the count of G. B. Starushenko in 1970, ten African and Asian countries "whose development is already noncapitalist" had formed or were in the process of forming national-democratic states.[112]

In addition to the national-democratic form, according to R. G. Landa, noncapitalist development could also take place in a "revolutionary democracy, in which all exploiting classes have been removed from economic and political power," or in a "people's democracy, where all property-owning classes" have been so removed. In the latter case noncapitalist and socialist development might even coincide.[113] Thus neither the form of state power nor the exact composition of the ruling elite appeared to be of critical importance as far as Soviet scholars were concerned; what mattered was whether the power of the state was being used to encourage capitalist development (as it currently was in India) or whether it was oriented toward promotion of a noncapitalist program.[114]

d. Difficulties along the "Noncapitalist Path"

The mere existence of a nonbourgeois leadership with "progressive" inclinations was by no means a guarantee that a country would succeed in its course of noncapitalist development; difficulties abounded and reversals were not unknown. According to Ul'ianovsky, the countries which had embarked on the noncapitalist path (he listed the UAR, Syria, Algeria, Burma, Mali, Guinea, the Congo [Brazzaville], and Tanzania) would require ten to fifteen years of "successful development" before their transition could be judged as "irreversible." A year later, he wrote that the "guarantee" of a continued advance toward socialism was a program which included economic measures to meet the needs of the masses, the grant of "democratic freedom," nonharassment of "those accepting scientific socialism," establishment of mass organizations, a purge of corrupt and counterrevolutionary elements from the state apparatus, and fi-

nally—but not least important—"close cooperation with the socialist countries." [115]

But just as there were dangers that the petty-bourgeois
leaders would be drawn into a deal with reaction, so also were
there real dangers that they would attempt to press on toward
"socialism" at too rapid a rate. Leaders such as Nkrumah in
Ghana had been ousted because of undue haste in remaking the
economy, the result of which had been popular disaffection and
internal chaos. Though the Soviets are less explicit about it,
Castro's Cuba is another case in point. There nationalization
and the cutting of ties with the capitalist world market had been
accomplished so suddenly that the Soviets had been forced to
take up the burden of keeping the Cuban economy afloat. They
have since made it quite clear that the "socialist camp" has no
intention of duplicating this rescue operation. Soviet economists now argue that nationalization of foreign capital should
not necessarily be "immediate and general"; for countries taking the "noncapitalist way" foreign capitalist investment is "inevitable but temporary." So long as power is in the hands of
"revolutionary-democratic" forces serving the interests of the
masses and seeking to build socialism, then the question of the
presence of foreign capital is "important but secondary." [116]

In assessing the character of the "noncapitalist way" and the
direction in which it will lead, Soviet scholars have recently
emphasized one point about which they had earlier been ambiguous. Even though noncapitalist development may simultaneously solve tasks both of a bourgeois-democratic and of a socialist nature, such a path can at most be labeled "semi-
socialist"; it should not (as it had been earlier) be equated
with the *socialist* path. Not only had nonproletarian leaders and
non-Marxist parties been proclaiming themselves as "socialists," but Soviet theorists and political leaders had also earlier
in the decade allowed of the possibility that noncapitalist development could simply "grow over" into socialist transformation
without prior attainment of proletarian hegemony or the existence of a vanguard party. It will be recalled that such a possibility had been suggested and then hastily rejected in the mid-
1950's with respect to "socialist" development in India under
the leadership of the national bourgeoisie. Now, in the late
1960's, Soviet scholars were again emphasizing the orthodox
view that, in Tiagunenko's words, "to identify the noncapitalist
way with the socialist one amounts to admitting the possibility

of socialist development without the dictatorship of the proletariat." [117] The noncapitalist path may at most involve the creation of the "prerequisites for the construction of socialism," [118]
and it may help to popularize the idea of socialism, but it does
not itself amount to "socialist development" nor does it even
guarantee that such a stage will be attained. Ul'ianovsky best
expresses the unanimous view on this point: "Socialism can
triumph only on the basis of scientific socialism, under the leadership of the working class closely allied with the working peasantry." [119] It should be noted that this apparently does not mean
that "revolutionary democrats" must be removed from power
before the transformation can take place; some of these leaders
might come to adopt a Marxist-Leninist viewpoint and to build
a vanguard party based on a program of scientific socialism. But
there must also be a profound change in the class basis of the
revolutionary movement, from petty bourgeois to proletarian,
and this will, of necessity, be accomplished only through intense class struggle.

Thus the noncapitalist path is truly a transitional phase, and
revolutionary leaders who have embarked on this path must
steer a careful course if they are eventually to move on to socialist development. They must avoid on the one hand the danger
of losing their ties with the working people, of degenerating
into a "bureaucratic bourgeoisie," of relying solely on army of-
ficers, or of "demagogically engaging in the dangerous game of
playing on the current differences in the Communist movement, as some national-democratic leaders have done." They
must on the other hand avoid the temptations of "reckless adventurism," of proceeding too fast, of seeking "instant hegemony for the proletariat, dumping all the national bourgeoisie
as a counterrevolutionary force," or of promoting "arbitrary,
subjectivist solutions for immature economic tasks." [120]

In evaluating the recent developments in the "creative" ad-
justment of the doctrine by Soviet scholars, it may be said that
they have placed more emphasis than ever before on the "intermediate stages" of revolutionary development in the third
world, while simultaneously tightening the requirements for ultimate admission of these states to the "socialist camp." What is
important for the present is that the newly independent countries break away from the capitalist path, end the political monopoly of the national bourgeoisie or of reactionary circles, and
enter into noncapitalist development. Once embarked on this

course, having chosen one of a number of acceptable forms for organizing state power, they should proceed with caution, not prematurely narrowing the united front, not breaking all links with the imperialist world market, and not underestimating the magnitude of the task of building the material base for the ultimate transition to socialism.

6. The Communist Parties of India: 1966–1972

This Soviet analysis of third-world development in general and of India in particular has been faithfully copied by the resolutions and program of the "right" Communist Party of India. At its Eighth Congress in February 1968 (at which time it claimed 173,000 members), this faction again echoed the Soviets in proclaiming the urgent necessity of leftist unity in India. Such unity, according to the congress documents, should assume the form of a National Democratic Front which would rally to itself "democratic elements" within the Congress party. This coalition, joining workers, peasants, the petty bourgeoisie, and non-monopolistic elements of the national bourgeoisie in an anti-imperialist, antifeudal, and antimonopoly struggle, would be under the exclusive leadership of neither the working class nor the national bourgeoisie.[121]

Through a combination of parliamentary and extraparliamentary "militant mass struggle," this coalition would overthrow Congress rule at the center, create a government of "national democracy," and lead India on the noncapitalist path of development. In the course of this advance, the balance within the coalition government would shift in favor of the worker-peasant alliance, paving the way for the assumption of leadership by the working class, and only then to the actual transition to socialism.

Although the Eighth Congress expressed confidence in the correctness of this approach, it warned against underestimating the difficulty of overcoming the forces of reaction in India and stressed—as the CPI had done throughout its history—the need to correct organizational shortcomings, including the "criminal neglect" of education of party members, the shortage of qualified cadres, the tendencies toward provincialism, and the "staggering" failures on the peasant front.[122]

In the last area the CPI has been pressured into direct action by the successful appeal of the Naxalite movement to landless peasants in areas of Eastern India. This movement, which began in the Naxalbari region of West Bengal in 1967, had seen thousands of agricultural laborers and peasants engage in looting, terrorism against landlords and government officials, and the seizure of land. To reestablish its credentials as a revolutionary party among the increasing numbers of radicals in the countryside, as well as to put additional pressure on the Gandhi government to implement its land reform program, the CPI in the summer of 1970 began a nationwide campaign for land redistribution. In the first stage of the campaign, state-owned cultivable wastelands were to be seized and distributed to the village poor; in the second stage, the party was to lead the peasants in taking over plots of land owned by landlords in violation of the law fixing maximum limits on holdings. Though it is doubtful that this campaign succeeded in reversing the serious weakness of the CPI in the countryside, the party itself expressed satisfaction with its results, describing it as a "great blow" to the power of big landlords.[123]

The weakness of the mass base of the party, as well as the costs of the split in the CPI, were dramatically evidenced in the 1967 and 1971 election results. Not only did the CPI and CPI (Marxist) put up rival candidates in most areas, but they differed fundamentally on the issue of electoral alliances with communal parties and on the priority to be given to achieving a Congress defeat at all costs. But both parties won posts in the united front coalition governments that emerged from the elections in several Indian states. In fact, in Kerala, E. M. S. Namboodiripad, a leader of the left CPI, assumed in 1967 the position of Chief Minister, an office he had held in 1957–1959.

Despite its continuing commitment to the establishment of "people's democracy," the left CPI in power has behaved in a relatively moderate fashion. Indeed, the party not only participated, as a part of the united front government in West Bengal, in the armed suppression of the peasant rebellion in the Naxalbari area of that state in 1967, but also expelled as "left-sectarian adventurist deviationists" a number of party dissidents who urged support of the rebellion. For the next two years the left CPI was rent with a divisiveness reminiscent of that which had characterized the entire party in the late 1940's. The issues were much the same: armed struggle or the peaceful road, a peasant or urban-based revolution, a focus against imperialism and feudalism or against capitalism.

In November 1968, in Kerala, a dissident Maoist faction

which had broken with the CPI(M) attempted an armed uprising against the Namboodiripad government in the state. The rising was crushed, and its leaders were denounced by the party as CIA agents. The CPI(M) party congress which met in Kerala a month later condemned the terrorism and called for a strategy which combined the tactics of parliamentarism and agitation among the masses. The following July two party leaders, Namboodiripad and Gopalan, worked out a further refinement of the party's course of action. According to this statement, the CPI (M) would continue to use the government machinery under its control to introduce measures which would "help the masses" and develop the "democratic movement," until the day arrived when the Indian constitution itself could be "totally changed."

But the CPI(M) was soon to lose its control of the government in the two crucial states of Kerala and West Bengal. A scandal involving party officials in Kerala caused the collapse of its coalition there in November 1969, allowing the right CPI to take advantage of the situation to form its own coalition and take control of the state's government. Continued fighting between the right and left communists led the central government to step in and place Kerala under President's Rule the following August, but by October the right CPI, heading a new coalition, was back in control of the cabinet.

In West Bengal the situation was even more chaotic. The unrestrained competition for influence among the partners in Bengal's coalition government dominated by the left communists had led to a series of bloody clashes. The CPI(M) had used its key positions at the head of the Home, Land, Labor, and Rehabilitation ministries to organize workers and peasants and to lead them in a variety of radical actions. The police, under the direction of Home Minister Jyoti Basu, a left communist leader, had refused to interfere with the activities of the "proletariat," and Basu himself had assured the workers that the police "will not interfere in democratic movements seeking the worker's legitimate rights." Unable to cope with the situation, the noncommunist Chief Minister had submitted his government's resignation and appealed for President's Rule to be imposed. Nine of the parties in the state formally refused to participate in any future government with the left CPI.

a. Competition between the CPI and CPI(M)

In such an atmosphere, cooperation between the left and right communists has proved impossible, despite efforts by the right CPI—at Moscow's urging—to establish a joint coordinating committee and work out a common platform. This inability to act on a united basis became even more critical for India's communists following the events of the autumn of 1969, which culminated in the formal split of the ruling Congress party. The right CPI, claiming that the crisis in the Congress had vindicated its position concerning the increasing differentiation in the national bourgeoisie and the need to establish a national democratic front, was again rebuffed by the CPI(M) in its appeals for cooperation.[124] The left CPI, however, though it perceived a "healthy trend" in Mrs. Gandhi's party, still claimed that the "old" and "new" Congress factions represented the same bourgeois and landlord classes, and thus pursued essentially identical policies.

In the eyes of the leaders of the right CPI, as well as in those of their Soviet patrons, the "supreme task" facing the party was to defeat the efforts of the right to bring down the Gandhi government. Right reaction in India, like a "wounded beast," was now more dangerous than ever before, and it had so far been unable to "reenact the drama of Indonesia and Ghana on Indian soil" only because of the country's strong democratic tradition and the growing anger of the working masses.[125] True, Mrs. Gandhi's government was "by no means Left and not socialist by any standard of measurement" though a number of leftist elements had been attracted to it. The leadership of the New Congress, which from the central to the district levels was either "bourgeois or kulak," would continue to vacillate and compromise, and the CPI would persist in its opposition, both in the parliament and through mass action, to the "antipeople measures" of the government. But when the Syndicate, the Jan Sangh, and the Swatantra parties seek to topple this government, then the CPI would stand by it, for if they succeeded in their efforts it would be the beginning of "downright reactionary, authoritarian, pro-imperialist rule in India." [126]

Though the CPI viewed the Congress split as opening the possibility of a broader united front against external and internal reaction, the party made clear that this did not imply the formation of a united front with the Gandhi government itself. Rather it meant attempting to gain increasing support from the masses which supported the New Congress, so that pressure could be brought on the government to take firmer measures against reaction and to "lean more on the left wing," and so that the ongoing process of "differentiation" within the present government could be aided. Finally, the CPI emphasized that its quarrel with Mrs. Gandhi concerned her domestic policies only. According to one of the party's leaders, the Prime Minister's foreign policy statements never failed "to stress the friendly relations between the Soviet Union and India, her support for the Arabs, for non-alignment, and so on." [127]

Though the CPI failed to make gains in the 1971 election, the results of that contest, in affirming Mrs. Gandhi's popularity and drastically reducing the parliamentary representation of the "right" parties, led the CPI to make a more positive estimate of political trends in India. The party declared at its Ninth Congress, held in Kerala in October 1971, that whereas the main task had previously been to check the further drift of the country to the right, the task in 1971 was to move the country toward the left. Again, the vehicle to be used for the purpose was a united front of the "leftist and democratic" forces, including the "progressive sections" of the ruling Congress faction. Condemning the CPI(M) for its "anti-Congressism," the right CPI took measures to weaken its rival by building coalitions with the New Congress parties in Kerala and West Bengal.[128] This strategy, together with the sharp increase in Mrs. Gandhi's popularity among Bengalis in the wake of the December war, resulted in a drastic defeat for the CPI(M) in the March 1972 elections in West Bengal. The New Congress, assisted by the CPI, was able to emerge with the first stable governing majority in the state in over a decade.

On issues concerning the international communist movement, the right CPI has remained a close supporter of the Soviet position. Dange so demonstrated at the international conference in Moscow in 1969, at which he insisted on condemning the Chinese schismatic activity as an "enormous danger" to the Indian revolutionary movement, while praising the Soviets for their assistance at Tashkent as well as their subsequent efforts in South Asia "to turn this area of tension" into an "area of peace and friendship." [129]

The left CPI, on the other hand, has remained critical of Soviet "modern revisionism" and even more hostile to the Soviet-supported concept of "national democracy," though it has never gone so far as to break formally with the CPSU. Concerning the Moscow Conference, the left Communists, pathetically echoing the slogans of the early 1950's, condemned its documents for placing the "struggle for peace" above the "struggle against imperialism." While disavowing the label "pro-Peking," and assuming an independent stance in the international movement, the left CPI's position on many issues has remained closer to the Chinese stance than to that of the Soviets.

Agreement on a number of doctrinal and organizational issues concerning the international movement did not, however, prove to be sufficient cement to hold Peking and the left CPI together. In 1967 they split over the issue of the left Communists' participation in the Kerala and West Bengal coalitions and over the attitude assumed by the CPI(M) toward the Peking-backed Naxalites. In August 1967, the party's leadership drew up a draft resolution criticizing the Chinese advocacy of the Naxalbari rebellion as violating "every Marxist-Leninist tenet of assessing a given political situation." Subsequent resolutions have accused the Chinese of interfering in internal party affairs and have condemned "the grave Left errors" of the CCP leadership.

The Chinese have been even less restrained in their language. A statement issued in March 1969 equated the left Communists with the "clique" of the "notorious renegade S. A. Dange." Like the right CPI, the CPI(M) had "degenerated into despicable lackeys of U.S. imperialism, Soviet revisionism and Indian reaction." Specifically condemning the left Communists for their "cruel victimization" of the Naxalbari revolutionaries, Peking concluded that "these renegades, who are colluding overtly and covertly with the new tsars in the Kremlin, are savage hatchetmen of the reactionary Indian Government in suppressing the people's revolution." [130]

During this period Peking was seeking to counter the Soviet containment policy not only by giving material support and moral encouragement to the Pakistanis, but also by attempting to tie down the Indian military forces through its assistance to peasant rebellions and separatist movements in India. According to the Chinese line, armed struggle was the only proper course of action against the Congress regime, which represented only big landlords and capitalists and which had, in the name of "socialism," thrown the Indian masses into an "abyss of misery." [131] To further the dissemination of this assessment, Peking in the beginning of 1969 introduced daily radio broadcasts in Bengali. At the same time, reports were circulating in India that Chinese instructors had begun to train guerrillas in the Pakistani-occupied areas of Kashmir.

b. The CPI (Marxist-Leninist)

In April 1969 *Peking Review* hailed the founding of the CPI (Marxist-Leninist)—a *third* Communist party which, according to the Chinese, had been in the works since late 1967. Its program was unmistakably the "Chinese path" that had been advocated by the Andhra committee in 1948 (though left-extremist communists in Andhra have subsequently criticized the new party for its failure to build a political base before launching a guerrilla war).

According to the new party's program, India is a semicolonial and semifeudal country run by big landlords and compradore-bureaucratic capitalists who toady to U.S. imperialism and Soviet social imperialism and collaborate with these forces against socialist China and the entire national-liberation movement. Armed struggle (primarily guerrilla warfare) would have to be utilized, under the leadership of the working class, to accomplish a people's democratic revolution, based on the rural areas and relying on the peasantry as the "main force." The revisionist leaderships of both the right and left CPIs, who had tried to create illusions among the Indian people about the "parliamentary road" in order to blunt their revolutionary consciousness, were thus conscious traitors to the cause. Armed with Marxism–Leninism–Mao Tse-tung Thought, the new party (led by Charu Mazumdar) took as its internationalist duty the kindling of peasant revolutions throughout India, which had long been a center of conspiracies against China.[132]

Following the "first phase" of the new party's activity in 1969, during which it claimed to have sparked peasant revolts in West Bengal, Andhra Pradesh, Orissa, Bihar, the Punjab, and Kerala, its leaders paused to take stock. They found that their experience had pointed up certain "erroneous notions," such as the idea that the peasantry could not be organized for political struggle without the use of economic inducements, as well as the tendency to place "excessive reliance on modern firearms." [133] Toward the end of 1970, while the Soviet press was voicing concern that such "adventurist" activities would be utilized by Indian reactionaries to whip up anticommunist feelings, the Chinese were continuing to hail "steady development" of what they termed "India's people's war." [134]

Only a year later, however, the traditional disease of Indian communism had overtaken this new entrant. The Indian press reported that an underground conclave of the proscribed

CPI(M-L) had resulted in the expulsion of its erstwhile leader, Mazumdar, for pursuing a "Trotskyist adventurist line"— specifically, for departing from the Maoist path of rural guerrilla struggle to advocate urban-based guerrilla activities.[135] By 1972, with its pipeline for arms supplies from Peking cut off as a result of the creation of Bangladesh, and with the Indian government's consequent surge of popularity in the main Naxalite base of West Bengal, the CPI(M-L) seemed to be a spent force. Mazumdar was dead and one-fifth of the party's 10,000 activists had been arrested.[136] Although this party, once purified, may yet play a significant role in any future plans Peking might have for encouraging violent and separatist struggles in India, the Chinese press, dropping its earlier enthusiasm for the CPI (M-L), has simply ignored its protégé since 1971.

7. Conclusion: The "De-eschatology" of Soviet Policy

The continuing disunity, instability, and occasional ineptitude of the Indian communists has probably been a contributing factor to the evident lack of Soviet enthusiasm for the (still unlikely) prospect of communist rule in India. Doctrinally, the long-term Soviet commitment is to the building of a communist India. Whether this doctrinal commitment is deeply felt and sincere among the Soviet leadership is impossible to determine. It is more certain that it must continue to be voiced if the remaining viability of Marxism-Leninism, both as an instrument of mass control and as a justification for the very rule of the Soviet leadership, is to be preserved. But, as we have seen, this commitment is qualified by the specification of a number of transitional stages and by the increasing emphasis on the need to develop wide popular support as a prerequisite for communist takeover.

As the Soviets have become progressively more committed to the present Indian government—at least for the foreseeable future—on the diplomatic, economic, and military levels, the time perspective for the achievement of the ultimate objective (and even of the intermediate goals) has lengthened. Thus E. M. Zhukov, who in 1949 had endorsed the "Chinese path" of violent revolution for India, could in 1963 go so far as to declare: ". . . *it would be absurd to advance the slogan of armed struggle* for countries, where political independence has been

won, the political position of imperialism has basically been undermined, but its economic position is still strong." [137]

In effect, what has occurred is the Soviet leadership's own
version of the "de-eschatology" of its policy towards India. Just
as the Christian version of "de-eschatology" developed with the
need to ensure the survival of the Church as a worldly community, so the most salient factor in the Soviet version has been
the dual threat to Soviet survival produced first by thermonuclear weaponry and second by the emergence of the Chinese
challenge to the balance of power in Asia and to the very
borders of the Soviet Union. The consequence with respect to
India has been the Soviet decision to concentrate less on the
"kingdom to come" and more on its present and quite concrete
investment in a staunchly anti-Chinese "national bourgeois"
government in New Delhi.

For, in fact, the old Soviet dream of a communist India must
now be a nightmare. Even at best, communist rule in poverty-
ridden and overpopulated India would prove to be an immense
material burden for the Russians. Western aid would cease, and
the Soviets would be faced with the "fraternal obligation" to
divert even more of their treasure to India in order to make
good on their own and the CPI's claims about the superiority of
the noncapitalist path to development. Recent Soviet warnings
against undue haste in cutting off imperialist aid, abolishing the
private sector of the economy, and embarking prematurely on
the revolutionary path reflect an acute awareness of this dilemma. Even more frightening, however, must be the spectre of
a communist India thumbing its nose at "bourgeois" Russia and
embarking hand-in-hand with Peking on Mao Tse-tung's path to
Utopia. Compared to either of these alternatives, the status quo
in India must seem quite palatable.

This attitude, of course, has been condemned by the Chinese
as heresy—a betrayal of the faith. For the Chinese are still, to
continue the analogy, in the position of the early Christians, not
yet sufficiently distracted by worldly successes and dependent
for the vitality of their faith on the belief in the imminence of
the coming of the new age.

While the present Soviet time-perspective may have lengthened well beyond Lenin's, and while the strength of the
present leaders' faith that the goal will be achieved may be less
than his, still this transformation in Soviet policy has been very

much a part of the Leninist tradition. That tradition, first and most dramatically evident at Brest Litovsk, accepted as its axiom that Soviet survival was the priority on which all else depended and had as its postulate that temporary alliances were permissible with those who shared the immediate objective of cooperation against a common enemy. Even in its choice of temporary allies, the post-1953 leadership has been more in the Leninist tradition than was the Stalinist regime. For Lenin and the post-Stalinist leadership demanded only that the potential ally manifest hostility toward imperialism, while Stalin had undermined Soviet flexibility by also requiring undeviating support for the USSR.

But it has been a constant practice of all Soviet regimes to assess the economic position or "class interests" of a noncommunist group as the dependent variable, secondary to the determination of its foreign-policy attitude. The above pages have documented in detail the successive shifts in the Soviet assessment of Indian social forces—in the late 1920's, the mid-1930's, the late 1940's, and the mid-1950's. Uniformly these shifts have been motivated by changes in the perceived requirements of securing and strengthening the Soviet Union rather than by changes in the productive forces or class relations within India itself.

The sensitivity demonstrated by Khrushchev and his successors to nationalist sentiments in the East was also squarely in the Leninist tradition. Lenin's warning in 1920 that communists must make concessions to petty-bourgeois prejudices in order to hasten the extinction of such attitudes was well heeded by Khrushchev both in his sensitivity to such factors as India's great-power ambitions and pride in the Gandhist tradition and in his later recognition of the worth of "socialisms of a national type." In dealing with the peculiarities and sensitivities of the third world, even the use of such un-Marxian concepts as the "noncapitalist path" had its origins in Lenin's time.

Another element of the tradition was the practice of sacrificing the interests and freedom of action of local communist cadres to overriding national interests of the Soviet state. It was not Khrushchev or even Stalin who first looked the other way when a nationalist "ally" chose to persecute native communists. Nor was it unnatural for later Soviet leaders to follow Lenin's practice of viewing foreign communists as obedient servants whose task was to exert pressure in support of Soviet-desired policies and against those deemed by the Russians to be contrary to their interests. But, as the case of the CPI illustrates, the result of such a modus operandi was often so to isolate local communists in the domestic political environment that, once the authority of Soviet instructions began to erode, they were unable to function in a unified and effective manner.

Thus, when the Chinese accuse the Soviet leadership of having betrayed both the interests of world revolution and the Leninist tradition, they are missing the point by proceeding from a faulty understanding of exactly what constitutes the Leninist tradition. To argue that what has been betrayed is the *Marxist* tradition comes closer to the mark. For the Soviets, in formulating their policies toward a particular state such as India, do not operate in a vacuum. A Marxian analysis of Indian social forces based chiefly on economic factors, phrased solely in terms of class struggle and aimed primarily at the speediest possible achievement of the socialist revolution, while it may serve the interest of local Marxist cadres, does not necessarily prescribe what is in the best interests of the Russian state. However, there have been long periods when Soviet energies have been concentrated on internal priorities or when Soviet attention has been focused on vital interests in the "main arena" of the struggle with imperialism; in such periods, when India was herself playing no independent role in the world arena, the Soviets— lacking either vital interests or an operational strategy—could afford to indulge in the more orthodox assessment of Indian social forces.

But in the postwar period, and especially with the stalemate in the "main arena" which was brought about by nuclear weapons, the countries of the "third world" became a major focus of Soviet attention. As there had been in Lenin's day, so again there was discussion of the possibility of striking a fatal blow at the imperialists by expelling them from (and even replacing them in) the "world village." In the postwar era, however, unlike the days in which Lenin was struggling to secure the victory of October, the Soviets had the resources to implement the strategy.

As countries such as India loomed larger in Soviet plans and became independent actors in world politics, the doctrinal assessment of Indian social forces left over from the days of inaction threatened to distort Soviet perception and to blunt the impulse toward an active policy. Only after Stalin's death were the

Soviet leaders able to remove this handicap. The new assessment which followed the decision to direct Soviet energies toward the "third world" was, however, far less wedded to traditional Marxist notions of class analysis and far more suited to the needs of Soviet foreign policy for effective action in the present and maximum flexibility in the future.

Thus the Chinese were presented with the opportunity to make a challenge to the Soviets not only in the diplomatic but also in the ideological realm and to justify the former offensive in terms of the latter. Speaking in the role of the conscience of the world revolutionary movement—which had seldom before found its voice—the Chinese communists denounced the new Soviet argument, serving notice that what furthered the best interests of Soviet foreign policy was no longer automatically assumed also to be in the best interests of the entire communist movement.

Appendix
Notes
Bibliography
Index

Appendix. Treaty of Peace, Friendship and Co-operation between the Union of Soviet Socialist Republics and the Republic of India

Wishing to expand and strengthen the existing relations of sincere friendship between them,

considering that the further development of friendship and co-operation meets the basic national interests of both states as well as the interests of a lasting peace in Asia and throughout the world,

being determined to contribute to strengthening world peace and security and to work tirelessly to bring about a relaxation of international tension and the final abolition of the remnants of colonialism,

reaffirming their firm belief in the principles of peaceful co-existence and co-operation between states with different political and social systems,

convinced that in the present-day world international problems can be solved only through co-operation and not through conflict,

reaffirming their determination to follow the objectives and principles of the United Nations Charter,

the Union of Soviet Socialist Republics, on the one hand, and the Republic of India, on the other, have decided to conclude the present Treaty and with this aim in view have appointed the following plenipotentiaries:

on behalf of the Union of Soviet Socialist Republics—the Foreign Minister of the U.S.S.R. A.A. Gromyko,

on behalf of the Republic of India—the Minister of External Affairs of India Swaran Singh,

who, upon presentation of their credentials, found in due form and proper order, agreed on the following:

Article 1

The High Contracting Parties solemnly declare that there shall be a lasting peace and friendship between their two countries and their peoples. Each shall respect the independence, sovereignty and territorial integrity of the other and refrain from interfering in the internal affairs of the other Party. The High Contracting Parties shall continue to develop and strengthen the relations of sincere friendship, good-neighborliness and all-round co-operation existing between them, on the basis of the above-mentioned principles as well as the principles of equality and mutual benefit.

Article 2

Guided by a desire to contribute in every way towards ensuring a lasting peace and the security of their peoples, the High Contracting Parties declare their determination to continue efforts towards maintaining and strengthening peace in Asia and throughout the world, ending the arms race and achieving general and complete disarmament covering both nuclear and conventional weapons under effective international control.

Article 3

Guided by their devotion to the lofty ideal of equality of all peoples and states, irrespective of race or creed, the High Contracting Parties condemn colonialism and racism in all forms and manifestations and reaffirm their determination to strive for their final and complete abolition.

The High Contracting Parties shall co-operate with other states in achieving these aims and to support the just aspirations of the peoples in their struggle against colonialism and racial domination.

Article 4

The Union of Soviet Socialist Republics respects India's policy of non-alignment and reaffirms that this policy is an important factor for maintaining universal peace and international security and for easing tension in the world.

The Republic of India respects the peaceful policy of the Union of Soviet Socialist Republics aimed at strengthening friendship and co-operation with all peoples.

Article 5

Being deeply interested in ensuring world peace and security, and attaching great importance to mutual co-operation in the international arena to achieve these aims, the High Contracting Parties shall maintain regular contacts with each other on major international problems affecting the interests of both states, through meetings and exchanges of opinion between their leading statesmen, visits by official delegations and special representatives of the two governments, and through diplomatic channels.

Article 6

Attaching great importance to economic, scientific and technical co-operation between them, the High Contracting Parties shall continue to strengthen and widen their mutually advantageous and all-round co-operation in these fields and also to expand their co-operation in the fields of trade, transport and communications on the basis of the principles of equality, mutual advantage and the most favoured nation principle in compliance with the existing agreements and special agreements with neighboring countries, as it is stipulated in the trade agreement between the Union of Soviet Socialist Republics and India of December 26, 1970.

Article 7

The High Contracting Parties shall promote the further development of the relations and contacts between them in the fields of science, art, literature, education, health care, the press, radio, television, cinema, tourism and sport.

Article 8

In accordance with the traditional friendship established between the two countries, each of the High Contracting Parties solemnly declares that it shall not enter into or participate in any military alliances directed against the other Party.

Each of the High Contracting Parties undertakes to refrain from any aggression against the other Party and not to allow the use of its territory for committing any act that may cause military damage to the other High Contracting Party.

Article 9

Each of the High Contracting Parties undertakes to refrain from giving any assistance to any third Party taking part in an armed conflict with the other Party. In the event that any of the Parties is attacked or threatened with attack, the High Contracting Parties will immediately start mutual consultations with a view to eliminating this threat and taking appropriate effective measures to ensure peace and security for their countries.

Article 10

Each of the High Contracting Parties solemnly declares that it shall not undertake any commitment, secret or open, with regard to one or more states incompatible with the present Treaty. Each of the High Contracting Parties declares further that it has no commitments towards any other state or states and shall not undertake any commitments that may cause military damage to the other Party.

Article 11

The present Treaty is signed for a term of twenty years and shall be prolonged automatically for every subsequent period of five years unless one of the High Contracting Parties declares its intention to terminate its operation by notifying the other High Contracting Party 12 months before the expiration of the term of the Treaty.

The Treaty is subject to ratification and shall come into force on the day the instruments of ratification are exchanged, which will be effected in Moscow within one month after the signing of the present Treaty.

Article 12

Any differences in interpreting any article or articles of the present Treaty that may arise between the High Contracting Parties shall be settled on a bilateral basis by peaceful means in a spirit of mutual respect and understanding.

The above-mentioned plenipotentiaries have signed the present Treaty in Russian, Hindi and English, all the texts being equally authentic, and affixed their seals thereto.

Done in New Delhi on August 9, 1971.

For the Union
of Soviet Socialist
Republics
A. GROMYKO,
Minister
of Foreign Affairs

For the Republic
of India
SWARAN SINGH,
Minister
of External Affairs

Notes

I. Marx and Lenin on India

1. See the collection of Karl Marx's writings, *Articles on India* (Bombay, 1945), p. 62.

2. In 1912 Lenin described Russia as "one of the wildest, most medieval and shamefully backward of Asian countries" ("Democracy and Narodism in China," in V. I. Lenin, *The National-Liberation Movement in the East* [Moscow, 1957], p. 42; this collection is hereafter cited as *National-Liberation*). For a discussion of the "dialectics of backwardness," see Alfred G. Meyer, *Leninism* (Cambridge, Mass., 1957), chap. 12.

3. V. I. Lenin, "Inflammable Material in World Politics," in *National-Liberation*, pp. 14–15.

4. Lenin, "Democracy and Narodism in China," p. 43.

5. V. I. Lenin, "The Socialist Revolution and the Right of Nations to Self-Determination," in *National-Liberation*, p. 109.

6. V. I. Lenin, "A Caricature of Marxism and 'Imperialist Economism,'" in *National-Liberation*, p. 184 (Lenin's emphasis).

7. V. I. Lenin, "The Right of Nations to Self-Determination," in *National-Liberation*, pp. 70, 79 (Lenin's emphasis).

8. V. I. Lenin, "Discussion on Self-Determination Summed Up," in *National-Liberation*, p. 176 (Lenin's emphasis).

9. Michael T. Florinsky, *Russia: A History and an Interpretation* (New York, 1947), II, 986.

10. K. A. Troianovsky, *Vostok i revoliutsiia* (The East and the revolution) (Moscow, 1918), quoted in X. J. Eudin and R. C. North, *Soviet Russia and the East, 1920–1927: A Documentary Survey* (Stanford, 1957), p. 92.

11. *Izvestiia*, May 8, 1919, p. 1.

12. *Zhizn' natsional'nostei* (Life of nationalities), no. 6, 1919, p. 2.

13. Amur Sanai, "Kliuchi k Vostoku" (Keys to the East), *Zhizn' natsional'nostei*, no. 19, 1919, p. 2.

14. To complete the cycle, the British would then cite as confirmation of *their* fears these same Soviet speeches and articles whose misinformation was based on British speculations. For an example see Savdar, "Indiia na VI Kongresse Kominterna," (India at the Sixth Congress of the Comintern), *Novyi Vostok* (The new East), no. 23–24, 1928, pp. l–lxxii.

15. In Jan Meijer, ed., *The Trotsky Papers, 1917–22* (The Hague, 1964), I, 623.

16. M. N. Roy, *Memoirs* (Bombay, 1964), pp. 420–421.

17. Shaukat Usmani, *I Met Stalin Twice* (Bombay, 1953), pp. 8–9.

18. Ibid., p. 14.

19. See Hodgson Note to Chicherin, September 17, 1921, quoted in

C. S. Samra, *India and Anglo-Soviet Relations (1917–1947)* (Bombay, 1959), pp. 60–61, and Soviet Government Reply to British Government, September 27, 1921, quoted in Eudin and North, *Soviet Russia and the East*, p. 192.

20. Roy, *Memoirs*, pp. 482–483.

21. M. L. Veltman (M. Pavlovich), *Sovetskaia Rossiia i kapitalisticheskii Angliia* (Soviet Russia and capitalist England) (Moscow, 1922), quoted in Eudin and North, *Soviet Russia and the East*, p. 160.

22. Usmani, *I Met Stalin Twice*, pp. 17–18.

23. Roy, *Memoirs*, pp. 377–380. Collections of Comintern documents included the unrevised version of Roy's theses until 1934, when the mistake was corrected. As Allen Whiting has noted (*Soviet Policies in China, 1917–1924* [New York, 1954], pp. 55–56) the fourteen-year survival of the error suggests that Roy's theses were not exactly the object of careful study after the Congress. The unrevised theses were included in *Vtoroi Kongress Kommunisticheskogo Internatsionala: Stenograficheskii otchet* (Second Congress of the Communist International: Stenographic report) (Moscow, 1920), pp. 603–606, and in Bela Kun, ed., *Kommunisticheskii Internatsional v dokumentakh 1919–1932* (The Communist International in documents) (Moscow, 1933), pp. 130–132. The revised version appeared in *Protokoly Kongressov Kommunisticheskogo Internatsionala: Vtoroi Kongress Kominterna iiul'-avgust 1920 g.* (Proceedings of the Congresses of the Communist International: Second Congress of the Comintern July–August 1920) (Moscow, 1934), pp. 496–499.

24. *Votoroi Kongress*, p. 603.

25. *Protokoly Kongressov*, pp. 116, 155, 158.

26. *Petrogradskaia pravda* (Petrograd truth), July 29, 1920, quoted in *The Second Congress of the Communist International as Reported and Interpreted by the Official Newspapers of Soviet Russia* (Washington, 1920), p. 44 (hereafter cited as *Petrogradskaia pravda*).

27. While this was clearly the position Lenin took at the Comintern Congress, in the context of concern with questions in both Europe and Asia, only six months earlier and to a different audience, composed solely of representatives of "peoples of the East," he had taken a position closer to Roy's 1920 stand. The proletariat of the advanced countries, he had said in December 1919, "will not be victorious without the aid of the toiling masses of all the oppressed colonial peoples, and of the Eastern peoples in the first place" (*National-Liberation*, p. 235).

28. *Protokoly Kongressov*, p. 496 (emphasis supplied).

29. *Vtoroi Kongress*, pp. 126–127.

30. *Petrogradskaia pravda*, p. 43.

31. *Protokoly Kongressov*, p. 498.

32. *Petrogradskaia pravda*, p. 44. Here, Lenin, too, was overstating communist strength, for there was not yet an organized communist party in India.

33. Alfred Rosmer, "In Moscow in Lenin's Days: 1920–1921," *The New International*, XXI, 2 (1955), p. 109.

34. *Petrogradskaia pravda*, p. 43.

35. Ibid., p. 44.

36. *National-Liberation*, p. 266.

37. *Protokoly Kongressov*, p. 498.

38. "Theses on the Agrarian Question," quoted in Jane Degras, ed., *The Communist International, 1919–1943: Documents* (London, 1956), I, 156–161.

39. *National-Liberation*, p. 268.

40. Lenin himself declared to the congress that the bases of his and Roy's theses were the same (*National-Liberation*, pp. 264–265). And Maring, in the debate, expressed the view that there was no difference between the two sets of theses: "They are alike in essence" (*Protokoly Kongressov*, p. 138).

41. Lenin, "On the Tenth Anniversary of *Pravda*," in *National-Liberation*, p. 297.

42. *Vestnik Narodnogo Komissariata po Inostrannym Delam* (Herald of The People's Commissariat for Foreign Affairs), no. 3–4, 1921, p. 25, quoted in Eudin and North, *Soviet Russia and the East*, p. 76.

43. See, for example, Tivel', "Puti i perspektivy Indiiskoi revoliutsii" (Paths and perspectives of the Indian revolution), *Novyi Vostok* (The new East), no. 1, 1922, pp. 104–118.

44. *Fourth Congress of the Communist International: Abridged Report* (London, n.d.), pp. 221–222.

45. Quoted in Degras, *The Communist International*, I, 389.

46. See Gene D. Overstreet and Marshall Windmiller, *Communism in India* (Berkeley, 1959), pp. 67–68.

47. "Trotsky's Manifesto on the Tenth Anniversary of the Outbreak of War," in Degras, *The Communist International*, II, 110.

48. Quoted in Degras, *The Communist International*, II, 106, 159.

49. *International Press Correspondence (Inprecor)*, IV (1924), 608.

50. Quoted in Eudin and North, *Soviet Russia and the East*, p. 330.

51. Ibid.

II. The Soviet Approach to India in the Stalin Era

1. J. V. Stalin, "Don't Forget the East," in *Works* (Moscow, 1953), IV, 174–176.

2. "To All the Toiling Moslems of Russia and the East," in *Lenin-Stalin, 1917: Selected Writings and Speeches* (Moscow, 1938), pp. 664–666.

3. Quoted in A. M. D'iakov, *Natsional'nyi vopros i Angliiskii imperializm v Indii* (The national question and English imperialism in India) (Moscow, 1948), p. 36.

4. Quoted in Elliot R. Goodman, *The Soviet Design for a World State* (New York, 1960), p. 157.

5. George Kennan, *Russia and the West under Lenin and Stalin* (Boston, 1960), p. 268.

6. ECCI Resolution, January 12, 1923, quoted in Eudin and North, *Soviet Russia and the East*, pp. 343–344.

7. Roy, *Memoirs*, p. 537.

8. The quotations which follow are from the translation in J. V. Stalin, *Marxism and the National and Colonial Question* (New York, n.d.), pp. 214–220.

9. Quoted in R. C. North, *Moscow and the Chinese Communists* (Stanford, 1953), p. 96.

10. Benjamin I. Schwartz, *Chinese Communism and the Rise of Mao* (Cambridge, Mass., 1952), p. 71.

11. Quoted in Eudin and North, *Soviet Russia and the East*, p. 396.

12. V. Kriazhin, "Rabochee i professional'noe dvizhenie v Indii" (The worker and trade union movement in India), *Novyi Vostok*, no. 5, 1924, pp. 230–231.

13. M. N. Roy, "Anti-Imperialist Struggle in India," *Communist International*, no. 6, 1925, p. 84.

14. Philip Spratt, *Blowing Up India: Reminiscences and Reflections of a Former Comintern Emissary* (Calcutta, 1955), p. 35.

15. "Theses of Sixth Enlarged Plenum of the ECCI," February 17–March 15, 1926, in Eudin and North, *Soviet Russia and the East*, p. 325.

16. Quoted in Degras, *The Communist International*, II, 558.

17. Spratt, *Blowing Up India*, pp. 39–44.

18. M. N. Roy, "Lessons of the Chinese Revolution," in *Masses of India*, III (September–October 1927), 19–20, quoted in Overstreet and Windmiller, *Communism in India*, p. 102.

19. Quoted in Eudin and North, *Soviet Russia and the East*, p. 391.

20. Leonard Schapiro, *The Communist Party of the Soviet Union* (New York, 1960), p. 367.

21. Quoted in X. J. Eudin and R. M. Slusser, *Soviet Foreign Policy, 1928–1934: Documents and Materials* (University Park, Pa., 1966), I, 21.

22. There is a discernible parallel between the militant isolationism Stalin imposed on Soviet foreign policy and the international communist movement in the face of internal challenges and difficulties, and in the direction in which Mao Tse-tung led Chinese foreign policy in the recent period of "Cultural Revolution."

23. Jawaharlal Nehru, *Soviet Russia: Some Random Sketches and Impressions* (Bombay, 1929).

24. *The Communist International between the Fifth and the Sixth World Congresses, 1924–8* (London, 1928), p. 469.

25. It has been suggested by two students of this period that Roy was sent to China precisely to allow the CPGB to take control of the Indian movement (Overstreet and Windmiller, *Communism in India*, p. 96).

26. Ibid., pp. 106–107.

27. Spratt, *Blowing Up India*, p. 41.

28. Usmani, *I Met Stalin Twice*, p. 23.

29. *Inprecor*, VIII, 80 (1928), 1518.

30. *The Communist International 1924–8*, p. 466.

31. N. Bukharin, Report of ECCI to 6th Congress, *Inprecor*, VIII, 41 (1928), 734.

32. *Inprecor*, VIII, 76 (1928), 1391.

33. "Theses on the Revolutionary Movement in the Colonies and Semi-Colonies," in Degras, *The Communist International*, II, 544.

34. Usmani, *I Met Stalin Twice*, pp. 28–29.

35. *Inprecor*, VIII, 78 (1928), 1461.

36. Spratt, *Blowing Up India*, p. 43.

37. Quoted in Degras, *The Communist International*, II, 560–561.

38. Spratt, *Blowing Up India*, p. 44.

39. Ibid., p. 51.

40. *Inprecor*, IX, 53 (1929), 1141 (emphasis supplied).

41. *Inprecor*, IX, 55 (1929), 1203.

42. *Inprecor*, IX, 48 (1929), 1040. See also G. Safarov, "The End of Mr. Roy (The Ideological Metamorphosis of a Renegade)" *Communist International*, VI, 28 (1929), 1108–1116.

43. "The Comintern in the East," *Communist International*, VI, 9–10 (1929), 286 (emphasis supplied).

44. P. Schubin, "Problems of the Revolutionary Movement in India," *Communist International*, VI, 11–12–13 (1929), 525.

45. Valia, "The Struggle for Indian State Independence: A Condition of Success of the English Proletariat," *Communist International*, VIII, 20 (1931), 697–698 (emphasis in original).

46. See, for example, R. P. Dutt, "The Road to Proletarian Hegemony in the Indian Revolution," *Communist International*, VII, 13 (1930), 282–288; K. Mikhailov and A. Pronin, "Uglublenie ekonomicheskogo krizisa i revoliutsionnyi pod'em v Indii" (The sharpening of the economic crisis and the revolutionary upsurge in India), *Revoliutsionnyi Vostok* (The revolutionary East), nos. 1–2, 1932, pp. 55–101; and Yu. Roslavlev [R. A. Ul'ianovsky], "Osnovnye voprosy sovremennogo agrarnogo stroia v Indii" (The basic problems of the contemporary agrarian order in India), in *Agrarnyi vopros na Vostoke* (The agrarian problem in the East), ed. A. Mineev et al. (Moscow, 1933), pp. 171–225.

47. P. Prager, "K postanovke voprosa o nekapitalisticheskom puti razvitiia ostalykh stran" (Toward a resolution of the problem of the non-

capitalist path of development of backward countries), *Proletarskaia revoliutsiia* (Proletarian revolution), no. 5, 1930, pp. 55–94; no. 6, 1930, pp. 73–102.

48. R. P. Dutt, "The Road to Proletarian Hegemony in the Indian Revolution," *Communist International*, VII, 14 (1930), p. 317.

49. Karl Radek, "Problems of the Revolution in India," *Inprecor*, X, 30 (1930), 545 (emphasis in original).

50. I. M. Reisner, "Klassovaia sushchnost' Gandizma" (The class essence of Gandhism), *Istorik Marksist* (Marxist historian), XVIII–XIX (1930), 63–82.

51. Degras, *The Communist International*, III, 99.

52. See, for example, I. M. Reisner, "Novyi etap v rabochem dvizhenii Indii" (A new stage in the worker movement of India), *Novyi Vostok*, no. 25, 1929, pp. 47–73.

53. See Democratic Research Service, *Indian Communist Party Documents, 1930–1956* (Bombay, 1957), pp. 1–21.

54. *Inprecor*, XII, 22 (1932), 436–442.

55. "Open Letter to the Indian Communists from the C.C. of the C.P. of China," *Inprecor*, XIII, 51 (1933), 1153–1158.

56. Quoted in M. R. Masani, *The Communist Party of India: A Short History* (New York, 1954), p. 73.

57. Ibid., pp. 51–52.

58. For the text, see Democratic Research Service, *Indian Communist Party Documents*, pp. 25–35.

59. "Orgwald," "A Conversation with Indian Comrades," *Inprecor*, XIV, 20 (1934), 521.

60. K. Mikhailov, "O sdvigakh v Indiiskom Natsional'nom Kongresse" (On the changes in the Indian National Congress), *Revoliutsionnyi Vostok*, no. 2, 1935, pp. 132–146. For similar attacks on the noncommunist left, see G. Safarov, "The Congress Socialist Party and the New Maneuvers of the National Congress in India," *Communist International*, XI, 22 (1934), 783–792, and "Whither Nehru?" *Inprecor*, XIV, 17 (1934), 443.

61. Masani, *The Communist Party of India*, pp. 54–55.

62. Ben Bradley, "The Government of India Bill," *Inprecor*, XV, 26 (1935), 683.

63. *VII Congress of the Communist International: Abridged Stenographic Report of Proceedings* (Moscow, 1939), p. 305 (emphasis in original).

64. Ibid., p. 299.

65. Ibid., p. 172.

66. R. P. Dutt and Ben Bradley, "The Anti-Imperialist People's Front," *Inprecor*, XVI, 11 (1936), 298.

67. Ibid., p. 300.

68. R. P. Dutt, Ben Bradley, and Harry Pollitt, "The United National Front," *Inprecor*, XVI, 50 (1936), 1343.

69. "The New Party of Bose and What Should Be Our Attitude to It," *Inprecor*, XIII, 52 (1933), 1185.

70. S. Krishna, "After the Lucknow Congress," *Inprecor*, XVI, 30 (1936), 803 (emphasis in original).

71. See G. Konchar'iants, "Indiiskii narod na puti k antiimperialisticheskomu edinstvu" (The Indian people on the path toward anti-imperialist unity), *Bol'shevik*, no. 21–22, 1938, p. 120, and S. M. Mel'man, "Indiia v bor'be za svoiu natsional'nuiu nezavisimost'" (India in the struggle for her national independence), *Mirovoe khoziaistvo i mirovaia politika* (World economy and world politics), no. 9, 1939, p. 96.

72. *National Front*, II (1939), 96, 189, quoted in Overstreet and Windmiller, *Communism in India*, pp. 168–169.

73. Harry Pollitt, "Greetings to the Indian National Congress," *World News and Views*, XIX, 10 (1939), 199.

74. Georgy Dimitrov, "The Tasks of the Working Class in the Present War," *World News and Views*, XIX, 53 (1939), 1079, 1081.

75. V. Bushevich [Balabushevich], "Natsional'no-osvoboditel'noe dvizhenie v Indii i bor'ba rabochego klassa," (The national-liberation movement in India and the struggle of the working class), *Mirovoe khoziaistvo i mirovaia politika*, no. 11, 1939, pp. 133–152.

76. Quoted in P. C. Joshi, *Communist Reply to Congress Working Committee's Charges* (Bombay, 1945), pp. 36–38 (emphasis in original).

77. Quoted in Masani, *The Communist Party of India*, p. 276.

78. G. Konchar'iants, "Voina i natsional'no-osvoboditel'noe dvizhenie indiiskogo naroda," (The war and the national-liberation movement of the Indian people), *Bol'shevik*, no. 14, 1940, pp. 59–75.

79. V. Bushevich [Balabushevich] and A. D'iakov, "Indiia i Vtoraia Imperialisticheskaia Voina" (India and the Second Imperialist War), *Mirovoe khoziaistvo i mirovaia politika*, no. 12, 1940, pp. 53–67.

80. R. J. Sontag and I. S. Boddie, eds., *Nazi-Soviet Relations, 1939–1941: Documents from the Archives of the German Foreign Office* (Washington, 1948), pp. 217–259. Throughout the talks with Ribbentrop, Molotov stubbornly returned to questions of German interests and activities in the Baltic and Balkans. It was clear that the Soviets' main interests were in these areas. The suggestions of a sphere centered "in the direction of the Persian Gulf" was a last-minute Soviet riposte to German suggestions of Soviet movement toward the Indian Ocean.

81. Quoted in Masani, *The Communist Party of India*, p. 277.

82. I. M. Lemin, "Rol' Britanskoi imperii v sovremennoi voine" (The role of the British empire in the present war), *Bol'shevik*, no. 20, 1941, p. 33.

83. Quoted in Overstreet and Windmiller, *Communism in India*, p. 194.

84. P. C. Joshi, *The Indian Communist Party: Its Policy and Work in the War of Liberation* (London, 1942).

85. A. M. D'iakov, *Indiia vo vremia i posle Vtoroi Mirovoi Voiny 1939–49* (India during and after the Second World War) (Moscow, 1952), pp. 33–34.

86. I. M. Lemin, "Anglo-Indiiskie otnosheniia i voina" (Anglo-Indian relations and the war), *Mirovoe khoziaistvo i mirovaia politika*, no. 5–6, 1942, pp. 76–84.

87. S. M. Mel'man, "Polozhenie v Indii" (The situation in India), *Mirovoe khoziaistvo i mirovaia politika*, no. 11–12, 1942, pp. 46–47.

88. P. C. Joshi, *Congress and Communists* (Bombay, 1944).

89. *Correspondence between M. Gandhi and P. C. Joshi* (Bombay, 1945).

90. Joshi, *Communist Reply*, pp. 1–16.

III. The Soviets and the CPI in Search of a Policy

1. B. Seigel', "Evoliutsiia Indiiskikh Natsional'nykh Kongressov" (The evolution of the Indian National Congress), *Novyi Vostok*, no. 6, 1925, p. 244.

2. Chattopadyaya, "Musul'manstvo i Buddizm na sluzhbe u imperializma" (Muslimism and Buddhism in the service of imperialism), *Revoliutsionnyi Vostok*, no. 3–4, 1932, pp. 282–288.

3. "Orgwald," "A Conversation with Indian Comrades," *Inprecor*, XIV, 20 (1934), 532.

4. A. M. D'iakov, "Natsional'naia politika Britanskogo imperializma v Indii" (The national policy of British imperialism in India), *Mirovoe khoziaistvo i mirovaia politika*, no. 12, 1939, pp. 77–92.

5. Quoted in G. Adhikari, *Pakistan and Indian National Unity* (London, 1943), pp. 31–32.

6. Ibid., pp. 1–32.

7. In *The Imperialist Alternative*, a ten-page pamphlet published in 1945, Adhikari spoke of Pakistan as the "freedom demand" of the Moslem League and called for a united India in the form of a "brotherly alliance of Free Pakistan and Free Hindustan achieved through a joint-front" of Congress and League. This appears to have represented only a brief CPI flirtation with the slogan of Pakistan, and it was soon replaced by the policy outlined in the election manifesto cited below.

8. P. C. Joshi, *For the Final Bid for Power! The Communist Plan Explained* (Bombay, 1946), pp. 89–92.

9. Quoted in S. S. Harrison, *India: The Most Dangerous Decades* (Princeton, 1960), p. 154.

10. A. M. D'iakov, "The Political Situation in India," *The War and the Working Class*, no. 7, 1945, p. 11; A. M. D'iakov, "After the Failure of the Simla Conference," *New Times*, no. 5, 1945, p. 14.

11. A. M. D'iakov, "Sovremennaia Indiia" (Contemporary India), *Bol'shevik*, no. 4, 1946, pp. 49–53.

12. A. M. D'iakov, "K voprosu o natsional'nom sostave naseleniia Indii" (On the question of the national basis of the population of India), *Uchenye zapiski Tikhookeanskogo Instituta* (Scholarly notes of the Pacific Institute), I (1947), 223–330.

13. "Kautilya," "Pakistan, Russia and the Communists," *National Herald*, February 10, 1946, p. 6.

14. A. M. D'iakov, "The New British Plan for India," *New Times*, no. 24, 1947, p. 14.

15. Quoted in Harrison, *India*, p. 155.

16. A. M. D'iakov, "The Indian Problem," *The War and the Working Class*, no. 2, 1945, p. 14.

17. D'iakov, "The Political Situation in India," p. 13.

18. E. M. Zhukov, "Porazhenie Iaponskogo imperializma i natsional'no-osvoboditel'naia bor'ba narodov Vostochnoi Azii" (The defeat of Japanese imperialism and the national-liberation struggle of the peoples of East Asia), *Bol'shevik*, no. 23–24, 1945, pp. 79–87.

19. E. M. Zhukov, "The Trusteeship Question," *New Times*, no. 14, 1945, pp. 3–6.

20. Milovan Djilas, *Conversations with Stalin* (New York, 1962), p. 182.

21. Joshi, *For the Final Bid for Power*, pp. 113–118.

22. G. M. Adhikari, *Resurgent India at the Cross Roads: 1946 in Review* (Bombay, 1947).

23. Quoted in Overstreet and Windmiller, *Communism in India*, p. 260.

24. E. M. Zhukov, "Velikaia Oktiabr'skaia Sotsialisticheskaia Revoliutsiia i kolonial'nyi Vostok" (The Great October Socialist Revolution and the colonial East), *Bol'shevik*, no. 20, 1946, pp. 38–47. See also A. M. D'iakov, "India after the War," *New Times*, no. 2, 1946, p. 11, and V. Bushevich [Balabushevich], "Bor'ba Indii na nezavisimost'" (The struggle of India for independence), *Mirovoe khoziaistvo i mirovaia politika*, no. 9, 1946, pp. 39–52.

25. M. S. Venkataramani, "The Soviet Union and the Indian Food Crisis of 1946," *International Studies* (Bombay), IV, 4 (1963), 395–403.

26. See F. C. Barghoorn, "The Varga Discussion and its Significance," *American Slavic and East European Review*, VII, 3 (1948), 214–236.

27. E. M. Zhukov, "K polozheniiu v Indii" (On the situation in India), *Mirovoe khoziaistvo i mirovaia politika*, no. 7, 1947, pp. 3–14. A footnote on page 3 notes the origin of the article, which was signed for the press on August 4.

28. John Kautsky, *Moscow and the Communist Party of India* (Cambridge, Mass., 1956), p. 25.

29. The works are John Kautsky's (see n. 28 above) and Overstreet and Windmiller, *Communism in India*.

30. Akademiia Nauk SSSR. Tikhookeanskii Institut. *Uchenye zapiski Tikhookeanskogo Instituta*, II: *Indiiskii sbornik* (Moscow, 1949).

31. The content of the "debate" is reconstructed by Kautsky and Overstreet through a juxtaposition of Zhukov's arguments in "On the Situation in India" with the contrasting assessments contained in D'iakov's and Balabushevich's contributions to the 1949 collection (Kautsky, *Moscow and the Communist Party of India*, pp. 24–28, and Overstreet and Windmiller, *Communism in India*, pp. 255–260. This mistake is repeated by C. B. McLane, *Soviet Strategies in Southeast Asia: An Exploration of Eastern Policy under Lenin and Stalin*, [Princeton, 1966], p. 256).

The examination of evidence not considered by Kautsky and Overstreet makes such confident accounts of sharp disagreement at the June 1947 joint session much less credible. For the editor of the 1949 Pacific Institute collection, in a footnote apparently overlooked by Kautsky and Overstreet, specifically identifies the volume in which Zhukov's report to the Academy had previously been published. The reader who turns to this volume will find *not* the politically significant article "On the Situation in India," but an innocent account of Zhukov's trip to a Pan-Asiatic Congress held in Delhi in the spring of 1947. See E. M. Zhukov, "Mezhaziatskii Kongress v Indii (mart-aprel' 1947 g) (Pan-Asiatic Congress in India [March–April 1947]) in Akademii Nauk SSSR, *Obshchee sobranie Akademii Nauk SSSR: 10–13 iiunia 1947 goda* (General meeting of the USSR Academy of Sciences: 10–13 June 1947) (Moscow, 1948), pp. 122–134. I would conclude that Zhukov delivered his report both at this general meeting of the Academy on June 10–13 and at the special session on India which followed on June 14–18.

Further confirmation that Zhukov did not present his views concerning the Indian political situation to the Academy conference can be found in another volume overlooked by Kautsky and Overstreet. This is the August 1947 issue of the Academy's *Vestnik* (Herald), which gives an unsigned summary report of the conference's proceedings ("Izuchenie Indii" [The study of India], *Vestnik Akademii Nauk SSSR*, no. 8 [August 1947], pp. 83–91). If Zhukov's August article "On the Situation in India" had indeed been the paper he delivered at the June joint session, one would have expected the *Vestnik* summary to take note of that article's significant conclusions concerning the causes and effects of the Mountbatten Plan. Yet in fact, according to the *Vestnik*, Zhukov's contribution to the June gathering consisted entirely of an account of the Delhi Congress on Pan-Asiatic Relations. Moreover, portions of the summary account are exact duplicates of the May 1948 article, "The Pan-Asiatic Congress."

32. Discovery of the *Vestnik* summary enables us to conclude that

the 1949 publication's version of D'iakov's and Balabushevich's views (relied upon by Kautsky and Overstreet to show the existence of a controversy in mid-1947) were not identical to the reports these men actually delivered in June 1947. Indeed, both reports, in their published form, contain references to events which occurred after the Academy's session. Balabushevich's article refers to a policy of terror against workers and peasants conducted by the governments of India and Pakistan (partition occurred only in August), and D'iakov quotes a resolution which he says was passed by the CPI in August 1947 (*Uchenye zapiski*, II, 28, 64. D'iakov's historical scholarship is suspect, for the resolution he quotes was actually passed in December 1947).

33. "Izuchenie Indii," p. 89.

34. "The division of India into two dominions . . . is the apparent result of an agreement of the Indian bourgeoisie and landlords with English imperialism . . . The Indian bourgeoisie and leadership of the National Congress have utterly crossed over into the camp of reaction and imperialism. . . . The toiling masses of India under the leadership of the Indian worker class and its party . . . are conducting a decisive struggle against the reactionary bloc of imperialists, bourgeoisie and landlords for full independence, for liquidation of all the survivals of feudalism, for people's democracy" (*Uchenye zapiski*, II, 28).

35. "Agreement on the basis of the English declaration will not be acceptable to the broad masses of Hindus and Moslems seeking real independence. There is reason to think also that part of the bourgeois elements (Bengalis and others) will be dissatisfied with the agreement since they fear the excessive strengthening of the position of the Gujarati-Marwari bourgeoisie" ("Izuchenie Indii," p. 88).

36. *Uchenye zapiski*, II, 65–66. The report of S. M. Mel'man on the economy of postwar India also appears to have been revised before publication. In place of the mild conclusion reported in the *Vestnik* summary, the 1949 version concluded that the bourgeoisie's acceptance of the Mountbatten Plan meant that "the Indian big bourgeoisie wholly went over to the camp of reaction and imperialism" (ibid., p. 53).

37. John Kautsky describes the "clash" in terms of disagreement among the scholars on whether to replace the "right" strategy in India with the "left" (D'iakov-Balabushevich) or "neo-Maoist" (Zhukov) strategies. Kautsky uses other, later writings to develop this theme further, and these—as well as the entire concept of "neo-Maoism"—will be considered below. Here it is important to note only that Kautsky's "striking" conclusion that the debate developed as early as June 1947, and that D'iakov and Balabushevich had by then become "adherents of the 'left' strategy," has no basis in the evidence available.

Likewise, Overstreet and Windmiller, misreading the sources in the same way, picture a confrontation with battle lines firmly drawn: Zhukov's "moderate" four-class strategy and D'iakov-Balabushevich's "very radical" three-class "program aimed at revolution." Moreover, they go on to link this fictitious debate to a dispute then raging between the Russians and the Yugoslavs on the meaning of "people's democracy." Balabushevich's use of this term in the conclusion of his article published in 1949 is interpreted as evidence that he and D'iakov were siding with the Yugoslav position. If, on the other hand, Balabushevich's use of the term is seen as a later addition to the report, then its appearance is not so striking, for by 1949 the issue was settled and both the Indian Communist Party and Soviet scholars (including Zhukov) were speaking freely of the goal of "people's democracy."

38. A. A. Zhdanov, *The International Situation: Report Made at the Conference of the Nine Communist Parties Held in Poland, September, 1947* (n.p., n.d.).

39. Summaries appear in "Velikaia Oktiabr'skaia Revoliutsiia i strany Vostoka" (The Great October Revolution and the countries of the East), *Vestnik Akademii Nauk SSSR,* no. 1, 1948, pp. 39–46, and B. Kremortat, "Sessiia Tikhookeanskogo Instituta Akademii Nauk SSSR" (Session of the Pacific Institute of the USSR Academy of Sciences), *Voprosy istorii* (Problems of history), no. 4, 1948, pp. 151–157.

40. E. M. Zhukov, "Obostrenie krizisa kolonial'noi sistemy" (The sharpening crisis of the colonial system), *Bol'shevik,* no. 23, 1947, pp. 51–64.

41. Kautsky (*Moscow and the Communist Party of India,* p. 30) again overstates the case when he describes Zhukov's article as a "very clear . . . unambiguous . . . thoroughly neo-Maoist interpretation." Zhukov is not "careful to include merely the 'big' bourgeoisie" among the opponents of communist parties. Kautsky is equally in error in describing an article by Balabushevich which appeared in the same month ("Indiia posle razdela" [India after partition], *Mirovoe khoziaistvo i mirovaia politika,* no. 12, 1947, pp. 41–62) as "still" advocating the "left" strategy, for Balabushevich uses the same group of terms as interchangeably and ambiguously as does Zhukov. In fact Balabushevich even describes the Mountbatten Plan as a "concession" by the English and quotes the June CPI resolution promising support to the Nehru government in its "democratic measures." An article by D'iakov in January ("Partitioned India," *New Times,* no. 3, 1948, pp. 3–9) can more justifiably be termed "left" for its suggestion that the Indian "bourgeoisie is incapable of carrying out even the elementary democratic reforms," but even D'iakov's analysis is not unambiguous, for it does distinguish between the "bourgeoisie" and the "upper bourgeoisie." Nor were articles by these two Indologists appearing in February any less ambiguous in their assessment of the Indian bourgeoisie (V. V. Balabushevich, "What is happening in India," *Trud,* February 18, 1948, in *Soviet Press Translations* [hereafter *SPT*], III, 11 (1948), 327, and A. M. D'iakov, "The Assassination of Gandhi," *New Times,* no. 7, 1948, pp. 13–15). Commenting on the assassination of Gandhi, Balabu-

shevich called him the "foremost political figure of India" and implied that the British ordered his assassination, while D'iakov stated that Gandhi, by promoting the "political awakening" of India and dedicating his life to her "complete independence" and "better conditions for her people," had played "a certain progressive part."

42. Quoted in Overstreet and Windmiller, *Communism in India*, p. 268.

43. Ibid., p. 269.

44. Ruth McVey, *The Calcutta Conference and the Southeast Asian Uprisings* (Ithaca, 1958).

45. Quoted in Overstreet and Windmiller, *Communism in India*, p. 271.

46. Communist Party of India, *Political Thesis of the Communist Party of India, Passed by the Second Congress at Calcutta, February 28–March 6, 1948* (Bombay, 1948), p. 54.

47. Ibid., p. 10.

48. A peasant uprising had begun in the Telengana area in 1946 and had soon come under the leadership of local communist groups. The semifeudal agrarian system existing under the Nizam of Hyderabad had been extremely brutal, and the peasant guerrilla warfare had spread rapidly. Its appeal was based not only on economic and social grievances but also on the particularist demands of the communist-influenced Andhra Mahasabha, which sought autonomy for the Telegu-speaking people of this part of South India. Joshi's strategy had opposed or ignored such armed struggle, but Ranadive at the Congress declared, "Telengana today means Communists and Communists mean Telengana."

49. Kautsky, *Moscow and the Communist Party of India*, p. 56.

50. Overstreet and Windmiller, *Communism in India*, p. 287.

51. "Speech by Mao Tse-tung," *Pravda*, January 6, 1948, in *SPT*, III, 5 (1948), 131–137, and "Mao Tse-tung's Report to the Central Committee of the Communist Party of China," *For a Lasting Peace, For a People's Democracy!* (hereafter *FLP, FPD*), January 15, 1948, p. 6.

52. "Agrarian Policy of the CP of China; Mao Tse-tung's Address to Cadres of Shansi-Suiyan Liberated Areas," *FLP, FPD*, July 1, 1948, p. 6 (emphasis supplied). See also Li-Shun, "Chinese Party in the Struggle for National Independence," *FLP, FPD*, May 1, 1948, p. 3.

53. For a detailed analysis see Kautsky, *Moscow and the Communist Party of India*, pp. 63–80.

54. Quoted in Tridib Chaudhuri, *The Swing Back: A Critical Survey of the Devious Zig-Zags of CPI Political Line (1947–1950)* (Calcutta, 1950), p. 70.

55. Quoted in Madhu Limaye, *Communist Party: Facts and Fiction* (Hyderabad, 1951), pp. 62–63.

56. "Congress of the Communist Party of India," *FLP, FPD*, May 15, 1948, p. 4.

57. T. Ershov, "The Truth about Kashmir," *New Times*, no. 10, 1948, pp. 24–29, and O. Orestov, "The War in Kashmir," *New Times*, no. 40, 1948, pp. 24–30.

58. M. Alekseev, "Indiiskii Soiuz i Pakistan posle raschleneniia Indii" (The Indian Union and Pakistan after the partition of India), *Bol'shevik*, no. 11, 1948, pp. 54–66.

59. R. P. Dutt, "Struggle of Colonial Peoples against Imperialism," *FLP, FPD*, October 15, 1948, p. 5, and "Right-Wing Social Democracy in the Service of Imperialism," *FLP, FPD*, November 1, 1948. John Kautsky wrongly suggests (*Moscow and the Communist Party of India*, p. 55n) that Dutt's references to Chinese influences had been omitted by Cominform editors.

60. A. M. D'iakov, *Natsional'nyi vopros i Angliiskii imperializm v Indii.*

61. An authoritative review by E. M. Zhukov ("Manevry Angliiskogo imperializma v Indii" [The maneuvers of English imperialism in India], *Bol'shevik*, no. 4, 1949, pp. 79–80) gave D'iakov's study a "positive rating." Zhukov endorsed D'iakov's conclusions on the reactionary nature of the "top national" bourgeoisie—the Gujarati-Marwari groups. But he felt that D'iakov had overstated the degree to which these groups had been able to wrest power from the imperialists, who still occupied the "commanding positions" both politically and economically. Nor had D'iakov sufficiently stressed that the landlords were part of the reactionary ruling stratum in India, in opposition to whom the "multimillion peasant masses" were struggling.

Interestingly, Professor Kautsky's study (*Moscow and the Communist Party of India*) fails to refer either to D'iakov's book or to Zhukov's review. Had he taken these works into account, Kautsky's conception of the "debate" between the two might have been altered. Whereas Kautsky characterizes D'iakov as less sensitive to the revolutionary potential of the bourgeoisie than Zhukov, it is of interest to note that Zhukov's review shows the opposite to be the case. His article criticizes D'iakov for overestimating the progressive role of the National Congress in the prewar liberation movement and states that D'iakov had been "methodologically incorrect and absolutely unsubstantiated by facts" when he asserted that all of India's nationality movements were anti-imperialist. This criticism, however, did not have the effect of denying absolutely D'iakov's suggestion of the possibility of worker-bourgeoisie alliances. It merely implied that such alliances would have to be made selectively.

62. Iu. Frantsev, "Natsionalizm—oruzhie imperialisticheskoi reaktsii" (Nationalism—the weapon of imperialist reaction), *Bol'shevik*, no. 15, 1948, pp. 45–55.

63. A. I. Levkovsky, "Nekotorye voprosy poslevoennogo ekonomicheskogo razvitiia Indii v svete Leninskogo-Stalinskogo ucheniia ob imperializme" (Some problems of the postwar economic development

of India in light of Leninist-Stalinist teachings about imperialism), *Vestnik Moskovskogo Universiteta* (Herald of Moscow University), no. 1, 1949, pp. 172–173.

64. S. M. Mel'man, "Rabochee dvizhenie Indii posle razdela strany" (The worker movement of India after the division of the country), *Professional'nye soiuzy* (Trade unions), no. 3, 1949, pp. 39–43.

65. The following quotations are from the English-language edition, Liu Shao-ch'i, *Internationalism and Nationalism* (Peking, 1948).

66. Ibid., pp. 46–47. There was no insistence on proletarian hegemony in this alliance. Indeed, Liu cited as the "clearest example of this type of collaboration," that between the Chinese Communists and Sun Yat-sen—a relationship in which the CCP had by no means been dominant. Earlier in the article, however, Liu had made the exaggerated claim that the CCP had always been the "leader and organizer" of the anti-imperialist front in China (ibid., pp. 10–11).

67. E. M. Zhukov, "Voprosy natsional'no-kolonial'noi bor'by posle Vtoroi Mirovoi Voiny" (Problems of the national-colonial struggle since the Second World War), *Voprosy ekonomiki* (Problems of economics), no. 9, 1949, pp. 55–59.

68. V. V. Balabushevich, "Novyi etap natsional'no-osvoboditel'noi bor'by narodov Indii" (A new phase in the national-liberation struggle of the peoples of India), *Voprosy ekonomiki*, no. 8, 1949, pp. 30–48.

69. A. M. D'iakov, "Krizis Angliiskogo gospodstva v Indii i novyi etap osvoboditel'noi bor'by ee narodov" (The crisis of English rule in India and the new stage of the liberation movement of her peoples), in E. M. Zhukov, ed., *Krizis kolonial'noi sistemy: natsional'no-osvoboditel'naia bor'ba narodov Vostochnoi Azii* (Moscow, 1949), pp. 87–123. Most of the articles were published in English by the CPI in 1951, as *Crisis of the Colonial System: National Liberation Struggle of the Peoples of East Asia* (Bombay, 1951).

70. Mao Tse-tung, "The Dictatorship of the People's Democracy," *Pravda*, July 6, 1949, in *SPT*, IV, 15 (1949), 454–461.

71. Chu Teh, "Chinese People's Struggle for Liberation," *FLP*, *FPD*, September 1, 1949, p. 3.

72. "Great Victory of People's Democratic Revolution in China," *FLP*, *FPD*, October 7, 1949, p. 1.

73. A. M. D'iakov, "Anglo-American Plans in India," *Pravda*, November 25, 1949, in *SPT*, V, 3 (1950), 80–83. See also "Chiang Kai-shek's Successor," *New Times*, no. 42, 1949, pp. 20–21.

74. "Speech by Liu Shao-ch'i to Conference of Trade Unions of Countries of Asia and Oceania," *Pravda*, January 4, 1950, in *SPT*, V, 6 (1950), 168–172. See also *FLP*, *FPD*, December 30, 1949, p. 2.

75. "Mighty Advance of the National Liberation Movement in the Colonial and Dependent Countries," *FLP*, *FPD*, January 27, 1950, p. 1.

76. Kautsky, *Moscow and the Communist Party of India*, chap. 1. See also Bernard Morris and Morris Watnick, "Current Communist

Strategy in Non-industrialized Countries," *Problems of Communism*, IV, 5 (1955), 1–6.

77. Schwartz, *Chinese Communism and the Rise of Mao*, p. 189.

78. Mao Tse-tung in October 1939, quoted in Stuart R. Schram, *The Political Thought of Mao Tse-tung* (New York, 1963), p. 257 (emphasis in original).

79. Stalin, *Marxism and the National and Colonial Question*, p. 218.

80. Quoted in Schram, *The Political Thought of Mao Tse-tung*, p. 56.

81. G. V. Astaf'iev, "Ot polukolonii k narodnoi demokratii" (From semicolony to people's democracy), in Zhukov, ed., *Krizis kolonial'noi sistemy*, pp. 29–86.

82. Ibid., p. 82. A year later an article by A. N. Kheifets utilized Mao's own words to show Stalin's superiority: ". . . now that there is a Stalin, things have gone well in this world." According to Kheifets, the Chinese comrades had been taught by Stalin to utilize the peasantry and even the national bourgeoisie as allies in their revolution (A. N. Kheifets, "Voprosy kitaiskoi revoliutsii v trudakh I. V. Stalina" [Problems of the Chinese revolution in the works of J. V. Stalin], *Voprosy filosofii* [Problems of philosophy], no. 3, 1950, pp. 53–74).

83. Professor Kautsky's contention that a debate began in mid-1947 between Soviet "leftists" and "neo-Maoists" concerning the proper strategy for India has already been shown to rest on a faulty reading of the evidence. Unfortunately, much of Kautsky's interpretation of the Soviet and Cominform writings on India in this period seems to be influenced by a desire to show the sharpest possible contrast between the "right" and "left" strategies and "neo-Maoism." Passages in the works of Zhukov, D'iakov, and Balabushevich are at times said to make careful and conscious distinctions, while those passages which on the surface appear to blur the distinctions are called "careless" and unintentional (Kautsky, *Moscow and the Communist Party of India*, esp. pp. 30, 90, 93, 127).

That such bending of the evidence is necessary in order to support the case for the uniqueness of "neo-Maoism" is testimony to the weakness of Kautsky's distinctions. In fact, he himself admits toward the end of his study that both the "right" and the "neo-Maoist" strategies can involve a combination of united front appeals "from above" and "from below" (ibid., pp. 160–163). Such a concession would seem to indicate that the form a united front takes is a matter of tactics, rather than—as Kautsky contends—the very hallmark of a "strategy."

84. *Colonial Peoples' Struggle for Liberation* (Bombay, 1950), p. 99 (emphasis supplied).

85. See, for example, the following articles in *New Times*: V. Berezhkov, "Foreign Policy Manoeuvres of Indian Reaction," no. 22, 1950, pp. 30–32; T. Ershov, "Indian Version of Bourgeois Pseudo-Democracy," no. 11, 1950, pp. 3–7; "Nehru's Smear Campaign," no. 25, 1950, pp. 21–22; V. Berezhkov, "Glorifiers of Colonial Rapine," no. 26, 1950, pp. 12–13.

86. "The Peoples of the Colonial and Dependent Countries in the Struggle against the Warmongers," *FLP, FPD,* May 19, 1950, p. 1.

87. According to Ranadive, the Second Congress was a "great step in the life of the party," the Report on Strategy and Tactics (the very document which had attacked Mao) had "correctly applied" many points, "considerable successes" had been made by the CPI in the past year, and the chief error of the party had been not its adventurism (Ranadive does not use the word) but its *"lagging behind* the rising tempo and sweep of the revolutionary struggle which the Indian people are waging." Such claims as these canceled the self-critical effect of admissions of the "rich experience" of the Chinese revolution, the need to distinguish potential "fellow travelers" among the Indian bourgeoisie, and the mistaken lumping of rich peasants with landlords ("Statement of the Editorial Board on the Editorial Article in the Organ of the Information Bureau on the National Liberation Movement in the Colonies," *Communist* [Bombay], III, 2 [February–March, 1950], 1–11. The same issue reprints the Cominform editorial, Liu's speech to the Peking Trade Union Conference, and the Conference Manifesto).

88. Quoted in Overstreet and Windmiller, *Communism in India,* p. 353.

89. Ibid., pp. 302–303.

90. "Neotlozhenye zadachi Sovetskikh istorikov-vostokovedov" (Urgent tasks of Soviet historians of the East), *Voprosy istorii* (Problems of history), no. 4, 1949, pp. 3–8, and "Ocherednye zadachi istorikov-vostokovedov" (The next tasks of historians of the East), *Voprosy istorii,* no. 12, 1950, pp. 3–7.

91. See Masani, *The Communist Party of India,* pp. 109–110; Overstreet and Windmiller, *Communism in India,* pp. 304–305; and Limaye, *Communist Party,* pp. 79–80.

92. "Talks with Comrade R. Palme Dutt and Other Impressions Gained Abroad by Deven and Bal Krishna," in Democratic Research Service, *Indian Communist Party Documents,* pp. 63–65.

93. Masani, *The Communist Party of India,* p. 115, and Democratic Research Service, *Indian Communist Party Documents,* p. 71. The "Tactical Line" is contained in the latter volume, pp. 72–85. Much of this document is identical with the "Statement of Policy," the primary difference being the former's greater certainty that guerrilla warfare and workers' uprisings would eventually have to be utilized in order to achieve the revolution. There is no reason to doubt that the trip to Moscow took place, but even if it did not, the publicity given the April documents of the CPI in the Soviet and Cominform press is evidence enough that Moscow fully approved of their contents. (See "Draft Program of the Communist Party of India," *FLP, FPD,* May 11, 1951, p. 3.) Gangadhar Adhikari wrote in 1964 (in *Communist Party and India's Path to National Regeneration and Socialism* [New Delhi, 1964], p. 118) that the 1951 program was arrived at only after a "sustained period of collective discussion into which international communist cir-

cles" were also drawn. The large role of "international circles" in shaping this document is reminiscent of the origins of the CPI's 1930 Draft Program.

94. "Draft Program," *FLP*, *FPD*, May 11, 1951, p. 3.

95. Communist Party of India, *Statement of Policy of the C.P. of India* (Bombay, 1951). The quotations are from the second edition, published in June 1951.

96. "Statement by Political Bureau, Communist Party of India," *FLP*, *FPD*, November 2, 1951, p. 6. The May Central Committee session also passed a resolution stating its readiness to negotiate the Telengana struggle, which it said had been aimed only at ending feudal oppression, and not at ousting the Nehru government. When Nehru refused to negotiate, the CPI found it necessary unilaterally to call off the fighting. This it did in October, on the pretense of depriving the government of an excuse for not holding elections in Telengana. (See Kautsky, *Moscow and the Communist Party of India*, pp. 143–144.)

97. A. K. Ghosh, "The Communist Party of India in Struggle for People's Democratic Government," *FLP*, *FPD*, October 19, 1951, pp. 2–3. In this article, Ghosh also wrote that 500 communists had been killed in Telengana and 25,000 party members had been imprisoned (with 3,000 still in jail at the time of his writing).

98. "Electoral Successes of People's Democratic Front in India," *FLP*, *FPD*, February 15, 1952, p. 4. A writer in *Bol'shevik* charged that persecution, terrorism, bribery, and ballot-stuffing had been employed by Congress forces (O. Orestov, "Parlamentskie vybory v Indii" [Parliamentary elections in India], *Bol'shevik*, no. 5, 1952, pp. 63–70).

99. Overstreet and Windmiller, *Communism in India*, p. 357.

100. Lu Ting-yi, "World Significance of Chinese Revolution," *FLP*, *FPD*, June 29, 1951, p. 2.

101. A. Sobolev, "People's Democracy as a Form of Political Organization of Society," *Bol'shevik*, no. 19, 1951, reprinted in *Communist Review* (London), January 1952, pp. 3–21.

102. "O kharaktere i osobennostiakh Narodnoi Demokratii v stranakh Vostoka" (On the character and attributes of People's Democracy in the countries of the East), *Izvestiia Akademii Nauk SSSR: Seriia istorii i filosofii* (News of the USSR Academy of Sciences: History and philosophy series), IX, 1 (1952), 81.

103. Ibid., p. 85.

104. V. V. Balabushevich, "Natsional'no-osvoboditel'naia bor'ba narodov Indii" (National-liberation struggle of the peoples of India), in V. A. Maslennikov, ed., *Uglublenie krizisa kolonial'noi sistemy imperializma posle Vtoroi Mirovoi Voiny: sbornik statei* (The deepening crisis of the colonial system of imperialism after World War Two: collected articles) (Moscow, 1953), pp. 265–342.

105. D'iakov, *Indii vo vremia i posle Vtoroi Mirovoi Voina 1939–49*, pp. 3–4. D'iakov was not the only Indologist whose scholarship was re-

trospectively poor. S. M. Mel'man, in her *Ekonomika Indii i politika Angliiskogo imperializma* (The economy of India and the policy of English imperialism) (Moscow, 1951), pp. 3–4, begins with a self-critical confession of these same mistaken positions in her earlier works.

106. K. A. Mikhailov, review article in *Voprosy istorii*, no. 6, 1953, p. 161.

107. V. Ia. Grashe, "Kratkii ocherk formirovaniia krupnykh promyshlennykh kapitalistov v kolonial'noi Indii" (A brief sketch of the formation of the big industrial capitalists in India), *Uchenye zapiski Instituta Vostokvedeniia* (Scholarly notes of the Oriental Studies Institute), X (1954), 97–160.

108. V. I. Levkovsky, review article in *Sovetskaia kniga* (Soviet book), no. 4, 1952, pp. 68–73.

109. Typical is the appraisal of S. M. Vakar in 1948, even the title of which, "Klassovaia sushchnost' Gandizma" (The class nature of Gandhism), echoed Reisner's article (*Voprosy filosofii*, no. 3, 1948, pp. 266–279).

110. D'iakov, *Indiia vo vremia*, p. 168.

111. I. M. Lemin, "The Fruits of British Rule in India and Pakistan," *Voprosy ekonomiki*, no. 1, 1952, in *SPT*, VII, 8 (1952), 211–220; A. Pronin, "Foreign Monopolies in India," *Pravda*, June 2, 1953, p. 3, in *Current Digest of the Soviet Press* (hereafter *CDSP*), V, 20 (1953), 13–14; A. I. Levkovsky, "Angliiskie upravliaiushchie agenstvia—orudie poraboshcheniia i ekspluatatsii narodov Indii" (The English managing agencies—an instrument of enslavement and exploitation of the peoples of India), *Kratkie soobshcheniia Instituta Vostokovedeniia* (Brief reports of the Oriental Studies Institute), no. 10, 1953, pp. 69–80.

112. See D'iakov, *Indiia vo vremia*, part II, chap. 3; G. G. Kotovsky, "K voprosu o roli rostovshchicheskogo kapitala v obezzemelenii krest'ianstva v Indii" (On the question of the role of usury capital in dispossessing the peasantry in India), *Kratkie soobshcheniia Instituta Vostokovedeniia*, no. 10, 1953, pp. 20–34; L. R. Gordon, *Agrarnye otnosheniia v Severo-Zapadnoi Pogranichnoi Provintsii Indii (1914–1947 gg.)* (Agrarian relations in the Northwest Frontier Province of India [1914–1947]) (Moscow, 1953).

113. G. G. Kotovsky, "Sotsial'no-ekonomicheskoe soderzhanie problemy 'Neprikasaemykh' " (The socio-economic content of the problem of the "Untouchables"), *Uchenye zapiski Instituta Vostokovedeniia*, V (1953), 75–152.

114. I. M. Lemin, *Obostrenie krizisa Britanskoi Imperii posle Vtoroi Mirovoi Voiny* (The sharpening crisis of the British Empire after World War Two) (Moscow, 1951), pp. 166–274.

115. See D'iakov, *Indiia vo vremia*, part II, chap. 5, and N. Sosina, "K voprosu o gosudarstvennom iazyke v Indiiskom Soiuze" (On the problem of a state language in the Indian Union), in I. M. Reisner and N. M. Gold'berg, eds., *Ocherki po novoi istorii stran Srednego Vos-*

toka: Indiia, Afganistan, Iran (Sketches on the modern history of the countries of the Middle East: India, Afghanistan, Iran) (Moscow, 1951), pp. 7–19.

116. A. K. Ghosh, "Some of Our Main Weaknesses," *FLP, FPD*, November 7, 1952, p. 5.

117. Communist Party of India, *Resolution on Party Organization* (New Delhi, 1954), p. 23.

118. R. K. Karanjia, *China Stands Up* (Bombay, 1952), p. 160, quoted in Morris and Watnick, "Current Communist Strategy," p. 3.

119. E. M. S. Namboodiripad, "Present Stage of Peasant Movement in India," *FLP, FPD*, December 18, 1953, pp. 3–4.

120. Communist Party of India, Central Committee, *Our Tasks among the Peasant Masses; Resolution Adopted by the Central Committee of the Communist Party of India April 1954* (New Delhi, 1954), p. 16.

121. Sankara Narayan, in *Cross Roads*, January 18, 1952, p. 10, quoted in Harrison, *India*, p. 176.

122. K. P. S. Menon, *The Flying Troika* (London, 1963), pp. 26–30.

123. Quoted in Harrison, *India*, p. 266.

124. Ibid., p. 265.

125. The trip is noted in M. C. Goodall, "Soviet Policy and India: Some Postwar Trends," *Journal of International Affairs*, VIII, 1 (1954), 49.

126. D. S. Carlisle, "Stalin's Postwar Foreign Policy and the National Liberation Movement," *Review of Politics*, XXVII, 3 (1965), 350–352.

127. "Industrialization of Underdeveloped Countries," *New Times*, no. 21, 1952, pp. 1–3.

128. Quoted in Carlisle, "Stalin's Postwar Foreign Policy," p. 355.

129. Marshall Shulman, *Stalin's Foreign Policy Reappraised* (Cambridge, Mass., 1963).

130. Supplement to *New Times*, no. 33, 1953, p. 15.

131. Quoted in Overstreet and Windmiller, *Communism in India*, p. 312.

132. "Andhra Thesis," in Democratic Research Service, *Indian Communist Party Documents*, p. 89.

133. Ghosh, "Third Congress of the CPI," *FLP, FPD*, February 5, 1954, p. 5.

134. A. A. Kutsenkov and A. B. Frumkin, "Indiia," in *Mezhdunarodnaia torgovlia* (International trade), ed. I. S. Potapov et al. (Moscow, 1954), pp. 614, 635. See also V. Solodovnikov, "The Soviet Union and the Underdeveloped Countries," *New Times*, no. 52, 1954, pp. 12–14.

135. N. Sergeieva, "America and India," *New Times*, no. 11, 1954, pp. 19–21; V. Iliushechkin, "Enemies of People's China—Enemies of Peace," *New Times*, no. 16, 1954, pp. 11–14; "China's Growing Influence in World Affairs," *New Times*, no. 28, 1954, p. 6; T. Ershov, "No-

vaia pobeda printsipa mirnogo sosushchestvovaniia" (A new victory of the principle of peaceful coexistence), *Mezhdunarodnaia zhizn'* (International affairs), no. 1, 1954, pp. 79–85; A. Leont'ev, "O mirnom sosushchestvovanii dvukh sistem" (On peaceful coexistence of the two systems), *Kommunist*, no. 13, 1954, pp. 43–58.

136. G. Bondarevsky, "Ekspansiia monopolii SShA v Indii" (Expansion of the monopolies of the USA into India), *Kommunist*, no. 12, 1954, pp. 121–128.

137. R. P. Dutt, "New Features in National Liberation Struggle of Colonial and Dependent Peoples," *FLP, FPD*, October 8, 1954, p. 6.

138. Quoted in Democratic Research Service, *Indian Communist Party Documents*, pp. 215, 271.

139. Quoted in Overstreet and Windmiller, *Communism in India*, p. 317 (emphasis supplied).

IV. Doctrinal and Operational Changes, 1955–1959

1. Quoted in M. W. Fisher and J. V. Bondurant, *Indian Approaches to a Socialist Society* (Berkeley, 1956), p. 5.

2. Ibid., p. 21.

3. E. M. Zhukov, "The Bandung Conference of African and Asian Countries and Its Historic Significance," *International Affairs*, no. 5, 1955, pp. 18, 28.

4. J. Nehru, *Soviet Russia*, p. 131.

5. "Joint Statement by the Chairman of the Council of Ministers of the USSR N. A. Bulganin and the Prime Minister of India Jawaharlal Nehru," *New Times* (supplement), no. 27, 1955.

6. Menon, *The Flying Troika*, p. 119.

7. "In the Interest of World Peace and the Security of the Peoples," *FLP, FPD*, June 24, 1955, p. 1.

8. "Statements by N. A. Bulganin and N. S. Khrushchev in India, Burma and Afghanistan," *New Times* (supplement), no. 52, 1955, p. 19 (hereafter, "Statements").

9. Ibid., p. 22.

10. Ibid., p. 16.

11. Ibid., p. 29.

12. Ibid., p. 27.

13. Quoted in Overstreet and Windmiller, *Communism in India*, p. 462.

14. N. A. Bulganin and N. S. Khrushchev, *Report to the Supreme Soviet on the Trip to India, Burma and Afghanistan* (New York, 1956), p. 56.

15. "May Friendship between Soviet and Indian Peoples Grow Stronger and Flourish!," *FLP, FPD*, November 18, 1955, p. 1.

16. F. C. Barghoorn, *The Soviet Cultural Offensive: The Role of Cultural Diplomacy in Soviet Foreign Policy* (Princeton, 1960), p. 77.

17. F. C. Barghoorn, *Soviet Foreign Propaganda* (Princeton, 1964), pp. 288–289.

18. V. V. Balabushevich, "Soviet-Indian Friendship," *New Times,* no. 10, 1962, p. 12.

19. This information appears periodically on the back cover of *New Times.*

20. This section is indebted to Marshall Goldman, *Soviet Foreign Aid* (New York, 1967), pp. 85–114.

21. See, for example, B. Voevodin, "The Bhilai Project," *New Times,* no. 6, 1956, p. 18.

22. M. Zenovich, "Second Bhilai," *Pravda,* January 30, 1965, p. 3, in *CDSP,* XVII, 5 (1965), 16, and V. Bolshakov, "Bokaro, Another Bhilai," *International Affairs,* no. 9, 1964, p. 87.

23. Goldman, *Soviet Foreign Aid,* p. 114.

24. B. Pichugin, "The Seven-Year Plan and the Soviet Union's Foreign Economic Relations," *International Affairs,* no. 10, 1959, p. 70.

25. Bulganin and Khrushchev, *Report,* pp. 40–42.

26. See O. Maev, "Amerikanskaia 'Pomoshch' Indii" (American "Aid" to India), *Mirovaia ekonomika i mezhdunarodnye otnosheniia* (World economy and international relations: hereafter *MEIMO*), no. 12, 1960, pp. 104–106; and R. G. Iskandarov, *K voprosu o pomoshchi slaborazvitym stranam* (On the question of aid to underdeveloped countries) (Moscow, 1960).

27. V. Rymalov, "Ekonomicheskoe sorevnovanie dvukh sistem i problema pomoshchi slaborazvitym stranam" (Economic competition of the two systems and the problem of aid to the underdeveloped countries), *MEIMO,* no. 2, 1960, pp. 34–35.

28. Nathan Leites, *A Study of Bolshevism* (Glencoe, Ill., 1953), p. 28.

29. Ibid., p. 29.

30. Quoted in Herman Achminow, "Khrushchev's 'Creative Development' of Marxism-Leninism," *Studies on the Soviet Union* (New Series) II, 3 (1962), 16.

31. N. S. Khrushchev, "Report of the Central Committee of the Communist Party of the Soviet Union to the Twentieth Party Congress," *New Times* (supplement), no. 8, 1956, p. 6.

32. Ibid., p. 13.

33. Ibid., p. 22.

34. Ibid., p. 21.

35. "Statements," p. 19.

36. Khrushchev, "Report," p. 23.

37. Ibid., p. 23.

38. Ibid., p. 14.

39. *Pravda,* February 20, 1956, p. 6, in *CDSP,* VIII, 10 (1956), 24.

40. Quoted in "XX S'ezd Kommunisticheskogo Partii Sovetskogo

Soiuza i zadachi izucheniia sovremennogo Vostoka" (The Twentieth Congress of the CPSU and the task of study of the contemporary East), *Sovetskoe Vostokovedenie,* no. 1, 1956, p. 6.

41. "Fifth Anniversary of the Republic of India," *Pravda,* January 26, 1955, p. 3, in *CDSP,* VII, 4 (1955), 33.

42. See A. M. D'iakov, "Indiia v bor'be za mir" (India in the struggle for peace), *Sovetskoe Vostokovedenie,* no. 1, 1955, p. 42, for a suggestion that a portion of the Indian "big bourgeoisie" were supporting the "peace-loving" foreign policy of the Nehru government; A. M. D'iakov, *Indiia v period obsehchego krizisa kapitalizma* (India in the period of the general crisis of capitalism) (Moscow, 1955), for limited praise, in a lecture to the Central Committee's Higher Party School, of Nehru's economic policies; and V. A. Maslennikov, "Nekotorye osobennosti ekonomicheskogo razvitiia kolonial'nykh i zavisimykh stran v epokhu imperializma" (Some peculiarities of the economic development of the colonial and dependent countries in the epoch of imperialism), *Sovetskoe Vostokovedenie,* no. 4, 1955, p. 42, for the statement that the Indian economy was no longer to be considered "semifeudal."

43. "Za dal'neishii pod'em Sovetskogo Vostokovedeniia" (For the further uplifting of Soviet Oriental Studies), *Kommunist,* no. 8, 1955, pp. 75, 78.

44. "Ob izuchenii ekonomiki stran Vostoka" (On the study of the economy of countries of the East), *Sovetskoe Vostokovedenie,* no. 4, 1955, pp. 5, 8.

45. "XX S'ezd," pp. 8–10.

46. E. M. Zhukov, "Gandhi's Role in History," *New Times,* no. 6, 1956, pp. 15–16 (emphasis in original).

47. A. M. D'iakov and I. M. Reisner, "Rol' Gandi v natsional'no-osvoboditel'noi bor'be narodov Indii" (Gandhi's role in the national-liberation struggle of the peoples of India), *Sovetskoe Vostokovedenie,* no. 5, 1956, translated as "Gandhi in Russia's New Mirror," *Thought* (New Delhi), March 23, 1957, pp. 4–5; March 30, 1957, pp. 7–8, 15; April 6, 1957, pp. 7–8, 16. Further examples of the new appraisal are A. M. D'iakov, *Natsional'no-osvoboditel'naia bor'ba narodov Indii i rabochee dvizhenie na pervom etape obshchego krizisa kapitalizma: uchebnyi material* (The national-liberation struggle of the peoples of India and the worker movement in the first stage of the general crisis of capitalism: teaching material) (Moscow, 1957), and V. V. Balabushevich and A. M. D'iakov, eds., *Noveishaia istoriia Indii* (Contemporary history of India) (Moscow, 1959).

48. *Thought,* March 23, 1957, p. 4.

49. Ibid., p. 5.

50. "Soviet-Indian Friendship Grows Stronger," *Pravda,* January 27, 1957, pp. 1–2, in *CDSP,* IX, 4 (1957), 19.

51. Pavel Yudin, "Can We Accept Pandit Nehru's Approach?" *World Marxist Review,* I, 4 (1958), 42–54.

52. V. Durdenevsky, "The Five Principles," *International Affairs,* no. 3, 1956, p. 46, and Eugene Korovin, "The Five Principles—A Basis for Peaceful Coexistence," *International Affairs,* no. 5, 1956, p. 53.

53. V. Avarin, "Asia in the Modern World," *New Times,* no. 4, 1956, p. 4, and L. Modzhorian, "Neutrality," *New Times,* no. 8, 1956, p. 12. See also D. Melnikov, "Neutrality and the Current Situation," *International Affairs,* no. 2, 1956, pp. 74–81, and T. M. Ershov, "Indiiskaia Respublika—vazhnyi faktor mira" (The Indian Republic—an important factor of peace), in V. V. Balabushevich and A. M. D'iakov, eds., *Nezavisimaia Indiia: sbornik statei* (Independent India: collected articles) (Moscow, 1958), p. 139.

54. D'iakov, *Indiia v period,* p. 29; T. Giiasov, *Indiia i bor'ba za oslablenie napriazhennosti v Iugo-Vostochnoi Azii i na Dal'nem Vostoke* (India and the struggle for relaxation of tensions in Southeast Asia and the Far East) (Tashkent, 1957), pp. 38–39; Ershov, "Indiiskaia Respublika," in Balabushevich and D'iakov, eds., *Nezavisimaia Indiia,* p. 144.

55. V. P. Nikhamin, *Ocherki vneshnei politiki Indii 1947–1957 gg.* (Sketches on the foreign policy of India 1947–1957) (Moscow, 1959), pp. 31–32.

56. Ibid., p. 200.

57. The Soviets had long viewed Goa as a NATO-SEATO base on Indian soil. See A. Usvatov, "A U.S. Military Base," *International Affairs,* no. 2, 1958, pp. 100–101; and N. Pastukhov, "Goa is an Integral Part of India's Territory," *Pravda,* September 18, 1957, in *CDSP,* IX, 38 (1957), 16–17.

58. "N. S. Khrushchev's Message to Jawaharlal Nehru," July 19, 1958, in *New Times* (supplement), no. 30, 1958, p. 15.

59. A. A. Mishin, *Gosudarstvennyi stroi Indii* (The state system of India) (Moscow, 1956), and T. F. Deviatkina and A. M. D'iakov, "Sozdanie shtatov po lingvisticheskomu printsipu i likvidatsiia kniazhestv" (Creation of states on a linguistic principle and the liquidation of the princely states), in Balabushevich and D'iakov, eds., *Nezavisimaia Indiia,* pp. 99–100.

60. Quoted in T. F. Deviatkina and A. M. D'iakov, "V. I. Lenin i Indiia," in B. G. Gafurov, ed., *Lenin i Vostok: sbornik statei* (Lenin and the East: collected articles) (Moscow, 1960), pp. 279–280.

61. K. Perevoshchikov, "Election in India," *Izvestiia,* April 9, 1957, p. 4, in *CDSP,* IX, 4 (1957), 27. See also *New Times,* no. 13, 1957, pp. 6–7.

62. A. I. Levkovsky, "Angliiskie pravliaiushchie," and *Nekotorye osobennosti razvitiia kapitalizma v Indii do 1947 g.* (Some peculiarities of the development of capitalism in India before 1947) (Moscow, 1956).

63. A. Vanin, "India's Industrial Prospects," *New Times,* no. 32, 1955, p. 12; G. Kolykhalova, "India's New Economic Plan," *New Times,* no. 15, 1956, p. 12.

64. "Diskussiia ob ekonomicheskikh i politicheskikh pozitsiiakh natsional'noi burzhuazii v stranakh Vostoka" (Discussion of the economic and political positions of the national bourgeoisie in countries of the East), *Sovetskoe Vostokovedenie*, no. 1, 1957, p. 175.

65. Ibid., pp. 176, 179.

66. See, for example, V. L. Tiagunenko, "Osnovye strukturnye sdvigi v ekonomike slaborazvitykh stran" (Principal structural changes in the economies of the underdeveloped countries), *MEIMO*, no. 3, 1960, pp. 56–70. See also the analysis in Stephen Clarkson, "Soviet Theory and Indian Reality," *Problems of Communism*, XVI, 1 (1967), 11–20.

67. Modeste Rubinshtein, "A Non-Capitalist Path for Underdeveloped Countries," *New Times*, no. 28, 1956, p. 4.

68. A. Ghosh, "On India's Path of Development," *New Age*, October, 1956, pp. 16–18.

69. B. G. Gafurov, "Aktual'nye zadachi sovetskogo Vostokovedeniia" (Vital tasks of Soviet Oriental Studies), *Vestnik Akademii Nauk SSSR*, no. 9, 1957, p. 23.

70. "Problemy gosudarstvennogo kapitalizma v slaborazvitykh stranakh Vostoka" (The problems of state capitalism in underdeveloped countries of the East), *Sovetskoe Vostokovedenie*, no. 4, 1958, pp. 213–214.

71. Ibid., pp. 218–219.

72. R. A. Ul'ianovsky, "Indiia v bor'be za ekonomicheskuiu nezavisimost' (Voprosy goskapitalizma)" (India in the struggle for economic independence [The problem of state capitalism]), in Balabushevich and D'iakov, *Nezavisimaia Indiia*, pp. 15–79.

73. R. A. Ul'ianovsky, "Ob osobennostiakh razvitiia i kharaktere gosudarstvennogo kapitalizma v nezavisimoi Indii" (On the peculiarities of the development and character of state capitalism in independent India), *Problemy Vostokovedeniia*, no. 3, 1960, p. 37.

74. See Ul'ianovsky, "Indiia v bor'be," pp. 51–52; S. M. Mel'man, *Inostrannyi monopolisticheskii kapital v ekonomiki Indii*, (Foreign monopoly capital in the Indian economy) (Moscow, 1959), chap. 4; V. Kondrat'ev, "Natsional'naia burzhuazia i promyshlennoe razvitie sovremennoi Indii" (The national bourgeoisie and industrial development of contemporary India), *MEIMO*, no. 8, 1959, pp. 61–72.

75. L. A. Gordon, "Nekotorye voprosy polozheniia promyshlennogo proletariata" (Some problems of the situation of the industrial proletariat), in A. M. D'iakov et al., eds., *Ekonomika sovremennoi Indii* (The economy of contemporary India), (Moscow, 1960), pp. 316–317.

76. M. N. Egorova, "Chislennost' i struktura fabrichnogo proletariata" (The number and structure of the factory proletariat), in D'iakov et al., eds., *Ekonomika*, pp. 258–283.

77. G. Kotovsky, "Agrarian Reform in India," *New Times*, no. 48, 1958, pp. 13–15.

78. R. P. Gurvich, "Nekotorye voprosy razvitiia sel'skogo kho-

ziaistvo" (Some problems of the development of agriculture), in D'ia-kov et al., eds., *Ekonomika*, pp. 5–51; and R. P. Gurvich, *Selskoe kho-ziaistvo Indii i polozhenie krest'ianstva* (The agriculture of India and the situation of the peasantry) (Moscow, 1960); Iskandarov, *K voprosu o pomoshchi*, pp. 7–8.

79. L. Shaposhnikova, "V Indiiskoi derevne: Pochampalli" (In the Indian countryside: Pochampalli), *Sovremennyi Vostok* (The contemporary East), no. 2, 1961, p. 25.

80. R. A. Ul'ianovsky, "Reform agrarnogo stroia" (Reform of the agrarian order), in D'iakov et al., eds., *Ekonomika*, pp. 117–119, 130.

81. "CC Resolution on Andhra Elections," in Democratic Research Service, *Indian Communist Party Documents*, pp. 216–223.

82. S. S. Harrison, "Caste and the Andhra Communists," *American Political Science Review*, L, 2 (1956), 378–404.

83. See D. R. Mankekar, *The Red Riddle of Kerala* (Bombay, 1965), and R. R. Nair, *How Communists Came to Power in Kerala* (Trivandrum, 1965).

84. Harrison, *India*, p. 204.

85. Communist Party of India, Central Committee, *Communist Party in the Struggle for Peace, Democracy and National Advance* (New Delhi, 1955), p. 26.

86. "Meeting of Central Committee, Communist Party of India," *FLP, FPD*, July 8, 1955, p. 3.

87. A. K. Ghosh, "National Independence and United Front," *New Age*, October 1955, pp. 17–24.

88. A. K. Ghosh, "The Internal Politics of the Government," *New Age*, November 1955, pp. 5–24.

89. A. K. Ghosh, "The Indian Bourgeoisie," *New Age*, December 1955, pp. 5–18.

90. A. K. Ghosh, "Problems of Industrialization," *New Age*, January 1956, pp. 5–15.

91. Adhikari, *Communist Party*, p. 9.

92. "Report of Ajoy Ghosh to the Fourth Congress of the CPI (1956)," in Democratic Research Service, *Indian Communist Party Documents*, p. 327.

93. A. Ghosh, "Letter to J. Narayan," *New Age* (weekly), November 18, 1956, p. 7.

94. "Report of Ajoy Ghosh," in Democratic Research Service, *Indian Communist Party Documents*, p. 257.

95. Ibid., pp. 281, 292.

96. E. M. S. Namboodiripad, *Agrarian Reforms: A Study of the Congress and Communist Approach* (New Delhi, 1956).

97. E. M. S. Namboodiripad, *Kerala: Problems and Possibilities* (New Delhi, 1957), pp. 65–66.

98. A. K. Ghosh, "Towards a Mass Communist Party," *New Age*, February 1958, pp. 1–14.

99. *Constitution of the Communist Party of India* (New Delhi, 1958), p. 3.

100. Quoted in Mankekar, *The Red Riddle of Kerala*, pp. 155–156.

101. Ibid., p. 157.

102. A. K. Ghosh, "Kerala," *World Marxist Review*, II, 11 (1959), 42–43.

V. From Tibet to Tashkent

1. W. E. Griffith, *Sino-Soviet Relations 1964–1965* (Cambridge, Mass., 1967), pp. 28–30. A similar Soviet response accompanied the serious border clashes in March 1969.

2. See Arnold Horelick and Myron Rush, *Strategic Power and Soviet Foreign Policy* (Chicago, 1966), esp. Parts Two and Three.

3. Alexander Kaznacheev, *Inside a Soviet Embassy: Experiences of a Russian Diplomat in Burma* (Philadelphia, 1962), p. 142.

4. A. Yakovlev, *The World Socialist System and the National Liberation Movement* (Moscow, n.d.), p. 30.

5. W. E. Griffith, *The Sino-Soviet Rift* (Cambridge, Mass., 1964), p. 12.

6. Goldman, *Soviet Foreign Aid*, p. 42.

7. Khrushchev, in a speech in Moscow in January 1961 declared: "If we are called the leader it gives no advantage either to our Party or to other parties. On the contrary it only creates difficulties" (quoted in David Floyd, *Mao against Khrushchev: A Short History of the Sino-Soviet Conflict* [New York, 1963], p. 310).

8. S. Mikoian, "Desiat' let vneshnei politiki Indii" (Ten years of the foreign policy of India), *MEIMO*, no. 2, 1957, p. 30.

9. "Revolution in Tibet and Nehru's Philosophy," *Jen-min Jih-pao* (People's Daily), May 6, 1959, in *Current Background*, no. 570, and John Rowland, *A History of Sino-Indian Relations* (Princeton, 1967), pp. 118–119.

10. "The Truth about How the Leaders of the C.P.S.U. Have Allied Themselves with India against China," *Jen-min Jih-pao*, November 2, 1963, in *Peking Review*, VI, 45 (1963), 19.

11. "TASS Statement," *Pravda*, September 10, 1959, p. 3, in *CDSP*, XI, 36 (1959), 14.

12. "The Truth," p. 19.

13. N. S. Khrushchev, "On the International Situation and the Foreign Policy of the Soviet Union," *Pravda*, November 1, 1959, pp. 1–3, in *CDSP*, XI, 44 (1959), 8.

14. "The Truth," p. 19.

15. Ibid.

16. "Whence the Differences?—A Reply to Comrade Thorez and Other Comrades," *Jen-min Jih-pao*, February 27, 1963, quoted in Floyd, *Mao against Khrushchev*, p. 378.

17. Menon, *The Flying Troika*, pp. 236, 253.

18. *Happiness and Peace for the Peoples: N. S. Khrushchev's Visit to India, Burma, Indonesia and Afghanistan, February 11–March 5, 1960* (Moscow, 1960), pp. 17–105.

19. Hemen Ray, "The Secret of Soviet Successes in Asia-Africa," *Aussenpolitik*, XII, 10, 668–675, translated in Joint Publications Research Service, no. 11,542.

20. See, for example, "The Indian Government Should Rein in on the Brink of the Precipice," *Jen-min Jih-pao*, July 9, 1962, in *Peking Review*, V, 28 (1962), 10–11; Chou Chun-li, "Sino-Indian Border Situation Worsens," *Peking Review*, V, 29 (1962), 14–16; "Observer," "The Indian Authorities Must not Miscalculate," *Jen-min Jih-pao*, July 21, 1962, in *Peking Review*, V, 30 (1962), 12–14. For a controversial and well-documented history, focusing on the Indian "forward policy," see Neville Maxwell, *India's China War* (London, 1970).

21. "Mr. Nehru, It Is High Time for You to Pull Back from the Brink of the Precipice!" *Jen-min Jih-pao*, October 14, 1962, in *Peking Review*, V, 42 (1962), 6–7.

22. "The Truth," p. 20.

23. "How Chinese Attack on Indian Frontier Was Reported," *CDSP*, XIV, 43 (1962), 16–18.

24. Ibid., p. 19.

25. *Pravda*, November 7, 1962, pp. 1–3, in *CDSP*, XIV, 45 (1962), 7.

26. Floyd, *Mao against Khrushchev*, p. 325, quotes contradictory statements appearing in *Pravda* and *Jen-min Jih-pao* on November 18. The former asserted that "Soviet policy saved world peace" while the latter declared: "It is pure nonsense to say that 'peace has been saved' by withdrawing Soviet missiles."

27. Albert Cantril, *The Indian Perception of the Sino-Indian Border Clash* (Princeton, 1967), pp. 16–17. Similar data are of course unavailable for the measurement of Soviet popularity in the communist world.

28. Roger Hilsman, *To Move a Nation: The Politics of Foreign Policy in the Administration of John F. Kennedy* (Garden City, 1967), pp. 331–332.

29. "More on Nehru's Philosophy in the Light of the Sino-Indian Boundary Question," *Jen-min Jih-pao*, October 27, 1962, in *Peking Review*, V, 44 (1962), 10–22.

30. Ibid., pp. 19–20.

31. *Pravda*, December 13, 1962, in *CDSP*, XIV, 52 (1962), 7–8.

32. Ibid., pp. 3–4.

33. Quoted in Floyd, *Mao against Khrushchev*, p. 339.

34. Quoted ibid., p. 366.

35. V. Korionov, "Left of Common Sense," *Pravda*, August 16, 1963, pp. 2–3, in *CDSP*, XV, 33 (1963), 13; A. Bovin, "The Revolutionary Process and Peaceful Coexistence," *New Times*, no. 42, 1963, p. 7; S. Nesterov, "Manevry Amerikanskogo imperializma v Iugo-Vostochnoi Azii"

(The maneuvers of American imperialism in Southeast Asia), *MEIMO*, no. 10, 1963, p. 74.

36. "Serious Hotbed of Tension in Asia," *Pravda*, September 19, 1963, pp. 2–3, in *CDSP*, XV, 38 (1963), 18–19, and "Proletarskii internatsionalizm—znamia trudiashchikhsia vsekh stran i kontinentov" (Proletarian internationalism is the banner of the working people of all countries and continents), *Kommunist*, no. 7, 1964, pp. 25–50.

37. E. M. Zhukov, "Significant Factor of Our Times—On Some Questions of the Present-Day National-Liberation Movement," *Pravda*, August 26, 1960, pp. 3–4, in *CDSP*, XII, 34 (1960), 18.

38. *Jen-min Jih-pao*, August 30, 1960, quoted in H. Sonnenfeldt, "Soviet Strategy in Africa," *Africa Report*, V, 11 (November 1960), 10, 14. Some of the sharpest Sino-Soviet disagreements concerning the proper communist stance toward the national-liberation movement at this time centered on the situation in the Middle East, especially Egypt, Syria, and Iraq. For a detailed account of this quarrel see D. S. Zagoria, *The Sino-Soviet Conflict 1956–1961* (Princeton, 1962), chap. 10.

39. An example of the ability of the new concept, by virtue of its ambiguity, to mislead noncommunist politicians as to Soviet intentions is Indian ambassador Menon's assertion in his diary (Menon, *The Flying Troika*, p. 278) that it was "an almost perfect description of the condition of India today"—a statement which the Soviets would have emphatically denied.

40. G. F. Hudson et al., *The Sino-Soviet Dispute* (New York, 1961), pp. 191–195.

41. See L. G. Stauber, "Recent Soviet Policy in Underdeveloped Countries: The Significance of the 'National-Democracy' Doctrine" (unpub. diss., Harvard University, 1964, pp. 110–117), for a discussion of the differences between the concepts "people's democracy" and "national democracy."

42. Quoted in Hudson et al., *The Sino-Soviet Dispute*, p. 216.

43. B. N. Ponomarev, "O gosudarstve natsional'noi demokratii" (Concerning the national-democratic state), *Kommunist*, no. 8, 1961, pp. 33–48. Ponomarev's relative caution concerning the progressive potentialities of nonproletarian elements may be attributable to his own occupational concerns, i.e., the supervision of relations with nonruling communist parties.

44. "The Program of the Communist Party of the Soviet Union," in C. Saikowski and L. Gruliow, eds., *Current Soviet Policies IV* (New York, 1962), pp. 10–12.

45. "XXII S'ezd KPSS i zadachi dal'neishego izucheniia problem mirovogo razvitiia" (The Twenty-second CPSU Congress and tasks of a further study of the problems of world development), *MEIMO*, no. 3, 1962, pp. 3–19.

46. "Proekt Programmy KPSS i nekotorye problemy natsional'no-os-

voboditel'nogo dvizheniia narodov Azii i Afriki" (Draft Program of the CPSU and some problems of the national-liberation movement of the peoples of Asia and Africa), *Narody Azii i Afriki*, no. 5, 1961, p. 4.

47. R. M. Avakov and G. I. Mirsky, "O klassovoi strukture v slaborazvitykh stranakh" (The class structure in the underdeveloped countries), *MEIMO*, no. 4, 1962, pp. 68–82, translated in T. P. Thornton, ed., *The Third World in Soviet Perspective: Studies by Soviet Writers on the Developing Areas* (Princeton, 1964), pp. 276–304.

48. Ponomarev, "O gosudarstve natsional'noi demokratii," p. 43.

49. V. L. Tiagunenko, "Tendentsii obshchestvennogo razvitiia osvobodivshikhsia stran v sovremennuiu epokhu" (The tendencies of social development in the liberated countries in the contemporary era), *MEIMO*, no. 3, 1962, p. 33.

50. G. I. Mirsky, "Tvorcheskii Marksizm i problemy natsional'noosvoboditel'nykh revoliutsii" (Creative Marxism and problems of the national-liberation revolution), *MEIMO*, no. 2, 1963, p. 65. Mirsky's erstwhile collaborator, Avakov, joined with Lev Stepanov ("Sotsial'nye problemy natsional'no-osvoboditel'noi revoliutsii" [Social problems of the national-liberation revolution], *MEIMO*, no. 5, 1963, pp. 46–54) to criticize Mirsky for overextending the limits in classifying leaders as "revolutionary democrats." They warned against forgetting the petty-bourgeois nature and political instability of the "middle strata," recalled the anticommunist persecution in such countries as the UAR and Iraq, and concluded that "revolutionary-democratic" slogans had "nothing in common with scientific socialism."

51. A. Sobolev, "National Democracy—The Way to Social Progress," *World Marxist Review*, VI, 2 (1963), 41–42, 46.

52. G. B. Starushenko, "Cherez obshchedemokraticheskie preobrazovaniia k sotsialisticheskim" (Through general democratic transformations to socialist transformation), *Kommunist*, no. 13, 1962, p. 108; V. Kudriavtsev, "Africa's Hopes and Anxieties," *International Affairs*, no. 11, 1963, pp. 44–45.

53. K. N. Brutents, "Sovremennyi etap natsional'no-osvoboditel'nogo dvizheniia" (The current stage of the national-liberation movement), *Kommunist*, no. 17, 1964, p. 29.

54. Starushenko, "Cherez obshchedemokraticheskie preobrazovaniia," p. 108 (emphasis supplied).

55. G. I. Mirsky, "The Proletariat and National Liberation," *New Times*, no. 18, 1964, pp. 8–9.

56. Starushenko, "Cherez obshchedemokraticheskie preobrazovaniia," p. 109.

57. V. L. Tiagunenko, "Aktual'nye problemy nekapitalisticheskogo puti razvitiia" (The urgent problems of the noncapitalist path of development), *MEIMO*, no. 11, 1964, pp. 23–24.

58. Ibid., p. 17.

59. "Sotsializm, kapitalizm, slaborazvitye strany" (Socialism, capi-

talism, the underdeveloped countries), *MEIMO*, no. 4, 1964, pp. 116–131, no. 6, 1964, pp. 62–81. Some of the "academicians" participating in conferences such as this one are in fact high-ranking members of the party apparatus, especially of the Central Committee Secretariat's departments. There is good reason to speculate that others, indeed, may be analysts for the Soviet intelligence apparatus.

60. Ibid., no. 6, p. 77.

61. "For the Unity and Solidarity of the International Communist Movement," *Pravda*, December 6, 1963, pp. 2–5, in *CDSP*, XV, 47 (1963), 17–18.

62. "N. S. Khrushchev's Replies to Questions Put by the Ghanaian Times, Alger Republicain, Le Peuple and Botataung," *New Times* (supplement), no. 52, 1963, pp. 42, 45.

63. Quoted in Uri Ra'anan, "Moscow and the 'Third World,'" *Problems of Communism*, XIV, 1 (1965), 28. This paragraph draws from the examples cited by Ra'anan.

64. Quoted ibid., p. 30.

65. ". . . prerequisites are already being laid down in a number of countries for development along the noncapitalist path, along the path of socialism" (Griffith, *Sino-Soviet Relations 1964–1965*, p. 228). In light of this quotation, it is difficult to understand how R. A. Yellon ("Shifts in Soviet Policy Towards Developing Areas 1964–1968," in W. R. Duncan, ed., *Soviet Policy in Developing Countries* [Waltham, Mass., 1970], p. 283) can argue that Suslov in this speech "carefully distinguished" the two paths.

66. F. Burlatsky, "The Liberation Movement and Scientific Socialism," *Pravda*, August 15, 1965, pp. 3–4, in *CDSP*, XVII, 33 (1965), 3–5.

67. G. I. Mirsky, "Developing Countries at the Crossroads," *New Times*, no. 48, 1966, p. 8.

68. R. A. Ul'ianovsky, "Nekotorye voprosy nekapitalisticheskogo razvitiia osvobodivshikhsia stran" (Some problems of the noncapitalist development of the liberated countries), *Kommunist*, no. 1, 1966, p. 112. For another clear statement of this theory, see "Natsional'no-osvoboditel'noe dvizhenie i sotsial'nyi progress" (National-liberation movement and social progress), *Kommunist*, no. 13, 1965, pp. 12–26.

69. It should be noted that Algeria had twice previously been hailed as "building an independent, *people's* democratic state," and the 1965 designation seemed to signify demotion in status. Brutents, in his *Kommunist* article of December 1964, had gone so far as to declare that a national-liberation revolution "may, as in Algeria, grow into a Socialist revolution." But the ouster of Ben Bella in July 1965 apparently gave the Soviets second thoughts about this. The UAR, Ghana, Guinea, and Mali were also—in the slogan for May Day 1965—once hailed for building "people's democratic" states. The 1965 Anniversary slogans can be found in *CDSP*, XVII, 43 (1965), 3–5. The 1966 Anniversary slogans (*CDSP*, XVIII, 42 [1966], 7–9) saw Ghana drop from the list

and Syria join the ranks of the "progressives." Syria was hailed as an "independent, national, democratic state"; Algeria, similarly addressed, was again apparently deemed to qualify as "democratic."

70. V. P. Nikhamin, "The Soviet Union and the Developing Countries," *International Affairs*, no. 4, 1966, p. 38.

71. B. N. Ponomarev, "Stroitel'stvo Kommunizma v SSSR—velikaia internatsional'naia zadacha Sovetskogo naroda" (The construction of Communism in the USSR is the great international task of the Soviet people), *Kommunist*, no. 11, 1964, pp. 52–54.

72. N. N. Inozemtsev, "Peaceful Coexistence and the World Revolutionary Process," *Pravda*, July 28, 1963, pp. 4–5, in *CDSP*, XV, 30 (1963), 8–9.

73. V. Kudriavtsev, "Into Whose Hands are They Playing—National Egoism of C.P.C. Leaders Merges with Neocolonialism," *Izvestiia*, August 2, 1964, p. 3, in *CDSP*, XVI, 31 (1964), 8.

74. "The Supreme International Duty of a Socialist Country," *Pravda*, October 27, 1965, pp. 3–4, in *CDSP*, XVII, 43 (1965), 6–9. Of course the implementation by force of one country's will upon another is not considered alien to Marxism-Leninism when the defense of the Soviet periphery is felt to be in danger, as the Czechoslovaks can attest.

75. Avakov and Mirsky, "O klassovoi strukture," in Thornton, *The Third World in Soviet Perspective*, pp. 298–299.

76. Mirsky, "Tvorcheskii Marksizm," p. 66.

77. G. G. Kotovsky, V. P. Pavlov, and I. B. Redko, "Some Economic and Political Problems," *New Times*, no. 1, 1964, pp. 18–22, and V. P. Pavlov and I. B. Redko, "From Jaipur to Bhubaneswar," *New Times*, no. 5, 1964, pp. 7–9.

78. "Speech by Comrade N. S. Khrushchev, May 27, 1964, on Moscow Radio and Television," *Pravda*, May 28, 1964, pp. 1–2, in *CDSP*, XVI, 21 (1964), 18.

79. I. Andronov, "Charting a Nation's Course," *New Times*, no. 28, 1964, pp. 29–31; P. Nikolsky, "Nehru's Party Without Nehru," *New Times*, no. 32, 1965, pp. 16–17.

80. O. V. Maev, "Indiiskii monopolisticheskii kapital" (Indian monopolistic capital), *Narody Azii i Afriki*, no. 1, 1964, pp. 21–36. See also R. M. Avakov and R. Andreasian, "Progressivnaia rol' gosudarstvennogo sektora" (The progressive role of the state sector), *Kommunist*, no. 13, 1962, pp. 95–96.

81. "The Agrarian Question in the Developing Countries of Asia," *World Marxist Review*, VIII, 9 (1965), 38–42. For another study of class relations in the Indian village, see R. P. Gurvich, "Nekotorye novye iavleniia v Indiiskoi derevne" (Some new phenomena in the Indian village), *Narody Azii i Afriki*, no. 3, 1964, pp. 16–25.

82. V. Chevrakov, "A Threat! To Whom?" *Literaturnaia Gazeta*, March 13, 1965, and Boris Urlanis, "Is There a Population Problem?"

Literaturnaia Gazeta, November 23, 1965, in *CDSP,* XVII, 52 (1965), 11–13.

83. O. V. Martyshin, "Toward a Definition of the Social Ideas of Gandhism," *Voprosy filosofii,* no. 1, 1965, pp. 95–106, in *CDSP,* XVII, 19 (1965), 15–19.

84. A. M. D'iakov, *Natsional'nyi vopros v sovremennoi Indii* (Moscow, 1963). The quotations which follow are from the English-language edition, *The National Problem in India Today* (Moscow, 1966).

85. L. A. Gordon and L. A. Fridman, "Osobennosti sostava i struktury rabochego klassa v ekonomicheski slaborazvitykh stranakh Azii i Afriki (na primere Indii i OAR)" (Peculiarities of the composition and structure of the working class in the economically underdeveloped countries of Asia and Africa [The examples of India and the UAR]), *Narody Azii i Afriki,* no. 2, 1963, pp. 3–22, translated in Thornton, *The Third World in Soviet Perspective,* pp. 154–188. See also M. N. Egorova in Akademiia Nauk SSSR, Institut Narodov Azii, *Rabochii klass stran Azii i Afriki* (The working class of countries of Asia and Africa) A. A. Iskenderov, ed. (Moscow, 1964), pp. 22–37.

86. R. A. Ul'ianovsky, in "Sotsializm, Kapitalizm," *MEIMO,* no. 4, 1964, pp. 125–126.

87. R. A. Ul'ianovsky, "Ekonomicheskaia nezavisimost' blizhaishaia zadacha osvoboditel'nogo dvizheniia v Azii" (Economic independence is the next task of the liberation movement in Asia), *Kommunist,* no. 1, 1962, pp. 96–102; V. V. Rymalov, "Ekonomicheski slaborazvitye strany v mirovom kapitalisticheskom khoziaistve" (The economically underdeveloped countries in the world capitalist economy), *MEIMO,* no. 3, 1962, pp. 48–49.

88. R. A. Ul'ianovsky, "Socialism and the National-Liberation Struggle—The Non-Capitalist Path of Development," *Pravda,* April 15, 1966, p. 4, in *CDSP,* XVIII, 15 (1966), 24–25.

89. "Natsional'no-osvoboditel'noe dvizhenie i sotsial'nyi progress" (The national-liberation movement and social progress), *Kommunist,* no. 13, 1965, p. 20.

90. Communist Party of India, *The India-China Border Dispute and the Communist Party of India: Resolutions, Statements and Speeches* (New Delhi, 1963), pp. 1–2, 3–6, 27 (hereafter cited as *India-China*).

91. Ibid., pp. 7–8. See also K. Nair, "Struggle against Splitters in India," *World Marxist Review,* VII, 7 (1964), p. 54.

92. *India-China,* p. 26; Harry Gelman, "The Communist Party of India: Sino-Soviet Battleground," in A. D. Barnett, ed., *Communist Strategies in Asia* (New York, 1963), p. 114.

93. *India-China,* pp. 12–15, 45.

94. Quoted in "Sathi," "The Strategic Triangle: India," *Survey,* no. 54, 1965, p. 107.

95. *India-China,* pp. 22–28.

96. Ibid., pp. 29–52.

97. "Sathi," "The Strategic Triangle: India," p. 109.

98. Quoted in Stauber, "Recent Soviet Policy in Underdeveloped Countries," pp. 298–301.

99. Gelman, "The Communist Party of India," p. 126; Savak Katrak, "India's Communist Party Split," *China Quarterly*, no. 7, 1961, pp. 143–147.

100. Ajoy Ghosh, "Some Features of the Situation in India," *World Marxist Review*, V, 2 (1962), 17–28. The article was published posthumously.

101. Marshall Windmiller, "Constitutional Communism in India," *Pacific Affairs*, XXXI, 1 (1958), 23.

102. *India-China*, p. 64.

103. Ibid., pp. 64–69.

104. Ibid., pp. 70–88.

105. "N. S. Khrushchev Meets with S. A. Dange," *Pravda*, December 13, 1962, p. 1, in *CDSP*, XIV, 50 (1962), 23.

106. John B. Wood, "Observations on the Indian Communist Party Split," *Pacific Affairs*, XXXVIII, 1 (1965), 52.

107. See, for example, "Behind the Persecution of Indian Communists," *New Times*, no. 5, 1963, pp. 14–15, and "World Public Opinion Condemns Repressions against Indian Communist Party," *Pravda*, November 30, 1962, p. 5, in *CDSP*, XIV, 48 (1962), 24.

108. *A Mirror for Revisionists: "Renmin Ribao" Editorial, March 9, 1963* (Peking, 1963), pp. 1–12.

109. S. A. Dange, "Neither Revisionism nor Dogmatism Is Our Guide," *New Age* (weekly), April 21, 1963.

110. See Communist Party of India, National Council, *Resolution on Splitters and Other Documents of the National Council of the Communist Party of India* (New Delhi, 1964), pp. 19–25.

111. "Expose the Conspiracy of Disruptors and Splitters! Defend the Unity and Sacred Honor of the Party," in *Resolutions on Splitters and Other Documents*, p. 2.

112. Quoted in Mankekar, *The Red Riddle of Kerala*, pp. 109–110, 141.

113. Communist Party of India, *Proceedings of the Seventh Congress of the CP of India, Bombay, 13–23 December, 1964* (New Delhi, 1965), I, 1–60.

114. G. Nadar, "The Sweep of the Mighty Mass Movement in India," *World Marxist Review*, VII, 10 (1964), 75; K. Nair, "Struggle against Splitters in India," *World Marxist Review*, VII, 7 (1964), 56.

115. "At Seventh Congress of the Indian Communist Party," *Pravda*, December 15, 1964, p. 3, in *CDSP*, XVI, 50 (1964), 18–19, and "Militant Program of Vanguard of India's Working People," *Pravda*, December 25, 1964, p. 3, in *CDSP*, XVI, 52 (1964), 19.

116. P. Kutsobin and N. Pastukhov, "Maneuvers of Reaction in

India," *Pravda*, August 10, 1963, p. 4, in *CDSP*, XV, 32 (1963), 20; I. Beliaev, F. Burlatsky, I. Gotlober, and O. Shalkin, "Meeting with Indian Communists," *Pravda*, March 28, 1966, p. 5, in *CDSP*, XVIII, 13 (1966), 24–25.

117. O. P. Kolikhalova and I. B. Redko, in Akademiia Nauk SSSR, Institut Narodov Azii, *Politika SShA i stranakh Iuzhnoi Azii* (The policy of the USA and the countries of South Asia) ed. B. G. Gafurov (Moscow, 1961), pp. 128–129.

118. Lev Stepanov, "Neutralism: Attack Repelled," *New Times*, no. 9, 1963, p. 5

119. A. Kuznetsov, "The Atom Bomb and Indian 'Ultras,' " *Pravda*, November 14, 1964, p. 4, in *CDSP*, XVI, 46 (1964), 19.

120. Goldman, *Soviet Foreign Aid*, p. 195. See also the useful and well-documented analysis in Charles B. McLane, "Foreign Aid in Soviet Third World Policies," unpub. paper delivered at the 1968 Annual Meeting of the American Political Science Association, Washington, September 2–7, 1968, pp. 16–26.

121. "Trade Agreement Signed," *Pravda*, January 8, 1966, p. 3, in *CDSP*, XVIII, 19 (1966), 26.

122. *Pravda*, May 14, 1965, in *CDSP*, XVII, 19 (1965), 26.

123. "May the Friendship and Cooperation between the Peoples of the Soviet Union and the Republic of India Develop and Grow Stronger," *Pravda*, May 16, 1965, pp. 1–2, in *CDSP*, XVII, 20 (1965), 9 (emphasis supplied).

124. "Observer," "What Shastri's Soviet Trip Reveals," *Jen-min Jih-pao*, May 27, 1965, in *Peking Review*, VIII, 23 (1965), 17–19.

125. Parallel efforts to woo Turkey and Iran away from the American orbit were vigorously pursued by Kosygin in 1966–1967.

126. "May the Friendship," p. 7.

127. Consult the following issues of *CDSP* for the slogans mentioned: XVII, 16 (1965), 3–4; XVII, 43 (1965), 3–4; XVIII, 15 (1966), 21; XVIII, 42 (1966), 7; XIX, 16 (1967), 12–13.

128. I. A [ndronov?], "Americans in the Rann of Kutch," *New Times*, no. 23, 1965, p. 28.

129. "Commentator," "Urgent Necessity—Stop Bloodshed in Kashmir," *Pravda*, August 24, 1965, p. 4, in *CDSP*, XVII, 34 (1965), 15–16.

130. *Peking Review*, VIII, 37 (1965), 7.

131. "TASS Statement," *Pravda*, September 14, 1965, p. 1, in *CDSP*, XVII, 37 (1965), 27.

132. "Who Backs the Indian Aggressors," *Jen-min Jih-pao*, September 18, 1965, in *Peking Review*, VIII, 39 (1965), 15.

133. Griffith, *Sino-Soviet Relations 1964–1965*, p. 115.

134. The Chinese intervention was not without an element of humor. In response to Peking's charge that 800 sheep, 50 yaks, and 4 Tibetans had been "abducted" by India at the Sikkim-Tibet border, a crowd of Indians paraded 800 sheep before the Chinese embassy in

New Delhi. Signs hung around the necks of the sheep pleaded: "Don't start a war: we are here" (Russell Brines, *The Indo-Pakistani Conflict* [London, 1968], pp. 375–376).

135. Quoted in Dev Sharma, ed., *Tashkent: The Fight for Peace* (Varanasi, 1966), pp. 107–108 (emphasis in original).

136. See "Coming Showdown over Arms," *New Republic*, September 17, 1966, p. 11.

137. Quoted in Sisir Gupta, "India and the Soviet Union," *Current History*, XLIV, 259 (1964), 143.

138. "Refutation of the New Leaders of the CPSU on 'United Action,'" *Peking Review*, VIII, 46 (1965), 14.

139. Quoted in Sharma, *Tashkent: The Fight for Peace*, pp. 63–65.

140. "Tashkent," *New Times*, no. 3, 1966, p. 1; Yuri Zhukov and Viktor Mayevsky, "Path to Peace in Hindustan," *Pravda*, January 16, 1966, in *CDSP*, XVIII, 3 (1966), 21; Lev Stepanov, "The Indo-Pakistani Accord," *New Times*, no. 3, 1966, p. 4; "Istoricheskaia Tashkentskaia Deklaratsiia" (The historic Tashkent Declaration), *Kommunist*, no. 1, 1966, pp. 40–41. See also Lev Stepanov, *Konflikt v Indostane i soglashenie v Tashkente* (Conflict in Hindustan and the agreement in Tashkent) (Moscow, 1966).

VI. From Mediation to Alliance

1. "The Tashkent Declaration," *New Times*, no. 3, 1970, p. 4.

2. "U.S. Aides in India Concerned over Sale of Arms to Pakistan," *New York Times*, October 11, 1970, p. 11.

3. Viktor Mayevsky, "Soviet-Indian Friendship is a Great Gain," *Pravda*, July 29, 1968, p. 4, in *CDSP*, XX, 30 (1968), 18–19.

4. See Elizabeth K. Valkenier, "New Soviet Views on Economic Aid," *Survey*, no. 76, 1970, pp. 17–29.

5. In the period from 1951–1952 to 1964–1965, Indian industrial production rose 138 percent, but industrial employment went up only 35 percent. Wages rose only 76 percent, and the cost of living increased by 57 percent (*Far Eastern Economic Review*, LXXII, 40 [1969], 20).

6. The Chinese have recently raised the charge that "predatory" Soviet aid to and "unequal" trade with India are turning India into a "raw material processing plant for Soviet revisionism." See *Peking Review*, XII, 30 (1969), 20–22.

7. "President Giri's Visit," *New Times*, no. 41, 1970, p. 16.

8. Yakov Etinger and Ovanes Melikian, *The Policy of Nonalignment* (Moscow, 1965), pp. 59–60.

9. V. Sidenko, "Non-Alignment: The Prospects," *New Times*, no. 36, 1970, pp. 18–20.

10. *New York Times*, July 14, 1970, p. 11.

11. *National Herald*, August 23, 1968.

12. For an interesting illustration of the asymmetry with which some Indian officials have viewed the two superpowers, see Michael Brecher, *India and World Politics: Krishna Menon's View of the World* (New York, 1968), especially chapters 6 and 8 for Menon's views on Suez and Hungary.

13. Amina Nizami, "Lessons of Democratic Upsurge in Pakistan," *World Marxist Review*, XII, 12 (1969), 57–63; and "General Secretary, C.C., C.P. of East Pakistan," "Leninism is our Guide," *World Marxist Review*, XIII, 5 (1970), 67–69.

14. "Joint Statement," *Pravda*, May 31, 1969, p. 4, in *CDSP*, XXI, 22 (1969), 14–15.

15. "Soviet-Pakistani Cooperation," *New Times*, no. 27, 1970, p. 15.

16. *New Times*, no. 15, 1971, p. 8.

17. *Pravda*, June 10, 1971, p. 1.

18. V. Vasin, "The Only Correct Path," *Izvestiia*, July 10, 1971, p. 3, in *CDSP*, XXIII, 28 (1971), 16 (emphasis supplied).

19. V. V. Matveyev, "A Filled 'Vacuum,' " *Izvestiia*, May 29, 1969, p. 3, in *CDSP*, XXI, 22 (1969), 14.

20. L. I. Brezhnev, *For a Greater Unity of Communists, For a Fresh Upsurge of the Anti-Imperialist Struggle* (Moscow, 1969), p. 53.

21. Peter Howard, " 'A System of Collective Security,' " *Mizan*, XI, 4 (1969), 201.

22. " 'System of Collective Security in Asia'—Soviet Revisionism's Tattered Flag for Anti-China Military Alliance," *Peking Review*, XII, 27 (1969), 22–23, 32–33.

23. Howard, " 'A System of Collective Security,' " p. 199.

24. Quoted in *Studies in Comparative Communism*, II, 3–4 (1969), 358–360.

25. A. A. Gromyko, "Questions of the International Situation and the Foreign Policy of the Soviet Union," *Pravda*, July 11, 1969, pp. 2–4, in *CDSP*, XXI, 28 (1969), 9.

26. Cited in Howard, " 'A System of Collective Security,' " p. 202.

27. "Statement by D. Singh," *Pravda*, September 21, 1969, p. 4, in *CDSP*, XXI, 38 (1969), 16.

28. B. Chekhonin, "Firm Guarantee," *Izvestiia*, December 17, 1969, p. 5, in *CDSP*, XXI, 51 (1969), 24.

29. Howard, " 'A System of Collective Security,' " p. 199, citing the *London Observer*, June 22, 1969.

30. "Bourgeois Dictatorship of the Soviet Revisionist New Tsars," *Jen-min Jih-pao*, June 6, 1969, in *Studies in Comparative Communism*, II, 3–4 (1969), 272.

31. M. Ukraintsev, "Asia and the Peking Empire-Builders," *New Times*, no. 23, 1970, p. 14.

32. Ibid., pp. 14–15.

33. "The Anti-China Encirclement Formed by the New Tsars in

League with US Imperialism Will Definitely Come to No Good End," Hsinhua Domestic Service, March 11, 1969, in *Studies in Comparative Communism*, II, 3–4 (1969), 249–252.

34. "Soviet Revisionist Social-Imperialism's Expansionist Activities on the Seas," *Jen-min Jih-pao*, May 18, 1969, in *Studies in Comparative Communism*, II, 3–4 (1969), 370.

35. "Reactionary Indian Government: Frantic Arms Expansion and War Preparations," *Peking Review*, XIII, 12 (1970), 29.

36. "Counter-Revolutionary Activities of USSR in Southeast Asia," Hsinhua International Service in English, March 14, 1969, in *Studies in Comparative Communism*, II, 3–4 (1969), 319.

37. Hsinhua International Service in English, July 13, 1969, in *Studies in Comparative Communism*, II, 3–4 (1969), 364.

38. *Peking Review*, XIII, 46 (1970), 12–13, and XIII, 47 (1970), 4–9.

39. G. S. Bhargava, "National Consensus or Bandwaggoning?" *The Overseas Hindistan Times*, XXII, 34 (August 21, 1971), 16. Bhargava attributes the information about the start of negotiations to External Affairs minister Swaran Singh. See also Max Frankel, "To India the U.S. Is a Bitter Disappointment," *New York Times*, November 30, 1971, p. 2.

40. Kissinger reportedly warned Mrs. Gandhi in the summer of 1971 that China might not remain aloof from a war in the subcontinent, and that the U.S. might not give its support as it had in 1962. Frankel, "To India the U.S. Is a Bitter Disappointment," p. 2.

41. Vasin, "The Only Correct Path," p. 3.

42. *Pakistan News Digest*, XIX, 18 (September 15, 1971), 1–2.

43. For the text of the treaty, see Appendix.

44. *New York Times*, August 14, 1971, p. 6.

45. It is worth noting the similarity between the absence of formal military obligations on the Soviets in this treaty and in the Soviet-Egyptian treaty of May 1971. In either case, however, there may exist secret protocols which spell out the Soviet commitment more explicitly.

46. *Pravda*, August 11, 1971, p. 1 (emphasis supplied).

47. *New York Times*, August 15, 1971, section 4, p. 2.

48. G. S. Bhargava, "National Consensus or Bandwaggoning?" p. 16.

49. Hiren Mukherjee, "The Indo-Soviet Pact: New Directions for Indian Foreign Policy," *The Mail* (Madras), reprinted in *Atlas*, XX, 11 (1971), 36. Mukherjee advised Mrs. Gandhi to follow up the treaty by extending full diplomatic recognition to North Vietnam, North Korea, East Germany, and the Provisional Revolutionary Government of South Vietnam. On January 7, 1972, India did upgrade to ambassadorial level its relations with Hanoi.

50. *Hindustan Times*, September 30, 1971 (emphasis supplied). I am indebted to Professor Richard Sisson for bringing this quotation to my attention. For a thorough assessment of this period in Soviet-Indian

relations, see Richard Sisson and Raju G. C. Thomas, "The Indo-Russian Treaty and the Creation of Bangladesh," unpub. paper delivered at the Twenty-fifth Annual Meeting of the Association for Asian Studies, 1973.

51. "Joint Soviet-Indian Statement," *New Times*, no. 41, 1971, p. 7.

52. "Friendship and Mutual Understanding," *Pravda*, September 29, 1971, pp. 1, 3, in *CDSP*, XXIII, 39 (1971), 9.

53. Quoted in A. Hariharan, "India: Bosom Friends," *Far Eastern Economic Review*, LXXIV, 41 (1971), 14.

54. Alexander Ulansky, "The Tragedy of East Pakistan," *New Times*, no. 42, 1971, pp. 13–15.

55. Alexander Ulansky, "Indian Subcontinent: Roots of the Crisis," *New Times*, no. 46, 1971, pp. 7–8.

56. I. Borisov, "Dark Skies over the Indian Subcontinent," *New Times*, no. 44, 1971, pp. 10–12.

57. Oleg Orestov, "Hindustan Needs Peace," *Pravda*, November 9, 1971, p. 3, in *CDSP*, XXIII, 45 (1971), 17–18; V. Kondrashov, "Hindustan Needs Peace," *Izvestiia*, November 16, 1971, p. 2, in *CDSP*, XXIII, 46 (1971), 20–21; P. Mezentsev, "Hindustan Awaits Peace," *Pravda*, November 23, 1971, p. 5, in *CDSP*, XXIII, 47 (1971), 26.

58. Frankel, "To India the U.S. is a Bitter Disappointment," p. 2.

59. *Peking Review*, XIV, 46 (1971), 5; *Peking Review*, XIV, 49 (1971), 5.

60. Henry Tanner, "Bhutto Denounces Council and Walks Out in Tears," *New York Times*, December 16, 1971, p. 17. In Bhutto's words, in the application of pressure "the Russians have outdone the Indians."

61. Dmitri Volsky and A. Usvatov, "War on the Indian Subcontinent," *New Times*, no. 50, 1971, pp. 7–9.

62. Dmitri Volsky, "The India-Pakistan Conflict and American-Chinese Collusion," *New Times*, no. 51, 1971, pp. 7–9.

63. "Text of Secret Documents on Top Level U.S. Discussions of Indian-Pakistan War," "Kissinger Parley Excerpts," and "Keating Cable to Rogers," *New York Times*, January 6, 1972, pp. 16–18. Kissinger was reported to have told the Washington Special Action Group that he was "getting hell" from Nixon because "we are not being tough enough" on India. The President "wants to tilt in favor of Pakistan." Later Kissinger instructed officials to show "a certain coolness" to the Indians. For the Soviet reaction see *Pravda*, January 7, 1972, p. 5, and *Izvestiia*, January 6, 1972, pp. 1–2, and January 7, 1972, p. 1.

64. Bernard Gwertzman, "U.S. Says Possibility of Canceling Moscow Trip is Not 'Live Issue,'" *New York Times*, December 16, 1971, p. 16. Admiral Zumwalt of the Joint Chiefs of Staff was quoted in the "secret" documents as predicting that the Soviets would push for permanent usage of the Indian naval base at Visag. See "Text of Secret Documents," p. 16.

65. "Huang Hua Condemns Soviet Union for Supporting Indian Aggression," *Peking Review*, XIV, 50 (1971), 8–10.

66. "Commentator," "Most Absurd Logic, Flagrant Aggression," *Jen-min Jih-pao*, December 10, 1971, in *Peking Review*, XIV, 50 (1971), 6–7.

67. "Statement of the Government of the People's Republic of China," December 16, 1971, *Peking Review* (supplement to XIV, 51 [1971]).

68. Volsky, "The India-Pakistan Conflict and American-Chinese Collusion," p. 9.

69. Volsky and Usvatov, "War on the Indian Subcontinent," pp. 8–9; Volsky, "The India-Pakistan Conflict and American-Chinese Collusion," pp. 8–9; Dmitri Volsky, "Now That the Guns Are Silent," *New Times*, no. 52, 1971, p. 10.

70. *Pravda*, March 21, 1972, p. 3.

71. D. Vostokov [pseud.?], "The Foreign Policy of the People's Republic of China Since the 9th Congress of the CPC," *International Affairs*, no. 1, 1972, pp. 23–25.

72. Henry Tanner, "Outgrowth of War: Major Loss is Seen for U.S. Influence," *New York Times*, December 20, 1971, p. 14.

73. "Into the Net," *The Economist*, December 11, 1971, p. 11.

74. *Pravda*, March 5, 1972, pp. 1, 4.

75. *Pravda*, March 18, 1972, p. 4.

76. James P. Sterba, "Pakistan Reported to Get Chinese MIG's and Tanks," *New York Times*, June 3, 1972, pp. 1, 5.

77. *Pravda*, December 22, 1972, p. 4.

78. "Text of Secret Documents," p. 16. In fact, reports from Dacca early in 1973 have noted that total Soviet aid ($136 million) was only slightly more than one-third of what the United States had provided in the same period. And Bangladesh officials were said to be anxious to attract even greater American interest and assistance, as a counterweight to the substantial Soviet presence. See Bernard Weinraub, "US Has Top Role in Bangladesh Aid," *New York Times*, March 10, 1973, pp. 1, 9.

79. G. Dudin and A. Usvatov, "Soviet-Indian Treaty in Action," *New Times*, no. 39, 1971, p. 21.

80. O. Borisov, "For Peace and Security in Asia," *New Times*, no. 39, 1971, pp. 10–11.

81. *Pravda*, September 29, 1971.

82. *Pravda*, March 21, 1972, p. 3.

83. *Pravda*, June 21, 1972, p. 4. Shortly after the Vietnam agreement was in fact signed, V. Yakovlev wrote in *New Times*, in the context of the Soviet collective security proposal: "It is natural that in many Asian countries public opinion and governments are anxious to create a 'post-Vietnam' structure of international relations in Asia that will en-

sure peace and security for the peoples of this largest of continents" ("Asia Wants Peace and Security," no. 10, 1973, p. 8).

84. V. Matveyev, "Aziia v sovremennon mire: vzgliad vpered" (Asia in the contemporary world: a glance forward), *Izvestiia*, April 8, 1972, p. 4.

85. D'iakov, *Indiia vo vremia*, p. 174.

86. P. Kutsobin, "The Indian Confrontation," *New Times*, no. 47, 1969, pp. 6–8.

87. A. Maslennikov and V. Shurygin, "Division of Forces," *Pravda*, December 24, 1969, p. 5, in *CDSP*, XXI, 47 (1969), 18.

88. A. Medovoi and V. Yashkin, "Problems of India's Socio-Economic Development," *International Affairs*, no. 10, 1970, pp. 64–65; L. Koriavin, K. Perevoshchikov, A. Ter-Grigorian, "International Survey," *Izvestiia*, September 14, 1969, p. 2, in *CDSP*, XXI, 37 (1969), 12.

89. B. Kalyagin, "Defeat for Indian Reaction," *New Times*, no. 12, 1971, pp. 6–7.

90. P. Viktorov, "India: Problems and Politics," *New Times*, no. 26, 1971, pp. 12–13.

91. P. Kutsobin, "India: New Phrase of the Struggle," *New Times*, no. 11, 1970, p. 7.

92. G. Mirsky, "Developing Countries at the Crossroads," pp. 6–9. See also V. Kudriavtsev, "A Blow to the Plans of Reaction in India," *Izvestiia*, November 15, 1969, p. 3, in *CDSP*, XXIII, 46 (1971), 16, which argues that the capitalist path can lead only to the "de facto recolonization" of India.

93. R. Ul'ianovsky, "Socialism and the National-Liberation Struggle—the Non-Capitalist Path of Development," *Pravda*, April 15, 1966, p. 4, in *CDSP*, XVIII, 15 (1966), 24–25.

94. "India: 20 Years of the Republic," *New Times*, no. 4, 1970, p. 24.

95. L. I. Brezhnev, "The Cause of Lenin Lives On and Triumphs," in *New Times*, no. 17, 1970, p. 19.

96. A. A. Iskenderov, "The Theory of Marxism and the National-Liberation Movement," in *The National-Liberation Movement: Vital Problems* (Moscow, 1967?), III, 38–72.

97. It is of interest to note that the blame for "dogmatic postulates" was no longer being assigned to Stalin personally, as it had been a few years earlier. The scapegoat in the post-Khrushchev years was rather the more impersonal one of "some Comintern documents."

98. Iskenderov, "The Theory of Marxism," pp. 87–89 (emphasis supplied).

99. Yakovlev, *The World Socialist System and the National-Liberation Movement*, pp. 99–100.

100. Conclusion to the forum on "Immediate Problems of the National-Liberation Movement," *International Affairs*, no. 5, 1967, p. 78.

101. Georgy Mirsky, in the forum on "The Theory and Practice of the Non-Capitalist Way of Development," *International Affairs,* no. 11, 1970, p. 16; G. Kim and A. Kaufman, "Non-Capitalist Development: Achievements and Difficulties," *International Affairs,* no. 12, 1967, p. 70.

102. B. S. Nikolayev, in the forum on "The Theory and Practice," p. 18 (emphasis supplied).

103. V. G. Solodovnikov, in "The Theory and Practice," pp. 12–13.

104. V. L. Tiagunenko, in "The Theory and Practice," p. 15.

105. Rostislav Ul'ianovsky, "The 'Third World'—Problems of Socialist Development," *International Affairs,* no. 9, 1971, p. 27.

106. Tiagunenko, in "The Theory and Practice," p. 15.

107. E. M. Zhukov, "Contemporary Pace of Development of National-Liberation Revolution," in "Immediate Problems," pp. 52–54.

108. D. Zarine, "Classes and Class Struggle in Developing Countries," *International Affairs,* no. 4, 1968, p. 48.

109. Kim and Kaufman, "Non-Capitalist Development," pp. 71–74.

110. Rostislav Ul'ianovsky, "At New Frontiers—On Some Features of the Present Stage of the National-Liberation Movement," *Pravda,* January 3, 1968, pp. 4–5, in *CDSP,* XX, 1 (1968), 9–11. See also his article, "Some Aspects of the Non-Capitalist Way for Asian and African Countries," *World Marxist Review,* XII, 9 (1969), 90.

111. Ul'ianovsky, "Some Aspects," p. 91; Ul'ianovsky, "The 'Third World,'" p. 30; R. A. Ul'ianovsky, in the forum "Once More about the Non-Capitalist Way," *World Marxist Review,* XIII, 6 (1970), 88.

112. G. B. Starushenko, in "The Theory and Practice," p. 21.

113. R. G. Landa, "More on the Non-Capitalist Path of Development," *Narody Azii i Afriki,* no. 6, 1966, pp. 30–38, in *Soviet Sociology,* IV, 3 (Winter, 1965–1966), p. 9.

114. Tiagunenko, "Immediate Problems," p. 57, has cited the examples of Mali and Senegal, where power was in the hands of forces of similar social origin, but was being used in precisely opposite directions.

115. Ul'ianovsky, "At New Frontiers," p. 9; Ul'ianovsky, "Some Aspects," p. 88.

116. R. N. Andresian, "Developing Countries and Foreign Capital," in "Immediate Problems," p. 73.

117. V. L. Tiagunenko, "World Socialism and the Character of the Liberation Struggle," in *The National-Liberation Movement: Vital Problems,* III, 59, 63; Tiagunenko, in "The Theory and Practice," p. 14 (emphasis in original).

118. Mirsky, in "The Theory and Practice," p. 16.

119. Ul'ianovsky, "Some Aspects," p. 87. The views of this prominent Soviet Indologist have recently been collected in his *Sotsializm i Osvobodivshiesia Strany* (Socialism and the Liberated Countries) (Moscow, 1972).

120. Ul'ianovsky, "Some Aspects," p. 93.

121. This view was reiterated in a joint statement issued by the CPSU and CPI in June 1972 which asserted that the cohesion of left-wing forces and formation of a "national-democratic front" were necessary conditions for the further struggle with "reactionary forces," leading to the "development and democratization of the state sector, radical agrarian reforms . . . and planning aimed at achieving economic independence and improving the working peoples' living standard." See *Pravda*, June 30, 1972, p. 2.

122. Mohit Sen, "Eighth Congress of the CP of India," *World Marxist Review*, XI, 5 (1969), 72–84.

123. For a perceptive analysis of the rural strength of Indian communism, see Bhabani Sen Gupta, "Indian Communism and the Peasantry," *Problems of Communism*, XXI, 1 (1972), 1–17.

124. S. G. Sardesai, "Political Struggle in India," *World Marxist Review*, XIII, 7 (1970), 54.

125. N. K. Krishnan, "On Recent Political Developments in India," *World Marxist Review*, XII, 12 (1969), 50–57.

126. Sardesai, "Political Struggle in India," pp. 52–53.

127. Ibid., p. 54.

128. "CPI to Strive for a Coalition at Center," *The Statesman Weekly*, October 9, 1971, p. 7. At the Ninth Congress, the CPI claimed a membership of 231,894—down from 243,238 the previous year. Many observers consider this figure to be greatly inflated.

129. S. A. Dange, Speech of June 12, 1969, to the Moscow Conference, in *CDSP*, XXI, 27 (1969), 6.

130. "Counter-Revolutionary Activities of U.S.S.R. in Southeast Asia," Hsinhua International Service in English, March 14, 1969, in *Studies in Comparative Communism*, II, 3–4 (1969), 319.

131. "Indian Reactionaries Heading for Collapse at Quicker Tempo," *Peking Review*, XIII, 9 (1970), 25–26.

132. "Political Resolution of the Communist Party of India (Marxist-Leninist)," *Peking Review*, XII, 28 (1969), 18–22.

133. "Indian Monthly 'Liberation' Sums Up Experiences of Armed Peasant Struggle in Mushahari," *Peking Review*, XIII, 5 (1970), 18–19; "Indian Armed Struggle Intensifies," *Peking Review*, XIII, 7 (1970), 15–16.

134. "Peasants' Armed Struggle Led by Communist Party of India (M-L) Develops Steadily," *Peking Review*, XIII, 39, (1970), 26, 28.

135. "CPI M-L Reported to Have Expelled Charu Mazumdar," *The Statesman Weekly*, November 13, 1971, p. 7.

136. Kasturi Rangan, "Maoist Movement Declining in India," *New York Times*, August 5, 1972.

137. E. M. Zhukov, "Natsional'no-osvoboditel'noe dvizhenie na novom etape" (The national-liberation movement in a new stage), *Kommunist*, no. 12, 1963, p. 28 (emphasis supplied).

Bibliography

"Abridged Draft of Political Theses of the C.C. of C.P. of India," *International Press Correspondence*, XIV, 40 (1934), 1024–1034.

Adhikari, Gangadhar. *Communist Party and India's Path to National Regeneration and Socialism.* New Delhi: New Age Printing Press, 1964.

—— *The Imperialist Alternative.* Bombay: People's Publishing House, 1945.

—— *Pakistan and Indian National Unity.* London: Labour Monthly, 1943.

"The Agrarian Question in the Developing Countries of Asia," *World Marxist Review*, VIII, 9 (1965), 38–42.

Akademiia Nauk SSSR. *Obshchee sobranie Akademii Nauk SSSR; 10–13 iiunia 1947 goda.* Moscow: Izdatel'stvo Akademii Nauk SSSR, 1948.

Akademiia Nauk SSSR, Institut Narodov Azii. *Politika SShA v stranakh Iuzhnoi Azii.* B. G. Gafurov, ed. Moscow: Izdatel'stvo vostochnoi literatury, 1961.

—— *Rabochii klass stran Azii i Afriki.* A. A. Iskenderov, ed. Moscow: Nauka, 1964.

Akademiia Nauk SSSR, Tikhookeanskii Institut. *Uchenye zapiski Tikhookeanskogo Instituta.* II: *Indiiskii sbornik.* Moscow: Izdatel'stvo Akademii Nauk SSSR, 1949.

Alekseev, M. "Indiiskii Soiuz i Pakistan posle raschleniia Indii," *Bol'shevik*, no. 11, 1948, pp. 54–66.

Andronov, I. "Charting a Nation's Course," *New Times*, no. 28, 1964, pp. 29–31.

Avakov, R. M., and G. I. Mirsky. "O klassovoi strukture v slaborazvitykh stranakh," *Mirovaia ekonomika i mezhdunarodnye otnosheniia*, no. 4, 1962, pp. 68–82.

Avakov, R. M., and Lev Stepanov. "Sotsial'nye problemy natsional'no-osvoboditel'noi revoliutsii," *Mirovaia ekonomika i mezhdunarodnye otnosheniia*, no. 5, 1963, pp. 46–54.

Avarin, V. "Asia in the Modern World," *New Times*, no. 4, 1956, pp. 3–6.

Balabushevich, V. V. "Novyi etap natsional'no-osvoboditel'noi bor'by narodov Indii," *Voprosy ekonomiki*, no. 8, 1949, pp. 30–48.

—— and A. M. D'iakov, eds. *Nezavisimaia Indiia: sbornik statei.* Moscow: Izdatel'stvo vostochnoi literatury, 1958.

—— *Noveishaia istoriia Indii.* Moscow: Izdatel'stvo vostochnoi literatury, 1959.

Barghoorn, F. C. *The Soviet Cultural Offensive: The Role of Cultural Diplomacy in Soviet Foreign Policy.* Princeton: Princeton University Press, 1960.

—— *Soviet Foreign Propaganda*. Princeton: Princeton University Press, 1964.

Bhargava, G. S. "National Consensus or Bandwaggoning?" *The Overseas Hindustan Times*, XXII, 34 (August 21, 1971), 16.

Bondarevsky, G. "Ekspansiia monopolii SShA v Indii," *Kommunist*, no. 12, 1954, pp. 121–128.

Borisov, I. "Dark Skies over the Indian Subcontinent," *New Times*, no. 44, 1971, pp. 10–12.

Borisov, O. "For Peace and Security in Asia," *New Times*, no. 39, 1971, pp. 10–11.

Bovin, A. "The Revolutionary Process and Peaceful Coexistence," *New Times*, no. 42, 1963, pp. 5–8.

Brecher, Michael. *India and World Politics: Krishna Menon's View of the World*. New York: Praeger, 1968.

Brezhnev, L. I. "The Cause of Lenin Lives On and Triumphs," *New Times*, no. 17, 1970, pp. 3–20.

—— *For a Greater Unity of Communists, for a Fresh Upsurge of the Anti-Imperialist Struggle*. Moscow: Novosti Press Agency Publishing House, 1969.

Brines, Russell. *The Indo-Pakistani Conflict*. London: Pall-Mall Press, 1968.

Brutents, K. N. "Sovremennyi etap natsional'no-osvoboditel'nogo dvizheniia," *Kommunist*, no. 17, 1964, pp. 23–34.

Bulganin, N. A., and N. S. Khrushchev. *Report to the Supreme Soviet on the Trip to India, Burma and Afghanistan*. New York: New Century, 1956.

Burlatsky, F. "The Liberation Movement and Scientific Socialism," *Pravda*, August 15, 1965, pp. 3–4, in *Current Digest of the Soviet Press*, XVII, 33 (1965), 3–5.

Bushevich, V. [V. V. Balabushevich], and A. M. D'iakov. "Indiia i Vtoraia Imperialisticheskaia Voina," *Mirovoe khoziaistvo i mirovaia politika*, no. 12, 1940, pp. 53–67.

Cantril, Albert H. *The Indian Perception of the Sino-Indian Border Clash: An Inquiry in Political Psychology*. Princeton: Institute for International Social Psychology, 1963.

Carlisle, D. S. "Stalin's Postwar Foreign Policy and the National Liberation Movement," *Review of Politics*, XXVII, 3 (1965), 334–363.

Chattopadyaya. "Musul'manstvo i Buddizm na sluzhbe u imperializma," *Revoliutsionnyi Vostok*, no. 3–4, 1932, pp. 282–288.

Chaudhuri, Tridib. *The Swing Back: A Critical Survey of the Devious Zig-Zags of CPI Political Line (1947–1950)*. Calcutta: Revolutionary Socialist Party, 1950.

Clarkson, Stephen. "Soviet Theory and Indian Reality," *Problems of Communism*, XVI, 1 (1967), 11–20.

Colonial Peoples' Struggle for Liberation. Bombay: People's Publishing House, 1950.

"The Comintern in the East," *Communist International*, VI, 9–10 (1929), 273–292.

"Commentator," "Most Absurd Logic, Most Flagrant Aggression," *Jen-min Jih-pao*, December 10, 1971, in *Peking Review*, XIV, 50 (1971), 6–7.

The Communist International between the Fifth and the Sixth World Congresses, 1924–8. London: Communist Party of Great Britain, 1928.

Communist Party of India. *Constitution of the Communist Party of India, Adopted at the Extraordinary Party Congress, Amritsar, 1958.* New Delhi: People's Publishing House, 1958.

—— *Election Manifesto.* Bombay: People's Publishing House, 1951.

—— *The India-China Border Dispute and the Communist Party of India: Resolutions, Statements and Speeches, 1959–1963.* New Delhi: Communist Party of India, 1963.

—— *Political Thesis of the Communist Party of India, Passed by the Second Congress at Calcutta, Feb. 28–Mar. 6, 1948.* Bombay: Kaul, 1948.

—— *Proceedings of the Seventh Congress of the CP of India, Bombay, 13–23 December 1964.* 3 vols. New Delhi: D. P. Sinha, 1965.

—— *Resolution on Party Organisation.* New Delhi: Communist Party of India, 1954.

—— *Statement of Policy of the CP of India.* 2nd ed. Bombay: Jayant Bhatt, 1951.

Communist Party of India, Central Committee. *Communist Party in the Struggle for Peace, Democracy and National Advance.* New Delhi: D. P. Sinha, 1955.

—— *Our Tasks among the Peasant Masses: Resolution Adopted by the Central Committee of the Communist Party of India, April 1954.* New Delhi: D. P. Sinha, 1954.

Communist Party of India, National Council. *Resolution on Splitters and Other Documents of the National Council of the Communist Party of India.* New Delhi: D. P. Sinha, 1964.

—— *Resolutions, 1963–66.* New Delhi: D. P. Sinha, 1966.

"Constructive Approach," *New Times*, no. 23, 1964, pp. 2–3.

Correspondence between M. Gandhi and P. C. Joshi. Bombay: People's Publishing House, 1945.

Dange, S. A. "Neither Revisionism nor Dogmatism Is Our Guide," *New Age* (weekly), April 21, 1963, pp. 1–2.

Degras, Jane, ed. *The Communist International, 1919–1943: Documents.* 3 vols. London: Oxford University Press, 1956–1965.

Democratic Research Service, Bombay. *Indian Communist Party Documents, 1930–56.* Bombay: Democratic Research Service, 1957.

D'iakov, A. M. "The Indian Problem," *The War and the Working Class*, no. 2, 1945, pp. 12–17.

—— *Indiia v period obshchego krizisa kapitalizma.* Moscow: Vysshaia Partiinaia Shkola pri TsK KPSS, 1955.

—— *Indiia vo vremia i posle Vtoroi Mirovoi Voiny 1939–49.* Moscow: Izdatel'stvo Akademii Nauk SSSR, 1952.

—— "K voprosu o natsional'nom sostave naseleniia Indii," *Uchenye zapiski Tikhookeanskogo Instituta*, I (1947), 223–330.

—— "Natsional'naia politika Britanskogo imperializma v Indii," *Mirovoe khoziaistvo i mirovaia politika*, no. 12, 1939, pp. 77–92.

—— *Natsional'no-osvoboditel'naia bor'ba narodov Indii i rabochee dvizhenie na pervom etape obshchego krizisa kapitalizma: uchebnyi material.* Moscow: Vysshaia Partiinaia Shkola pri TsK KPSS, 1957.

—— *Natsional'nyi vopros i Angliiskii imperializm v Indii.* Moscow: Gospolitizdat, 1948.

—— *Natsional'nyi vopros v sovremennoi Indii.* Moscow: Izdatel'stvo vostochnoi literatury, 1963.

—— "The New British Plan for India," *New Times*, no. 24, 1947, pp. 12–15.

—— "The Political Situation in India," *The War and the Working Class*, no. 7, 1945, pp. 10–13.

—— "Sovremennaia Indiia," *Bol'shevik*, no. 4, 1946, pp. 49–53.

—— and I. M. Reisner. "Rol' Gandi v natsional'no-osvoboditel'noi bor'be narodov Indii," *Sovetskoe Vostokovedenie*, no. 5, 1956, translated in "Gandhi in Russia's New Mirror," *Thought* (New Delhi), March 23, 1957, pp. 4–5; March 30, 1957, pp. 7–8; April 6, 1957, pp. 7–8, 16.

D'iakov, A. M., et al., eds. *Ekonomika sovremennoi Indii.* Moscow: Izdatel'stvo vostochnoi literatury, 1960.

Dimitrov, Georgy. "The Tasks of the Working Class in the Present War," *World News and Views*, XIX, 53 (1939), 1079–1082.

"Diskussia ob ekonomicheskikh i politicheskikh pozitsiiakh natsional'noi burzhuazii v stranakh Vostoka," *Sovetskoe Vostokovedenie*, no. 1, 1957, pp. 174–184.

Djilas, Milovan. *Conversations with Stalin.* New York: Harcourt, Brace and World, 1962.

"Documents: The Sino-Soviet Dispute," *Studies in Comparative Communism*, II, 3–4 (1969), 149–412.

Duncan, W. R., ed. *Soviet Policy in Developing Countries.* Waltham, Mass.: Ginn-Blaisdell, 1970.

Durdenevsky, V. "The Five Principles," *International Affairs*, no. 3, 1956, pp. 45–50.

Dutt, R. P. "The Road to Proletarian Hegemony in the Indian Revolution," *Communist International*, VII, 13 (1930), 282–288.

—— and Ben Bradley, "The Anti-Imperialist People's Front," *International Press Correspondence*, XVI, 11 (1936), 297–300.

—— and Harry Pollitt. "The United National Front," *International Press Correspondence*, XVI, 50 (1936), 1342–1344.

"XX S'ezd Kommunisticheskogo Partii Sovetskogo Soiuza i zadachi izucheniia sovremennogo Vostoka," *Sovetskoe Vostokovedenie,* no. 1, 1956, pp. 3–12.

"XXII S'ezd KPSS i zadachi dal'neishego izucheniia problem mirovogo razvitiia," *Mirovaia ekonomika i mezhdunarodnye otnosheniia,* no. 3, 1962, pp. 3–19.

Ershov, T. "The Truth about Kashmir," *New Times,* no. 10, 1948, pp. 24–29.

Etinger, Yakov, and Ovanes Melikian. *The Policy of Nonalignment.* Moscow: Progress Publishers, 1965.

Eudin, X. J., and R. C. North. *Soviet Russia and the East, 1920–1927: A Documentary Survey.* Stanford: Stanford University Press, 1957.

Eudin, X. J., and R. M. Slusser. *Soviet Foreign Policy, 1928–1934: Documents and Materials.* vol. I. University Park, Penna.: Pennsylvania State University Press, 1966.

Fisher, M. W., and J. V. Bondurant. *Indian Approaches to a Socialist Society.* Berkeley: Institute of International Studies, 1956.

Florinsky, Michael T. *Russia: A History and an Interpretation.* 2 vols. New York: Macmillan, 1947, 1953.

Floyd, David. *Mao against Khrushchev: A Short History of the Sino-Soviet Conflict.* New York: Praeger, 1963.

"For the Unity and Solidarity of the International Communist Movement," *Pravda,* December 6, 1963, pp. 2–5, in *Current Digest of the Soviet Press,* XV, 47 (1963), 17–18.

Fourth Congress of the Communist International: Abridged Report. London: Communist Party of Great Britain, 1923 (?).

Frankel, Max. "To India the U.S. Is a Bitter Disappointment," *New York Times,* November 30, 1971, p. 2.

Frantsev, Iu. "Natsionalizm—oruzhie imperialisticheskoi reaktsii," *Bol'shevik,* no. 15, 1948, pp. 45–55.

Gafurov, B. G. "Aktual'nye zadachi Sovetskogo Vostokovedeniia," *Vestnik Akademii Nauk SSSR,* no. 9, 1957, pp. 13–24.

————, ed. *Lenin i Vostok: sbornik statei.* Moscow: Izdatel'stvo vostochnoi literatury, 1960.

Gelman, Harry. "The Communist Party of India: Sino-Soviet Battleground," in *Communist Strategies in Asia.* A. D. Barnett, ed. New York: Praeger, 1963. Pp. 101–147.

"General Secretary, C.C., C.P. of East Pakistan." "Leninism is our Guide," *World Marxist Review,* XIII, 5 (1970), 67–69.

Ghosh, A. K. "The Indian Bourgeoisie," *New Age,* December 1955, pp. 5–18.

———— "The Internal Politics of the Government," *New Age,* November 1955, pp. 5–24.

———— "Kerala," *World Marxist Review,* II, 11 (1959), 35–43.

———— "National Independence and United Front," *New Age,* October 1955, pp. 17–24.

———— "On India's Path of Development," *New Age,* October 1956, pp. 16–18.

———— "Problems of Industrialization," *New Age*, January 1956, pp. 5–15.

———— "Some Features of the Situation in India," *World Marxist Review*, V, 2 (1962), 17–28.

———— "Toward a Mass Communist Party," *New Age*, February 1958, pp. 1–14.

Giiasov, T. *Indiia i bor'ba za oslablenie napriazhennosti v Iugo-Vostochnoi Azii i na Dal'nem Vostoke*. Tashkent: Izdatel'stvo vo SAGU, 1957.

Goldman, Marshall I. *Soviet Foreign Aid*. New York: Praeger, 1967.

Goodall, M. C. "Soviet Policy and India: Some Postwar Trends," *Journal of International Affairs*, VIII, 1 (1954), 43–51.

Goodman, E. R. *The Soviet Design for a World State*. New York: Columbia University Press, 1960.

Gordon, L. R. *Agrarnye otnosheniia v Severo-Zapadnoi Pogranichnoi Provintsii Indii (1914–1947 gg.)*. Moscow: Izdatel'stvo Akademii Nauk SSSR, 1953.

Grashe, V. Ia. "Kratkii ocherk formirovaniia krupnykh promyshlennykh kapitalistov v kolonial'noi Indii," *Uchenye zapiski Instituta Vostokovedeniia*, X (1954), 97–160.

Griffith, W. E. *Sino-Soviet Relations, 1964–1965*. Cambridge: The MIT Press, 1967.

———— *The Sino-Soviet Rift*. Cambridge: The MIT Press, 1964.

Gromyko, A. A. "Questions of the International Situation and the Foreign Policy of the Soviet Union," *Pravda*, July 11, 1969, pp. 2–4, in *Current Digest of the Soviet Press*, XXI, 28 (1969), 4–11.

Gupta, Sisir. "India and the Soviet Union," *Current History*, XLIV, 259 (1964), 141–146.

Gurvich, R. P. *Sel'skoe khoziaistvo Indii i polozhenie krest'ianstva*. Moscow: Izdatel'stvo vostochnoi literatury, 1960.

Happiness and Peace for the Peoples: N. S. Khrushchev's Visit to India, Burma, Indonesia and Afghanistan February 11–March 5 1960. Moscow: Foreign Languages Publishing House, 1960.

Hariharan, A. "India: Bosom Friends," *Far Eastern Economic Review*, LXXIV, 41 (1971), 14.

Harrison, Selig S. "Caste and the Andhra Communists," *American Political Science Review*, L, 2 (1956), 378–404.

———— *India: The Most Dangerous Decades*. Princeton: Princeton University Press, 1960.

Hilsman, Roger. *To Move a Nation: The Politics of Foreign Policy in the Administration of John F. Kennedy*. Garden City, N.Y.: Doubleday, 1967.

Horelick, Arnold, and Myron Rush. *Strategic Power and Soviet Foreign Policy*. Chicago: University of Chicago Press, 1966.

"How Chinese Attack on Indian Frontier Was Reported," *Current Digest of the Soviet Press*, XIV, 43 (1962), 16–18.

Howard, Peter. " 'A System of Collective Security,' " *Mizan*, XI, 4 (1969), 199–204.

Hudson, G. F., Richard Lowenthal, and Roderick MacFarquhar, eds. *The Sino-Soviet Dispute.* New York: Praeger, 1961.

"Immediate Problems of the National-Liberation Movement," *International Affairs*, no. 5, 1967, pp. 51–78.

"Industrialization of Underdeveloped Countries," *New Times*, no. 21, 1952, pp. 1–3.

Inozemtsev, N. N. "Peaceful Coexistence and the World Revolutionary Process," *Pravda*, July 28, 1963, pp. 4–5, in *Current Digest of the Soviet Press*, XV, 30 (1963), 8–9.

Iskandarov, R. G. *K voprosu o pomoshchi slaborazvitym stranam.* Moscow: Izdatel'stvo VPSh i AON pri TsK KPSS, 1960.

"Istoricheskaia Tashkentskaia Deklaratsiia," *Kommunist*, no. 1, 1966, pp. 40–41.

"Izuchenie Indii," *Vestnik Akademii Nauk SSSR*, no. 8, 1947, pp. 83–91.

"Joint Soviet-Indian Statement," *New Times*, no. 41, 1971, pp. 6–7.

"Joint Statement by the Chairman of the Council of Ministers of the USSR N.A. Bulganin and the Prime Minister of India Jawaharlal Nehru," *New Times* (supplement), no. 27, 1955.

Joshi, P. C. *Communist Reply to Congress Working Committee's Charges.* Bombay: People's Publishing House, 1945.

————— *Congress and Communists.* Bombay: People's Publishing House, 1944.

————— *For the Final Bid for Power! The Communist Plan Explained.* Bombay: People's Publishing House, 1946.

————— *The Indian Communist Party: Its Policy and Work in the War of Liberation.* London: Communist Party of Great Britain, 1942.

Kalyagin, B. "Defeat for Indian Reaction," *New Times*, no. 12, 1971, pp. 6–7.

Katrak, Savak. "India's Communist Party Split," *China Quarterly*, no. 7, 1961, pp. 143–147.

Kautsky, John H. *Moscow and the Communist Party of India.* Cambridge: The Technology Press of MIT, 1956.

Kaznacheev, Alexander. *Inside a Soviet Embassy: Experiences of a Russian Diplomat in Burma.* Philadelphia: Lippincott, 1962.

Kennan, G. F. *Russia and the West under Lenin and Stalin.* Boston: Atlantic–Little, Brown, 1961.

Khrushchev, N. S. "On the International Situation and the Foreign Policy of the Soviet Union," *Pravda*, November 1, 1959, pp. 1–3, in *Current Digest of the Soviet Press*, XI, 44 (1959), 3–12.

————— "Report of the Central Committee of the Communist Party of the Soviet Union to the Twentieth Party Congress," *New Times* (supplement), no. 8, 1956.

"N. S. Khrushchev's Replies to Questions Put by the Ghanaian Times,

Alger Republicain, Le Peuple, and Botataung," *New Times* (supment), no. 52, 1963.

Kim, G., and A. Kaufman. "Non-Capitalist Development: Achievements and Difficulties," *International Affairs*, no. 12, 1967, pp. 70–76.

Kolykhalova, G. "India's New Economic Plan," *New Times*, no. 15, 1956, pp. 12–13.

Konchar'iants, G. "Indiiskii narod na puti k antiimperialisticheskomu edinstvu," *Bol'shevik*, no. 21–22, 1938, pp. 120–131.

—— "Voina i natsional'no-osvoboditel'noe dvizhenie Indiiskogo naroda," *Bol'shevik*, no. 14, 1940, pp. 59–75.

Kondrat'ev, V. "Natsional'naia burzhuazia i promyshlennoe razvitie sovremennoi Indii," *Mirovaia ekonomika i mezhdunarodnye otnosheniia*, no. 8, 1959, pp. 61–72.

Korovin, Eugene. "The Five Principles—A Basis for Peaceful Coexistence," *International Affairs*, no. 5, 1956, pp. 46–53.

Kotovsky, G. G. "Agrarian Reforms in India," *New Times*, no. 48, 1958, pp. 13–15.

——, ed. *Bibliografiia Indii*. Moscow: Izdatel'stvo Nauka, 1965.

—— "K voprosu o roli rostovshchicheskogo kapitala v obezzemelenii krest'ianstva v Indii," *Kratkie soobshcheniia Instituta Vostokovedeniia*, no. 10, 1953, pp. 20–34.

—— "Sotsial'no-ekonomicheskoe soderzhanie problemy 'Neprikasaemykh,'" *Uchenye zapiski Instituta Vostokovedeniia*, V (1953), 75–152.

——, V. P. Pavlov, and I. B. Redko. "Some Economic and Political Problems," *New Times*, no. 1, 1964, pp. 18–22.

Kremortat, B. "Sessiia Tikhookeanskogo Instituta Akademii Nauk SSSR," *Voprosy istorii*, no. 4, 1948, pp. 151–157.

Kriazhin, V. "Rabochee i professional'noe dvizhenie v Indii," *Novyi Vostok*, no. 5, 1924, pp. 230–237.

Krishnan, N. K. "On Recent Political Developments in India," *World Marxist Review*, XII, 12 (1969), 50–57.

Kun, Bela, ed. *Kommunisticheskii Internatsional v dokumentakh 1919–1932*. 2 vols. Moscow: Partiinoe izdatel'stvo, 1933.

Kutsenkov, A. A., and A. B. Frumkin. "Indiia," in *Mezhdunarodnaia torgovliia*. I. S. Potapov et al., eds. Moscow: Vneshtorgizdat, 1954. Pp. 614–635.

Kutsobin, P. "India: New Phase of the Struggle," *New Times*, no. 11, 1970, pp. 7–8.

—— "The Indian Confrontation," *New Times*, no. 47, 1969, pp. 6–8.

Landa, R. G. "More on the Non-Capitalist Path of Development," *Narody Azii i Afriki*, no. 6, 1966, pp. 30–38, in *Soviet Sociology*, IV, 3 (Winter 1965–1966), 3–10.

Leites, Nathan. *A Study of Bolshevism*. Glencoe, Ill.: The Free Press, 1960.

Lemin, I. M. "Anglo-Indiiskie otnosheniia i voina," *Mirovoe khoziaistvo i mirovaia politika*, no. 5–6, 1942, pp. 76–84.

———— "The Fruits of British Rule in India and Pakistan," *Voprosy ekonomiki*, no. 1, 1952, in *Soviet Press Translations*, VII, 8 (1952), 211–220.

———— *Obostrenie krizisa Britanskoi imperii posle Vtoroi Mirovoi Voiny.* Moscow: Izdatel'stvo Akademii Nauk SSSR, 1951.

———— "Rol' Britanskogo imperii v sovremennoi voine," *Bol'shevik*, no. 20, 1941, pp. 27–37.

Lenin-Stalin, 1917: Selected Writings and Speeches. Moscow: Foreign Languages Publishing House, 1938.

Lenin, V. I. *Imperialism, the Highest Stage of Capitalism.* New York: International Publishers, 1939.

———— *The National-Liberation Movement in the East.* Moscow: Foreign Languages Publishing House, 1957.

Levkovsky, A. I. "Angliiskie upravliaiushchie agentsvia—orudie poraboshcheniia i ekspluatatsii narodov Indii," *Kratkie soobshcheniia Instituta Vostokovedeniia*, no. 10, 1953, pp. 69–80.

———— *Nekotorye osobennosti razvitiia kapitalizma v Indii do 1947 g.* Moscow: Gosudarstvennoe izdatel'stvo politicheskoi literatury, 1956.

———— "Nekotorye voprosy poslevoennogo ekonomicheskogo razvitiia Indii v svete Leninskogo-Stalinskogo ucheniia ob imperializme," *Vestnik Moskovskogo Universiteta*, no. 1, 1949, pp. 171–180.

Limaye, Madhu. *Communist Party: Facts and Fiction.* Hyderabad: Chetana Prakashan, 1951.

Liu Shao-ch'i. *Internationalism and Nationalism.* Peking: Foreign Languages Press, 1948.

McLane, Charles B. "Foreign Aid in Soviet Third World Policies," unpub. paper delivered at the 1968 Annual Meeting of the American Political Science Association, Washington, September 2–7, 1968.

———— *Soviet Strategies in Southeast Asia: An Exploration of Eastern Policy under Lenin and Stalin.* Princeton: Princeton University Press, 1966.

McVey, Ruth T. *The Calcutta Conference and the Southeast Asian Uprisings.* Ithaca, N.Y.: Cornell Modern Indonesia Project, 1958.

Maev, O. V. "Amerikanskaia 'Pomoshch' Indii," *Mirovaia ekonomika i mezhdunarodnye otnosheniia*, no. 12, 1960, pp. 104–106.

———— "Indiiskii monopolisticheskii kapital," *Narody Azii i Afriki*, no. 1, 1964, pp. 21–36.

Mankekar, D. R. *The Red Riddle of Kerala.* Bombay: Manaktalas, 1965.

Martyshin, O. V. "Toward a Definition of the Social Ideas of Gandhism," *Voprosy filosofii*, no. 1, 1965, pp. 95–106, in *Current Digest of the Soviet Press*, XVII, 19 (1965), 15–19.

Marx, Karl. *Articles on India.* Bombay: People's Publishing House, 1945.

Masani, M. R. *The Communist Party of India: A Short History.* New York: Macmillan, 1954.

Maslennikov, V. A., ed. *Uglublenie krizisa kolonial'noi sistemy imperializma posle Vtoroi Mirovoi Voiny: sbornik statei.* Moscow: Gospolitizdat, 1953.

Matveyev, V. V. "A Filled 'Vacuum,' " *Izvestiia*, May 29, 1969, p. 3, in *Current Digest of the Soviet Press*, XXI, 22 (1969), 14.

Maxwell, Neville. *India's China War.* London: Jonathan Cape, 1970.

"May the Friendship and Cooperation between the Peoples of the Soviet Union and the Republic of India Develop and Grow Stronger," *Pravda*, May 16, 1965, pp. 1–2, in *Current Digest of the Soviet Press*, XVII, 20 (1965), 7–11.

Medovoi, A., and V. Yashkin. "Problems of India's Socio-Economic Development," *International Affairs*, no. 10, 1970, pp. 62–65.

Meijer, Jan, ed. *The Trotsky Papers, 1917–22.* Vol. I. The Hague: Mouton, 1964.

Mel'man, S. M. *Ekonomika Indii i politika Angliiskogo imperializma.* Moscow: Izdatel'stvo Akademii Nauk SSSR, 1951.

―――― "Indiia v bor'be za svoiu natsional'nuiu nezavisimost'," *Mirovoe khoziaistvo i mirovaia politika*, no. 9, 1939, pp. 92–103.

―――― *Inostrannyi monopolisticheskii kapital v ekonomike Indii.* Moscow: Izdatel'stvo vostochnoi literatury, 1959.

―――― "Polozhenie v Indii," *Mirovoe khoziaistvo i mirovaia politika*, no. 11–12, 1942, pp. 41–47.

―――― "Rabochee dvizhenie Indii posle razdela strany," *Profesional'nye soiuzy*, no. 3, 1949, pp. 39–43.

Menon, K. P. S. *The Flying Troika.* London: Oxford University Press, 1963.

Meyer, Alfred G. *Leninism.* Cambridge: Harvard University Press, 1957.

Mikhailov, K. "O sdvigakh v Indiiskom Natsional'nom Kongresse," *Revoliutsionnyi Vostok*, no. 2, 1935, pp. 132–146.

―――― and A. Pronin. "Uglublenie ekonomicheskogo krizisa i revoliutsionnyi pod'em v Indii," *Revoliutsionnyi Vostok*, no. 1–2, 1932, pp. 55–101.

Mikoian, S. M. "Desiat' let vneshnei politiki Indii," *Mirovaia ekonomika i mezhdunarodnye otnosheniia*, no. 2, 1957, pp. 26–32.

A Mirror for Revisionists: 'Remnin Ribao' Editorial, March 9, 1963. Peking: Foreign Languages Press, 1963.

Mirsky, G. I. "Developing Countries at the Crossroads," *New Times*, no. 48, 1966, pp. 6–9.

―――― "The Proletariat and National Liberation," *New Times*, no. 18, 1964, pp. 8–9.

―――― "Tvorcheskii Marksizm i problemy natsional'no-osvoboditel'nykh revoliutsii," *Mirovaia politika i mezhdunarodnye otnosheniia*, no. 2, 1963, pp. 63–68.

Mishin, A. A. *Gosudarstvennyi stroi Indii.* Moscow: Izdatel'stvo iurid. literatury, 1956.

"Mr. Nehru, It Is High Time for You to Pull Back from the Brink of the Precipice," *Jen-min Jih-pao,* October 14, 1962, in *Peking Review,* V, 42 (1962), 6–7.

Modzhorian, L. "Neutrality," *New Times,* no. 8, 1956, pp. 12–15.

"More on Nehru's Philosophy in the Light of the Sino-Indian Boundary Question," *Jen-min Jih-pao,* October 27, 1962, in *Peking Review,* V, 44 (1962), 10–22.

Morris, Bernard, and Morris Watnick. "Current Communist Strategy in Non-Industrialized Countries," *Problems of Communism,* IV, 5 (1955), 1–6.

Mukherjee, Hiren. "The Indo-Soviet Pact: New Directions for Indian Foreign Policy," *The Mail* (Madras), in *Atlas,* XX, 11 (1971), 36–38.

Nadar, G. "The Sweep of the Mighty Mass Movement in India," *World Marxist Review,* VII, 10 (1964), 73–76.

Nair, K. "Struggle against Splitters in India," *World Marxist Review,* VII, 7 (1964), 52–57.

Nair, R. R. *How Communists Came to Power in Kerala.* Trivandrum: Kerala Academy of Political Science, 1965.

Namboodiripad, E. M. S. *Agrarian Reforms: A Study of the Congress and Communist Approach.* New Delhi: D. P. Sinha, 1956.

———— *Kerala: Problems and Possibilities.* New Delhi: D. P. Sinha, 1957.

The National-Liberation Movement: Vital Problems. Vol. III. Moscow: Novosti Press Agency Publishing House, 1967 (?).

"Natsional'no-osvoboditel'noe dvizhenie i sotsial'nyi progress," *Kommunist,* no. 13, 1965, pp. 12–26.

Nehru, Jawaharlal. *Soviet Russia: Some Random Sketches and Impressions.* Bombay: Chetana, 1929.

"Neotlozhenye zadachi Sovetskikh istorikov-vostokovedov," *Voprosy istorii,* no. 4, 1949, pp. 3–8.

Nesterov, S. "Manevry Amerikanskogo imperializma v Iugo-Vostochnoi Azii," *Mirovaia politika i mezhdunarodnye otnosheniia,* no. 10, 1963, pp. 66–77.

"The New Party of Bose and What Should Be Our Attitude to It," *International Press Correspondence,* XIII, 52 (1933), 1181–1187.

Nikhamin, V. P. *Ocherki vneshnei politiki Indii 1947–57.* Moscow: Gospolitizdat, 1959.

———— "The Soviet Union and the Developing Countries," *International Affairs,* no. 4, 1966, pp. 33–39.

Nikolsky, P. "Nehru's Party without Nehru," *New Times,* no. 32, 1965, pp. 16–17.

Nizami, Amina. "Lessons of Democratic Upsurge in Pakistan," *World Marxist Review,* XII, 12 (1969), 57–63.

North, R. C. *Moscow and the Chinese Communists.* Stanford: Stanford University Press, 1953.

———— and X. J. Eudin. *M. N. Roy's Mission to China: The Communist-Kuomintang Split of 1927.* Berkeley: University of California Press, 1963.

"O kharaktere i osobennostiakh Narodnoi Demokratii v stranakh Vostoka," *Izvestiia Akademii Nauk SSSR: Seriia istorii i filosofii,* IX, 1 (1952), 80–87.

"Ob izuchenii ekonomiki stran Vostoka," *Sovetskoe Vostokovedenie,* no. 4, 1955, pp. 3–10.

"Observer." "What Shastri's Soviet Trip Reveals," *Jen-min Jih-pao,* May 27, 1965, in *Peking Review,* VIII, 23 (1965), 17–19.

"Ocherednye zadachi istorikov-vostokovedov," *Voprosy istorii,* no. 12, 1950, pp. 3–7.

"Once More about the Non-Capitalist Way," *World Marxist Review,* XIII, 6 (1970), 85–90.

"Open Letter to the Indian Communists," *International Press Correspondence,* XII, 22 (1932), 436–442.

"Open Letter to the Indian Communists from the C. C. of the C. P. of China," *International Press Correspondence,* XIII, 51 (1933), 1153–1158.

Orestov, O. "The War in Kashmir," *New Times,* no. 40, 1948, pp. 24–30.

"Orgwald." "A Conversation with Indian Comrades," *International Press Correspondence,* XIV, 20 (1934), 519–531.

Overstreet, Gene D., and Marshall Windmiller. *Communism in India.* Berkeley: University of California Press, 1959.

Pavlov, V. P., and I. B. Redko. "From Jaipur to Bhubaneswar," *New Times,* no. 5, 1964, pp. 7–9.

"Political Resolution of the Communist Party of India (Marxist-Leninist)," *Peking Review,* XI, 28 (1969), 18–22.

Ponomarev, B. N. "O gosudarstve natsional'noi demokratii," *Kommunist,* no. 8, 1961, pp. 33–48.

———— "Stroitel'stvo kommunizma v SSSR—velikaia internatsional'naia zadacha Sovetskogo naroda," *Kommunist,* no. 1, 1964, pp. 36–61.

Prager, P. "K postanovke voprosa o nekapitalisticheskam puti razvitiia ostalykh stran," *Proletarskaia revoliutsiia,* no. 5, 1930, pp. 55–94; no. 6, 1930, pp. 73–102.

"Problemy gosudarstvennogo kapitalizma v slaborazvitykh stranakh Vostoka," *Sovetskoe Vostokovedenie,* no. 4, 1958, pp. 213–225.

"Proekt Programmy KPSS i nekotorye problemy natsional'no-osvoboditel'nogo dvizheniia narodov Azii i Afriki," *Narody Azii i Afriki,* no. 5, 1961, pp. 3–14.

Program of the Communist International. New York: Workers Library Publishers, 1936.

"Proletarskii internatsionalizm—znamia trudiashchikhsia vsekh stran i kontinentov," *Kommunist*, no. 7, 1964, pp. 25–50.

Protokoly Kongressov Kommunisticheskogo Internatsionala: Vtoroi Kongress Kominterna iiul'-avgust 1920 g. Moscow: Partiinoe izdatel'stvo, 1934.

Ra'anan, Uri. "Moscow and the 'Third World,'" *Problems of Communism*, XIV, 1 (1965), 22–31.

"Refutation of the New Leaders of the CPSU on 'United Action,'" *Peking Review*, VIII, 46 (1965), 10–21.

Reisner, I. M. "Klassovaia sushchnost' Gandizma," *Istorik Marksist*, no. 18–19, 1930, pp. 63–82.

"Revolution in Tibet and Nehru's Philosophy," *Jen-min Jih-pao*, May 6, 1959, in *Current Background*, no. 570.

Rink, I. "Problemy oborony Indii," *Novyi Vostok*, no. 23–24, 1928, pp. 25–34.

Roslavlev, Iu. [R. A. Ul'ianovsky]. "Osnovnye voprosy sovremennogo agrarno stroia v Indii," in *Agrarnyi vopros na Vostoka: sbornik statei*. A. Mineev et al., eds. Moscow: Mezhdunarodnyi Agrarnyi Institut, 1933. Pp. 171–225.

Rosmer, Alfred. "In Moscow in Lenin's Days: 1920–1921," *The New International*, XXI, 2 (1955), 98–120.

Rowland, John. *A History of Sino-Indian Relations: Hostile Coexistence*. Princeton: Princeton University Press, 1967.

Roy, M. N. "Anti-Imperialist Struggle in India," *Communist International*, no. 6, 1925, 80–85.

——— *Memoirs*. Bombay: Allied Publishers Private Ltd., 1964.

——— *Our Differences*. Calcutta: Saraswaty Library, 1938.

Rubinshtein, Modeste. "A Non-Capitalist Path for Underdeveloped Countries," *New Times*, no. 28, 1956, pp. 3–6.

Rymalov, V. V. *Economic Cooperation between the U.S.S.R. and Underdeveloped Countries*. Moscow: Foreign Languages Publishing House, 1962 (?).

——— "Ekonomicheskii slaborazvitye strany v mirovom kapitalisticheskom khoziaistve," *Mirovaia ekonomika i mezhdunarodnye otnosheniia*, no. 3, 1962, pp. 34–50.

Safarov, G. "The End of Mr. Roy (The Ideological Metamorphosis of a Renegade)" *Communist International*, VI, 28 (1929), 1108–1116.

Saikowski, Charlotte, and Leo Gruliow. *Current Soviet Policies IV: The Documentary Record of the 22nd Congress of the Communist Party of the Soviet Union*. New York: Praeger, 1962.

Samra, Chattar S. *India and Anglo-Soviet Relations(1917–1947)*. Bombay: Asia Publishing House, 1959.

Sanai, Amur. "Kliuchi k Vostoku," *Zhizn' natsional'nostei*, no. 19, 1919, p. 2.

Sardesai, S. G. "Political Struggle in India," *World Marxist Review*, XIII, 7 (1970), 50–55.

"Sathi." "The Strategic Triangle: India," *Survey*, no. 54, 1965, pp. 105–112.

Savdar. "Indiia na VI Kongresse Kominterna," *Novyi Vostok*, no. 23–24, 1928, pp. l–lxxii.

Schapiro, Leonard. *The Communist Party of the Soviet Union*. New York: Random House, 1960.

Schram, Stuart R., ed. *The Political Thought of Mao Tse-tung*. New York: Praeger, 1963.

Schubin, P. "Problems of the Revolutionary Movement in India," *Communist International*, VI, 11–12–13 (1929), 502–526.

Schwartz, B. I. *Chinese Communism and the Rise of Mao*. Cambridge: Harvard University Press, 1952.

The Second Congress of the Communist International As Reported and Interpreted by the Official Newspapers of Soviet Russia. Washington: Government Printing Office, 1920.

Seigel', B. "Evoliutsiia Indiiskikh Natsional'nykh Kongressov," *Novyi Vostok*, no. 6, 1925, pp. 226–244.

Sen, Mohit. "Eighth Congress of the CP of India," *World Marxist Review*, XI, 5 (1968), 72–84.

Sen Gupta, Bhabani. "Indian Communism and the Peasantry," *Problems of Communism*, XXI, 1 (1972), 1–17.

"Serious Hotbed of Tension in Asia," *Pravda*, September 19, 1963, pp. 2–3, in *Current Digest of the Soviet Press*, XV, 38 (1963), 18–19.

VII Congress of the Communist International: Abridged Stenographic Report of Proceedings. Moscow: Foreign Languages Publishing House, 1939.

Shaposhnikova, L. "V Indiiskoi derevne: Pochampalli," *Sovremennyi Vostok*, no. 2, 1961, pp. 25–27.

Sharma, Dev. *Tashkent: The Fight for Peace*. Varanasi: Gandhian Institute of Studies, 1966.

Shulman, Marshall D. *Stalin's Foreign Policy Reappraised*. Cambridge: Harvard University Press, 1963.

Sidenko, V. "Non-Alignment: The Prospects," *New Times*, no. 36, 1970, pp. 18–20.

Sobolev, A. "National Democracy—The Way to Social Progress," *World Marxist Review*, XI, 2 (1963), 41–46.

——— "People's Democracy as a Form of Political Organization of Society," *Bol'shevik*, no. 19, 1951, reprinted in *Communist Review* (London), January 1952, pp. 3–21.

Sontag, R. J., and I. S. Boddie, eds. *Nazi-Soviet Relations, 1939–1941: Documents from the Archives of the German Foreign Office*. Washington: Government Printing Office, 1948.

Sosina, N. "K voprosu o gosudarstvennom iazyke v Indiiskom Soiuze," in *Ocherki po novoi istorii stran Srednogo Vostoka: Afganistan, Iran, Indiia*. I. M. Reisner and N. M. Gold'berg, eds. Moscow: Izdatel'stvo Moskovskogo Universiteta, 1951. Pp. 7–19.

"Sotsializm, kapitalizm, slaborazvitye strany," *Mirovaia ekonomika i mezhdunarodnye otnosheniia,* no. 4, 1964, pp. 116–131; no. 6, 1964, pp. 62–81.

"Soviet-Pakistani Cooperation," *New Times,* no. 27, 1970, p. 15.

"Speech by Liu Shao-ch'i to Conference of Trade Unions of Countries of Asia and Oceania," *Pravda,* January 4, 1950, in *Soviet Press Translations,* V, 6 (1950), 168–172.

Spratt, Philip. *Blowing Up India: Reminiscences and Reflections of a Former Comintern Emissary.* Calcutta: Prachi Prakashan, 1955.

Stalin, J. V. *The Foundations of Leninism.* New York: International Publishers, 1932.

——— *Marxism and the National and Colonial Question.* New York: International Publishers, n.d.

——— *Works.* 9 vols. Moscow: Foreign Languages Publishing House, 1953.

Starushenko, G. B. "Cherez obshchedemokraticheskie preobrazovaniia k sotsialisticheskim," in the forum, "Natsional'no-osvoboditel'noe dvizhenie na sovremennoi etape," *Kommunist,* no. 13, 1962, pp. 89–109.

"Statement of the Government of the People's Republic of China," December 16, 1971, in *Peking Review* (supplement), XIV, 51 (1971).

"Statements by N. A. Bulganin and N. S. Khrushchev in India, Burma and Afghanistan," *New Times* (supplement), no. 52, 1955.

Stauber, Leland G. "Recent Soviet Policy in Underdeveloped Countries: The Significance of the National-Democracy Doctrine." Unpub. diss., Harvard University, 1964.

Stepanov, Lev. *Konflikt v Indostane i soglashenie v Tashkente.* Moscow: Izdatel'stvo politicheskoi literatury, 1966.

——— "Neutralism: Attack Repelled," *New Times,* no. 9, 1963, pp. 3–5.

"The Supreme International Duty of a Socialist Country," *Pravda,* October 27, 1965, pp. 3–4, in *Current Digest of the Soviet Press,* XVII, 43 (1965), 6–9.

" 'System of Collective Security in Asia'—Soviet Revisionism's Tattered Flag for Anti-China Military Alliance," *Peking Review,* XII, 27 (1969), 22–23, 32–33.

"Tashkent," *New Times,* no. 3, 1966, pp. 1–2.

"The Tashkent Declaration," *New Times,* no. 3, 1970, p. 4.

"TASS Statement," *Pravda,* September 10, 1959, p. 3, in *Current Digest of the Soviet Press,* XI, 36 (1959), 14.

"TASS Statement," *Pravda,* September 14, 1965, p. 1, in *Current Digest of the Soviet Press,* XVII, 37 (1965), 27–28.

"Text of Secret Documents on Top Level U.S. Discussions of Indian-Pakistani War," *New York Times,* January 6, 1972, p. 16.

"The Theory and Practice of the Non-Capitalist Way of Development," *International Affairs,* no. 11, 1970, pp. 11–25.

Thornton, T. P., ed. *The Third World in Soviet Perspective: Studies by Soviet Writers on the Developing Areas.* Princeton: Princeton University Press, 1964.

Tiagunenko, V. L. "Aktual'nye problemy nekapitalisticheskogo puti razvitiia," *Mirovaia ekonomika i mezhdunarodnye otnosheniia*, no. 11, 1964, pp. 13–25.

———— "Osnovnye strukturnye sdvigi v ekonomike slaborazvitykh stran," *Mirovaia ekonomika i mezhdunarodnye otnosheniia*, no. 3, 1960, pp. 56–70.

———— "Tendentsii obshchestvennogo razvitiia osvobodivshikhsia stran v sovremennuiu epokhu," *Mirovaia ekonomika i mezhdunarodnye otnosheniia*, no. 3, 1962, pp. 20–33.

Tivel'. "Puti i perspektivy Indiiskoi revoliutsii," *Novyi Vostok*, no. 1, 1922, pp. 104–118.

"The Truth about How the Leaders of the C.P.S.U. Have Allied Themselves with India against China," *Jen-min Jih-pao*, November 2, 1963, in *Peking Review*, VI, 45 (1963), 18–27.

Ukraintsev, M. "Asia and the Peking Empire-Builders," *New Times*, no. 23, 1970, pp. 14–15.

Ulansky, Alexander. "Indian Subcontinent: Roots of the Crisis," *New Times*, no. 46, 1971, pp. 7–8.

———— "The Tragedy of East Pakistan," *New Times*, no. 42, 1971, pp. 13–15.

Ul'ianovsky, R. A. "At New Frontiers—On Some Features of the Present Stage of the National-Liberation Movement," *Pravda*, January 3, 1968, pp. 4–5, in *Current Digest of the Soviet Press*, XX, 1 (1968), 9–11.

———— "Ekonomicheskaia nezavisimost' blizhaishaia zadacha osvoboditel'nogo dvizheniia v Azii," *Kommunist*, no. 1, 1962, pp. 96–102.

———— "Nekotorye voprosy nekapitalisticheskogo razvitiia osvobodivshikhsia stran," *Kommunist*, no. 1, 1966, pp. 109–119.

———— "Ob osobennostiakh razvitiia i kharaktere gosudarstvennogo kapitalizma v nezavisimoi Indii," *Problemy Vostokovedeniia*, no. 3, 1960, pp. 23–41.

———— "Socialism and the National-Liberation Struggle—The Non-Capitalist Path of Development," *Pravda*, April 15, 1966, p. 4, in *Current Digest of the Soviet Press*, XVIII, 15 (1966), 24–25.

———— "Some Aspects of the Non-Capitalist Way for Asian and African Countries," *World Marxist Review*, XII, 9 (1969), 86–93.

———— "The 'Third World'—Problems of Socialist Development," *International Affairs*, no. 9, 1971, pp. 26–35.

Usmani, Shaukat. *I Met Stalin Twice*. Bombay: K. Kurian, 1953.

Valia. "The Struggle for Indian State Independence: A Condition of Success of the English Proletariat," *Communist International*, VIII, 20 (1931), 694–699.

Valkenier, Elizabeth K. "New Soviet Views on Economic Aid," *Survey*, no. 76, 1970, pp. 17–29.

Vanin, A. "India's Industrial Prospects," *New Times*, no. 32, 1955, pp. 11–13.

Vasin, V. "The Only Correct Path," *Izvestiia*, July 10, 1971, p. 3, in *Current Digest of the Soviet Press*, XXIII, 28 (1971), 15–16.

"Velikaia Oktiabr'skaia Revoliutsiia i strany Vostoka," *Vestnik Akademii Nauk SSSR*, no. 1, 1948, pp. 39–46.

Venkataramani, M. S. "The Soviet Union and the Indian Food Crisis of 1946," *International Studies* (Bombay), IV, 4 (1963), 395–403.

Viktorov, P. "India: Problems and Politics," *New Times*, no. 26, 1971, pp. 12–13.

Volsky, Dmitri. "The Indian-Pakistan Conflict and American-Chinese Collusion," *New Times*, no. 51, 1971, pp. 7–9.

—— and A. Usvatov. "War on the Indian Subcontinent," *New Times*, no. 50, 1971, pp. 7–9.

Vtoroi Kongress Kommunisticheskogo Internatsionala: Stenograficheskii otchet. Moscow: Izdatel'stvo Kommunisticheskogo Internatsionala, 1920.

Whiting, A. S. *Soviet Policies in China, 1917–1924.* New York: Columbia University Press, 1954.

Windmiller, Marshall. "Constitutional Communism in India," *Pacific Affairs*, XXXI, 1 (1958), 22–35.

Wood, John B. "Observations on the Indian Communist Party Split," *Pacific Affairs*, XXXVIII, 1 (1965), 47–63.

Yakovlev, A. *The World Socialist System and the National Liberation Movement.* Moscow: Novosti Press Agency Publishing House, n.d.

Yudin, Pavel. "Can We Accept Pandit Nehru's Approach?" *World Marxist Review*, I, 4 (1958), 42–54.

"Za dal'neishii pod'em Sovetskogo Vostokovedeniia," *Kommunist*, no. 8, 1955, pp. 74–83.

Zagoria, D. S. *The Sino-Soviet Conflict 1956–1961.* Princeton: Princeton University Press, 1962.

Zarine, D. "Classes and Class Struggle in Developing Countries," *International Affairs*, no. 4, 1968, pp. 47–62, 83.

Zhdanov, A. A. *The International Situation: Report Made at the Conference of the Nine Communist Parties Held in Poland, September, 1947.* n.p., n.d.

Zhukov, E. M. "The Bandung Conference of African and Asian Countries and its Historic Significance," *International Affairs*, no. 5, 1955, pp. 18–32.

—— "K polozheniiu v Indii," *Mirovoe khoziaistvo i mirovaia politika*, no. 7, 1947, pp. 3–14.

—— *Krizis kolonial'noi sistemy: natsional'no-osvoboditel'naia bor'ba narodov Vostochnoi Azii.* Moscow: Izdatel'stvo Akademii Nauk SSSR, 1949.

—— "Natsional'no-osvoboditel'noe dvizhenie na novom etape," *Kommunist*, no. 12, 1963, pp. 23–32.

—— "Obostrenie krizisa kolonial'noi sistemy," *Bol'shevik*, no. 23, 1947, pp. 51–64.

—— "Porazhenie Iaponskogo imperializma i natsional'no-osvoboditel'naia bor'ba narodov Vostochnoi Azii," *Bol'shevik*, no. 23–24, 1945, pp. 79–87.

———— "Significant Factor of Our Times—On Some Questions of the Present-Day National-Liberation Movement," *Pravda*, August 26, 1960, pp. 3–4, in *Current Digest of the Soviet Press*, XII, 34 (1960), 18–19.

———— "The Trusteeship Question," *New Times*, no. 14, 1945, pp. 3–6.

———— "Velikaia Oktiabr'skaia Revoliutsiia i kolonial'nyi Vostok," *Bol'shevik*, no. 20, 1946, pp. 38–47.

———— "Voprosy natsional'no-kolonial'noi bor'by posle Vtoroi Mirovoi Voiny," *Voprosy ekonomiki*, no. 9, 1949, pp. 54–61.

Index

Russian Research Center Studies

* Out of print.
† Publications of the Harvard Project on the Soviet Social System.